D1538588

Richard Bradford is Research Professor in English at Ulster University and Visiting Professor at the University of Avignon. He has published over 30 acclaimed books, including: a biography of Philip Larkin, which was an *Independent* Book of the Year; the authorised biography of Alan Sillitoe; a life of Kingsley Amis; and a biography of Kingsley's son, Martin. He has written for the *Spectator* and the *Sunday Times* and has been interviewed on his work for various BBC Radio Arts programmes, as well as appearing on the Channel 4 series *Writers in their Own Words*, talking mainly on Martin Amis and the post-1960s generation of British novelists. The BBC TV programme *Through the Lens of Larkin*, in which he appeared, was inspired by his *The Importance of Elsewhere: Philip Larkin's Photographs.*

'*The Man Who Wasn't There* will make even very knowledgeable Hemingway readers want to re-examine what they believe they know about the man and his work. Many familiar episodes in Hemingway's life are seen afresh as Bradford shrewdly reassesses previous biographers' work in the light of Hemingway's own testimony, most significantly the shocking disclosures of unpublished letters and other unseen documents. For Bradford, Hemingway was constitutionally unable to tell truth from fiction – not simply in his declining, fame-wracked years but from the beginning of his adult life. This is revisionist biography at its best – well informed and fearless.'

– Carl Rollyson, author of *Beautiful Exile: The Life of Martha Gellhorn*

'Richard Bradford is as dynamic a writer as his subject and brings Hemingway and his remarkable worlds – for there were many, from Paris to Cuba, from Mombasa to Madrid – to life with zest and wit. Bradford bases his new study on years of meticulous research in the archives, revealing the significance of numerous previously unpublished letters. Bradford not only helps us understand the deeply flawed, larger-than-life Hemingway but also offers intriguing insights into his lovers and wives, his literary friends and his enemies. Above all, he offers some powerful correctives to what have become powerful myths about the "man who wasn't there".'

– Anna Beer, author of *Milton: Poet, Pamphleteer and Patriot*

'Vivid and pugnacious, like its subject, this book addresses head-on the topic most of Hemingway's biographers have found embarrassing: his lying. It is not news, of course, that he was a self-fantasist. What is startling here is the *extent* of his fabrications, often designed to defame formerly close friends: Dos Passos and Fitzgerald in particular. Anyone who dared to challenge him, male or female, was knocked down, physically or in print. In this portrait we have Hemingway the sexist, racist, foul-mouthed egomaniac who ultimately goes mad with persecution mania. It will ruffle a few feathers among those wedded to the image of him as all-American literary hero.'

– Martin Stannard, Professor of Modern English Literature, University of Leicester, and author of *Evelyn Waugh: The Early Years 1903–1939*; *Evelyn Waugh: No Abiding City: 1939–1966* and *Muriel Spark: The Biography*

THE MAN WHO
WASN'T THERE

A Life of Ernest Hemingway

RICHARD BRADFORD

I.B. TAURIS
LONDON · NEW YORK

For Gerard Burns, who inspired it
And for Amy

Published in 2019 by
I.B.Tauris & Co. Ltd
London • New York
www.ibtauris.com

ISBN: 978 1 78831 158 8
eISBN: 978 1 78672 546 2
ePDF: 978 1 78673 546 1

A full CIP record for this book is available from the British Library
A full CIP record is available from the Library of Congress

Library of Congress Catalog Card Number: available

Typeset in Stone Serif by OKS Prepress Services, Chennai, India
Printed and bound by CPI Group (UK) Ltd, Croydon, CR0 4YY

Contents

Plates

1 Grace Hall Hemingway, photographed in 1905 when Ernest was six years old.

2 Hemingway in an American Red Cross Ambulance in Italy, 1918.

3 Hemingway in uniform, Milan, 1918.

4 Hemingway recuperating in the Milan hospital where he met Agnes Von Kurovsky.

5 Hemingway in uniform in Oak Park, 1919.

6 Hemingway and Hadley's wedding day, 1921. To the left of the couple are his sisters Carol and Marcelline, and to the right his mother Grace, his younger brother Leicester, and his father Clarence, 'Ed'.

7 Hemingway and Hadley with their son John Hadley Nicanor (aka 'Jack' and 'Bumby'), Schruns, Austria, Spring, 1926.

8 Ticket stub saved by Hemingway from a bullfight he attended in Pamplona, 1926.

9 Hemingway with his second wife Pauline (nee Pfeiffer) at their home in Key West, circa early 1930s.

10 John Dos Passos reads aloud to his wife Katy when the couple were visiting the Hemingways in Key West, 1932. They are on board the *Anita*, a boat used by Hemingway for sailing and fishing.

11 Hemingway on his own boat the *Pilar*, 1935. Before the war he sometimes used the tommy gun against sharks. Later, when he turned *Pilar* into a 'U-Boat hunter', more powerful weapons were added to its armoury.

12 Hemingway with his third wife Martha Gellhorn in Chunking, China, 1941, accompanied by various Chinese military officers and men.

13 Hemingway with his friend Colonel Charles T "Buck" Lanham, with captured German artillery piece, 18 September, 1944.

14 Hemingway aboard the *Pilar*, 1950.

15 Hemingway and his fourth wife Mary on safari in Africa, shortly before their near-fatal plane crashes, 1954.

16 Bullfighter Antonio Ordonez and Hemingway, by the pool at La Consula, the Davis estate, near Malaga, 1959. The Davis's had recently hosted Hemingway's extravagant sixtieth birthday party.

Abbreviations

HIW *How It Was*, by Mary Hemingway. New York: Alfred A Knopf, 1976.
JFK Ernest Hemingway Collection, John F. Kennedy Presidential Library and Museum, Boston, Massachusetts.
PUL Department of Rare Books and Special Collections, Princeton University Library, Princeton, New Jersey.

Correspondence quoted without a specified source has come either from *Selected Letters, 1917–1961*, edited by Carlos Baker, London, Granada, 1981, or from the *The Letters of Ernest Hemingway*, Four Vols, 1907–1931, ongoing, edited by S. Spanier et al., Cambridge, Cambridge University Press, 2011–.

Acknowledgements

Lisa Verner has been of great help. The Northern Ireland Cardiologists, Charles Jack and Alastair Graham, made sure that I survived to write the book. Martin Stannard, a fellow literary biographer, has provided invaluable assistance. Tatiana Wilde and David Campbell have been helpful editors. As usual Amy Burns was splendid.

Introduction

Halfway through writing this book a question occurred to me: why bother? When I began I was aware of the amount of biographical work already in print: seven conventional lives, along with numerous sidelong accounts of his various activities and preoccupations, involving women, war, his family, espionage (pure speculation), bullfighting, his cats, cocktails, travel in general, Spain in particular, and his boat. There is even a biographical account by a forensic psychiatrist entitled, with no hint of irony, *Hemingway's Brain*. There was such a wealth of information in the public arena that I began to wonder why I'd started to write another life, let alone what I thought I could offer that was not already available. Watching a Coen Brothers film-noir I became aware of why Hemingway fascinated me and of what was lacking in everything else written about him, something that explained who he was and why he wrote as he did. The movie was of no relevance but its title suddenly caused the Hemingway enigma to unravel: *The Man Who Wasn't There*.

Most of his later biographers have taken account of his inclination to tell lies, but all treat this as an imperfection that affected Hemingway only a little more than it does the rest of us. The premise seems to be that mendaciousness is part of the human condition and Hemingway's inordinate tendency to make things up renders him extravagantly human, along with his addiction to the killing of animals, warfare, the consumption of alcohol and his disagreeable treatment of women. We might not approve of everything he did but we should see the composite spectacle of excess – dissembling included – as an expedient necessity: only a man given to immoderation could produce an opus of such unrestrained originality. The problem with this thesis is that it overlooks the fact that his lying was far more endemic and quintessential than the rest of his extremities. Hemingway perverted the truth so frequently and habitually that he all but erased his own existence. The verifiable facts used by biographers as the essential framework for their speculations and conclusions are abundant and undeniable. His life, made up of places he visited, people he knew, things he experienced and of course the books he wrote, leaves little opportunity for dispute – but when we search among this material for the essence of Hemingway's personality we find only shadows and contradictions. From his teenage years onwards he fantasised to the point of self-delusion. It is not uncommon for young men to attempt to improve their profile in this way, or so psychologists would have it, but Hemingway's inclination to falsehood went much deeper than a wish to flatter himself. Sometimes he seemed happily oblivious to the difference between what went on in his head and the world in which, for others, truths were largely agreed upon and undisputed. If he had not become a writer his predisposition to sophistry would have remained a matter for those who shared their lives with him. But he is celebrated as one of the great modern American novelists, a Nobel Prize winner. It goes without saying that fiction belongs to a class of fakery that is uniquely its own. There is an unspoken agreement between novelist and reader that the words on the page are an acceptable form of duplicity, since both parties are aware that the world of the novel is created and consumed as an escapist alternative to real life. Yet what would happen if the novelist had already formed a rather unusual relationship with what the rest of us would regard as actuality? What kind of novels would they produce? I ask these questions because Hemingway drifted into literary writing as a man who was already unclear about the difference between disingenuousness and fidelity.

Apart from *The Old Man and the Sea*, all of Hemingway's fiction is perversely autobiographical, involving portraits of himself and those he knew, often accompanied by projections of what might have been, what he would greatly have preferred, and acts of revenge or self-justification. Novels based on actual events, usually those experienced by the author, probably outnumber those composed of purely fictional characters and episodes. Most writers who make use of the world as the raw material for their work alter it to allow themselves space for conjecture, a means of exploring what they might otherwise take for granted. Their skills are tested by how well they deal with and disguise the puzzling, confounding panorama of their lives. But in Hemingway's case something unusual occurred. An author's success in reframing and disguising reality as fiction presupposes an ability to consciously differentiate between the two. For Hemingway the boundaries between life and writing were sometimes poorly defined.

Hemingway is one of the few major authors of the modern era who wrote hardly anything about his vocation. His own comments on the so-called 'iceberg theory' of fiction are asides turned into an allegedly coherent model for his fiction by later critics, mainly academics, keen to design a frame for the study of his work. Two years before he died he produced a Foreword to a Scribner's collection that was published posthumously as 'The Art of the Short Story' (*The Paris Review*, Issue 79, Spring 1981); Scribner's refused to publish it. Scholars and commentators have treated it with embarrassed tolerance, saying nothing in particular but leaving it to the reader to discern it as symptomatic of his degraded mental condition. It is indeed a strange document, so impenetrable that one is surprised that the deconstructionists of the 1980s did not treat it as a precursor to their zealous lunacies. However, when we read it alongside many of the letters he dispatched from the 1940s onwards it becomes evident that he had not lost his mind, at least in the conventional sense. Throughout, he deals with the characters in his short stories as, to an extent, real, but we should not regard this as a confession, a disclosure that he had based the stories on life lived. Not quite. Because he also presents real people, notably writers such as Fitzgerald, Faulkner and Anderson as partial figures, as if they depend for their existence on his particular view of them. Often, he seems to be on the verge of saying something disarmingly candid about his use of actual people and events in his own short fiction, only to lead the reader along a maze of blind alleys and obfuscations. Forty years later, in the playfully self-serving world of metafiction, such chicanery might be celebrated, by some, but for Hemingway in 1959 it is painfully evident that he is as perplexed as we are. He concedes that Margot, wife of the eponymous character in 'The Short and Happy Life of Francis Macomber', is based on someone he knew (Jane Mason, with whom he had an extra-marital affair), but then he loses track of the distinction between autobiographical recollection and making things up. 'The woman called Margot Macomber is no good to anybody now except for trouble. You can bang her but that's about all.' Is he projecting his invention into the future or does he have in mind the real and now rather sad Jane? We do not know, but more significantly, nor does he. 'The man [Francis, of the story? Or Grant, Jane's husband?] is a nice jerk.' He was, in the sense that Hemingway regarded Grant as an easy cuckold. 'I knew him very well, so invent him too from everything I know. So he is just how he really was, only he is invented.' Was he 'just how he really was' or was he 'invented'? Who knows? Certainly not Hemingway. The reason why Hemingway did not write *about* literature was that he was uncertain about what it involved; his fiction was a natural extension of his life and his life involved a considerable amount of make-believe.

His arrival in Paris is routinely regarded as the beginning of his career as an author, and the chronology of events appears to bear this out. What is generally overlooked is the fact that Hemingway joined the party of aesthetic radicals in the 1920s not only as an uninvited guest but as a figure who had only a vague idea of what his fellow revellers were doing or striving towards. He exulted in being part of it – the new pal of Stein, Pound, Beach, Joyce, Picasso, Fitzgerald et al. – but 'it' was beyond his comprehension. He fitted in without understanding the nature of the club that, bizarrely, accepted him. His letters to Stein during this period are fascinating because he often adopts a style that echoes the inchoate, stylistically dissolute manner of the former's *The Making of Americans*, which he helped to get into print. On 15 August 1924 he wrote to Stein and Toklas on the progress of what would become one of his best-known short stories, 'Big Two-Hearted River'. 'It is about 100 pages long and nothing happens and the country is swell, I made it all up, so I see it all and part of it comes out the way it ought to, it is swell about the fish, but isn't writing a hard job though?' This is perversely unlike the manner of, say, his letters to his wife Hadley's financial adviser, which are informed by coherence and ruthless precision, or to his parents – informal but respectfully grammatical. It was as though he had become a version of the speaking presence of Stein's rambling monologue, though not, I think, out of obsequiousness. More likely, he had come to treat Stein's prose style as a feature of her personality – a further indication that he saw fiction more as an existential condition than an aesthetic medium. His comments on how he had 'made it all up' so that it 'comes out the way it ought to' appear bizarre given that Stein would not need to be instructed that fiction is something that we 'make up'. However, when she read the story she suddenly understood what he meant. The original version carried a lengthy coda in which Nick Adams muses on what 'making it all up' actually involves, and he concludes that there is no essential difference between experience, truth-telling and fiction writing. Stein, wisely, advised him to cut this ending, which he did, but it tells us a great deal about a man for whom novels and short stories were a state of mind rather than something merely produced or undertaken. Hemingway from his twenties onwards began to treat fiction as a medium he loved and as an escape route from life that had in various ways let him down.

The novel that resulted from his Paris years is routinely regarded as a contribution to the modernist ethos, but *The Sun Also Rises* is driven by something far more personal and vindictive. He was getting rid of his recent past and the pared down manner of the prose was not a contribution to the era of innovation; he was looking for the most efficient way in which to extinguish and humiliate his erstwhile friends. He did not properly comprehend let alone care about the artistic ambitions of his Parisian companions, and in the novel he dispatched them to oblivion. Startlingly original, yes, but it was as much an act of wish-fulfilment as a work of fiction.

Across the River and Into the Trees marked the nadir of his career as a writer. It is a self-glorifying conceit that blends macho fantasy with a hint of paedophilia. By comparison Nabokov's *Lolita* stands out as acceptable family reading. Every part of the novel – from Cantwell's overweening pride in his military past to his relationship with the unreservedly adoring 'girl', Renata – draws on the stories Hemingway peddled to his friends about his past; the work is animated by his refusal to accept disappointing overtures from the real world, including the unwillingness of the actual 'girl', Adriana Ivancich, to behave like Renata. Hemingway was not asking his readers to suspend disbelief; rather, he had incubated his own, preferred, fictional universe. Before he put Cantwell and Renata on the page Hemingway had already performed in a similarly lurid fantasy involving himself and Adriana, a horrible embarrassment for all who witnessed it, his wife Mary in particular.

The Old Man and the Sea, his least autobiographical novel, won him the Nobel Prize but, ironically, it had hardly anything in common with the rest of his work. It was, in part, an act of contrition. He had subjected Mary to his nightmarish regime of wishing the real world, his wife included, into something else. He hoped that a novel which was not a distillation of his phantasmal existence would allow each of them some relief. It did, but only for a short period. Afterwards things became much worse, with his letters to potential biographers, journalists and Mary, along with his conversations, testifying to the fact that his sense of his identity and his past was fluid, illusory and inconsistent with the recollections and observations of everyone else. He continued to write fiction, but he knew that these novels would remain unfinished; they were versions of his self-deceits and reformulated memories and it would have been impossible for them to have any sense of an ending. Fictional narrators can by various means be allowed to enter some speculative hinterland of existence once their stories close. But Hemingway had become part of his stories; they would end, despite their being incomplete, only when he ceased to exist.

Cambridge University Press is presently putting together the complete letters of Hemingway. The unpublished correspondence runs to something like 25 times the length of Baker's *Selected Letters*

(1981), and so far the Cambridge volumes have reached the end of the 1920s. The remainder is stored in various American archives, but the John F. Kennedy Hemingway (JFK) centre has the most substantial amount of original documents and can make available copies of virtually all the other letters, incoming and outgoing, whose originals are stored elsewhere. Without access to this unpublished material this book would not have been possible and I here express my unreserved thanks to the JFK staff for their patience and assistance. Ulster University generously provided me with the funds that enabled me to see the archives.

The unpublished letters provide an extraordinary insight into the true nature of Hemingway as a man and a writer. They confirm my suspicion that his mendaciousness was more than an idiosyncrasy. One example might, I hope, whet your appetite for what follows. The final letter written to him by Martha Gellhorn, which he kept but which was never published, is almost tear-jerking. She is under no illusions about the demise of their relationship, but her affection for the man she once loved is authentic and moving. She writes of the two of them in the past tense and wishes him well for his new life with Mary. Gellhorn was not a hapless sentimentalist. Quite the opposite; she prefigured more recent feminists in her perception of what women might expect from men. Yet in the letter she is poignantly candid in her recollections of life in the Finca, involving places and objects that encapsulated the uniqueness of their time there together. There is no evidence that she expected him to respond in kind, or that she felt disappointed when he did not reply. In fact, he composed a polite, moderately affectionate response but did not post it. Instead, his letters to others about her from the same period are made up largely of malicious falsehoods. This in its own right would be sufficient evidence of their incompatibility, but it is more extraordinary than that. Gellhorn, in her letter, was closing down an intimate dialogue, or so she believed. She thought she knew the man with whom she had shared the prospect of injury, even violent death, in Spain, had spent almost a decade as lover and wife, and who would read the words of her final letter to him. Her goodbye note is transparent to the extent that she entrusted her feelings to someone whose responses she thought she could predict, despite the fact that she was resolved that the two of them would probably never meet again. But it was a dialogue of one. She had never really known her erstwhile partner because he was a constantly mutable presence, a law unto himself. Even before the marriage ended he had begun to treat her in the same way that a novelist would deal with one of his characters, as a person who seemed autonomous but was ultimately his own creation. He could not distinguish between the real Martha and the woman he eventually decided was deserving of his contempt.

CHAPTER 1

The Young Deceiver

Ernest Hemingway was born on 1 July 1899 in Oak Park Illinois. Oak Park was near enough to Chicago to be classed as a suburb, and indeed many of its worthy, male inhabitants commuted to and from the city, but it would be more accurate to see it as a collective rejoinder to the corruption and immorality of the metropolis. From the mid-nineteenth century its inhabitants seemed intent on creating the exact antithesis of its sprawling urban neighbour. It looked like a buttoned-down alternative to a New England village. Timber-framed colonial-style houses were a little too 'English' in their quaint homeliness; Oak Park residents preferred so-called Prairie Style, echoing the independent pioneering spirit of the first settlers in the Midwest, an effect belied by the fact that they stood in rows of up to 50 along neatly paved streets. Some churches were allowed the solidity of brick or stone and all were Protestant. There were no bars, a prohibition brought about by a consensus of the citizenry and local edicts enforced by the ten-man police force. An adjacent assembly of homes, barely a quarter of a mile along the dust-ridden main road, was in 1901 obliged by the elders of Oak Park to announce itself formally, with sign posts, as a separate entity – 'Cicero'. Oak Park's unilateral declaration of independence from its nearest neighbour was prompted by fear of infection, if only by association. The majority of Cicero's residents were Irish Catholics, and served by several saloon bars.

By the time Ernest Hemingway was 12 his home town was caught in a time warp between various states of progress, denial and rabid conservatism. His parents' house on North Kenilworth was electrified and its servants has access to vacuum cleaners and washing machines. The fire brigade had abandoned the horse-drawn appliance in favour of one pulled speedily to emergencies by two Harley Davidson motorcycles. Main Street was becoming clogged by automobiles built by Ford, Franklin, Packard, Winton and Cadillac. Yet in October 1913 the local paper, *Oak Leaves*, launched an hysterical warning to citizens against an 'evil that reaches the suburban family', the equivalent of the 'disease germ' which will 'aggravate tendencies which civilisation demands be held in sure control'. These dreadful threats to the common good were Latin American music, Parisian 'gowns' for women and the waltz. Theatres and the two cinemas were obliged to close on Sundays. No blacks, not even servants, existed in the region before World War I, and Jews were politely discouraged by house agents from purchasing properties in the town. At school formals teenagers might sometimes be allowed to perform the steps of particular dances but they were forbidden from touching each other. The spectacle would certainly have been memorable.

Both of Hemingway's grandfathers, his mother's father Ernest Hall and his paternal grandfather Anson T. Hemingway, had served with distinction as officers in the Union army during the Civil War. Hall had commanded one of the few regiments made up of free blacks and was regarded by his peers as an outstanding soldier, a hero. Neither men spoke much of their experiences to their families. Indeed, Hall seemed to adhere to a self-imposed vow of silence. But their respective histories hung like a dark cloud above the forcefully placid atmosphere in which they had settled and brought up their families.

Ernest Hall's daughter, Grace, was (if early photographs are good records) the sort of young woman most commonly associated with the upper middle classes of Victorian England; ample-bodied, blue eyed, matronly-before-her-time. She once nearly escaped the parochial confines of Oak Park, her fine control of vocal melody securing her roles in high opera, first in Chicago and later in

Madison Square Garden, New York. Her talent as a singer did not falter but scarlet fever, contracted in childhood, weakened her eyes to the extent that floodlights in the major opera houses caused her unbearable pain. On returning to Oak Park she met a boy she'd known at Oak Park High School, Clarence Edmonds Hemingway, or 'Ed' as he was known to his friends, and to Grace. In the six years since their schooldays Ed had graduated as a medical practitioner from Oberlin College and Rush Medical College, Chicago, and was now practising in their home town. Their courtship and engagement were brief, less than six months, and they married in 1896. Their first child, Marcelline, was born on 15 January 1898, and their second, Ernest, on 21 July 1899. Four more children would follow, in 1902 (Ursula), 1904 (Madelaine), 1911 (Carol) and 1915 (Leicester).

Ed's income as a general practitioner was buttressed by money from both sides of the family. Anson had made a small fortune by dealing in real estate, particularly in the booming prosperous outskirts of late nineteenth-century Chicago, and Ernest Hall founded and ran a successful wholesale cutlery business in the city. Both had profited greatly from Chicago and each had invested their wealth in a haven of secure separateness. Here too they helped their respective children, now married, to purchase the sprawling house on Kenilworth Avenue, where each child would have their own bedroom. At one end Grace had a room to herself where she would sing and play musical instruments, and at the other Ed presided over his own small medical laboratory.

Family money also helped Ed to purchase another house, a lakeside 'cottage' first called 'Grace' and later renamed 'Windemere' (as Grace's tribute to her alleged ancestral roots in the English Lake District; no one was certain of why the 'r' was lost). The Michigan version of Windermere was Walloon Lake, reached by ferry and train and the retreat of the Hemingway family every summer from 1900 onwards.

This was where Hemingway formed a taste for the wild outdoors and the slaughtering of its non-human inhabitants. The lake and its tributary streams held a good stock of brown trout, which he fished for with an array of flies and lures, and the surrounding woods and prairies presented game birds, rabbit, hare and sometimes deer that he pursued with shotgun and rifle.

From the moment that Hemingway could first cast a fly or lift a gun his father insisted that fishing and shooting must be governed by a single edict: kill only what you intend to eat. The question of why and when Hemingway became an inveterate transgressor, wilfully different from his peers, remains a matter for speculation but one has to wonder if the paternal insistence on fairness and decency in the killing of animals stirred within him some rebellious curiosity regarding the rest of his environment, with its seemingly inconsistent platitudes and conventions. Clarence had shown him a world where only the rules of nature seemed to obtain, where the Oak Park customs of dressing properly, dancing without physical contact, attending church and praying before meals (both branches of the family were pious Episcopalian Protestants) were if not suspended then at least temporarily forgotten. Yet by insisting that some quasi-biblical morality should obtain even in the killing of wildlife his father had half opened a door upon an exciting uninhibited elsewhere and then rapidly closed it. In the light of this it is less than surprising that Hemingway should later have invested such energy in the pursuit of creatures which Clarence would have placed at the head of his 'forbidden' list; at least if shark fishing in the Caribbean, lion hunting in Africa, ceremonial bull slaughtering in Spain and bear shooting in Ohio had not seemed improbable prospects for an Illinois teenager.

In the summer of 1915, around the time of Hemingway's sixteenth birthday, he rowed out into the lake with his sister Sunny and took particular care to put up from the reeds and shoot a blue heron. The bird was a protected species and never eaten even by the most desperate country dwellers. Hemingway later claimed that he was ignorant of the regulations and was not certain of the species he'd shot. In both instances he was dissembling. He was challenged first on the shore of the lake by the son of a game warden, who discovered the dead bird under the seat of the rowing boat. He denied knowledge of it and later Windemere was visited by two wardens, who were seen off with a firm rebuttal by Grace. His father learned that the wardens were making further enquiries and he advised Hemingway to flee, first to the home of a local blacksmith Jim Dilworth and next across the state border to his Uncle George's summer home near Ironton, Michigan. After about a month, once the wardens had given up their chase, his father insisted that he declare himself the perpetrator before a judge in Boyne City. He did so, pleaded guilty, and paid a fine of 15 dollars.

The adventure would play a significant part in the creation of Hemingway's longest-serving alter ego, Nick Adams, who came into existence in stories produced while he was still in his teens and outlived his creator in numerous sprawling fragments, most of which were based on incidents from Hemingway's life.

The story that owes most to the heron-shooting episode is 'The Last Good Country', a cut-and-paste job assembled by his executors from various fragments and revisions and published after his death. The heron is replaced by a 12-pointed deer and Nick is joined on his flight from authority by Littless, his younger sister. Aside from the incident in the wilderness involving incestuous sex between the siblings – which has sated the appetites of psycho-analytical theorists for decades – we should take note of something more significant in Hemingway's transformations of fact into fiction. Nick's mother, unlike Grace, does not see off the wardens. Instead she answers their questions dutifully, and even provides them with lunch and supper before retiring to her room with a headache. There is no Uncle George to provide him with refuge and a father is never referred to. Nick seems to have become isolated from his family and his sense of resentment against them – with the exception of Littless – permeates the story. This image of Nick as a man alone is the keynote of all of his stories from the very earliest onwards. Often he seems to have no family at all and treats the wilderness as his true home, a place where he can be at one with himself and, he heavy-handedly implies, be released from the rules and stagnating routines of organised humanity. The 16-year-old knew precisely that he was committing a crime. Moreover, he chose this particular offence – the killing of a protected species of bird – because it was against the regulations that his father has imported from Oak Park and imposed on the potential wilderness of the lake. He wanted to trigger a chain of events that went against the predictabilities of his life. Throughout the rest of his existence he would be plagued by an obsession with breaking away, testing the patience of his friends, wives and fellow writers, seemingly intent on never allowing contentment or obedience to play a role in what he did and thought. Why precisely he was drawn to this incessant, often self-destructive mindset is an unanswerable question, but the fact that it encapsulated his personality and was the engine for his writing is the key to any understanding of each.

Most writers, and most people who aspire to be writers, show something more than a casual interest in literature by the time they reach their teens; an affiliation that mutates into a preoccupation and quite soon a vocation. Biographers have picked through circumstantial details in search of the young Hemingway as an avid reader of literature, and one detects in their endeavours a slight hint of anxiety, even desperation. Records survive of the Freshman English Course (1913–14) at Oak Park High School, listing, among other set texts, passages from the New Testament, Tennyson's *Idylls of the King* and Benjamin Franklin's *Autobiography*. In their sophomore years, junior and senior, Marcelline and Ernest would have been offered Shakespeare, Bunyan's *Pilgrim's Progress*, essays by Addison and Macaulay, and at least some fiction: most probably George Eliot's *Silas Marner* and Dickens's *David Copperfield*. So, implies Lynn (p. 23), Hemingway entered his late teens as a well-read literary sophisticate. But this heady mix of fiction and non-fiction, verse and discursive prose, promises no sense of a discrimination between 'literature' and other forms of writing. The fact that in surviving documents – including his own earliest letters and recollections by his siblings – there is no reference whatsoever to his having even a remote interest in literature is cautiously avoided. One might also wonder about the manner in which high-school students were taught 'English' in the early years of the twentieth century, irrespective of the prescribed texts. Even in universities, where English Literature was still in its infancy as an academic discipline, there was no consensus on what exactly literature, particularly novels, meant and involved.

As we will see, there is evidence that his earliest attempts at fiction, some of which would go into print, indicate a creative version of bipolar disorder. Specifically, he was prone to involuntary blendings of fact and invention. In an undated letter to his wife Mary, thought to have been written in the mid-1940s, Hemingway makes some pertinent though by no means entirely coherent comments on the nature of truth: 'It is not unnatural that the best writers are liars' (JFK). He shifts the focus back and forth between the notion of 'lying' as the telling of untruths in the world we share with others and the invention of another world in which the 'lie' is all-encompassing – in short, the work of fiction. Then he appears to reach, or at least grasp at, a conclusion: 'Lying to themselves is harmful [to writers] but this is cleansed away by the writing of a true book.'

His first recorded piece of writing was entitled 'My First Sea Vouge' (the last word being a misspelling of 'voyage'). He was 12 and it was inspired by stories told to him by his father's younger brother, Dr Willoughby Hemingway, of his experiences as a medical missionary in China, Tibet and India, a second-hand account, from his mother, of his maternal grandmother's mysterious journey to Australia, and by a series of books called 'Little Journeys' by Elbert Hubbard designed to educate young Americans on the nature of life in Europe. All involved locations that were fantastically imaginable, yet inconceivable for a boy whose only excursion beyond Illinois and Michigan was a train journey with his mother to Woods Hole, Massachusetts. It was his first, brief encounter with the ocean, the route to those places he'd read about and been told of, and so different from Oak Park as to again blur the distinction between the fictional and the actual. They had stayed for a night in Martha's Vineyard – and in Hemingway's story he tells of his voyage to Cape Horn, en route to Australia, recalling that he had been born in a small white house in Martha's Vineyard where 'my mother died when I was four years old'. We can never be certain if his choice to rid himself of his mother was triggered by some subliminal desire to stay on in Martha's Vineyard and then board the ship for ever more exciting destinations. He was certainly showing an early inclination to turn fiction and falsifying his life and circumstances into a strange hybrid, one that would preoccupy him thereafter.

Hemingway's relationship with his parents is a well-documented and heartily debated feature of his later existence. He rarely had serious arguments with them when he lived at Oak Park or when he visited and wrote to them later. But they appear, thinly disguised, in his writing and feature in exchanges with his friends as figures he seems – depending on his mood– to pity, love and loathe.

Grace and Clarence embodied a community, a state of mind, that Hemingway soon began to perceive as a mass of contradictions. His problem, especially during his teens and early twenties, was that he was part of it too, and this feeling of discomfort and involuntary attachment would plague him for the remainder of his days. Even during the late 1950s, Nick Adams, the same age as he was when Hemingway invented him almost four decades earlier, was still trying to make sense of it all and find a way out.

Further disparities between Oak Park and the rest of the world became evident during his visits to the farm of Henry Bacon, close to Windemere. There were dense woods on both sides of the road between the two houses and, hidden by the trees, Indians lived in a camp with hardly more resources than would have been available for such settlements a century earlier. Hemingway had first encountered a native American when Simon Green – who was fully 'assimilated' and owned his own large farm four miles from Windemere – would join him and his father on shooting expeditions. He was dimly aware that Simon was somehow different, though neither Clarence nor anyone else was given to acts of prejudice, but it was not until he got to know a friend of Simon, Nick Boulton, that he found himself in the company of people utterly unlike those of his home town. Nick lived in the camp and hired himself out as a utility labourer to farmers and second-home owners. For the Hemingways he was sometimes paid to cut up logs that had drifted on to the beach from the booms that were towed past towards the sawmills. Local gossip had created for Nick a mythology that was almost otherworldly. Some said he was a half-breed though no one could say which parent had indulged in a (shameful) interracial liaison because no one knew who his parents were. Another story had it that he was a white man – he looked lighter than others from the camp – who preferred life in the wild because of the opportunities for licentiousness. He spoke openly of how he had a son by one woman in the camp and a daughter by another, seemingly as an act of provocation to the people he worked for but was disinclined to respect. Kenneth Lynn (1987) refers to him as 'a muscular and thoroughly disagreeable lout', making it sound as though he had met him. There is no evidence that he was either disagreeable or loutish and one must assume that Lynn the biographer, like Clarence the patriarch, disapproved of their charge's friendship, even fascination, with a moral and intellectual inferior. Hemingway got on well with him and became friends with his two children, Prudy and Billy. The three of them went hunting squirrels with .22 rifles and the legend that Prudy introduced him to sex is based on two stories. Nick Adams, yet again, tells in 'Fathers and Sons' of how he and two Indians, Trudy and her brother, are hidden in the bushes listening for squirrels; Trudy puts her hand into Nick's pocket, explores further, and the two of them roll over into a bed of pine needles for what appears to be a bout of sex. Mary Hemingway claims in her memoirs that in London in 1944 Hemingway offered her a convincingly vivid recollection of how he had lost his virginity to an Indian girl called Prudy Boulton, three years his junior, in the woodlands of Michigan. He was, he claimed, 16 years old. For all we knew, both stories, Nick's and his creator's, are inventions: no one involved in the alleged incidents, apart from Hemingway, said anything of them and all others to whom he spoke, Nick included, are long dead. Yet we can be certain that Prudy, her brother Billy and their disreputable father Nick were very real, and that the actual Nick carried his name into Hemingway's most puzzling and enduring creation. More significantly they offered Hemingway an exciting alternative to the dull, regulated environment of Oak Park.

There, aged 15 and a half, he had been allowed to escort one Dorothy Davies to a school basketball game, an event supervised and scrutinised by teachers and a considerable number of parents. The following year he invited Frances Coates for a canoe ride on the Des Plaines river, with the proviso, as both were aware, that they would not be alone. The notion of canoeing hinted at escape, a surrender to the destiny and uncertainty of the river. Chaperoned canoeing, involving senior family in an accompanying boat, was farcical, part of the weird sense of tyranny bred from insecurity that pervaded Hemingway's home town.

Grace seemed obsessed with creating for Ernest and Marcelline something other than a standard brother and sister relationship. In their early years she had dressed them in a manner that today would be seen as casually transsexual. Sometimes both appeared to be female and on other occasions male. When they reached their teens she encouraged them to coexist, socially, to the exclusion of interlopers. Famously, at the Oak Park High Junior-Senior Prom of 1915 (the same year that Hemingway had his alleged sexual encounter with Prudy) she insisted that they attend as a couple. Common sense, rather than psychological insight, would lead one to conclude that Grace was attempting to corral her two youngest children against something that might lead them elsewhere, with other people – specifically sex.

Throughout his life in Oak Park Hemingway was becoming gradually alert to the existence of worlds that his parents and everyone else in his community appeared intent on pretending did not exist.

In 1916 the family returned from Windemere to find that their house had been broken into and some valuables stolen, notably Clarence's collection of old coins. The police arrested a teenager who turned out to be the son of a near neighbour, a prominent lawyer. Rumour spread that the young man had recently been warned by his father about associating with youths from Cicero who sometimes ventured into Oak Park carrying bottles of lemonade that might well have contained something more intoxicating and who were given to tempting local youngsters into back-alley gambling dens involving dice and cards. It seemed to all that the lawyer's son must have been corrupted by outsiders, at least until he confessed that his associates had been two others from the locality, both from respectable families.

From his infancy onwards everything Hemingway encountered would have appeared to be composed of inconstancies, delusions and hypocrisies. What he made of this at the time is a matter for pure speculation, complicated by two factors. First, his numerous biographers have attempted to impose a coherent narrative upon these years with Hemingway as the principal character. Second, they have done so by making up for a scarcity of reliable evidence from stories told later by Hemingway himself – in fiction, and in life – and by the time he left Oak Park for the first time, he was cultivating a habit that would characterise all of his adult existence: he was becoming a habitual dissembler.

A classic example is the story told by Baker (pp. 50–1) of how Hemingway and his two friends, Jack Pentecost and Morris Musselman, had been camping on the banks of the Des Plaines river and in the middle of the night been attacked by 'prowlers' who slashed their tent ropes and made off with some of their equipment. Baker reported that Hemingway had hurled an axe at one of these villains and missed his head by only a few inches.

The only authentic account of the incident appeared in the high-school journal *Trapeze*, which told of how a group of misbehaving seniors who were holding a stag party close to a group of campers had mounted a 'hoax' attack on the tents. No names were mentioned and there was no hint that the act might have led to violence. This was part of a fantasy concocted by Hemingway himself when he was 50 – never written down but repeated to indulgent listeners – in which he featured as a teenager who had come close to killing someone. All subsequent biographers omit any mention of this incident and fail to comment on its inclusion by Baker because it is a glaring example of how even the well-documented facts of their subject's life are compromised by his distortions of truth and recollection. The autobiographical traces in his fiction are a powerful magnet for speculation and it has long been accepted that novelists frequently borrow from and reformulate aspects of their experience. However, with Hemingway this is complicated by the fact that he regarded fabrication as a commonplace of all brands of communication; little that he said or wrote – from letters, through second-hand accounts of his conversational asides and fables, to notebooks and memoirs– can be regarded as reliable. It is an overexercised cliché that some writers are born to their vocation. Hemingway lends to this otherwise simplistic notion some credibility but in a most bizarre manner. In this regard religion was particularly significant. According to

Hemingway's sister, Sunny, every day before breakfast there would be compulsory family prayers 'accompanied by a bible reading and a hymn or two'. Grace was said before all meals and any evident of lack of pious enthusiasm for these rituals would result in the girls being spanked by their mother with a hairbrush and Clarence taking a razor strap to Ernest. Lying or swearing resulted in their mouths being washed out with bitter soap, followed by the requirement that they kneel and beg God for forgiveness.

For Hemingway some relief from this regime came from his friendship with Bill and Katy Smith, whom he met when he was 16. Katy would later marry John Dos Passos, which initiated a long-term friendship between the two men, poisoned by Hemingway in the late 1930s. In 1916 the Smiths were anomalies in the Oak Park region. Their father, an atheist academic, had written a book in which he sought to prove that Jesus Christ had never existed and his children were content to share his opinions. Hemingway had never encountered their like before, but rather than importing their radicalism into the family home he chose to divide his affiliations between his new friends and their parents, who held all forms of organised religion in contempt, and the parental home where he maintained the demeanour of an Evangelical Christian. When he wrote to his mother from Kansas (16 January 1918) he reassured her that he was still a devout follower of Christ: 'Now dry those tears Mother [...] Don't worry or cry or fret about my not being a good Christian. I am just as much as ever and pray every night and believe just as hard so cheer up!' Some might see this as an act of kindness towards his mother and father but in truth it was a symptom of Hemingway's growing addiction to existing simultaneously in two contradictory worlds. As late as the 1920s he was assuring his mother in letters that he was still a 'good Christian', in the full knowledge that it would eventually become evident to her that he was not. His bizarre pseudo-conversion to Catholicism when he married his second wife, Pauline, has been explained in terms of his wish to accommodate a faith fervently espoused by his new partner and her family. It was far more capricious than that. Part of the attraction of Catholicism, at least for Hemingway, was its association with the rituals of Spanish society and culture – bullfighting in particular involved a quasi-sacrificial connotations – and equally he found in it the opportunity to become or appear to become the kind of Christian that his parents abhorred. As adherents to a branch of Protestantism that traced its origins to the original Puritan settlers they would have found agnosticism more tolerable that the teachings and practices of the Church of Rome. Beneath Hemingway's performance as a Catholic convert – which he often foreswore to friends as a falsehood – there is no clearly detectable sense of what he really felt or believed, if anything. He was not even a convincing atheist. At various points in this voyage from the boy he was to the man he would become he gradually lost the ability or the inclination to discriminate between the actual and the manufactured.

The high-school magazine noted in the summer of 1917 that Hemingway was due, in the fall, to enter the University of Illinois and to major in journalism. No one knows why he chose not to go to college but by late summer his father's brother Alfred Tyler Hemingway had secured him a job on the *Kanas City Star*. Tyler lived in Kansas and Hemingway stayed at his uncle's house during the first few months of his career as an apprentice journalist. Before Christmas he moved to the apartment of Carl Edgar whom he'd known in Horton Bay, a small town near Walloon Lake, and soon afterwards took 'lodgings' – a single room – of his own and began to spend time with Theodore Brumback who also worked at the *Star*.

Accepted wisdom has it that Hemingway's move to Kansas City was a transformative gesture: the moment at which he asserted his independence from Oak Park and began to grow as an individual. Once again this perception is buttressed by later accounts of the period from Hemingway who perpetually reinvented his past. In Kansas he was geographically detached from the stifling controlled environment of his home town, but initially he showed no inclination to be or do anything radical and unorthodox. That came when he met Brumback.

Brumback was a Cornell University graduate who treated with scepticism the notion of a college education as an aid to intellectual maturity. He had spent the summer of 1917 driving ambulances in France for the American Field Service, and though he never preached any kind of ideology he epitomised a blend of disillusionment and heedless romanticism that Hemingway had never previously encountered. He entranced his young friend with stories of his life on the Western Front, without serving as a combatant, and of the moral irresponsibility that had informed France, facing imminent defeat. He told Hemingway of a nation behaving badly.

Accounts of Hemingway's enthusiasm for active service and his attempts to join the regular army vary radically in terms of what actually occurred. His most recent biographer, Mary Dearborn (2017), states that 'father and son both knew that Ernest's poor eyesight, according to family legend inherited from his mother, would keep him out of any US unit' (p. 53). Dearborn does not try to authenticate this exchange between Hemingway and his father because there is no evidence that it took place. Like much else involving the former's early life it is the product of hearsay and speculation. Other biographers have stated that it was Brumback who advised him that he might fail an eyesight test, but again these claims are based on purely circumstantial evidence. There is no evidence that Brumback told Hemingway that his eyesight problem would prevent him from enlisting because Brumback had no firsthand experience of what the medical examination for enlistment involved. He had not attempted to enlist because he assumed that at some point it would be noticed that he had only one eye, the result of an accident when he was 17. In a letter to Marcelline (*circa* 30 October to 6 November 1917) Hemingway announces that he has been in touch with Major Biggs and Lieutenant Simmie at the Canadian Mission in Kansas and intends to join the Canadian army. Canadians, along with Australians and New Zealanders, had served on the front line in France since 1914. Nowhere in the letter, nor anywhere else, does he state that he has chosen the Canadian forces because he has been rejected by their US counterparts. He does, however, inform Marcelline that he has also joined the Missouri National Guard and purchased a full uniform and overcoat. The US government had already made clear that National Guard Units would make up a major part of the Expeditionary Force soon to leave for France. They would see action alongside their full-time comrades and, one assumes, would subject new conscripts to the same examination of their suitability for military service. Records of how such examinations were employed suggest a certain degree of randomness and inconsistency. There were no specified regulations regarding eyesight tests. It is, for example, well known that Harry S. Truman enrolled for front-line duty despite the fact that without his glasses he could make out little beyond a distance of 12 feet. No one noticed this because he did not tell them. Certainly Hemingway's left eye was imperfect – by his thirties he would, reluctantly and occasionally, wear glasses – but there is no record of it causing him to be refused entry to the regular army. The stories that it did are entirely anecdotal, such as the recollection by his sister Marcelline of what he told her during his return to Oak Park in Christmas 1917. He entered in her journal: 'We all have that bad eye like Mother's, but I'll make it to Europe some way, in spite of the optic.'

It was not that Hemingway was attempting to cover up any deliberate avoidance of front-line service. He had many regrettable traits but cowardice was certainly not one of them; on numerous occasions during his life he was suicidally courageous. Thurber's Walter Mitty would not come to glorious fictional life until 1939 but Hemingway was at once his precursor and his complete opposite. While Mitty substituted fantasy for the real world, Hemingway had a tendency to project aspects of a life imagined or as yet unlived into the letters or stories as a kind of rehearsal for what he would attempt to make real. In this regard Ted Brumback was far more significant for him than anything he had read. He was a living story, something greater than the enticements brought about by fiction, and Hemingway began to insinuate himself into the narrative of his friend's life. Brumback had decided that he wanted to return to Europe, this time not as part of the US Field Service but as a driver for the American Red Cross. This would enable him to go beyond France, to the Italian front. He told Hemingway this and his young friend imitated him, counterfeiting the eyesight problem and becoming Brumback's dedicated acolyte during their trip to Europe. Both men volunteered, on the same day in January 1918, in Manhattan. Hemingway returned to Kansas in February, but he and Brumback were back in New York in early May to receive their uniforms and visas and prepare for embarkation to Europe later that month. It was during this period that he began to write prose fiction, albeit involuntarily. His letters, principally to his family, are bizarre in that he went further than attempting to create an image of himself as the newly commissioned heroic narrator, something one might not be too surprised of from an 18-year-old Midwestern teenager now in New York and sporting an officer's uniform. He begins his report to his 'Folks' on 14 May with a meticulously detailed account of the hotel in Greenwich Village, 'half a block from 5th Avenue', where he is quartered, along with the 'Howard Bunch'. His roommate is Brumback and his listing of the items of 'US officers uniform', from shoulder insignia to woollen socks, borders on the obsessive. He sounds like a child who has just unwrapped his Christmas presents and feels that he needs to keep some record of his good luck, just in case the wonderful spectacle might suddenly vanish. The high-octane temper of the letter carries us on through his visits with Brumback to the top storey of a skyscraper, and a boat trip on the river, where he is enraptured by the 'Libber of Godderty' (Statue of Liberty) and Grant's Tomb, and again we sense that he can't quite believe that it is all happening to him. Then:

> It is a wonderform I have an engagement the Mrs. And have already investigated the possibility of the Little Church around the corner. I've always planned to get married if I could ever get to be an officer, you know.

The 'Mrs' was Mae Marsh, one of the first stars of the silent movie era. In 1918, then aged 24, she had already appeared in more than 30 films, most notably D.W. Griffith's classic *The Birth of a Nation* (1915), and Hemingway had in an earlier letter informed his family that he met her soon after his arrival in New York and that within a week they were engaged to be married. Aside from having watched her on the screen, Hemingway had never even seen her and was apparently ignorant of the fact that she had recently married a Goldwyn Films publicity agent.

His mother wrote to him on 18 May reminding him that 'marriage is a wonderful thing' involving 'prayerfulness', and that the one he was about to enter into seemed to her 'unnatural and apt to bring great sorrow'. She continued: 'You may come home disfigured and crippled; would this girl love you then'. Grace clearly regarded the sort of 'girl' who made a living from the movies as innately untrustworthy and fickle. On the 18th she wrote to him again, this time appealing to him as the 'little yellow-headed laddie' who used to 'hug me tight', implicitly comparing her unconditional love for him with that of the rather doubtful Miss Marsh, and asking him to wait for a girl 'worth waiting for and working for'. On 19 May, Hemingway began to realise that his family had become so unsettled by his news that they might go so far as to visit New York before he departed for Europe and attempt to persuade him in person to break off his engagement with Miss Marsh. He telegraphed his father: 'CHEER UP AM NOT ENGAGED MARRIED OR DIVO-RCED [...] JUST JOKING'. Despite his jovial tone he did not deny that he had been seeing her, and only confessed that he had exaggerated the true nature of their relationship. On the same day that he sent the telegram, he wrote and posted a letter to Dale Wilson, fellow novice reporter on the *Star*, telling his friend of how, during a stroll along Broadway, in his officer's uniform he had been saluted 367 times by other ranks. He continues:

> By virtue of his manly form and perfect complexion the one and only Hemsteith has been made Ye Top Cutter [...] Me duties consist largely of being ye right guide of ye 1st or initial platoon. Today as ye right guide I stalked all alone down the old avenue and felt lonesome as hell. But at eyes right I had a fine look at Woodrow

The parade of 75,000 servicemen down 5th Avenue was indeed reviewed by President Woodrow Wilson. It took place not 'Today', as he reported to his friend, but the previous one, the 18th, and apart from his account in the letter there is no record of his having taken part, let alone of having been selected by virtue of his impressive physical presence as formation leader, the officer effectively in charge of the unit who delivers a salute to the president.

In the next paragraph it is evident that he has already informed Wilson of his relationship with Mae Marsh and he updates him: 'am out there [apparently at her apartment] for dinner tomorrow

evening [. . .] Miss Marsh no kidding says she loves me'. He continues
the fantasy he has already spun for his parents regarding the
imminent wedding in the 'little church around the corner' and
embellishes this with a subplot borrowed from the real world,
specifically his mother's warning that a woman such as Marsh might
not be dependable partner if he returned severely wounded, or
even worse:

> she opined as how ye war widow appealed not to her. So I spent the
> 150 plunks [dollars] Pop gave me in a ring so I am engaged anyway.
> Also broke. Dead. I did have about another 100 but I bought a pair of
> 30 buck cordovan leather boots.

He did buy the boots, adding a dashing quality to his officer's
uniform, and one cannot but be amazed by his ability to interweave
truth with complete fabrication. In the closing passages of the letter
he tells of how Mae 'loves me and she believes I am going to be a
great newspaper man', adding that Wilson 'can tell Punk Wallace'
(who also worked at the *Star*) 'about my being engaged' and, as if
in reply to his mother's sceptical comments, '[Mae] says she will
wait for me'.

That he managed to write this letter within hours of sending the
telegram which disentangled him from some of the lies he had told
to his family might seem astonishing, even a symptom of some
mental imbalance, but it also offers us a vital insight into the
bizarre relationship between Hemingway and much of his writing.
His made-up relationship with Mae was not a Walter Mitty fantasy
in that Mitty was a tragi-comic extension of an endemic human
predisposition. Most of us entertain brief rhapsodical leaps from
what we are to what we would like to be, while recognising that the
latter is attractive *because* it is all but impossible. For Hemingway his
fabulations were perversely authentic. He treated the stories he
made up as anticipations of what was about to occur, a projection of
who he was into what might happen to him. He was a good-looking
officer about to be dispatched to the front line and he saw it as
inevitable that someone as glamorous as Mae would be attracted to
him. The fact that this had not yet occurred did not prevent him
from treating it as a forthcoming episode in the narrative that he

both inhabited and controlled. Mae was not so much an invention as a rehearsal for things to come, and he was treating his life much as a novelist would deal with a story over which he had omnipotent control. In Italy he would meet the real-life version of Mae, Agnes von Kurowsky – second-generation aristocrat rather than film-star but equally *beau monde*. Things did not go as he planned and he wrote her out of the narrative. She would remain all but invisible until evidence of her existence began to emerge after his death.

All of Hemingway's biographers treat the 'sketches' he wrote during his first months back in the US in 1919 after military service as his first forays into literature. He sent them to magazines and all were returned with rejection slips. The impression that he was attempting to write short stories – that is, consciously formed works of fiction – is based mainly on the fact that most, if not all, of the characters' names were invented. But aside from this, the stories themselves amount to confections of autobiographical material from his time in Italy and tales he had made up for friends and family. Clearly the letters were a prototype for his first attempts to get into print, but whether he was fully conscious in both instances of the boundary between telling the truth and pure invention is unclear.

At the beginning of June he, Brumback, another ambulance driver Howell Jenkins and two Polish officers, both counts whose aristocratic forebears had emigrated to the US in the previous century, boarded the French merchant ship *Chicago* and set sail for Bordeaux. He wrote to his parents, reporting on how they had, so far, avoided the attention of U-boats and admitting that he, like most of his comrades, was subject to seasickness. The only female aboard was a Frenchwomen, called Gaby, an amiable prostitute who serviced clients in one of the ship's lifeboats. Or so we are led to believe. The Polish aristocrats and Gaby flit like ghosts through various biographies of Hemingway, though notably Reynolds does not mention them, and the assumption that they existed at all is based entirely on anecdotes, originating from stories told by Hemingway in the 1950s when he was still treating his life and his fiction as identical.

Hemingway and Brumback spent a night in Bordeaux before boarding the train for Paris, which was a city under siege. German units were 120 kilometres to the north-east but Parisians were being bombarded throughout the summer of 1918 by rail-mounted long-range German artillery that could hurl high-explosive 240 lb shells into the capital. The story that Hemingway, on his only full day in Paris, hailed a chugging two-cylinder taxi, insisted that Brumback accompany him and ordered the driver to take them to where the shells were falling has become legend. Allegedly, the driver was initially gripped by terror and persuaded to set off only when Hemingway offered him a generous wad of francs. He then transported them to Place de la Madeleine just in time to see the magnificent neoclassical church damaged by a giant shell. It might all have happened, but we should take into account that this tale of addiction to danger was told much later when Hemingway was enjoying a reputation as a gregarious man-of-letters and adventurer. The driver would have had no idea whatsoever of how to locate specifically targeted regions of the city because the Germans were shelling at random. After 120 kilometres in the air shells could fall at any point over a six-kilometre radius. Perhaps the driver knew that his passengers were credulous newcomers and it was due to pure luck that the shell struck the church as they approached it. On 3 June he reported to his family that Parisians had come to 'accept the shells as a matter of course [...] We had our first shell arrive soon after Breakfast', adding that despite the noise of explosions throughout the day, 'no one evinced any alarm or even interest'. The rest of the letter is an account of how he and Brumback had visited Napoleon's Tomb, 'the Champs Elysees', 'Louvre', 'Arc D'Triomphe etc' while listening to the sounds of shells landing at various points across Paris, at some distance from them.

There are two stories here, one he told many years later and one he posted to his family in a letter written during his only full day in the city. Given his tendency to present himself to his parents and siblings as a Romantic hero, why would he have left out his shell-chasing adventure to Place de la Madeleine?

On 5 June, Hemingway and Brumback left Paris by train for Milan where they were roughly eight kilometres away from the battle lines established in the ongoing conflict between Italian and Austrian forces. On 7 June, Austrian artillery targeted a Swiss-owned munitions factory in Bollate, north of Milan. Thirty-five civilian workers were killed immediately and more than a hundred severely wounded, some fatally. Hemingway and Brumback were close by but the most vivid, frequently quoted record of his involvement appeared almost 15 years later in *Death in the Afternoon*. The passage is shockingly precise and seems driven by his swings between fascination and cold resignation, remarking that a dead, dismembered woman wore her hair fashionably short and on how the human body could fragment in such an untidy way with no respect for dignity or symmetry. He does not explain why this passage appears in a book on bullfighting, but he no doubt assumes the reader will discern uneasy parallels between one form of slaughter and another. While he never suggests that his first encounter with the horrific effects on civilians of mechanised warfare is in any way comparable with his enthusiasm for the ritual killing of bulls, his maintenance of a detached mood in both pieces of writing enables him to construct a persona. In each he is demonstrating inner strength where others might admit to anguish. In a letter to his father written the day after his experiences at the munitions factory explosion he says nothing at all of the event. Instead his manner is jovial and enthusiastic. 'We've been treated like kings. Been two days here. Wonderful in Alps' (9 June 1918). In all of the letters he wrote and posted to family and friends in America over the following few days he mentions the incident only once, in a postcard to an unnamed colleague at the *Kanas City Star*:

> Having a wonderful time!!! Had my baptism of fire my first day here, when an entire munition plant exploded. We carried them in like at the General hospital Kansas City [...] Oh boy!!! I'm glad I'm in it. They love us down here in the mountains. (9 June 1918)

It seems that the teenage Hemingway was exempting his family and friends from the horrors he'd witnessed while storing away the traumatic details of the explosion for 14 years to be reported in suitably unsparing prose. Throughout this period he would switch personae, sometimes concealing or suspending his emotional registers and on other occasions dramatising events that were themselves invented or exaggerated. He had yet to explore the potentialities of writing beyond journalism, but his behaviour resembled the manner in which fiction writers observe and privately incubate events.

Three weeks after he wrote to his father a very different experience would turn Hemingway into a minor celebrity. We know for certain that at the end of June he was released from his ambulance unit after volunteering to serve in canteens that the Red Cross had set up in Piave Valley to offer coffee, soup, sweets and cigarettes to off-duty soldiers serving on the nearby front line. Earlier he had informed Brumback that he was bored and wanted to 'find out where the war is'. His pursuit of it prompted him to volunteer for a more dangerous role; specifically, he would be one of the Red Cross officers who would bicycle to the trenches and transport provisions to troops under fire. On 15 July a Red Cross telegram informed his family that on 8 July he had been injured by a 'trench mortar'. All of this is true, but thereafter the story of the exact nature of his injuries, of the events immediately following the explosion and during the subsequent weeks is riddled with anomalies and self-contradictions.

His parents received their first detailed account of what had happened in a letter from Brumback. This was posted the day before they received the telegram but arrived more than a week later. He tells of how the explosion had rendered his friend unconscious, and that Hemingway awoke to find the beheaded corpse of an Italian infantryman close by. Another soldier had lost both legs and was in Hemingway's opinion fatally wounded, but he picked up an injured man he thought might survive and carried him to the nearest dugout. The following day he found himself in hospital with no recollection of these events, but an Italian officer had informed him of what had happened and what he had done and 'said that it had been voted upon to give him a medal for the act of valour'. The legend of Hemingway the wounded war hero then began to acquire a momentum of its own. Hemingway sent his own cable to the family on 16 July:

> Wounded in legs by trench mortar; not serious; will receive valour medal.

On 20 July, *Oak Leaves* published a report, based on an interview with Grace and Ernest senior, that their son had 'received a baptism of fire' and has 'won a citation for bravery'. Other local papers, along with the *Chicago Evening Post*, carried a version of the same story, all emphasising his decoration for valour. It should be noted that the details of the narrative are based exclusively on Brumback's letter to Hemingway's parents, and that Brumback himself had witnessed nothing, spoken to no one involved in the aftermath of Hemingway's injury and had based his letter exclusively on what his friend had told him when he visited Hemingway in hospital in Milan.

Hemingway sent his first detailed account of events to his family on 21 July, seven days after Brumback's, and while it is possible that he had recovered from amnesia in the interim it is odd that he does not mention having suffered it at all. He does, however, offer a minutely detailed description of his injuries. Aside from countless shell fragments he had been hit by several machine-gun bullets. The one in his knee had, miraculously, caused only a flesh wound by lodging 'under the side of the knee cap'. A second bullet was in his right foot, but had not caused significant damage. He explained that both pieces of metal had been removed without leaving him with any permanent disability, as had the 'other bullets' – locations unspecified – and often bulky shell fragments. One of these 'about the size of a Timken roller bearing' had been taken from his left knee, but again had not had a major impact on his patella. He concluded the letter with a rough sketch of his bandaged body, adding: '227 wounds'. He also reported that he was the 'first American wounded in Italy', which was technically true but, as Hemingway was aware, Edward McKey of the Canteen Service had been killed by shellfire on 16 June.

On 4 August he informed his family that, though still bedridden, a 'body guard of about six Italian officers' had lifted him out onto the Plaza in Milan so that he could review troops at a 'big parade':

> The crowd cheered me for about ten solid minutes and I had to take off my cap and bow about 50 times. They threw flowers all over me and everybody wanted to shake my hand and the girls all wanted my name so they could write to me.

He was, he states, 'known to the crowd as the American Hero of the Piave'. Next, he claims that his recommendation for the 'medal of valor' had come not from the officer he'd encountered after his injury but from 'the Duke of Aosta [...] brother of the king', and that it is of equal esteem to the Victoria Cross and the French Légion d'Honneur, Médaille Militaire and the Croix de Guerre.

Writing on 18 August, he informs his family of what occurred ten days earlier on the 8th. His recollection is clear and meticulous, as if everything had happened 24 hours earlier: from how the 'machine gun bullet just felt like a sharp smack on my leg with an icy snow ball', through how he had 'got my wounded to the dugout', to the Italian officers who rescued him but who 'couldn't figure out how I had walked 150 yards with a load [the wounded infantryman] with both knees shot through and my right shoe punctured in two big places'. One must sympathise with the Italian officers' incredulity. It was well-nigh impossible for the 2,500 feet-per-second rifled shells of the Austrian guns not to have shattered, or more likely disintegrated, bone tissue in his knee and foot, let alone at those places struck by the unspecified 'other bullets'.

Hemingway would for the remainder of his life wear his scars as proudly as he did his medals, but no one could prove conclusively if any of the former were caused by a machine gun; or, as we shall see, whether he came to be recommended for the medals, and by whom.

Eric 'Chink' Dorman-Smith was an Ascendency Irishman, scion of minor gentry with an estate in County Cavan. He was Acting Major with the Royal Northumberland Fusiliers, had served in Belgium and France since 1914 and been awarded the Military Cross with two bars. This spare, self-deprecating man could have walked out of a novel by Kipling. He was little more than three years older than Hemingway, and a friendship that would last until the 1950s began when they met on the day of the Armistice in the Anglo-American Club in Milan. Carlos Baker interviewed Dorman-Smith about their conversations in the club 50 years later, and quotes him verbatim on 'this harmless-looking Red Cross youngster [who] had been badly wounded leading Arditi troops on Mount Grappa' (p. 79). In Baker's unpublished notes Dorman-Smith's recollections are much longer than the passages quoted and present us with a man entranced by the story offered by his young brother-in-arms of his time with the Arditi, the Italian storm troopers. Hemingway had no connection with the Italian regular army, let alone the elite Arditi troops, but not once does Dorman-Smith display any doubts about the veracity of his lifelong friend's account, perhaps a prescient clue to his eventual vocation as a convincing storyteller. On 19 August 1961, a month after Hemingway's death, Dorman-Smith wrote: 'When Hem was 21 – and I Was Rising 25', for *Today* magazine. It is a brief, warmly nostalgic account of their time in Italy, in which Chink retells his new-found friend's stories of battles with the Arditi and Hemingway's tale of when, in Sicily, the nymphomaniac hostess of a small hotel had hidden all his clothes so that she could have her way with him day and night for a week. He had not even visited the island. Baker knew the truth and perhaps his decision not to disclose it to Dorman-Smith or to the readers of his biography is laudable. Aside from lying to Dorman-Smith about how he acquired his injuries serving at Vittorio Veneto, the last major battle of the Italian front, he had also spun an elaborate fantasy on his abandonment of ambulance driving and enrolment as a soldier in the Italian Army. He had certainly entertained thoughts of travelling to Vittorio Veneto, yet it seems bizarre that he could have sustained for himself and his friend a falsehood that involved him being injured in a battle that occurred two months after he was admitted to hospital in Milan. Perhaps Dorman-Smith's stories of his experiences on the Western Front made Hemingway feel inadequate. He reported to family (1 November 1918) that he 'had the satisfaction of being in the offensive' against the Austrian army, despite this experience being shortened by an attack of jaundice. It was intriguing enough that he had pretended to be part of something that had already taken place. More disquieting is the evidence that he had planned the lie before he told it. Seven weeks earlier he had informed his father (11 September) that rather than returning to ambulance driving he would now be part of the Italian regular army: 'I will probably take command of some 1st line post up in the mountains.' To his sister Ursula (16 September): 'Your brother is now a full fledged 1st Lieut. and all the 2nd Lieuts salute him.' Marcelline and Madelaine were told (21 September) that 'I have been commissioned as 1st Lieut. But know that I will have chance of a front line post'. He had entertained the fantasy of his front-line service with the Arditi long before he created it.

It is of course not uncommon for a teenager who ventures from his closeted provincial environment into a war on another continent to exaggerate and embellish reports of his experiences. Indeed, in a letter to Marcelline (8 August 1918) he projects the persona he is cultivating for his family into the image of a glorious homecoming. 'If but the girls of our village could see me in my dress uniform, I am of great fear that the men would be wifeless.' But for Hemingway something more unusual accompanied, perhaps motivated, his compulsive fabrications: he had embodied a fiction long before he created one for publication.

His second novel, *A Farewell to Arms* (1929), is perversely autobiographical. The locations and the principal characters are all based on his experiences in Italy. Hemingway appears as the hero and narrator Frederic Henry, and his description of how he is injured in action is a near replica of what happened to his author. I emphasise 'near' because Hemingway seems preoccupied with those parts of the episode that he had made up. In the novel Henry does his best to carry a severely injured Italian soldier to safety but finds that his own leg injuries prevent him from properly standing let alone hoisting his comrade on to his shoulder. Was he in someway exhibiting remorse for the self-aggrandising letters, even confronting himself in fiction, with the implausibility of his having carried a man more than 150 yards, when his leg injuries would leave him bedridden for the subsequent two months? The novel also includes an account of how Henry's comrade, Passini, has both legs blown off and begs to be shot dead, a version of the stories that Hemingway would tell of his injury. One of the most farcical, embarrassing passages in the book is the conversation between Henry and an Italian officer on what grade of medal he deserves for his heroic acts – bronze or silver – and on whether he should also be consulted by English officers regarding his eligibility for a medal recognising his courage in a battle involving British troops. Frederic, despite what we, the readers, know, refuses to say anything of his courageous activities. Hemingway is having his cake and eating it, apologising, via Henry's denials of bravery, for his fantasies, while presenting them in the same novel as the truth. When he wrote the book he had no idea of what the legacy conferred by literary greatness would involve.

The intractable power of the Hemingway myth has blinded writers and editors to the anomalous relationship between what he said and the truth. On 29 November 1918 he wrote to his family of his visit to Lake Maggiore, where he stayed in an opulent hotel which he does not name but whose stationary he used for the letter: 'Grand Hotel Et Des Iles Borromees'. He has, he reports, met Signor Bellia, 'one of the richest men in Italy [...] here with three beautiful daughters'. He adds that Bellia 'and mother Bellia have adopted me and call themselves my Italian mother and father'. In subsequent letters he tells of how Pier Bellia has invited him to stay at his home in Turin, without informing them of whether or not he went there, and that Bellia had sent him a conspicuously expensive box of chocolates after his return to the convalescent hospital in Milan. His 'friendship' with the Bellia's acquired a self-affirming legitimacy after Hemingway's death, but when we examine the evidence it is as suspect as his claims about serving with the Arditi. In volume one of the ongoing Cambridge edition of the *Letters*, Pier Bellia is listed in the index of recipients. In 1922 Hemingway had addressed a postcard to 'Carrissmo Papa' during his motor trip to Switzerland. The card, depicting a nearby chateau, informs Bellia that 'We are near here and having a good time', which indicates that he was writing to a man with whom he was on familiar terms, or at least it would had he posted it. He did not. Instead he took it back to Paris, claiming that he had forgotten to send it, at the same time that he was entertaining Hadley with stories of his wartime exploits and encounters with the Italian aristocracy. The only evidence that Hemingway's acquaintanceship with the Bellias was anything more than brief and inconsequential comes from his own claims in his letters. Decades of credulity and self-delusion are distilled into Richard Owen's *Hemingway in Italy* (2017). Owen quotes a journalist who claims to have interviewed Bianca, one of the Bellia daughters, around whom Hemingway had spun stories of courtship and romance, extending to his visit to the family home in Turin. The interview took place more than 60 years after her encounter with Hemingway in 1918, and her most resonant comment is that 'we knew almost nothing about him'. Quite, because in 1918 nor did anyone else. Perhaps she meant that the man she encountered briefly in 1918 and might otherwise have forgotten, suddenly sprang to life through a combination of global fame and a journalist's insistence that she had fallen for him. After his dispatching of stories to his parents in 1918 the only link between Hemingway with the Bellias is a vague, unspecific comment he made to Hotchner when they visited Turin in 1954: 'I almost married a girl here'. Hotchner was his adoring, credulous confidant and Hemingway knew that anything he told him would be recorded unquestioningly in the former's forthcoming account of their friendship. Owen also tells of how in 1978 the Italian film director Mario Soldati had interviewed a woman, then in her nineties, who had been head nurse in the Milan hospital. Her junior colleague, an Italian girl, had become pregnant during Hemingway's stay and, following a period in the Catholic equivalent of Purdah, given birth to a boy who bore an exact likeness to 'Ernesto'. Adding to this the rumour of yet another brief *liaison amour*, Owen concludes that Hemingway 'fell for at least four young women in Italy while still in his late teens'. Hemingway did not calculatedly engineer the dense fabric of stories that now obscure any clear notion of what happened during his life. The former gained a momentum of its own, but it all began with his habitual fabrications.

In the letter from Lake Maggiore he informs his family that 'The second night I was here the Old Count Grecco who will be a 100 years old in March took charge of me and introduced me to about 150 people.' The Count who 'took me under his wing' had, apparently, dined with 'Maria Theresa the wife of Napoleon the 1st'. No one has explained why Count 'Grecco' would eventually mutate into Count 'Greppi', except that the latter would later feature in Hemingway's letters about his past, and it might be assumed that this is an instance of Hemingway's habit of deliberately misspelling names, usually as an indication of close acquaintanceship. In the late 1940s and early 1950s he frequently mentioned Greppi in correspondence, once telling his editor Max Perkins that the aristocrat and diplomat had acted as his close adviser on Italian and

European politics, and informing Evelyn Waugh that Greppi had 'adopted' him during his time in Italy, the role he had originally assigned to Bellia. Greppi certainly existed, and if they did meet on his 'second night' there is no evidence that they saw each other again. Carlos Baker and Michael Reynolds cooperated in attempting to solve the puzzle of whether Count Greppi was Giusseppi or his younger relative Emanuele: they decided on the former. The problem arose from the fact that Hemingway was equally uncertain of whom he had briefly encountered, never once using the nobleman's Christian name in his letters. The two biographers were determined to identify the real Greppi because Hemingway had reinvented him as the sagacious Count Greffi in *Farewell to Arms*. During the eighteenth century, when the English novel was in its infancy, many readers were so perplexed by this new manner of imitating life in words that they assumed the characters were real and the stories true. Hemingway's web of private fabrications and fictional inventions was so beguiling that it seems to have had a similar effect on his most eminent biographers. The strange conversations he conducted with himself and others in 1918 and the 1920s would later spiral into something even more nebulous and inchoate, in which the distinction between his fiction and the lies he told to himself and others would all but disappear.

When he left Italy, Hemingway carried in his rucksack a short notebook of what can best be described as creative fragments. Some bear the hallmarks of fiction, being third-person narratives, but the storyteller, Nick Granger of Petoskey, Michigan, is a weird combination of who Hemingway really was and the individual he created for his family and friends. Nick, in hospital at the time of the Armistice, reads through the citations for his two medals. Despite being wounded in action he volunteers once more for active service and leads his platoon into an attack against enemy lines during his final battle of the war. 'Wounded twice by the machine guns of the enemy he continued to advance [...] until struck in the legs by the shell of a trench mortar'. Hemingway's story of having served with the Arditi following his mortar shell injuries becomes for Nick a life lived in the strange hinterland between memory and invention.

It is likely that Hemingway consulted these fragments when he began his drafts for *A Farewell to Arms*, at least as a form of an aide memoire, but the most fascinating aspect of these unpublished pieces is what they tell us of a man who seemed unable to properly differentiate between what he'd experienced and what he'd made up.

Nick is far more seriously injured than his creator. The wound to his arm leads to amputation and both of his legs are so horribly mutilated by the mortar shell that there is little left to repair. The horror of the attack is no doubt bound up with Hemingway having witnessed the Italian soldier whose legs were blown off by the same shell that wounded him: but for a few yards he too could have been permanently disabled or killed. Nick reflects on the nature of war, mortality and death: 'I had a rendezvous with Death – but Death broke the date and now it's all over. God double crossed me' (JFK).

The story is a condensed, dramatised version of a letter he wrote to his parents:

> We all offer our bodies and only a few are chosen. They are just the lucky ones. I am very happy that mine was chosen [...] All the heroes are dead [...] Dying is a very simple thing. I've looked at death, and really I know. If I should have died it would have been very easy for me. Quite the easiest thing I ever did. (18 October 1918)

Hemingway's homily on the grandeur of death echoes Nick's lament at being cheated of it, left for the rest of his existence maimed and denied the opportunity to again face the prospect of gallant annihilation on the battlefield. He has secreted a bottle of mercury bichloride, a deadly poison, in his box of medals and when the nurse leaves him he drinks it. The two documents are variations on Hemingway's growing preoccupation with a nihilistic form of heroism. His declared appetite for the arbitrary, visceral nature of danger was genuine – as he put it to Brumback, he joined the Canteen Service simply to be part of 'the war' – but this was underpinned by an equally strong addiction to delusional self-aggrandisement. His earliest fiction was distilled from this strange mixture and throughout his life as a writer the formula endured.

Consider his medals. We begin with Brumback, who tells Hemingway's parents of how the Italian officer promises to recommend their son for the Silver Medal of Military Valor minutes after he rolled into the dugout. Brumback was speaking for his friend but there is no evidence that anyone on the front line actually witnessed his acts and nominated him for them. The legend of the brother of the King being so impressed by the heroism of the young American that he insisted on the award is ludicrous, in that apart from Hemingway's own report there is no record of the Italian Royal Family being remotely connected with the bestowing of military awards, let alone a special citation for a courageous American. In fact, Hemingway left Italy without having received the medals. He had acquired ribbons, of questionable authenticity, which he stitched to his tunic, but he was not awarded the medals until 1921.

Shortly after the Armistice he was befriended by Nick Neroni. Neroni was a decorated Italian Army veteran whose family, minor aristocrats, had a small estate in the Abruzzo region of central Italy to which he invited Hemingway for hunting and trout fishing. He was a Latin variation on Dorman-Smith and once more he stirred in Hemingway a blend of hero worship and stumbling narcissism. He offered Neroni an inflated version of his experience in the Piave Valley with the Arditi when they met again in Chicago in 1921, where Neroni had been appointed to a post in the Italian Legation. The latter was shocked to hear that his friend had yet to receive his decorations and promised to make use of his contacts to ensure that the Silver Medal of Military Valor would be presented to him in the US. It would, along with the citation, become part of the Hemingway mythology. The citation was composed when the medal was delivered in 1921 and was based entirely on the story Hemingway told Neroni in Chicago involving how, 'before taking care of himself, he rendered generous assistance to the Italian soldiers more severely wounded by the same explosion and did not allow himself to be carried anywhere until after they had been evacuated'.

Nick Adams would accompany Hemingway as his alter ego and confessor through much of his short fiction. He inherited his forename from Nick Granger, who came to life shortly after Hemingway met Nick Neroni. Granger treats his medals with something close to scorn, as reminders of his destiny as a cripple, and later in *A Farewell to Arms* Frederic Henry affirms his utter indifference towards the two awards he is due to receive for his exploits at the Battle of Caporetto (in 1917), where Nick Neroni had won his Gold Medal of Military Valor. This is not an accidental pattern of nuances and overtones. Hemingway's fiction reflected his private addiction to dissimulation.

Agnes von Kurowsky would spend most of her life in contented obscurity until Hemingway's brother Leicester told of her relationship with Ernest in a memoir published with disconcerting speed in 1961, just months after Hemingway's suicide. Leicester provided scandal-hungry readers with the story of their romantic entanglement in 1918–19, her allegedly heartless abandonment of Hemingway and her re-emergence as Catherine Barkley in *A Farewell to Arms*. Kurowsky came from a family of German gentry who emigrated to America in the nineteenth century. Her parents were comfortably wealthy and she was something of a nonconformist, abandoning her career as a librarian to train and volunteer as a Red Cross nurse for no other reason than she was captivated by the conflict in Europe. In this last respect she had much in common with Hemingway, whom she met several weeks after his hospitalisation in Milan. She was beautiful, witty, assertively independent and one of the two women, along with Martha Gellhorn, who caused Hemingway to feel uncomfortably inferior. What we know of their relationship is based mainly on the interviews she submitted herself to during the 1960s, prompted by Leicester's revelations, and later from the disclosure of letters she wrote to Hemingway when she was posted to other parts of Italy.

Her love for him is self-evident: they spent time alone together, initially in his hospital room, and when he could walk with a crutch they took meals and drank wine in the cafes of Milan; eventually they would have a sexual relationship. When she was posted away to another hospital south of Milan her letters to him are candid and unreserved on how much she adores him: 'Dear, I sometimes wonder at myself, because I think so much of you and want you so badly [...] It certainly is a new sensation for me – I never cared for anybody before in my life' (29 October 1918, JFK). 'I guess every girl likes to have someone tell her how nice she is [...] when *you* say these things I love it and can't help but believe you' (17 October 1918, JFK).

'I miss you so dear and I love you so much' (2 November 1918, JFK). 'I just buried my head in the pillows and laughed for joy I am going to see you in Milan when I get back' (1 November 1918, JFK). She loved him, but a question remains regarding her decision to abandon him.

He refers to her on 12 occasions in his letters to his parents and siblings but, curiously, not once does he mention her name or provide any information on her age or background. He is uninhibited, sometimes histrionic about his joyous mood, but its source is simply 'the girl' or in one moment of candour 'my wonderful American girl'. His enthralment with her is clear in virtually every letter to his family written during their relationship but there is a contrasting, obsessive desire to keep her secret, as someone whose name and character is known only by him. In one letter to his mother he assured Grace that he was not engaged to the mysterious 'girl' and he did so in a manner that is almost an exact replica, in style and phrasing, of his assurance that he was not planning to marry the film-star Mae Marsh. The latter was, of course, a lie born from a fantasy. They were not engaged because they had never met. Strangely, the woman with whom he did have a relationship, and to whom he proposed marriage shortly before he wrote to his mother denying that he had, must have sounded to his family as oddly unreal.

On 26 October, Agnes responded to his letter of the 24th. His letter is lost but it is evident that she is impressed by his reports of his involvement with the Arditi battalion during the last major action of the war: 'I know now for sure that you have gone back to be in the thick of the action' (26 October 1918). At some point after writing this she discovered inconsistencies between his account of front-line experience and her knowledge of where he actually was at that time. When she broke with him she wrote to explain why she thought the relationship would be disastrous for both of them. She prevaricates, soothes, praises him and then comes to the point:

> So kind (still kind to me and always will be) can you forgive me some day for unwittingly deceiving you? You know I'm not really bad, and don't mean to do wrong, and now I realize it was my fault in the beginning that you cared for me, and regret it from the bottom of my heart. But, I am now and always will be too old, and

that's the truth, and I can't get away from the fact that you're just a boy, a kid [...]

I tried hard to make you understand a bit what I was thinking on that trip from Padua to Milan, but, you acted like a spoiled child, and I couldn't keep on hurting you. Now, I only have the courage because I'm far away. (7 March 1919)

At first Agnes believed everything he that he told her of his acts of heroism, including his service with the Arditi, but now her image of him as a precocious hero was beginning to disintegrate. 'I am still very fond of you but it is more as a mother than as a sweetheart'. On 23 November 1918 he had written to Marcelline. He disapproves of her 'being so strong for Sam Anderson' who 'seem an awful simp to my humble view'. While conceding that his sister was two years older than him he claims seniority by virtue of his experience as a soldier and lover. 'Really Kid I'm immensely older. So when I say I'm in love with Ag it doesn't mean that I have a case on her. It means that I love her [...] I've wondered what it would be like to really meet a girl you will really love always and know I know. Furthermore she loves me'. He asks her to impress her Italian teacher with the news that her 'kid brother' is 'tre volte ferrite, decoratio due volte per valore ance promosso Tenente per merito di Guerra' (three times wounded, decorated twice for valour, promoted First Lieutenant for merit of war service). Marcelline was the only member of his family to whom he had confided the true depth of his commitment to 'Ag', and the only one who knew her name, albeit abbreviated. He goes further and insists that he and Ag will marry, but he adds, 'don't say anything to the folks because I'm confiding in you'. While not stating why exactly he wishes her to keep this from their parents, panic and uncertainty begin to inform the letter: 'when I do marry I know who I'm going to marry and if the family don't like it they can lump it and I never will come home. But don't say anything'. The love-struck war hero seems as much in fear of his parents' disapproval as the adolescent who had yet to leave Oak Park, and one begins to appreciate why Agnes decided to end their relationship: as she put it, 'you're just a boy, a kid'. The only others to whom he confided details of his feelings for Agnes were three men with whom he had served in Italy in the Red Cross: Bill Horne, James

Gamble and Howell Jenkins. Again, he asked each to keep things to themselves, at least until Agnes returned to the US and he became formally engaged to her. He refers to her routinely as his 'Missus'. He rarely told outright lies about her but eventually, when the relationship was drawing to a close, he began to ration out and redistribute details of it and accounts of his emotions, as though his old comrades had become a means of testing variations on the truth. On 5 March he wrote to Horne asking him to be his best man at the 'Little Church' after Agnes's arrival in the US. At this point she had already told him that she had accepted an offer out to dinner from an officer in the Italian artillery, that she was considering further dates. She was, as kindly as she could, asserting her independence; she could go out with whomever else she wished to. Three weeks later he received her unequivocal announcement that she no longer wished to see or communicate with him and he wrote to Horne, at length, of his dejection. 'She doesn't love me Bill. She takes it all back. A "mistake" [...] All I wanted was Ag and happiness. And now the bottom has dropped out of the whole world [...] Aw Bill I can't write about it. 'Cause I do love her so damned much' (30 March 1919). Little more than two weeks after that James Gamble was informed that 'There is a good deal of news which should be retailed to you tho. First I am now a free man. All entangling alliances ceased about a month ago and I know now I most damnably lucky' (18 April 1919). It is difficult to take this announcement of relief seriously, given that in his later correspondence with Horne he continued to stress the possibility of the renewal of their relationship. Bizarrely, he said nothing at all in his letters to Marcelline and the rest of the family. For them it was as if he was attempting to sweep the recent past into oblivion, something he acknowledges in a letter to Horne later that year. 'After I wrote you last I went through a process of cauterization [...] And "Ag" doesn't recall any image in my mind at all. It has just been burnt out' (2 July 1919). This last comment is eerily prophetic, given that Hemingway never referred to her again to anyone. His sustained act of erasure has been overlooked by his biographers, despite the fact that Agnes features nowhere in future correspondence and nor is she mentioned by wives and lovers, friends, literary associates or family members who would speak to researchers and writers after his death. He wrote to Agnes only once more, from Paris, telling her of his marriage to Hadley and his forthcoming debut novel, but we know of this only from her amicable reply, and the first person to see her letter was Baker who found it among Hemingway's private papers after his death. Describing his visit to Milan with Hadley in 1922, Reynolds remarks that 'maybe he even told her more about Agnes von Kurowsky' (p. 54, *Hemingway: The Paris Years*). Reynolds' presumption that he offered any information to his wife about the woman with whom he'd fallen in love in that same city less than four years earlier is based entirely on speculation. Like Hemingway's other biographers he would have found it difficult to accept that he effectively annulled his first emotional adventure. In her book *The Hemingway Women*, Bernice Kert is revealing in that while she too does not state specifically that Hemingway consigned his first love to a void she provides circumstantial evidence that he did. None of her other interviewees – Hadley included – had any knowledge of Agnes during Hemingway's lifetime. In August 1959 press agencies carried news that Hemingway had fallen ill at a bull ring in Malaga, probably with a heart attack. Within a week he wrote to his then wife Mary advising her to inform the press that the reports were false. In the interim, Betty Bruce, then working in the public library in Key West, was asked by her colleague if it was true that 'Ernie' had indeed suffered a heart attack. Betty, whose husband Toby had been close to Hemingway since the 1930s, knew that only his friends referred to him as Ernie and asked her fellow librarian if she had met him. Agnes Stanfield, nee von Kurowsky, answered that, yes, she'd known him quite well, in Italy, four decades ago. The next day Agnes brought in photographs of the two of them together in Milan and later asked Betty if she'd contact Hemingway to see if he'd like to have them. Eventually Hemingway replied to Betty advising her to send them to Scribner's to be filed confidentially with other material related to his life and work. He had kept letters from Agnes but concealed them, and he did not wish to explain to Mary the identity of the woman in the photographs. This faintly bizarre episode was not disclosed until after his death. Hemingway had caused Agnes to disappear, for everyone he knew, but she lived on vibrantly in his novels and short stories, notably as Catherine in *A Farewell to Arms*. The early letters to his friends and family on their ongoing relationship and its demise read like drafts by a fiction writer who can't quite decide on how he feels about his creation and how the narrative they share might continue, or close. When he wrote *A Farewell to Arms* he re-enacted the 'what if', 'if only', and 'what might have been', permutations in the letters on the actual relationship by continually revising the end of the novel. Catherine dies, and though Agnes lived on, Hemingway performed a private, morbid rite of extinction. From his teens onwards he would continue to tread a very narrow line between existence and invention.

On 4 January 1919 Hemingway was discharged from the Red Cross, and on the same day left Italy for New York on board the *Giuseppe Verdi*. By the end of the month he had joined his family in Oak Park.

Several sons of the town had distinguished themselves in the war. Lieutenant John Cadman returned with a Croix de Guerre, Lieutenant Roy Peck, Air Corps, had become an ace and gained a Distinguished Service Cross, Lieutenant John Gleeson earned himself the same honour by leading an attack through a minefield against a machine-gun post. Baldwin Reich received a posthumous Distinguished Service Cross. All had served in western France. Before leaving Italy, Hemingway had bought an Italian Army officers' cape, and as he learned of the exalted status of his peers in the community he wore it every day, and promoted himself to a First Lieutenant in the Italian Army. Invited to speak at the high school he told of how he had been alongside Arditi commandos who had stuck cigarettes into their bullet wounds to cauterise the blood and enable them to keep on fighting. At the Longfellow Women's Club he distressed the ladies of the town with his story of how, when he was first injured, he offered his pistol to a fatally wounded Italian infantryman who begged to be relieved of his pain. None in the audience knew that Red Cross personnel were not allowed side arms. Soon afterwards he was interviewed for the *Oak Parker* newspaper and told of his miraculous survival after being hit by 32 45-calibre bullets, 28 of which had been extracted without anaesthetic. One must ask when self-aggrandising mendacity segues into fiction, and while some of the stories that gripped the ladies of the Longfellow Club would resurface in *A Farewell to Arms*, far more convincing evidence of his ability to blur the difference between lies and literary invention would emerge in a short story written five years later and published in 1925. 'Soldier's Home' is an extraordinary piece of writing, treated by critics and biographers as a harrowing anticipation of the post-traumatic stress disorder suffered by servicemen, a minor master-piece which captures the consequences of mental breakdown in the tightened, inexpressive style that would soon become Hemingway's trademark. No one has recognised its true significance. Krebs returns to his Oklahoma home town after his time on the Western Front. 'He felt the need to talk but no one wanted to hear about it. His town had heard too many atrocity stories to be thrilled by actualities.' Like Hemingway, Krebs finds that his fellow servicemen had got home first and transfixed the community with tales of courage, medals and almost unimaginable scenes of horror. So what does he do? Like his creator, he makes things up:

> Krebs found that to be listened to at all he had to lie [...] His lies [...] consisted in attributing to himself things other men had seen, done or heard of, and stating as facts certain apocryphal incidents familiar to all soldiers [...] Krebs acquired the nausea in regard to experience that is the result of untruth or exaggeration, and when he occasionally met another man who had really been a soldier and they talked a few minutes in the dressing room at a dance he fell into the easy pose of an old soldier among other old soldiers: that he had been badly, sickeningly frightened all the time. In this way he lost everything.

At the opening we are told that he had 'been at Bellau Wood, Soissons, the Champagne, St Mihiel', but we know nothing of what happened to him, of whether he saw action at all. We suspect that he had been at the front only because we fall prey to the game of self-delusion and mendacity by which he creates for himself an image comparable to the real soldiers with whom he associates. We are not even clear about the nature of his lies, other than that they are untruths. The sentence that links Krebs with his creator is 'In this way he lost everything'. He is not protecting himself from his memories; rather he is attempting to forget that he has made them up.

Two years after this story he wrote one called 'In Another Country'. The unnamed first-person narrator is an American, injured while serving with the Italian regular army and recovering in hospital in Milan. Again this involves a blend of authenticity and fantasy identical to Hemingway's accounts of his experiences in Italy. His Italian comrades ask him how he obtained his medals and he shows them 'the papers, which were written in very beautiful language [...] but which really said, with the adjectives removed, that I had been given the medals because I was an American', which is patent nonsense given that the Italians did not decorate soldiers because they were foreigners. 'I was a friend, but I was never really one of them [...] because it had been different with them and they had done very different things to get their medals'. The narrator seems to be implying, modestly, that while each of them is equally deserving of their awards he, as an outsider, is less worthy of his. This might seem an admirable conceit, making us think again about routine conceptions of identity, honour and patriotism, but in actuality we find Hemingway once more using fiction to revisit, privately, his legacy of mendacity. The narrator draws a shroud over what actually happened to him, substituting for this a numinous and collective sense of trauma. Hemingway had lied about his medals and the heroic exploits that brought him such recognition, and in the story he exchanges the facts about his narrator's war service for something he appears too decent and honourable to boast about. It is commonplace to treat fiction as an exaggeration, a refashioning of its author's experience – never before, as far as I'm aware, had it been used as a means of burying their lies and self-delusions.

His audiences believed him, his family believed him, but by spring 1919 his mother had begun to regard him as feckless and dissolute. She encouraged him to go to university and he refused, without explanation. Nor did he look for work in the locality. Instead he spent time in the family home and at Windemere, relying on his family for financial support. When he wasn't fishing or hunting he wrote but said nothing to family or friends of what he was writing or what kind of writer he hoped to become. At the end of February he sent a story to the *Saturday Evening Post*, which the paper rejected without comment. During 1919 he composed several more short pieces, all of which were returned by the *Post* and the *Redbook*. The only one that survived was 'The Woppian Way', an assembly of the exaggerations and outright inventions he peddled to friends and family about his experiences in Italy.

Biographers treat this period as Hemingway's literary apprentice-ship, but it is evident from the surviving material that he was either evolving an utterly radical genre of his own, a combination of reportage and invention, or that he was not quite certain of how one differed from the other. The *Toronto Star* published his first news article, 'Circulating Pictures a New High-Art Idea in Toronto' (unsigned), on 14 February 1920, and for the next 18 months paid him as a freelance for features on various events in Michigan and Canada. He still relied on his family for regular subventions but he could at least advertise journalism as a potentially viable career: in July 1920 Grace had evicted him from Windemere and told him not to return until he had shown some inclination to do more than entertain local groups and societies with stories of his heroism. From 1919 to mid-1921 he lived in Chicago and introduced himself to all he encountered as the city correspondent for the *Star*, a lie but one which opened doors, most importantly to Sherwood Anderson, whose first two novels had introduced a brutalist strand of realism into US fiction. Anderson's letters of introduction would enable Hemingway to enter the coterie of avant-garde artists and writers of 1920s Paris.

Ralph and Harriet Connable were a wealthy Toronto-based couple – Ralph was head of Woolworth's in Canada – who in January 1920 employed Hemingway as tutor and companion to their disabled 19-year-old son, Ralph Junior. A few months after his arrival in Toronto Ralph Senior introduced Hemingway to Gregory Park, the *Star*'s feature editor, and the editor J.H. Cranston. He offered his services to them as a freelance correspondent but both, initially, perceived him as unstable and immature, Clarke treating his trademark narrative of recent military heroics with scepticism. As he later recalled, he appeared to be 'a [...] weird combination of quivering sensitiveness and preoccupation with violence'. Eventually, however, both were worn down by his relentless energetic presence, and they invited him to submit copy. Harriet Connable had first encountered him at one of his talks on his exploits in Italy, at the Petoskey Public Library. Impressed and credulous, she felt that this young man, only a year older than her son, would for Ralph Junior be an ideal exemplar of confidence and courage. Thus Hemingway's route to Paris, without which provincial obscurity and freelance journalism would have been his likely destiny, began with a convincing exercise in fibbing.

In October 1920 Hemingway moved to Chicago. He still received money from his parents, supplemented by modest payments for his pieces for the *Star* and 50 dollars a week as assistant editor of the *Co-operative Commonwealth*, a magazine purchased mainly by the working-class investors in the Co-operative Society of America. He shared apartments with old friends, Bill Horne and Kenley Smith, and, along with others involved in journalism – notably Krebs Friend, Don Wright and Bobby Rouse – cultivated an image as a young men on the edge of a decadent, criminal hinterland: Chicago. The city was riven with gang-based lawlessness and prostitution was widespread, as was police corruption, and supposedly honest citizens turned boxing matches into drink-fuelled celebrations of violence for its own sake. Hemingway revelled in the city's growing reputation as dangerous and anarchic, and the Toronto readers of the *Post* enjoyed, with prurient relief, his reports on the dreadful state of their southern neighbour.

In November 1920 Hemingway met Hadley Richardson at a party in the Smiths' apartment. She was from St Louis and her friend Katy, Kenley Smith's sister, had suggested that a visit to Chicago might provide some solace after years of emotional turmoil in her home city. Hadley was 28, her mother had died in October, her father had committed suicide 17 years earlier and her family appeared stricken by a particularly malevolent branch of fate: her younger sister expired horribly when her clothing was ignited by a candle. In her youth Hadley herself had fallen from a window and been confined to a wheelchair. Although she was not seriously injured, her mother insisted that she would forever be disabled or at best physically abnormal. She went to Bryn Mawr, a prestigious college for largely upper-class young women, but dropped out in her first year; her mother persuaded her that higher education had limited benefits.

In 1919 she dated Leo Loeb, a 48-year-old physician, who at first seemed besotted by her but suddenly, after three months, abandoned her without explanation.

A comfortable trust fund secured her financially but aside from that she seemed in a state of limbo, caught between awful memories and a future that betokened little more than respectable spinster-hood. She was attractive in a way that some might describe as comely – reassuringly well proportioned and quite different from the classically beautiful Agnes.

Her encounter with Hemingway at the party is treated by all biographers as a quintessential case of love at first sight, an impression drawn from Hadley's sympathetic portrait of her husband long after their divorce, and from Leicester Hemingway's questionable recollections of conversations with his brother. Something did happen that evening: their exchanges of intimate, earnestly committed letters after her return to St Louis testify to that. But it would be more correct to see them as drawn to each other in a mutually desperate attempt to resolve their personal dilemmas. The men at the party seemed to Hadley to be speaking a different language, based mainly on an idiolect that Hemingway had cultivated in his letters. Food was 'eatage', death 'mortage' and absurdity 'laughage'. They exchanged their actual names for invented versions that seemed like the cast list from a gothic pantomime. Hemingway was the most prolific, renaming himself Ernie, Oinbones, Nesto, Hemmy, Hemingstein, Stein, Wemedge and several more.

Hadley was enchanted by the clubbish, rather adolescent atmosphere. Everyone seemed to be performing, pretending to be part of a gang with its own rituals, a harmless echo of the various mafiosi groups which were already establishing an underworld in Chicago. Hemingway was constantly in motion, shifting back and forth on the balls of his feet and accompanying conversational exchanges with sparring, punches always pulled, and holding everyone's attention, Hadley's included. He was, self-evidently, making his presence felt as team leader and impresario, and it is quite likely that Hadley recognised beneath his performance a sense of isolation and insecurity similar to her own. They knew something special had happened, and despite having said little they made up for this during the remainder of Hadley's visit, little more than a week, and arranged to exchange letters and meet again following her return to St Louis. Their courtship was wholly conventional, and chaste, and when Hemingway visited St Louis he made a point of taking with him his Italian military tunic, medal ribbons attached, and his glamorous – though entirely inauthentic – cape. A few servicemen wore their uniforms after the cessation of hostilities, but only because they were still members of the armed forces.

For Hadley he was the kind of romantic hero she might otherwise only have read about, while Hemingway had found a woman who was both intelligent and willingly credulous. She loved drink – spirits especially – and dancing, and she wanted to travel. Both craved a licence to transform themselves and each sensed an opportunity to do so in their courtship. Hemingway lied even more outrageously than before about his past and his exploits, and Hadley, eager for a fantasy she could make real, accepted it all with awestruck naivety.

They married in Horton Bay, Michigan in May 1921, less than six months after they had met. The ceremony went some way to resolving Hemingway's alienation from his family, especially his mother, given that he presented Hadley to them, and she presented herself, as quintessentially decent, upper middle class; the kind of woman who might restore some equilibrium to his recent bouts of recklessness. She moved with him to an apartment in Chicago and two events there would change both of their lives forever.

Despite the fact that Hemingway had produced nothing resembling fiction or verse, Sherwood Anderson assumed that he had literary ambitions, though his grounds for doing so remain unclear. Neither of them left any record of what they talked about, but Hemingway is certain to have known of Anderson's recently earned acclaim. *Winesbery, Ohio* (1919), a novel made up of interconnected short stories, combined this experimental structure with unadorned portraits of the mundane lives and conditions of lower-middle-class and blue-collar Americans. It became associated with the evolving mood of counter-orthodoxy in the US and Europe that as yet had no shape or identity and would later be classified as modernism. During his writing of the book he exchanged letters with Gertrude Stein, who provided anecdotes of her association with a motley group of painters, musicians and writers who were united in a disrespect for everything associated with the artistic establishment. All of this was happening in Paris where Stein now lived as an American expatriate. Anderson had no firsthand knowledge of the place, but we can assume that he passed on to his young friend these tales of an alluring cultural nirvana, a cauldron for a revolution which would have radical consequences for the future of art – literary, visual and otherwise – and for the individuals who were part of the insurrection. He entranced Hemingway with Stein's accounts of her friends – James Joyce, Ezra Pound, Ford Madox Ford, Sylvia Beach, Picasso and others – and promised to write letters of introduction to all, so that if Hemingway chose to go to Paris he would be welcomed as a fecund apprentice to the new cause of the avant-garde. Anderson was a kind, generous man and Hemingway's sheer vivacity convinced him that this young writer was a modernist in the making. In truth Hemingway had never heard of Stein's companions and nor had he any understanding of the intellectual and artistic upheavals that were brewing in Europe.

The second occurrence seemed more expedient. The *Toronto Star* offered him the post of European correspondent, based in Paris. He was expected to report on the aftermath of World War I, on how Europe was restoring a form of order following what was supposed to be the war to end all wars. Paris would beget Hemingway as a writer, but never before or since has a literary celebrity been delivered by such a series of bizarre coincidences. He set out for Europe as a journalist with a vague sense of literature as an adjunct, recreational activity. The French capital and its personnel turned him into something unique, as a man and a writer.

CHAPTER 2

An American in Paris

At 5 rue Daunou, in Paris's Grands Boulevards, the mahogany interior of Harry's Bar dates from the nineteenth century; it was shipped over from Manhattan in 1911. On the wall a framed advertisement for Harry's, aimed at American expats of the 1920s and placed in the *International Herald Tribune*, reads, 'Tell the Taxi Driver Sank Roo Doe Noo'. One such customer, a table inscription informs us, was Scott Fitzgerald, and the next seat, we read, regularly supported the ample rear of Ernest Hemingway. Less than a kilometre away we find Andre Breton's favourite haunt, Les Deux Magots; Hemingway enjoyed many an afternoon here too, or so a notice informs us. A short walk from the bar takes us to Montparnasse and La Closerie des Lilas, where Picasso and his friends held court. The brass table tags do not document the exact dates of Picasso's visits, but in all likelihood his and Hemingway's paths would have crossed in the cafe. Hemingway is memorialised on a tag here too and they mixed regularly on the same social circuit. In these streets and in the Latin Quarter and the Left Bank the determined ghost hunter will find seemingly limitless records of the favourite bars, sometimes the preferred drinks, of a cornucopia of thinkers, writers and artists. What is extraordinary is the frequency of Hemingway's appearances. He was not ubiquitous – not quite – yet his seemingly viral presence within almost a hundred imbibing intellectuals tells us something of the imprint he left upon the artistic community of Paris during the 1920s.

Hemingway and Hadley left New York for Europe on the *Leopoldina* in November 1921, two months after their marriage. Two weeks earlier Hemingway had secured the post of European correspondent on the *Toronto Star*, and following that he had contacted Anderson and asked him to dispatch the promised letters of introduction. They are lost but we know that Stein, Pound, Ford Madox Ford and Sylvia Beach had been advised that they would soon meet a young man who would surprise and enthral them. On their arrival in Paris on 22 December the couple took a room at the Hotel Jacob, arranged by Anderson in advance. The establishment was well kept and respectable, and the day after Boxing Day a note arrived there from Lewis Galantiere, American by birth but French by assimilation. Galantiere, businessman, playwright and translator, would, he wrote, be happy to take them to dinner at the Pre aux Clercs in the rue Bonaparte and during the subsequent days arrange for them to view apartments in the city. He too was acting on behalf of Anderson. Following the meal Galantiere accepted Hemingway and Hadley's invitation to accompany them back to their hotel room for a drink and was perplexed, post-Cognac, to be handed a pair of boxing gloves and thereafter engaged in a bout of sparring with his host. He was used to the idiosyncrasies of the artists and bohemians who had flocked to the city after the war but he had never come across a ritual of greeting such as this. Odder still was Hemingway's apparent reluctance to treat the exchange as a casual token of bonhomie. Galantiere was a short, very lightly built man with poor eyesight – Hemingway towered above him by a foot and was almost twice his weight – but even when Galantiere removed his gloves his opponent took this as an invitation to go for a knockout and despite Hadley's plea for restraint succeeded in laying out his new companion. He apologised when Galantiere's spectacles broke on his fall and insisted on paying for a new pair but never did he explain his inclination to visit physical violence upon a genial, unprovocative man whom he had known only for only a few hours. A week after that Galantiere arranged for them to move into a fourth-floor apartment at rue du Cardinal Lemoine. He had not, it should be pointed out, recommended it. Hemingway, he knew from Anderson, was on a decent salary which, combined with Hadley's trust fund, brought them around $3,000, which would allow them to live comfortably, if not ostentatiously, in a continent crippled economically by the war; their hotel had charged them the equivalent of $1 per night. The flat cost little more than that. It was a foul place, with a single, open lavatory on each landing, shared by the residents of that floor – not a water closet, but a hole shipping human waste to the sewers. The Hemingways had a bathroom, of sorts; it was a curtained closet with a slop bucket for emergencies when the communal lavatory was occupied. Orwell, during the following decade, lived in rooms a street away and even he, a connoisseur of misery, was astounded by the depths to which humanity could sink. By spring 1922 Hemingway had rented a separate room at 39 rue Descartes for his exclusive use, selecting the property after hearing that Verlaine had died there in poverty and wretched dissolution in 1896. He announced that he needed privacy to type up his articles for the *Star* and to prepare his poems and stories. What of Hadley, one might ask; the solidly middle-class lady now introduced by her husband to the squalid environment of his choice? She was the good wife. She indulged Hemingway's performance as penniless bohemian, and at the time did not comment on the farcical contrast between their lifestyle and the comfortably appointed flats of expatriates where they spent many evenings. In her regular letters to her parents-in-law she painted a false picture of their situation. 'Dear Mother' she began, to Grace, 'we have been having a wonderful time […] working out the possibilities of our new apartment […] [which is] spacious and comfortable. I have my piano in what was the dining room […] and the dining table is used as a work and writing table as well as meal-table' (Hadley to Clarence and Grace Hemingway, 22 February 1922, JFK). This was a total fabrication, but whether she was sparing her husband's parents the knowledge that he had deliberately pretended to be a pauper or if he had persuaded her to tell lies on his behalf will remain a mystery.

In 1922, after reporting on the Greco-Turkish war, Hemingway returned to Paris without having shaved or washed for several days; his clothes were still caked with mud and dust from when he had sheltered in the hills and watched the Turks bombard the retreating

Greeks. He had treated himself to a seat on the Orient Express and after disembarking at the Gare du Lyon decided to walk home, savouring glances from those fascinated by the spectacle of an apparent down-and-out with rucksack striding through the boulevards with such mighty insouciance. Hadley's initial moment of shock at his appearance was soon exchanged for affection tinged with amusement. He unpacked gifts and presented his wife with three necklaces of ivy and amber, a silk headscarf, and a bottle of attar of roses, all purchased in Constantinople and kept with him while he sent reports from the front line. She was reminded of why she had fallen in love with this capricious fool who was determined to do anything but conform. Despite his bizarre first evening with the Hemingways, Galantiere remained on good terms with them and was with Hadley in the flat to greet Ernest on his return. Much later in interviews he recalled the homecoming as entrancingly ambiguous – it seemed to him both heartfelt and theatrical – and told of how this figure was by similar means becoming the most capricious and mercurial in the Parisian landscape. More than 40 years afterwards he reviewed Hemingway's posthumously published memoir, *A Moveable Feast*, for the *New York Times* and throughout he maintains a mood of admiration for a man who had, it seemed, excused himself from the ordinariness of the human condition; he refers to him as a version of Faust.

Virtually every week following his arrival Hemingway would find himself in the presence of another of his fellow countrymen who had set off for Europe in search of adventure, artistic and otherwise. In January 1922, in the American Press Club, he was befriended by Guy Hickok, European correspondent of the *Brooklyn Eagle*, and veteran reporter of various parts the continent beset by discord, anarchy and revolution. Hickok introduced him to another regular at the Club, Lincoln Steffens, then aged 56, and Hemingway was awestruck. Steffens had, 20 years earlier, disclosed levels of fraud and corruption in US business and politics sufficient to guarantee his exile, which he relished, first by covering the Mexican Civil War, and writing in favour of the revolutionary cause, and then sending to the West firsthand reports of the Bolshevik revolution and the subsequent civil war in Russia: he enthusiastically espoused the benefits of communism for the future of humanity. At the time Hemingway's concern with politics can best be described as apathetic, but Steffens excited his more visceral attachment to renegadism: the US Communist Party was less than three years old and its adherents regarded as traitors, even among some liberals. Two months later in a bar in Montparnasse, Hemingway encountered Steffens' antithesis, Charles Sweeny. Sweeny, after deserting from West Point, had fought with Madero's revolutionary army in Mexico and then apparently switched allegiances by pledging his services to the authoritarian forces of Gomez in Venezuela. He was a soldier of fortune with a somewhat fickle attitude to principle and ideology, and once more Hemingway was enthralled. Sweeny, impatient with America's neutrality, had joined the French Foreign Legion in 1915, transferring to the US Army when it entered the war and rising to the rank of lieutenant colonel. One afternoon in Spring 1922 Hemingway and Hickok were joined in the Press Club by William Bolitho. Hickok introduced him to his companion as a fellow journalist, South African by birth and a veteran of the Western Front. Prompted by Hickok, Bolitho told of how, as a mining engineer, he had been responsible for planting explosives under German trenches. Following an early detonation of one of these, his 'body', as he put it, was excavated and buried once more in a mass shallow grave with the rest of the deceased. Eventually, a member of the burial party noticed slight but regular movements of the earth. 'So', concluded Bolitho, offering Hemingway his hand once more, 'meet the walking dead'. In early April Hemingway and Hadley were invited to a party at the club to honour the brief presence in Paris of Max Eastman. Eastman epitomised the so-called 'lost generation', a term that Hemingway stole from Gertrude Stein and refashioned. Stein overheard it from a car mechanic, who was speaking of France's dead of World War I. Hemingway thought it more appropriate to the generation of, mostly American, writers, thinkers and adventurers who welcomed him to Paris in 1922. America, in its ordinariness, had 'lost' them to the war-torn excitements and intellectual radicalism of Europe. He was, initially, flattered and enthused by being part of this cultural diaspora, but by the time he left France he had come to treat his fellow expatriates with contempt. Anderson, a close friend of Eastman, engineered his protégée's invitation to the party, attended also by Steffens. Eastman, along with John Reed, was principally responsible for inciting support for Soviet-style communism among the American intelligentsia of the early to mid-twentieth century. He lived in Moscow for two years in the 1920s, had earned esteem as a pro-modernist poet and critic, and for many embodied a natural sympathy between revolutionary politics and artistic radicalism. Initially, Eastman was impressed by Hemingway's nonconformist attitude to virtually everything, but this would soon fade to pessimism and disillusionment: in 1927 he would, with weary resignation, face up to him in a fist fight. Eastman was not particularly fearful of the prospect; it seemed to him, by then, something of a farcical routine to which virtually every expatriate of Hemingway's acquaintance was obliged to subject themselves. Only those deemed unsuitable as foils for his self-cultivated image as scrapper-intellectual were exempt. Joyce was excused by his near blindness, while Ford Madox Ford was too infirm and the contest would clearly appear too one-sided with someone of delicate middle age. One of the latter, Max Beerbohm, also present at the party, came to regard Hemingway as a rowdy curiosity, an improbable counter-balance to the years of his youth, when combat amounted exclusively to verbal exchanges between the likes of Wilde and Beardsley. Fifteen years later, during the Spanish Civil War, Hemingway would become an unswerving supporter of the Stalinist-Communist faction of the splintered anti-Franco coalition. He had not experienced an ideological epiphany. Whatever entranced Reed and Eastman in the 1920s was quite different from the unflinching brutality of the Soviet Communists in 1930s Madrid. With the latter Hemingway found a politically correct home for his rough-house predisposition and a channel for his ever-growing vindictiveness towards his erstwhile friends, particularly John Dos Passos. Eastman's discovery of the thug beneath the radical façade was prescient.

Within a few days of the party, Hemingway, accompanied by many of the journalists present, took the train to Genoa to cover the International Economic Conference, where the major powers of Europe, along with the US, would debate the catastrophic consequences of the war. Hemingway's dispatches to the *Star* were peripheral to the exchanges between the conference delegates; these bored him, and as he shrewdly guessed his readers, particularly in America, were hungry for meatier stories. He found plenty of material in the city where groups of Italian Communists engaged daily in pitched battles with what he called 'a brood of dragons' teeth' led by one Benito Mussolini. Hemingway's pieces read more like extracts from bestsellers than journalistic reports and his employers were overjoyed with the output of their young correspondent. He portrayed the typical 'Northern Italian Red' as 'father of a family and a good workman six days out of seven [...] on the seventh he talks politics'. Sometimes, however, he must leave aside this peaceful routine, find a weapon and face the bullyboys, sporting their black tasselled caps and armed with revolvers and grenades, the 'young, tough, ardent intensely patriotic [...] fascisti'; men who are 'generally good looking with the youthful beauty of the southern races'. Hemingway betrays an intuitive sympathy for Mussolini's renegades, but just as significantly one detects parallels between his tale and the basic formula of the Western, such as where the eponymous 'Virginian', of Wister's 1902 bestselling story of cowboys on the plains, is reluctantly drawn from his settled existence to a gun-fight with the vulpine criminal, Trampas. Hemingway's American readers would have been transfixed by the apparent similarity between the political tribalism of Europe and the folklore of the Wild West.

In October Hemingway, again with US Press Corps companions, went further east, where the defeated Greek Army was being driven north by the Turks. After Constantinople he found himself in the ghastly Maritza valley through which a quarter of a million Christians were desperately fleeing, in fear of reprisals by Turkish irregulars for alleged massacres by Greek soldiers a year earlier. Suffering from a severe bout of malaria, following his stay in a mosquito- and bug-ridden hotel in Constantinople, he was taking quinine, laced with as much wine and ouzo as he could find, which lent the already terrible spectacle in the valley an apocalyptic air.

Hemingway was in no condition to file good copy so he borrowed pieces from fellow correspondents and from general bulletins of the International News Agency. Two weeks later, back in Paris, he began to do something that would have a formative effect on his early short fiction. He blended his newspaper copy on the Maritza valley with half-recalled impressions and what he felt it was suitable to add from his imagination. Before *In Our Time*, his first collection, was published a few of the key pieces appeared in an April 1923 edition of the *Little Review*. Perhaps the most memorable is a rewriting of his *Star* article that includes an image that many other news correspondents had incorporated: 'Women and kids were in the carts crouched with mattresses, mirrors, sewing machines, bundles. There was a woman having a kid with a young girl holding a blanket over her and crying. Scared sick looking at it. It rained all through the evacuation.' It is enchanting prose, especially since it enables us to question what Hemingway thought about the difference between reporting facts and creating effects. We will never know if it is the narrator who is 'scared sick' at watching the wretched birth, or the girl with the blanket. The next sentence, on the rain, seems to involve him turning away from what has recently upset him, but still we remain uncertain of who is joining us as witness to the pregnant woman's labour, the narrator or the girl. During the next few years Hemingway the man and Hemingway the writer would slip incautiously between what was verifiably true and what he felt able to pretend or invent. It would be his making as an author, and sometimes his nemesis as an individual.

He fitted in well enough with the cadre of journalists he had met during these first months and accompanied to Genoa and Greece, but at the same time many thought him a role-player. His performance on returning from Greece became a habit. Regularly he grew his hair long, was often unshaved, dressed casually and seemed to give the impression he had escaped from somewhere remote and dangerous virtually every week. He emphasised his wartime experiences in Italy in a way that caused his new acquaintances to suspect he was desperately seeking acceptance among the coterie of battle-hardened correspondents and political essayists. His encounters with so many individuals with a collective experience of life at its most raw and vital – reporting directly from events such as the Mexican war, the Russian revolution and World War I, many often serving in the Great War – would have made him look again at the personal history he presented to these individuals. Each embodied the ideal, the myth, towards which Hemingway aspired. Robert McAlmon, whom Hemingway met in August, was a close friend of James Joyce and had typed most of the final draft of *Ulysses*. He would soon found the Contact Press, an outlet for some of the most pioneering modernist writers; it would bring out Hemingway's first literary pamphlet, *Three Stories and Ten Poems*, in 1923. McAlmon had dropped out of college, worked as a nude model and married an English bisexual aristocrat, and one might easily misperceive him as dilettante and aesthete. But, as he reported to Hemingway, he had also served during the war as a pilot in the US Army Air Corps.

In his 1968 memoir McAlmon provided one of the most judicious portraits of Hemingway of the early 1920s. 'At times he was deliberately hard-boiled and case-hardened. Again he appeared deliberately innocent, sentimental, the hurt, soft, but fairly sensitive boy trying to conceal hurt, wanting to be brave, not bitter or cynical but somewhat both'. When he wrote this McAlmon felt neither pity nor scorn for his late, erstwhile companion; rather, he recalled him as a young man who was cultivating an image while not quite able to conceal his vulnerability. 'He approached a cafe with a small-boy, tough-guy swagger, and before strangers of whom he was doubtful, a potential snarl of scorn played on his large-lipped, rather loose mouth.' Everywhere he went Hemingway encountered men who combined cerebral maturity with a streak of heroism. He felt out of his depth and sought compensation with his 'tough-guy swagger' and his boxing gloves.

Anderson did not choreograph all of Hemingway's introductions but I stress his assistance in the newcomer's expeditions because he would become the principal target for Hemingway's first crusade against those who had shown him affection and treated him with respect. The woman to whom Hemingway had devoutly attached himself in these early months, via Anderson, would be visited with an even greater degree of loathing.

It was Anderson's letter to Gertrude Stein, with whom he was a close friend, that prompted Hemingway and Hadley's first invitation to visit Stein's apartment on the rue de Fleurus in February 1922. Their relationship thereafter can best be described a bizarre comedy of manners. The Stein salon had become the magnet for almost everyone involved in the project of modernism, literary writers and painters included. Since her arrival in Paris in 1903 she and her brother Leo had begun acquiring works by the most significant painters of the late nineteenth and early twentieth centuries, beginning with pieces by Gauguin, Cezanne, Matisse and Renoir and later collecting work by their new friends, Pablo Picasso and Juan Gris. Leo departed, mysteriously, for Italy in 1914, their collection was divided up and Stein began to cultivate friendships with writers who were visiting Paris during and shortly after the war, most of whom would pioneer literary modernism. She became particularly close to Ezra Pound, and by the time of the Hemingways arrived in early 1922 the Saturday evening soirees at the Stein flat had become legendary. Hemingway gives an account of his first visit to 27 rue de Fleurus in *A Moveable Feast*:

> My wife and I had called on Miss Stein, and she and the friend who lived with her had been very cordial and friendly and we had loved the big studio with the great paintings. It was like one of the best rooms in the finest museum except there was a big fireplace and it was warm and comfortable and they give you good things to eat and tea and natural distilled liqueurs made from purple plums, yellow plums or wild raspberries. These were fragrant, colourless alcohols served from cut-glass carafes in small glasses and whether they were *quetsche*, *Mirabelle* or *framboise* they all tasted like the fruits they came from, converted into a controlled fire on your tongue that warmed you and loosened it.
>
> Miss Stein was very big but not tall and was heavily built like a peasant woman. She had beautiful eyes and a strong German-Jewish face that also could have been *friulano* and she reminded me of a northern Italian peasant woman with her clothes, her mobile face and her lovely thick, alive, immigrant hair which she wore put up in the same way she had probably worn it in college. She talked all the time and at first it was about people and places. (p. 18)

If you are reasonably familiar with the style that Hemingway made his own – a spare, tight prose built from uncomplicated syntax –

you will experience here a feeling of blurred recognition, but there are discordances. The amount of attention he gives to Ms Stein's build, the colour of her eyes, her choice of clothing and her hairstyle is unusual and involves a surprising abundance of detail. Generally Hemingway is impatient with describing things; he prefers their action and effect. Now, he is taking his time to be less than flattering. One detects also, throughout the chapter given over to his recollections of Stein, an enforced note of naivety, hinting almost at backwardness.

The chapter is the belated final act in the festering dispute that followed Hemingway's initial, seemingly amicable years in the company of Stein. She had already been dead for more than a decade when he composed it in the late 1950s. The key to a full appreciation of the depth of his loathing for her can be found in an article, 'The Dumb Ox', by Wyndham Lewis published in 1934. Later it appeared in a collection called *Men Without Art*, an undisguised disparaging allusion to one of Hemingway's early collections of short stories, *Men Without Women* (1927). Lewis is merciless on Hemingway's indebtedness to Stein: 'This brilliant Jewish lady has made a *clown* of him by teaching Ernest Hemingway her baby talk! [. . .] [She has] [. . .] hypnotised him with her repeating habits and her faux naïf prattle.' The result being that 'Hemingway invariably invokes a dull-witted, bovine, monosyllabic simpleton, a lethargic and stuttering dummy [. . .] a super-innocent, queerly sensitive, village idiot of a few words and fewer ideas.' Few if any winners of the Nobel Prize in Literature can have received such an execrating review. It stayed with him, because although Lewis is a little harsh in his condemnation of the early Hemingway prose there are passages in his recollection of Stein which do indeed resemble the work of a 'dull witted [. . .] simpleton'. The chapter is called 'Miss Stein Instructs', and while there are few specific references to her role as a literary sage the true irony of the title is implicit: he wrote it as if he *were* the 'bovine' automaton that, according to Lewis, Stein had created. The image of him as Stein's pupil caused him, in *A Moveable Feast*, to conduct an exercise in self-caricature that was targeted at her. He implied that if she had played a significant part in his early development as a writer then he would have produced prose just as infantile and primitivist as hers – so dire was his mental state in 1959 that he was blind to the fact that for some of his career, he had.

On 9 March 1922 he wrote to Sherwood Anderson to report on who he'd met during his first month in the city, for which Anderson's fulsome letters of introduction were largely responsible. 'Gertrude Stein and me are just like brothers and we see a lot of her', he begins. His jocular allusion to her lesbianism is innocuous enough yet his presentation of her as his new intimate friend belies the fact that during these early months he was in awe of her. For example, later that summer he wrote to her, and Alice Toklas, in the respectful manner of the anxious subordinate, opening with 'Dear Miss Stein and Miss Toklas' and going on to report on 'playing the races with tremendous success'. Even his description of the horses is reserved and unambitious. 'Still it's fun to see them run with their tails all plaited up and the mud scudding' (11 June 1922). There is little difference between the style of this letter and the unctuous formality of his correspondence with his father. This causes one to suspect that his earlier report to Anderson is, if not fabricated, rather extravagant in its emphasis on his having joined the fashionable set of artists and writers who regularly visited the Stein flat. He name-drops energetically, beginning with Joyce, who 'had a most god damn most wonderful book'. This was *Ulysses*. He presents Joyce as a close companion and they would indeed become occasional drinking partners during Hemingway's time in Paris, but he did not actually meet him until later that month, after he had written the letter, when they were introduced by Sylvia Beach of the already famous *Shakespeare and Company*. He had met Ezra Pound, via Stein, but in the letter to Anderson they seem like long-term friends. 'Pound took six of my poems and sent them with a letter to Taylor Schofield [co-editor of *The Dial*] [...] Pound thinks I'm a swell poet'. Hemingway then adopts the persona of one of the hardy male ruffians who would come to feature persistently in his most successful novels:

> I've been teaching Pound to box with little success. He habitually leads his chin and has the general grace of the crayfish or the crawfish. He's willing but short winded. Going over there this afternoon but there aint much jab in it as I have to shadow box between rounds to get up a

sweat. Pound sweats well though, I'll say that for him. Besides its pretty sporting of him to risk his dignity and his critical reputation at something he don't know nothing about.

Hemingway never had much time for irony, which causes us to wonder about the effect he intended here for Anderson. The spectacle of the founder of Imagist poetry working up a sweat while exchanging punches with a figure whose addiction to violent sport matches his enthusiasm for grammatical brutishness certainly leaves an impression. What is even more intriguing, though not evident in this letter, is Hemingway's naivety. He would remain on good terms with Pound, even during the latter's imprisonment as a World War II Fascist sympathiser, but when he first met him in Pound's flat – less than a year before his report on them as boxing buddies – his first instinct was to compose a savagely satirical portrait of the pioneer of modernist verse as a 'presumptuous' dilettante, a performer, a self-conscious bohemian. Hemingway showed the article to Galantiere and asked if he thought the *Little Review* might be interested; Galantiere advised, with polite restraint, that he would be committing a social and professional faux pas. He was asking one of the organs of modernism to print a caricature of its most esteemed pioneer. Hemingway was a full-blown American male – boxer, footballer, fisherman – who was unclear of how to respond to the alien cultural landscape of postwar Paris – by parts radical and decadent – and the unfathomable nature of its residents. Pound had welcomed him congenially at this first encounter, neither patronising his guest nor in any way hinting at his own prestige. But Hemingway was perplexed and daunted. Instead of asking his host honest questions about what he barely understood (modernism in general and Pound's work in particular) he left the meeting unenlightened and deflected his embarrassment in the article by mocking Pound's appearance – notably his wild hair, unclipped goatee, *fin de siècle* clothing and Byronic open collar.

Hemingway's job as overseas correspondent for the *Star* enabled him to travel regularly through Italy, Switzerland, Spain, Germany and other parts of France, from where he sent articles back to his editor John Bone. As we have seen, he also took notes and recorded impressions that he would pore over in his Paris studio, hoping to find inspiration for his newly developing ambition, to write publishable fiction and verse. Day by day he tried to build bridges between his world among journalists and political commentators and the atmosphere of invention and creativity that informed his circle of literary acquaintances, yet what is fascinating is his apparent ignorance of what exactly the latter were actually up to. Nowhere in extant documents is there evidence that he had heard of any of the diverse trends which comprised modernism before his arrival and his encounter with Pound and Joyce, and the latter's 'god damn most wonderful book'. Occasionally he seems to sense that something unusual was going on but he rarely has the time or patience to reflect on the nature of this period of artistic turmoil. One suspects, however, that at a more instinctual level he felt like an uninvited guest at a party, one who was happy to both insinuate himself and shock those present.

On 16 November 1922 he wrote to Harriet Monroe, not someone he knew well but an influential editor and patron of avant-garde writers. He tells her that Gertrude Stein is in Provence and will return to Paris after Christmas, that 'Hueffer [Ford Madox Ford] is coming to town tomorrow', that 'Frank Harris has been trying to get Sylvia Beach to publish his autobiography' and despite her reservations he, Hemingway, has told 'her it will be the finest fiction ever written'. He concludes with a general account of what people feel about 'T.S. Eliot's new quarterly – The Criterion' and overall offers a convincing performance as a man at the centre of things, on friendly terms with the best and brightest and comfortably satisfied with his own status, at least until one notes his avoidance of any informed opinions on the nature of the work of his peers. It should also be noted that at this point he had, aside from a few abysmal poems, published no literary works at all. What we now routinely refer to as the Hemingwayesque style evolved via a series of accidents, beginning with what seemed to him a disaster.

In January 1922 he and Hadley had spent a week in the Swiss Alps, in Chamby, north-west of Montreux, with Chink Dorman-Smith. The three of them had skied, and in May the Hemingways and Dorman-Smith visited the region again, this time to sample the trout streams. In November Hemingway travelled to Lausanne to cover the peace conference on the Greco-Turkish war, ahead of his wife who would follow from Paris with extra luggage including a suitcase that contained everything that Hemingway had written since 1919, mostly short pieces which combined the techniques of fiction with journalism and travel writing. The suitcase was stolen from Hadley's carriage before the train left the Gare de Lyon and none of its contents was recovered. (Bizarrely, some papers that Hemingway thought had been in his luggage were discovered in the cellar of the Paris Ritz in the 1950s, fortifying his ongoing obsession with his past.) Hadley had not been careless but Hemingway responded as though she had acted with calculated malice. Much later the Spanish painter Quintanilla reported that Hemingway had told him of his exchanges with Hadley when she arrived in Lausanne. At first she was too afraid to disclose anything more than that a 'terrible event' had occurred in his absence and eventually Hemingway could only guess at the nature of this thing that seemed too vile for words. Eventually she told him the truth, but only after he had blurted 'Then you've slept with a Negro, tell me!' According to Quintanilla her having slept with a person of African descent would have been forgivable in comparison with what she now confessed. Most of his biographers treat the incident as a dreadful sin against their subject, and against art. Meyers states that her 'inexcusable negligence [...] [and] The fact that she had been so careless about his most precious possession – the tangible expression of his deepest thoughts and feelings [...] and had shown so little understanding of his life as a writer dealt the first disastrous blow to their marriage' (pp. 69–70). This portrayal of Hadley as feckless and insensitive is ludicrous, as is Meyers' conviction that Hemingway would eventually leave her because of this first sign of indifference to his vocation as a literary artist.

We know nothing of the content of the lost manuscripts but it is reasonable to assume that most of them would have reflected the narrow range of reading of the pre-Paris years and be based mainly on his experiences in the US and Italy. He had been in Europe for less than 12 months and of the two pieces left in drawers in the Paris flat – notably 'Up in Michigan' – the imprint of Anderson is evident, laden with a clumsy dose of immature, brutal and very male sexuality. It remains a matter for debate as to whether the lost manuscripts hindered or energised his progress as a writer. Even without his previous works-in-progress he would have some recollection of his original objectives and methods, but at the same time this new, albeit uninvited, confrontation with carte blanche caused him to look again at what the new continent might offer him as inspiration and raw material, and in the end he would seek assistance and instruction from Stein.

By the end of 1922 he was becoming genuinely close to Pound but in truth he found him intellectually intimidating. Their letters rarely refer to literature; instead he exchanged the highbrow chit-chat of his letters to Monroe for a self-consciously masculine manner:

> This high altitude has made me practically sexless. I don't mean that it has removed the sexual superiority of the male but that it has checked the activity of the glands [...] [There is an] increasing scarcity of prostitutes above 2000 metres u/s and a strange winter concentration of prostitutes is effected in the Engadie Valley. (Hemingway to Pound, 29 January 1923)

Less than three weeks later he wrote to Stein, still addressing her respectfully as 'Miss Stein' (Pound was, variously, 'Prometheus' and 'Carino') and maintaining the deferential, cautious manner of his earlier correspondence. He tells her of his and Hadley's travels in Italy, and then we come upon a passage in which he sounds like the studious pupil:

> I've been working hard and have two things done. I've thought a lot about the things you said about working and on starting that way at the beginning. If you think of anything else I wish you'd write it to me. Am working hard about creating and keeping my mind going about it all the time. (Hemingway to Stein, 18 February 1923)

He is referring to what would become one of his first published short stories, 'Big Two-Hearted River', on which Stein offered him a great deal of advice. The early draft is very different from the version that would eventually appear in the collection *In Our Time*. In the former Nick reflects anxiously and at length on his ambitions to become a writer and he even refers to specific competitors, an act of name dropping that recalls Hemingway's letters to Anderson and Monroe.

All, notably, are individuals he has met through his association with Stein: Joyce and E.E. Cummings appear to concern him particularly. Following Stein's advice he cut out these passages completely and what remains bears a close resemblance to the rather shambolic manner of his mentor's *The Making of Americans*. Hemingway went along with Stein's comments on the story without any clear understanding of her rationale, which she did not explain. In truth he had no clear sense of what he wanted to write or how he might evolve a style that was an authentic reflection of his temperament – this last was a difficult task since his temperament was a fabric of masks and evasions. By the time he began to pour contempt on Stein, as a writer and a woman, he was becoming conscious of quite how amateurish, even preposterous, he had appeared to many during his Paris years and of the part she had played in this, but in 1922–3 he felt grateful to her for having introduced him to the cadre of experimentalists and felt it his duty to repay the debt.

During the same months that he completed 'Big Two-Hearted River', in early 1924, he began work with Ford Madox Ford as assistant editor of the latter's short-lived *Transatlantic Review*. He offered Pound his opinion of Ford:

> I suspect Ford of writing in praise of his own work under various pseudonyms in Transatlantic Review […] Ford ought to be encouraged, but Jesus Christ. It is like some guy in search of a good money maker digging up Jim Jeffries at the present time as a possible heavy weight contender.

> The thing to do with Ford is to kill him […] I am fond of Ford's running the whole damn thing as compromise. In other words anything Ford will take and publish can be took and published in Century Harpers etc, except Tzara and other shit in French. That's the hell of it. Goddam if he hasn't any advertizers [*sic*] to offend or subscribers to discontinue why not shoot the moon? (Hemingway to Pound, 2 May 1924)

It is difficult to pick out from this rant the precise nature of Hemingway's complaint about Ford's editorship. On the one hand he appears to regard his policies as woefully uneconomic, while at the same time he accuses him of having too much money to worry about publishing the likes of 'Tzara and other shit in French'.

Beneath the discontinuities lurks the true cause of his displeasure, and his motive. He wanted control. British, French and US culture during the first three decades of the century was driven by the emergence of small magazines and journals, most enabling their editors to announce themselves as leading figures in the new age. Hemingway was not certain of what he wanted to do but he relished the opportunity to leave his mark, which came when Ford visited America in spring 1924 and left him in charge. Hemingway succeeded in raising far more sponsorship than his co-editor, notably with contributions from his US acquaintance Krebs Friend, recently married to an affluent heiress. His acuity as an editor was, however, a little more suspect, especially regarding his patronage of Stein. Despite the fact that Stein had achieved almost legendary status in the Europe of the early 1920s as hostess and patron of the visual arts, she had published hardly anything of importance. The novel that is now regarded as her most significant contribution to the avant-garde was composed between 1903 and 1911. She had sent parts of it to journals and publishers known to be sympathetic to innovative writing but none would take it. It is clear that she had shown it to Hemingway before he took over from Ford because his first act as editor was to prepare lengthy passages from it for inclusion in the *Review*, and parts of it appeared in every issue of his editorship. Stein herself – made wealthy by family inheritances and her art collection – contributed monies to keep the journal afloat but there is no evidence that Hemingway feigned enthusiasm for the book in return for a bribe. He wrote to Sherwood Anderson: 'This Making of Americans book of Gertrude Stein's is a wonderful one. Did you see the part of it that was in the Translatlantic Review? McAlmon is publishing it.' McAlmon's Paris-based Contact Press put out a limited run of 500 copies of the novel in 1925. Hemingway's sponsorship of the book in an economically fragile but well respected journal was the trigger for its full-length publication and there is good reason to assume that without his support it would never have appeared in print in any form.

The 1920s was a period of indulgence. Virtually everything unconventional and unprecedented seemed worthy of advertisement and, among converts, esteem. Yet even today in the corridors of academia, where evaluation has long been overtaken by theoretical distraction, Stein's *The Making of Americans* is treated with weary sympathy, much as one might a deranged, incontinent relative. The following is an extract:

> Always each thing should come out completely from me leaving inside me just then gently empty, so pleasantly and weakly gently empty, that is a happy way to have it come out of me each one that is making itself in me, that is the only way it can come to be content for me in me, it can come out fairly quickly very slowly with a burst or gently, any way it feels a need of coming out of me, but being out of me I must be very pleasantly most gently, often weakly empty, this one then Mr. Arragon is not so happily then out of me, he is still then still there inside me, I will let him come again when he is more completely ready.

Some have seen it as a precursor to Molly Bloom's interior monologue in Joyce's *Ulysses*, but it should be pointed out that this quotation comes from page 586 and that its unfocussed, ungrammatical manner is sustained throughout the book, which is nearly 900 pages long with no detectable plot. In 1924 Hemingway was preparing *In Our Time* for publication at the same time that he was promoting Stein's incoherent monolith. Some stories left out of the former would eventually appear in *Men Without Women* (1927) but one, 'Summer People', would be suppressed by Hemingway for the rest of his life. The following extract hints at why he hid it: 'It was liking, and liking the body, and introducing the body, and persuading and taking chances, and never frightening, and assuming about the other person, and always taking never asking, and gentleness and liking, and making liking.' And so on. It is a near facsimile of Stein. By the time *Men Without Women* went to press even the more indulgent commentators were expressing doubts about *The Making of Americans* and, without recorded explanation, correspondence between Hemingway and Stein ceased completely. It seems likely that when he put this collection together Hemingway had come to realise that only three years earlier he was devoid both of original ideas of his own and of any proper ability to evaluate the work of others. Instead he had hitched himself to what seemed like favourable trends without considering their intrinsic qualities, or otherwise. Stein had seemed to him the enabler and impresario of new writing and by virtue of this her own work would, he expected, be exceptional. Her influence on his early work is slight but by burying 'Summer People' he was trying to obliterate any notion of what might have been.

When Hadley found herself pregnant in spring 1923 she insisted that they return to Canada for the birth of the child. Aside from this practical distraction Hemingway treated the prospect of fatherhood as a cruel annexation of his right to self-interest. During the term of his wife's pregnancy he composed a story called 'Cross-Country Snow' in which Nick (Hemingway) informs George that he has made Helen pregnant. The exchange verges upon the tragi-comic, albeit unintentionally. The clipped, weary resignation of their utterances evokes two men sharing a condemned cell. They gaze at two empty glasses and an empty bottle on the table between them – a case-study in lumbering symbolism – and Nick observes 'It's hell, isn't it?'

Hemingway did not disguise from Hadley his disappointment at her news but he allowed matters to take their course. He and Hadley loved the energy and unpredictability of Paris but when it came to the real world of medical care they put more trust in the expertise and survival rates of North American hospitals, irrespective of cost. They left France in August and sailed back to Europe in January 1924, with John Hadley Nicanor Hemingway, soon to be known as 'Bumby', who had been born on 10 October 1923 in Ontario: Nicanor Villata was a celebrated Spanish bullfighter. Hemingway had met him briefly five months earlier during two visits to Spain, first with McAlmon and Bill Bird, then with Hadley. Why, one might ask, would he name his first-born child after someone he barely knew? As we shall see, bullfighting transformed him utterly.

On their return they found a flat in Paris that was even worse than the one they had vacated five months before. It had neither gas nor electricity; hot water was available only from a steel pot placed above an open fire; initially, there was no bed, only a borrowed mattress spread on the floor. They would eventually purchase a basic metal frame. Washing was available via an ancient sink and the 'lavatory' was a hole in the floor of the tiny storeroom. The ground

floor was occupied by a sawmill. While Hadley's trust fund had been
depleted by her executors' mismanagement of the estate it would
still secure the family against destitution. So, one must ask why
Hemingway chose to house his wife and newly born son in such a
place? The flat was in the Montparnasse quarter, very close to
Pound's spare but well-appointed residence, and it guaranteed a
sense of shock from other expatriates and writers of various
backgrounds. William Carlos Williams, Stein and Dorman-Smith
attended Hemingway Junior's baptism and each, later, recorded
their disbelief, and horror, at what the child would have to live with.
Hemingway was, once more, role-playing. He was certainly not
poverty-stricken but he made sure that his friends and fellow writers
knew little or nothing of the financial security blanket that
protected him from what appeared to be a descent into pauperism.
The near collapse of the franc allowed those expatriates with regular
access to other currencies to live comfortably, often in luxury, but
Hemingway was, even before he had published hardly any fiction,
creating a narrative for himself, a story that would, he hoped, set
him apart from his new community. From his childhood onwards
he had set individualism and rough self-sufficiency above any
abstract political ideals or codes of behaviour. When as an
apprentice journalist in Kansas, hungrily absorbing himself in
stories of violence and gang criminality, or driving an ambulance in
Italy, and fishing and hunting in wild countryside, he could act out
his private myths in suitably bracing environments. But he was in
fear of Paris. Its affordable delights and its abundance of
opportunities for artistic indulgence seemed capable of depleting
his creative energies. True, he enjoyed his drink-fuelled afternoons
in the American Press Club or the numerous bars, cafes and
restaurants that had virtually become the colony of the expatriate
set. Yet he was terrified of being absorbed by something – albeit a
very disparate and liberal something – that was not his preferred
domain. He would seek out the latter in his excursions to Italy,
Germany and Spain but throughout his early years in Paris he
was involved in a struggle between the figure he fantasised as his
ideal self and the environment he would, as a consequence, come
to alienate.

One of the more intriguing stories of Hemingway's behaviour came from the poet and critic Archibald MacLeish who had taken him and Wyndham Lewis for lunch at a Left Bank restaurant in 1927. Lewis's waspish 'The Dumb Ox', on Hemingway, would not appear for four years but he had already made clear, in conversation and print, his thoughts on the pretensions to greatness of many American expatriate writers. Lewis had said goodbye at the restaurant and Hemingway accompanied MacLeish on a stroll along the Seine, remarking pointedly that 'Did you notice? He kept his gloves on all through lunch'. MacLeish found the observation 'lurid and memorable' given that Lewis had removed his gloves on arrival. Both were aware of rumours about Lewis's alleged obsessive-compulsive habits but there was no evidence of these, MacLeish later testified, during their two hours in the restaurant. MacLeish was alarmed because Hemingway had not merely misrepresented Lewis's behaviour. He had invented the incident with the gloves; both of them knew this but Hemingway seemed to expect MacLeish to connive in the blatant alteration of truth. Creating a fiction was one thing but assuming that one's companion would treat it as fact, seemed, at least for MacLeish, symptomatic of a very curious character disorder. It is worth comparing this incident with a number of Hemingway's other blurrings of the line between invention and honesty. In August 1922, seven months after their arrival in Paris, the Hemingways' arranged a visit to Germany. First they would take a holiday in the Black Forest, accompanied by Galantiere, his fiancée Dorothy Butler, and the American journalist Bill Bird and his wife Sally. At Hemingway's behest he and Hadley bought air tickets to Strasbourg with the Franco-Romanian Aero Company, an outfit that ran three draughty biplanes from Le Bourget to random destinations. Their four friends chose to take the ten-hour train journey. Hemingway's devil-may-care mode of transport chimed perfectly with his plans for two weeks' hiking through the Black Forest – clothes and fishing tackle in haversacks, freshly caught trout cooked over bonfires. Things did not quite go as planned. His companions recoiled from living rough, insisted on rooms in the most bearable small-town inns, reached by rail. The strict German laws on fishing only by permission of estates and through complex licensing regulations took the edge off his ideal of losing himself within the wilderness. He rented a well-stocked stretch of the Elz from a local landowner, in contrast with his carefully cultivated image as reckless poacher. By all accounts the others saw his inconstancies as amusing, at least until he tripped on a log when returning from an afternoon on the river. His back was severely bruised, his proud stature now bent, and he dreaded the prospect of prolonged embarrassment, even with compensatory doses of pity from the others. His wisest option would probably have been self-caricature but instead he cultivated the image of tragic hero, taking to his bed and informing them that when they returned from their picnic the following day he would 'probably be dead' – all without a hint of irony. The next afternoon he rejoined the party seemingly in good health and made no further reference to the incident. It was farcical, and prescient. Two years later he wrote to Dorothy of the holiday, stating that 'Even though I kissed you Dorothy, even while I kissed you, I never liked you but I was willing to make the effort [...] for the sake of seeing Lewis.' Dorothy was perplexed, but not because he had insulted her as a past *inamorato*. The kiss, indeed the mild flirtation, had never occurred.

At the beginning of September Hemingway and Hadley saw the others off to Paris and took the train to Cologne where they met up again with Chink Dorman-Smith who was a member of the British Army occupation garrison. While Germany remained an independent state after the Armistice key parts of it were occupied by Allied troops throughout the 1920s, a situation that encouraged civil disorder and political extremism. Dorman-Smith had promised to show him a city on the brink of anarchy. It would, he implied, be a rerun of their experiences in war-torn Italy but this time Hemingway was the freelance front-line correspondent, with the opportunity for his copy, if thrilling enough, to be sold internationally via Reuters and other agencies. To his disappointment, however, Cologne seemed duller than Paris, its citizens more concerned with the hyperinflated cost of bread than with civil unrest. Dorman-Smith showed him a vandalised equestrian statue of the now exiled Kaiser. A mob, he reported, had attacked it with sledgehammers and later, it was rumoured, fatally injured a policeman who attempted to intervene. The death of the policeman, unnamed, was a vague story which seemed to gain in macabre detail as it circulated among customers in bars. The account that Hemingway sent to his editor at the *Star*, John Bone, and which Bone published, gives the impression that the intrepid reporter witnessed the events as they occurred, when in fact he had assembled the story from unaccountable gossip and rumour. He describes how the mob attempts to throw the policeman into the Rhine, and of how he manages to hang on to an abutment of the bridge, shouting up that he could and would identify them, ensuring their punishment. 'Then', reports Hemingway, 'the mob chopped his fingers loose from the stone with the hatchet with which they had been attacking the statue.' One might of course grant him some indulgence as an ambitious young hack determined to make what he could from the turmoil of postwar Europe: journalism in those days was made up more of vivid reportage than authenticated evidence. The article, like several others he authored at this time, is important because it is all but indistinguishable from the so-called 'miniatures' or 'vignettes' that would eventually become the core stories of the first edition of *In Our Time*. All have the vigour and immediacy of fiction but equally Hemingway grounded them in experience, witnessed directly or reported to him by friends such as Dorman-Smith. The question that endures, which no biographer or critic has addressed, is whether Hemingway was at the time making a conscious distinction between literary and non-literary writing. In the sixth very brief short story of *In Our Time* we are told in meticulous detail of the execution of six cabinet Greek ministers at the close of the Greco-Turkish war. The incident was reported widely in the press and Hemingway spoke with many who knew of it when he covered the postwar conference at Lausanne and borrowed from their copy to report on it to the *Star*. His story is lurid and vivid, to the extent that he dwells on the shooting of one of the ministers who was suffering from typhoid and who could not stand up to offer the firing squad a proper target. 'The other five stood very quietly against the wall. Finally the officer told the soldiers it was no good trying to make him stand up. When they fired the first volley he was sitting down in the water with his head on his knees.' It is impossible to distinguish, stylistically, between this and the article on the, alleged, murder of the policeman in Cologne. Perversely, the latter is journalism riddled with pure invention while the former sounds like a journalistic account of an event that no one contested as untrue, yet which is offered as a short story. Sometimes fiction can, when properly handled, provide us with a pitilessly accurate record of what we might wish to forget, in terms of the human condition being something we share – and here *Schindler's Ark* is the prime example – and journalists often exploit their creative talent to electrify the truth. But Hemingway causes us to wonder if he was alert to any clear difference between truth-telling and making things up. *In Our Time* is composed of pieces that are indistinguishable from the articles he sent to the *Star*, and even those which involve his intermittent proxy Nick Adams read more like an animated travelogue than fiction. In this respect Stein's advice that he should cut the passage from the original manuscript of 'Big Two-Hearted River' is revealing but not because she thought it a piece of writing that was below standard or redundant. Rather she encountered some-thing a little more disquieting. Nick reflects on the nature of writing and gradually becomes unable, or unwilling, to differen-tiate between the actual and the imagined. 'The only thing that was any good was what you made up, what you imagined. That made everything come true.' (The passage was eventually published as a separate piece called 'On Writing' in the 1972 edition of the *Nick Adams Stories*.) In the JFK archive there is an untitled, undated prose fragment which circumstantial evidence suggests was composed when he was planning the eventually abandoned coda to the story. He opens, 'When you first start writing stories in the first person if the stories are made so real that people reading them nearly always think the stories really happened to you.' He is idealising a brand of writing so transparent that it causes writing to be redundant:

> That is natural because while you were making them up you had to make them happen to the person who was telling them [...] If you can do this you are beginning to get what you are trying for which is to make the story real that it is beyond any reality [...]. (JFK, Roll 19. T 178)

This is the closest we will come to finding Hemingway's single, uncontrived working mantra. Conventionally, logically, fiction represents life, but Hemingway's principal character transcends that state: things must be made to 'happen to the person' before they can tell us about them. The ultimate objective is a 'story' so 'real that it is beyond reality'. He wrote this before he had begun his first full-length novel, but Hemingway would go on to become a novelist whose relationship with his medium is unique: for him, life and fiction were two dimensions of the same continuum.

Hemingway the letter writer was something of a chameleon. Often in Paris he would mimic the conversational familiarities of those he claimed as his confidants and these letters tell us something, albeit inadvertently, of a man who had chosen to forget the difference between art and life. On 17–18 July 1923 he sent a report to Bill Horne, with whom he had served in Italy, on his recent adventures. The following is a typical passage: 'And we flew to Strasbourg and hiked all through the Black Forest and fished for trout and caught lots and lived in little Inns and loved each other [...] and came down the Rhine from Frankfurt to Cologne and visited Chink and came back to Paris – and saw Siki nearly kill Carpentier and I got a cable from the Star to go to Constantinople and went and was with the Greek Army in the big retreat – and three weeks in Constant itself – 3 very fine weeks when just as it was getting light you'd all get into a car and drive out to the Bosphorous to see the sun rise and sober up and wonder if there was going to be a war that would set the world on fire again [...]' and on and on for several hundred words, unpunctuated but for an occasional dash. Never before had he written like this to Horne and nor would he again. Hemingway had recently become acquainted with the stream-of-consciousness techniques of Stein and Joyce and, without explanation to Horne, visited his pal with an example of them. Frequently his letters to Stein and Toklas would sound like extracts from *The Making of Americans* but these were not good-humoured recognitions of her uniqueness as a novelist. They were involuntary. He was continually searching for a persona that suited his predispositions as an individual and a writer, and always he was borrowing from others. Quite soon he would find a means of reinventing himself that was premeditated, and the consequences for many of those he knew would be painful. He would begin with Anderson and Stein and later, in *The Sun Also Rises* and other fictions, target other blameless friends and fellow writers.

On 25 November 1923 he replied to the critic Edmund Wilson who had read and praised several of the stories that had been published in magazines and would soon appear in *In Our Time*. We have no record of Wilson's letter but it obviously included some reference to Sherwood Anderson. Hemingway responded: 'No I don't think *My Old Man* [a Hemingway story] derives from Anderson. It is about a boy and his father and race-horses. Sherwood has written about boys and horses. But very differently. It derives from boys and horses. I don't think they're anything alike. I know I wasn't inspired by him.' Having failed to provide a coherent case for his own originality, let alone the quintessential features of Anderson's work, he goes on to deprecate him, rather in the manner of a floundering adolescent: 'I know him pretty well but I have not seen him for several years [actually 18 months]. His work seems to have gone to hell, perhaps from people in New York telling him too much how good he was. Functions of criticism. I am very fond of him. He has written good stories.' He knows that he does not want to be seen as in some way indebted to Anderson but he can't transform this into a rational argument. Within five sentences he turns full circle, from unfounded bitterness – 'his work seems to have gone to hell' – to a guilty retrenchment of feeling: 'I am very fond of him. He has written good stories.'

In 1925 he decided to undermine further suggestions that his writing owed anything to Anderson. *The Torrents of Spring* is a novel of around 15,000 words which Hemingway completed with astonishing speed between 20 and 26 November and it is one the cruellest parodies of one writer by another. Hemingway's caricature opens with Scripps, alone, walking down an Illinois railway track in midwinter. He comes upon an almost dead bird that he hopes he might revive. 'The bird nestled close to his warm body and pecked at his chest gratefully. "Poor little chap," Scripps said. "You feel the cold too." Tears came into his eyes.'

Scripps is more than a spoof of Anderson's typical characters. The story, of his own beginnings as a writer, of how he had left his wife and children and walked more than 30 miles down the railway track to Chicago to live in a hostel with a second-hand typewriter, had become a legend for aspiring young novelists. Scripps is Anderson and as the account of his lonely journey continues it becomes clear that Hemingway is targeting something more than his erstwhile mentor's writing; he finds him lacking in the toughness and brutality that is, in Hemingway's view, a prerequisite for good, male, prose:

> Scripps read the sign again. Could this be Petoskey? A man was inside the station, tapping something back of a wicketed window. He looked out at Scripps. Could he be a telegrapher? Something told Scripps that he was.
>
> He stepped out of the snow-drift and approached the window. Behind the window the man worked busily away at his telegrapher's key.
>
> 'Are you a telegrapher?' asked Scripps.
>
> 'Yes, sir', said the man. 'I'm a telegrapher.'
>
> 'How wonderful!'
>
> The telegrapher eyed him suspiciously. After all, what was this man to him?
>
> 'Is it hard to be a telegrapher?' Scripps asked ...
>
> The telegrapher looked at him curiously.
>
> 'Say,' he asked, 'are you a fairy?'
>
> 'No,' Scripps said. 'I don't know what being a fairy means.'
>
> 'Well,' said the telegrapher, 'what do you carry a bird around for?'
>
> 'Bird?' asked Scripps. 'What bird?'

The Torrents of Spring is horribly clever in that few who'd read Anderson would fail to recognise him as Hemingway's victim. Anderson has his imperfections. They are certainly not as glaring as Hemingway would have us believe but he causes us to suspect that they might be.

Curiously, the tone of the book alters in Part Four where the overwrought imitation of Anderson is counterpointed against

far more recklessly experimental passages which could have been
lifted directly from the novel by Stein he had just put into print
and indeed from his own unpublished 'Summer People'. For less
avid readers of the latest experimental fiction he offered a clue in
the title 'The Passing of a Great Race and the Making and Marring of
Americans'. Hemingway later stated that the book had made Stein
'very angry', not because she featured in it but since he had 'attacked
someone that was part of her apparatus'.

There is no record of any exchanges on the book between
Hemingway and Stein but he wrote to Anderson on 21 May 1926.
He appears unable to make up his mind on whether he feels contrite
or blameless:

> You see I feel that if among ourselves we have to pull our punches, if
> when a man like yourself who can write very great things writes
> something [he has referred already to Anderson's recent *Dark Laughter*]
> that seems to me rotten. I ought to tell you so.

In the next paragraph we come upon an embarrassing example of
him seeming to look for the right words while remaining shiftily
evasive:

> I guess this is a lousy snooty letter and it will seem like a lousy snooty
> book. That wasn't the way I wanted this letter to be – nor the book.
> Though I don't care so much about the book because the book isn't
> personal and the tougher it is the better.

For Anderson, so nastily satirised, the only hint of atonement might
have come in reading a letter that was beyond parody. A little later
Hemingway makes another, hapless attempt to rationalise his act
and justify his position:

> It goes sort of like this: 1 Because you are my friend I would not want to
> hurt you. 2 Because you are my friend has nothing to do with writing.
> 3 Because you are my friend I hurt you more. 4 Outside of personal
> feelings nothing that's good can be hurt by satire.

Hemingway's closing reference to Stein would surely have stupefied
him completely: 'I haven't seen Gertrude Stein since last fall. Her
making of Americans is one of the very greatest books I've ever read.'
Aside from the fact that he had also derided this book in his caricature
of Anderson the statement is preposterous in its own right. Even

during the 1920s, die-hard advocates of modernism indulged the book more as a bizarre curiosity than a serious contribution to the new aesthetic.

Anderson and his wife visited Paris in December 1926. During their time there they regularly called on Stein and Toklas, and Stein arranged a number of receptions at the houses of fellow patrons – including that of the wealthy American feminist Nancy Clifford Barney – at which in general he was lionised as a major literary presence. Pound and Gide, among others, called upon him and paid their compliments. He was slightly puzzled by the absence of Hemingway who, for no explicit reason, no longer visited Stein and seemed determined to avoid any events that Anderson and Stein were likely to attend. He recalls in his *Memoirs* talking with Stein about Hemingway, who lived with his wife and son barely two kilometres away. They agreed that he had been 'a good pupil' yet they felt 'a little proud and a little ashamed of their product'. Stein remarked that he was 'a pupil who does it without understanding it' and what she appears to mean is that irrespective of his having learned nothing from his time among the new writers, painters and thinkers his ego had carried him to success. Anderson seemed more perplexed by Hemingway's letter than the book, finding it 'a kind of funeral oration delivered over my grave. It was so raw, so pretentious, so patronizing, that it was amusing but I was filled with wonder'. Stein explained to him that Hemingway was unable to distinguish his new-found vocation as a literary artist from the aggressive competitive instinct that drew him to sport, fishing, bullfighting and hunting, and that as a writer he had 'staked out the whole field of sports for himself' and set about killing off his potential rivals. He had chosen Anderson as his first and most conspicuous victim.

Later that month he and Hemingway would meet, briefly and for the last time. No one knows who initiated the encounter but accounts by both parties of what happened differ considerably. Hemingway remarked in a letter to Max Perkins that they had 'a fine time' and that Anderson was 'not at all sore' about what he had done. According to Anderson in his *Memoirs*, Hemingway had arrived unannounced at their hotel on the final day of their visit and asked 'How about a drink?' They crossed the road to a bar and ordered beers. Hemingway lifted his glass, said 'Well, here's how', and emptied it in one. Anderson responded with 'Here's how' but before he had time to take the exchange further, let alone taste his drink, Hemingway 'turned and walked rapidly away'. To his credit Anderson made no other recorded mention of the novel or their meeting. As we will see it was Stein who exacted retribution, for both of them.

Hemingway first attended a bullfight in June 1923, in Madrid. Shortly before, Stein had instructed him that bullfighting was the nexus of Spanish culture and beyond that something inherently visceral, almost pagan. She knew him well enough to suspect he would be flattered by her notion of him as an ideal novitiate to a rite that most of his highly cultured associates would find abhorrent. In private she and Toklas were amused by his predictable, enthusiastic response. Within a few days he had persuaded his friends and potential publishers, Bill Bird and Robert McAlmon, to accompany him on his voyage of discovery; they too had never before witnessed bullfighting. Bird agreed to meet his two companions after they had taken the train there together. As usual the plateau of mid-Spain was extraordinarily hot and, when they drew into the station in Madrid, windows open, they were greeted by the sight and smell of a recently dead dog, already part-eaten by maggots. McAlmon swallowed a mouthful of vomit and turned his head away, prompting Hemingway to remind him that he had been hardened to such spectacles during the war in Italy, when the maggot-ridden corpses were human. Two days later Hemingway was taking a seat for his first bullfight. Aside from his own excitement he was alert to McAlmon's response – Bird had not yet arrived. McAlmon gives a creditably sincere account in his memoirs, 15 years later, of how he felt: 'At first it seemed totally unreal, like something happening on the screen.' His mixture of unease and fascination segues into a sense of being a participant in the ritual: 'Instead of a shock of disgust, I rose in my seat and let out a yell.' Eventually he reflects on what he has become and feels disgusted that he had allowed himself to enjoy it. Hemingway, next day, composed an article for the *Star*: 'Bullfighting is not a Sport – It is a Tragedy'. 'He seemed like some great prehistoric animal, absolutely deadly and absolutely vicious. And he was silent. He charged silently and with a soft galloping rush. When he turned he turned on his four feet like a cat. When he charged the first thing that caught his eye was the picador on one of the wretched horses.' He had written nothing like this before. The prose has a natural energy and momentum that draws upon, and draws us into, the events in the ring. Hemingway himself does not comment. He does not need to because he has become the medium for the spectacle he is witnessing. In Paris he had searched desperately for something within the intellectual radicalism of the city that would accommodate his primitivist temperament. In Spain he found it. McAlmon was horrified most by the gored horse who was left to gallop desperately around the ring treading on its own bloody, trailing entrails, apparently disregarded by the audience who were concerned only with the dramatic contest between man and bull. Thereafter Hemingway provoked and ridiculed McAlmon for his unmanly response. After they were joined by Bird and left for Seville for the Feast of Corpus Christi bullfights he continued to treat him as a man who had failed some inaugural test. Most evenings he left his expatriate companions to themselves and tried out his colloquial Spanish with groups of matadors, absorbing himself in the terminology of their profession. Almost ten years later in *Death in the Afternoon* Hemingway resorted to what had by then become his routine of deriding in print those who had befriended him in the 1920s. In the book McAlmon becomes 'X.Y.': '27 years old; American; male, college education [...] when bull charged picador and hit horse, X.Y. gave sudden screeching intake of breath'. Throughout, 'X.Y.' is presented as a man whose claim to maleness is suspect. Hemingway was particularly appalled by McAlmon's flirtations with young Spanish men – he was openly bisexual – which seemed to confirm for him that those who were unable to stomach the spectacle of the bullfight were weak and decadent. He found it easy to forget, when he ridiculed McAlmon's response to the rotting dog and later the disembowelled horse, that his companion had seen action as a pilot in the war. Hemingway was always ready to reframe the actual according to his prejudices and preferences. McAlmon later offered a dry laconic account of his erstwhile friend's new infatuation. 'Before leaving Paris, Hemingway had been much of a shadow-boxer. As he approached a cafe he would prance about, sparring at shadows, his lips moving, calling his imaginary opponent's bluff. Upon returning from Spain, he substituted shadow-bullfighting for shadow-boxing. The amount of imaginary cape work and sword thrusts he made in those days was formidable.'

Over the next five years he became a regular aficionado of the season of fights, in 1924 taking with him Hadley, Bumby and others from Paris to the Pamplona festival where traditional matadorial contests were set against the 'run' through the streets of bulls and reckless young men. One day Hemingway grabbed the horns of a bull and appeared to wrestle with the animal. Its horns were well padded and at worst he faced the danger of bruised or broken ribs but Hemingway wanted to portray himself as an honorary member of the elect society of matadors. Constantly he was inspecting his associates for those who were with him and those who might replicate McAlmon's sense of revulsion, and from this emerged a plan for what would be his first novel. *The Sun Also Rises* is not really about Spain and bullfighting. Rather, these settings and events become filters for its author's desire to dispatch himself, with a considerable degree of loathing, from the community of Paris-based writers and intellectuals.

The biographical resonances of the book have been scrutinised to the point of surpassing tedium. Jake, the narrator, is Hemingway. The motley crew of expatriates Jake associates with, first in Paris and then during a visit to Spain, notably to Pamplona to witness the annual festival of bull-running and bullfights, is based on Hemingway's impressions of individuals he knew. There are few one-to-one parallels between real and made-up characters, with two conspicuous exceptions. The volatile, alcoholic and sexually alluring Lady Brett Ashley is an unflattering version of the English aristocrat Mary Duff Twysden, and Jake's associate and fellow writer Robert Cohn is a cruel, unamusing caricature of Harold Loeb, scion of a wealthy New York Jewish family and a man who, at least until the novel appeared, regarded Hemingway as a close friend.

The status of the book as a literary classic is now beyond dispute, at least if you respect the legions of critics entrusted as accreditors of the modern 'greats'. Hemingway makes use of his proxy, Jake, to eviscerate the world and its inhabitants in which he had existed, usually as a welcome guest, for the previous three years, and to excuse himself from any association with them. In early September 1925 Hemingway, Harold Loeb and Bill Smith, each of whom had been in the group that had visited Spain earlier in the summer, attended a dinner in Paris hosted by Kitty Cannell, a wealthy dance and fashion correspondent who had known Hemingway for two years and taken an interest in his writing. He arrived last. 'Hey Kitty', he announced, 'I'm taking your advice. I'm writing a novel full of plot and drama'. He then nodded towards Loeb and Smith: 'I'm tearing those bastards apart [...] I'm putting everyone in it and that kike Loeb is the villain. But you're a wonderful girl Kitty and I wouldn't do anything to annoy you.' He had completed the first draft of the novel, provisionally entitled *Fiesta*, in six weeks during the July and August, and was now revising it.

It was not an empty threat – he would deliver as promised – but *The Sun Also Rises* diverged radically from the standard practices of satire and caricature. The figures observed by Jake, first in Paris and then during the trip to Spain, are not the subjects of ridicule. Rather, they are, in varying degrees, hopeless, directionless and pitiable. Hemingway's considerable achievement involves his management of the relationship between Jake and everyone else. Jake never appraises his peers: he takes a step back and allows them to condemn themselves. More than half of the book is made up of dialogue, sometimes involving Jake but more often as if he has ceased to be present. He gives the impression that he participates in these exchanges only as a matter of necessity; he prefers to share with the reader the role of listener. When he does enter the story Jake's manner is brittle, impatient. His prose is the prototype for Hemingway's mature fiction, and the following is brief and exemplary: 'Together we walked down the gravel path in the park in the dark, under the trees and then out from under the trees and past the gate into the street that led into the town.'

The speaking characters, Jake included, do not talk in a manner remotely similar to the way he writes. He builds himself an island of immunity from the witty, abrasive, erudite exchanges that inform the lives of his fictional co-habitants. His prose conveys a message: I, as a writer, am no longer content among this group of artistic aspirants. I exempt myself from their world by adopting a style that is exclusively my own, so much so that the reader will not find parallels with it in anything they have previously encountered. This quest for individuality – crafted during a period of less than two months – is, depending upon the reader's disposition, unendurably painful to read or a turning point in the history of English prose fiction. Listening to someone who repeats the same phrase lazily or insistently and who litters their conversation with scatterings of rhyme and alliteration would surely prompt us to excuse ourselves as soon as possible. Similarly, in *The Sun Also Rises* we flee from the narrator back to the dialogue, but perhaps this is what Hemingway intended. It is possible that he was replicating Jake's wish to detach himself from his world in the reader's feelings of alienation. If so the novel must be treated as a masterpiece inspired almost exclusively by its author's vindictiveness.

When the novel closes we find that although Jake has been with us for the duration of the story we know hardly anything of him. This is a remarkable technical accomplishment but we should consider his motivation. All of the male characters are made up of the temperamental characteristics that drew Hemingway to the artistic community of Paris, many of which he shared. Lady Brett Ashley, while inspired by Lady Duff Twysden, was a composite of a selection of women Hemingway had desired, idolised and some-times grown to loathe, Hadley included. Prior to the Spanish trip he had attempted to seduce Duff Twysden, unsuccessfully, begun an affair with the American heiress and recent arrival in Paris, Pauline Pfeiffer, and become acquainted with Scott Fitzgerald and his wife Zelda. From the beginning he treated the latter with utter contempt, which she gladly reciprocated, and did his best to convince Scott that Zelda was intent on ruining him as a man and a writer. Jake is the only character who is not sexually attracted to Brett Ashley. He confesses to a heroic form of 'impotence', caused by a wartime injury, though we remain uncertain of whether he is incapable of sex or procreation. Either way it makes credible his indifference to Brett's ubiquitous sexual allure. Hemingway, via his proxy, is releasing himself from all of his emotional investments. Instead, Jake watches as the other men, including a young matador, are transfixed and betrayed by her. The novel was his first attempt to realise the ideal of his unpublished JFK fragment on the novel in general, so 'real that it is beyond reality' – fiction as omnipotence with more than a hint of malice.

The most revealing disclosure of his motive comes in a letter he wrote to Pound (30 November 1925). He refers to *The Torrents of Spring* as a caricature of Sherwood and Stein, along with 'Lewis, Cather, [and] Hergo [Hergesheimer, a popular US novelist]'. Hemingway compares himself with Henry Fielding, who in the eighteenth century parodied and undermined the instructive, puritanical fiction of Samuel Richardson, but he was as much concerned with the novel about to appear as the one in press: 'I'm going to write a Joseph Andrews [...] I don't see how Sherwood will be able to write again. Gertrude isn't worth the bother to show up'. He promises that the 'next one' will be even more devastating. It would be. His *Joseph Andrews* was *The Sun Also Rises*. Just as Fielding began to write novels that went against the popular consensus established by Richardson, Hemingway uses his first two novels to, respectively, ridicule and alienate those writers who had come to form the new literary establishment of the 1920s. His perception of himself as a modern version of Fielding is fascinating, not least because it points up the striking differences between the two men. Fielding was dismayed by the treatment of the novel by Richardson and others as a means of proselytising public decency; he treated his opponent with respectful indulgence. For Hemingway something far more personal and vindictive had contributed to his distancing of himself from Europe. As we will see, he regarded all of his peers as potential competitors and by the 1930s he would turn upon his erstwhile friends, notably Dos Passos and Fitzgerald, with unreserved contempt. Neither had visited anything insulting or unfriendly upon him but they had dared to offer constructive critical comments on his work and by implication classified themselves as his equals.

His comment in the letter that 'I don't see how Sherwood will ever be able to write again' is telling. He wanted to eliminate competitors rather than merely supersede them.

Hemingway was nurturing other motives for dispatching Europe to his past. He had set out upon a *ménage à trois* involving Hadley and Pauline, eventually to be conducted by the three of them in a gruesomely open manner in Antibes during the summer of 1926, while the novel went to press. He was considering his long-term options, comparing the prospects of competing forms of commitment, and treating each woman in the way a potential purchaser might weigh up the attractions, and reliability, of different cars on a dealership forecourt. Hadley had never been a classically attractive woman – wholesome prettiness would be a better description – and after her first child she had grown larger in figure and more homely in temperament. But neither could Pauline – 'Fife' as she would be known – be regarded as the sexual magnet who would cause Hemingway to suddenly abandon his otherwise happy and stable marriage. Those who witnessed and reported on the events of 1925–6 seem puzzled by Hemingway's behaviour. Pauline was, as all agreed, acceptable in appearance but certainly not tantalising. Most descriptions of her are measured, almost apologetic: 'small boned and lively as a partridge'; 'a vivacious women rather than a pretty one'. She was clever and enjoyed talking to Hemingway about his work, but she was also a committed Roman Catholic whose worldview was shaped by her faith – or so she claimed. If accounts by contemporaries can be trusted, Hemingway in Paris was a man who could have taken his pick from barmaids, dancers, singers of all nationalities and expatriate heiresses of redoubtable beauty, and sometimes did so. The question of why he began an affair with Pauline and eventually chose to desert Hadley for her is one that his biographers have elected to leave unanswered. Her money might have played a part. His resignation from the *Star* came shortly after the birth of Bumby in Canada, and though he passed it off to many as his choice to exchange the role of reporter for that of freelance journalist and independent writer, the true cause was beyond his control. When he was in Ontario, Bone, his indulgent open-minded editor, was replaced by Harry Hindmarsh, a man who expected the

reporting of current affairs and politics to be rigorously unostenta-
tious and devoid of opinionated comment. Hindmarsh imposed
regulations on Hemingway that he knew would impoverish his will
to write anything at all. No longer would he be able to combine the
bluntness of truth-telling with vivid imaginative nuances, the
keynote of his early short stories, and with reluctance he gave up his
job. He faced the prospect of relying on Hadley's resources to
support him as an aspiring novelist, and during the 18 months
following their return to Paris the likelihood of gaining an income
from the latter seemed clear enough: nil. Moreover, by the time he
met Pauline, Hadley's fortune had suffered even further following
the disastrous fall in its value a year earlier, caused by the financial
incompetence of her executor-uncle: their most reliable source of
funds was becoming even more precarious. *The Sun Also Rises* would
eventually provide him with esteem and money but while he was
waiting for the book to go into print, and beginning his affair with
Pauline, he had no reason to foresee this. He had begun to
contemplate his latest mistress as his long-term financial safety net.

Kitty Cannell, at whose soiree Hemingway would announce the
savage character assassinations of *The Sun Also Rises*, hosted a dinner
in March 1925 at which she introduced two expatriate newcomers to
members of the cultural in-crowd of Paris. They were Jinny and
Pauline Pfeiffer, sisters, recently arrived in France and part of a US
trend that had begun to resemble the 'Grand Tour' undertaken by
members of the British aristocracy and nouveau riche two centuries
before. Neither of the Pfeiffers had ambitions to write, paint or do
anything remotely creative. Pauline had worked for various
newspapers in the US before leaving for Europe but not as a
journalist. She was an office worker never taxed with dogsbody
activities but secured as what we would now call an intern by virtue
of family sponsorship. Her father, Paul, was one of the wealthiest
landowners and industrialists in the Midwest. He owned and farmed
60,000 acres of Arkansas, had made a fortune as a commodity broker
in St Louis and invested his profits in various banks, cotton
companies and gigantic timber enterprises. He was happy to support
his daughters' excursion to Europe; the Pfeiffer sisters were to be
introduced to an artistic and social elite of mostly US expatriates.

In Paris Pauline worked as an 'assistant' to the editor of the French edition of *Vogue* magazine, a role that involved her as a lauded guest at fashion shows and theatre openings. She would deliver 'reports' on these events to the scribes based at 2 rue Edouard VII but not once did she herself write anything for the magazine. Soon after being introduced to the Hemingways at the Cannell party the Pfeiffer sisters visited them in their ramshackle apartment above the sawmill. Ostensibly they had come to see Hadley, and Hemingway maintained a stance of gruff indifference as they conversed with his wife. When Pauline reported on the visit to Kitty Cannell she said nothing of her exchanges with Hadley, telling instead of her perplexity at how this woman could put up with a man who lay in an unmade bed in his undershirt, torso partly exposed, unshaven and with uncombed hair. It was clear enough to Kitty that the recumbent 'lout' who had hardly bothered to acknowledge her presence was the true object of Pauline's attention.

Thereafter she set out on a Machiavellian strategy to win Hemingway, but not simply as a lover. She would insinuate herself into his relationship with Hadley, destroy it, and take him as her husband. Moreover, she would succeed in enshrouding him in the delusion that he was the guilty seducer – a fantasy that he enjoyed. It suited his appetite for a blend of sexual hubris and visceral unreason. In truth, he was the puppet and Pauline was the puppet master. She began her campaign by becoming what we would today treat as a stalker – a refined equivalent of Glenn Close in *Fatal Attraction*, but without the boiled rabbit.

In December 1925 Cannell came across Pauline in a Paris street, bent double beneath a recently purchased bag of top-quality skis, boots and winter clothing. She was, she announced to Kitty with a smile, travelling to Schruns, Austria, for Christmas and the New Year. 'Ernest' had invited her to share a chalet with his family and promised he would teach her to ski. How exactly the 'lout' she had observed earlier that year had now become her host and instructor is still unclear, but evidence indicates that she was playing a calculating, proactive role in making herself a friend of the family. When they returned to Paris in January 1926, Pauline wrote to Hadley to ask if she would return a kimono and a hairbrush which she had mislaid in Schruns and enclosed a generous amount of cash for a belated Christmas present for Bumby. Praising Pauline's skills as a pianist, she also included an account of how she had talked at length with her husband on whether he should alter the draft of *The Sun Also Rises* from first to third person. She had urged against and Hemingway, it seemed, had followed her advice. Two weeks later Pauline learned that Hemingway planned a brief visit to New York to find the most reliable, and profitable, publisher for the novel, and she announced to the author and his wife that she would be happy to accompany him on the trip. The innocent implication was that she might make use of family contacts to secure the best contract, but a more unsettling subtext was evident to many, with the exception of Hadley.

From Schruns, Hemingway had written a bizarre letter to Fitzgerald, in which for no evident reason he explains the true inspiration for two short stories, 'Cat in the Rain' and 'Out of Season', written when he and Hadley had visited Italy in 1923. He insists that Hadley features in neither and then contradicts himself: 'Hadley was 4 months pregnant with Bumby [...] Hadley never made a speech in her life about wanting a baby because she had been told various things by her doctor and I'd –. No use going into all that' (*circa* 24 December 1925). During their visit to Rapallo, Hemingway and Hadley had argued because he told her once more that he regretted her pregnancy. Fitzgerald knew nothing of this and would not have assumed that her fictional proxy had 'made a speech' about wanting a baby, given that the woman in 'Cat in the Rain' beseeches her husband to allow her to have a kitten. Why, one might ask, would Hemingway suddenly return to this moment of using fiction as a means of protecting himself from an uncomfortable truth? The fact that Schruns marked the beginning of his sexual relationship with Pauline might have played a part. At Schruns, Hemingway found himself caught between the life he was living and the one he was lying about to his wife. Thus he wrote to his friend about an episode two years before when he had sought refuge from the worst aspects of himself in the cleansing mechanisms of fiction. As a codicil to his mendacious explication of 'Cat in the Rain' he tells of why 'Out of Season' is only an 'almost literal transcription of what happened'. In the story a drunken gardener in the Italian hotel had promised the main character good trout fishing and had taken him to an unfishable part of a local river. On their return he had complained to the hotel owner of his employee's behaviour. He had, he told Fitzgerald, 'not put in' the fact that the actual, now jobless, gardener had hanged himself in a nearby barn. He had not included it because it had not happened. He had made it up two years later when he wrote the letter in Schruns. For an author to revisit the events behind a story and have one of the real characters commit suicide seems morbid to say the least. But Schruns involved Hemingway in the meshing of adultery, lying to his wife and dealing with his conscience, and the letter to Fitzgerald was a weird exploration of this, an experiment in blurring the distinctions between honesty and outright invention.

In Easter 1926, Pauline and Jinny invited Hadley to join them on a tour of the Loire valley. Jinny was be the main driver of their luxurious Peugeot saloon and their explorations of the chateaux and villages were interrupted only by evenings in hotels chosen for their elegance and the quality of their cuisine. At the beginning Hadley had no reason to suspect that the trip was anything other than the cementing of a new friendship between three young women, but gradually the sisters embarked on a campaign of mental torture which by the end of the holiday left their companion in little doubt that her life, her future, would soon be subject to the insidious, manipulative control of others. During their car journeys the sisters would pose seemingly innocuous enquiries about Hemingway's ongoing activities and, following Hadley's responses, would indicate with sadistic subtlety that they knew a little more of her husband than she did.

Hadley seems to have been outstandingly resilient and civilised, particularly during the summer of 1926 when Pauline was openly involved in a sexual relationship with her husband, despite Hadley's daily presence. In May the Hemingways took up what was left of a short lease on a villa in Juan-les-Pins, soon to be joined in the locality by Archie and Ada MacLeish, Gerald Murphy (a wealthy Yale graduate) and his wife Sara, and Scott and Zelda Fitzgerald. Fitzgerald was drifting erratically between embarrassing public displays of alcoholism – on one occasion he was ejected from a restaurant after hurling ashtrays at fellow diners – and intense debates with his new friend, Hemingway, on their works-in-progress. Bumby was recovering from whooping cough and spent most of the summer quarantined with his nanny, Madame Rohrbach, in a nearby studio-sized bungalow. At the beginning of June a note arrived from Pauline reassuring them that she had suffered from this same condition as a child, was now immune and would therefore be joining them shortly. Hadley was puzzled by who had reported to Pauline on Bumby's health and invited her south, but she did not press the question and it endured as the preamble to a strange combination of bedroom farce and danse macabre. The three of them would share breakfast on the terrace and for the remainder of the morning sunbathe or swim together. After lunch, again eaten together, they would take siestas followed by cocktails with neighbours, notably the MacLeishes and the Fitzgeralds. When the lease to the villa expired they took adjoining rooms in a nearby hotel. Hadley would sometimes break away from the trio to deal with such practicalities as Madame Rohrbach's needs, Bumby's medical care and arrangements for the deliveries of food suitable for the child but unobtainable in the hotel. Neither Pauline nor Hemingway ever joined her on these excursions and Pauline appeared to derive quiet satisfaction from having replaced her as the woman 'at home'. For July the Hemingways had planned a trip to the bull-runs and fights in Pamplona. Pauline accompanied them, again staying in an adjoining room in the Hotel Quintana, and once more it is unclear as to whether some kind of invitation was issued or if she simply assumed that no one would object to the continuance of what had become a weird fait accompli. Two weeks later the Hemingways left for San Sebastian and Pauline announced, regretfully, that much as she would love to join them she had arranged to meet her sister in Paris. En route she took time to dispatch a postcard from Bayonne: 'Well, well, it's all over [...] *A bientot!*' Hadley felt some relief, which was fleeting given that throughout the rest of their time in Spain they would on their arrival at each hotel find notes and cards from her rival. It remains a mystery as to how Pauline obtained times and addresses, and the content of her missives were ambiguous verging upon the sinister. To the couple, then in Madrid, she wrote, following her report on her intention to buy a bicycle, 'I am going to get everything I want. Please write to me. This means YOU Hadley.' Of the three, Hadley was the one who was being tested to breaking point. If his wife insisted that he broke with Pauline, Hemingway would probably have backed down: he was prone to irresponsible acts but disinclined to deal with long-term consequences. In such circumstances Pauline too would have abandoned her campaign. She was causing discomfort to both of them but she could not wait much longer for a decisive outcome. Hemingway had spoken to Hadley of divorce, but in an irresolute and cowardly manner, waiting for her to seize the initiative. Instead, Hadley proposed that if he and Pauline remained attracted to each during a period of 100 days while she and her husband lived apart she would allow for a divorce. Pauline elected to sail for the US for the trial period and Hemingway, prompted by Hadley, borrowed from the Murphys a well-appointed flat in the rue Froidevaux on the Left Bank. The Murphys, among others, later testified to Hemingway's performance as a man beset by guilt, despair and irresolution, sometimes confessing that he had made a dreadful mistake while just as frequently exchanging remorse for drink-fuelled bitterness. He came across as an adolescent in the body of a man, ill-tempered at dealing with the consequences of his compulsions.

At the end of October 1926 the MacLeishes hosted a party at their Paris flat attended mainly by American expatriates, and though *The Sun Also Rises* had not quite reached the bookshops Hemingway was unofficial guest of honour. After downing several large whiskies he announced that he would give a public reading, not from the novel but of a poem he had composed over the past few days, entitled 'To the Tragic Poetess'. It is a garbled free verse piece, and while its subject is not named she was easily recognisable. Hemingway had been introduced to Dorothy Parker during his voyage to Europe from the US earlier that year, and they got on well. He found that her actual talent as a wit more than matched the legend and she was equally enchanted by his rough-house charm. There is no record of any discord between them and, though he later claimed that the poem was a harmless riposte to her having borrowed and failed to return his typewriter, this story was an outright lie, a pitiable attempt to explain what all agreed was a repulsive gesture. During the voyage, in March, he had shown her the typescript of his forthcoming novel. She was amused, much in the manner of someone who treats profundity as by its nature hilarious, a response that would later be echoed in her review of the book. During 1926 Parker had become pregnant by the playwright Charles MacArthur, had an abortion, and shortly afterwards attempted suicide by cutting her wrists. The poem opens:

> Oh thou who with a safety razor blade
> A new one to avoid infection
> Slit both her wrists
> The scars defy detection

Later, Hemingway compounds images of attempted suicide with those, imagined by Parker, of the unborn foetus. Such experiments might be credited as radical insights into the consequences of being a woman in the early twentieth century, but Hemingway's words are grotesquely malicious:

> But always vomited in time
> And bound your wrists up
> To tell how you could see his little hands
> Already formed
> You'd waited months too long
> That was the trouble
> But you always loved dogs and other people's children
> And hated Spain where they are cruel to donkeys

The reference to Spain indicates the true cause of his wrath. Parker thought the country backwards and barbaric, its primitive rituals – bullfighting included – bound up with Catholicism. Hemingway kept two letters from Parker. The first, undated but dispatched in 1926, refers to *The Sun Also Rises*, which she would later treat unsympathetically in print. 'Isn't it a least bit too sweet?' she asks him. 'It seems to me as if [you] endeavour to pander to popular taste' (1926, undated, JFK). Four years later she wrote again, providing a bleakly ironic prose account of her physical and mental state, implying that little had changed since his rendering of both in the poem. She closes: 'Have you got a copy, or where can I get one, or can you remember it enough to write it out[?] [...] It's the one about people you know never succeeding in committing suicide (by H Hemingway, the Boy Prophet.) I want to quote it in my dandy pamphlet' (1929, undated, JFK). As a practitioner of bleak, self-directed irony she is unsurpassable, but the letters tell us much more than this. Parker had earned his savagery for daring to state that his writing was imperfect. Others – not least Dos Passos and Fitzgerald – would reap an equally dire fate for doing the same.

Hemingway had tolerated rather than practised Christianity but Pauline's devout Catholicism had caused him to treat the religious intensity of Catholic countries, Spain in particular, with awed fascination. In the poem on Parker he refers to her visit to Spain: 'You'd seen it with the Seldes/One Jew, his wife and a consumptive'. Gilbert Seldes, sometime editor of *The Dial*, and Jewish, had rejected a story from Hemingway two years earlier. At the close of the poem Hemingway reports on the true cause of Parker's disaffection with Spain.

> Spaniards pinched
> The Jewish cheeks of your plump ass
> In Holy Week in Seville

Every guest at the MacLeish party was stunned. Donald Ogden Stewart, who had helped and befriended Hemingway throughout his time in Paris, swore never to speak to him again. Within a few weeks most of those present had also read *The Sun Also Rises* and even those not pre-warned of Hemingway's boast that some of his friends might feature in it were astonished by the cruelty of his portrayals, particularly of Harold Loeb as Robert Cohn. Kitty Cannell, who had had a brief relationship with Loeb, was disgusted and perplexed. She knew both men well and had never witnessed any discord between them. Loeb himself was confounded by the cause of his friend's malice. Much later in his 1959 memoir he told of how he and Hemingway had argued one evening during the 1925 visit to Pamplona and almost come to blows. The cause, he vaguely recalled, was his own confession that Spain bored him and that he found the national obsession with bullfighting symptomatic of something ubiquitous and uncivilised. But, he also remarked, exchanges such as this, sometimes with violence, usually cemented rather than undid friendships with Hemingway. They were part of a very masculine bonding ritual. Loeb implied that their argument hardly explained let alone justified Hemingway's assault on him in the book. Hemingway marshals the narrative and its characters as a pogrom in fiction. Cohn, gradually but incessantly, becomes the outsider with each of the other male members of the group cultivating a sense of resentment against him. No obvious reason for this is presented but the reader is given the opportunity to draw their own conclusions. Cohn has had an affair with Lady Brett Ashley (as did Loeb with Duff Twysden). He, the 'kike', is trespassing on territory that the other men, all Gentiles, regard as their own. Hemingway even takes the trouble to present Cohn as a bully. He beats up Jake (Hemingway), Mike (Brett's fiancée) and the young matador Romero. Loeb had boxed at Princeton but, being 40 pounds lighter than Hemingway, thought it wisest to avoid a contest. By comparison with this novel *The Merchant of Venice* seems like a sermon on multiculturalism. The fact that all available copies of the novel were publically burned in Germany in the 1930s – because it was thought to advertise US decadence – tells us something of Hemingway's brand of antisemitism. It was not that the Nazi's failed to notice his treatment of Loeb; rather, Hemingway's presentation of him was seen as little more than a reflection of commonplace social mores. Before the Holocaust, in America and throughout Europe, Jews were routinely classified as outsiders. In some instances this was the basis for prejudice and discrimination – at its most extreme, in Eastern Europe, resulting in fatal violence – but even educated middle-class liberals combined their acceptance of members of this disparate tribe with a tinge of smug self-congratulation – a kind of enlightened separatism. Similarly, Hemingway's antisemitism was casually selective. Jews who had naturalised themselves as members of the intellectual and cultural establishment of the US and Europe often bought themselves prejudice by improving it. Hemingway had come to despise virtually all members of the intelligentsia, especially in Paris, and Jews seemed to offer themselves to him as easy targets for his contempt.

One subject gripped the expatriate community of Paris at the close of 1926: did they see versions of themselves or their friends in Hemingway's novel? Pat Guthrie was content enough to appear as Mike Campbell, not least because Mike is one of the few characters who is neither completely obnoxious nor inadequate, and Duff Twysden rather enjoyed her role as the first 'new woman' in literature, albeit with more than a hint at the louche and dissolute about her. Others detected something of themselves, only to find these deflected by unfamiliar features. Donald Ogden Stewart noted that Bill Gorton sometimes mimicked his chummy manner, especially during the fishing trip with Jake, but Hemingway's seemingly fraternal gesture could not undo Stewart's enduring sense of shock and disgust at the poem on Parker. Despite his promise to Kitty at her party that she would be spared she found she too was listening to herself, as if via a ventriloquist, speaking as Frances Cline, Cohn's jealous mistress. Kitty was enraged because the bilious caricature was not so much aimed directly at her as against her as a philosemite. In 1924 Loeb, convinced of Hemingway's potential, had taken him for drinks with Leon Fleischman, the publisher Horace Liveright's overseas agent who had recently arrived in Paris to scout for new talent among the expatriate community. Fleischman had rented a sumptuously furnished flat near the Champs Elysees where he received Loeb and Hemingway genially, stating to the latter that he came highly recommended by Loeb and others and that he looked forward to seeing his work. Hemingway puzzled both of his companions by paying only cursory attention to their enquiries about his writing. The cause of his discomfort was made evident to Loeb in the street following the meeting, when he raged against Fleischman as a 'fucking low-life kike'. Hemingway could not tolerate what he saw as a mismatch between power, wealth, cultural authority and Judaism – Fleischman had done nothing else to offend him – and there was some unintentional dark comedy in his overlooking of the fact that the close friend who was listening to this antisemitic rant was Jewish. Yet Loeb, to his enormous credit, treated Hemingway's behaviour as simply an element of his self-cultivated ungenteel persona, more a performance than an expression of something genuinely horrible. When Loeb spoke of it to Kitty Cannell she confessed her concern that beneath the rough-house presence that endeared so many to their mutual friend there ran a streak of pure malicious brutality.

Liveright did eventually publish *In Our Time*, but Hemingway blamed its modest sales during 1925 on the fact that he had been careless enough to entrust his work to a publishing house co-owned and run by a Jew who would, he ought to have realised, let him down. He took revenge by composing a short story, 'Fifty Grand', in which the decent American family man and boxer Jack Brennan is conspired against by potential opponents, managers and trainers, among whom are a considerable number of Jews. Kitty Cannell had advised Loeb that his faith in Hemingway, his enduring tolerance and his Jewishness would eventually guarantee his fate as a victim, that those closest to this man would suffer worst of all. She took no satisfaction in being proved horribly correct with *The Sun Also Rises*.

In early November 1926, soon after the novel was published, Hadley sent word that in her view the exercise in a trial separation, which still had a month to run, was proving to be more a masochistic endurance test than an act of settlement and stated that if her husband wished to end the marriage she would not obstruct legal procedures. They were divorced on 27 January 1927 and Hemingway married Pauline in May 1927. This was effectively the final year of his extended visit to Europe, and it framed acts and inclinations that began to disclose the true Hemingway – and show that he was slightly deranged. January began with him hearing rumours of the effect that his novel had had upon those he had previously regarded as his friends. In truth, for Loeb, Kitty and others, sadness and perplexity overruled anger, but Hemingway locked himself away from social interactions and nursed neurotic scenarios involving conspiracies against him. As a gesture of farcical heroism he sent out notes stating that if those who saw versions of themselves in the novel were planning to shoot him they could find him at Lipp's Brasserie between two and four on particular afternoons. He added that if his vengeful erstwhile friends did not arrive and discharge shots this would confirm his suspicion that they were all cowards. His unsettled state was worsened when he received, again in January, a letter from one Chard Powers Smith, with whom he and Hadley had become friends three years earlier. Hemingway's story, 'Mr and Mrs Elliot', originally entitled 'Mr and Mrs Smith', had featured in *In Our Time* but had first appeared a year earlier, October 1924, in the *Little Review*. Hemingway's fictional depictions of people he knew rarely flattered them but here he plumbed a new level of arbitrary vindictiveness. The real Smith, an alumnus of Harvard and Yale with a considerable private income, was the kind of New England figure that Hemingway had now decided to treat with scorn. As an individual he was kind and courteous, which made things worse. Chard Smith and his wife Olive had in 1924 rented a modest, well-appointed chateau in Provence for the summer months. The Hemingways spent time there as their guests and the two couples continued to socialise in Paris. During this period Hemingway planned and completed the story, which involves a rich American couple on the European Grand Tour and is littered with small details unique to the Smiths, including desperate attempts by the fictional and the actual couple to have children. Other elements are distorted grotesquely: a family friend is turned into a lesbian who begins an affair with Mrs Smith/Mrs Elliot while Smith/Elliot himself, facing life without offspring, turns to drink. It is unlikely that Smith read the story in the *Little Review* since he did not contact Hemingway about it, by letter, until January 1927, and at the time he was concerned with other matters. By a hideous coincidence Olive Smith had died in childbirth two weeks before the story first appeared in 1924. Perhaps Smith had blinded himself to this act of horrible cruelty while he took proper account of his more immediate experience of grief. It is more probable, however, that he was first alerted to the story during the month, January 1927, when many of Hemingway's other compatriots were finding disturbing portraits of themselves in his work. There is no record of Chard Smith's letter beyond a phrase quoted by Hemingway in his reply; Smith had allegedly referred to him as a 'contemptible worm'. The reply (21 January 1927) echoes his delusion that Loeb was hunting him down with a handgun. The piece is a catalogue of juvenile salvos against Smith's courage, manhood and his – in Hemingway's view – inability to construct a sentence. He invites Smith to Paris, promises to 'knock you down a few times' and predicts that he will arrive 'carrying numbers of pistols [and] sword canes'. Smith, to his credit, said nothing publically of these events even after Hemingway's death, but the effect of the story upon him are easy to speculate on. Seeing his life foully distorted in fiction is bad enough but the manner of its execution must have caused him a special form of distress. The clipped syntax is typical of early Hemingway but he uses it here sadistically, as a means of framing and contemplating the minute particulars of a sad, doomed relationship. 'Mr and Mrs Elliot tried very hard to have a baby. They tried as hard as Mrs Elliot could stand it. They tried in Boston after they were married and they tried coming over on the boat. They did not try very often on the boat because Mrs Elliot was sick.' Soon after sending the letter to Smith he was invited to dinner with the writer Louis Bromfield and his wife Mary, a couple who remained untroubled by the rumours surrounding their guest. This trust was soon proved unfounded when Hemingway began to refer to Bromfield not as Louis – they had been on first name terms for some time – but 'Bloomfield'. Bromfield's given name was Brumfield but he had exchanged the 'u' for 'o' only because his first publisher had misspelt it on the dust jacket of his debut novel. Hemingway implied that another name with Semitic resonances was hidden even deeper in his past. He supplemented this by openly criticising the quality of the wine and commenting to another guest that Mary's pet cats usually roamed freely across the dining table feasting on fish (only kosher dishes were available) and were left to defecate in various corners of the well-appointed dining room.

Pauline's family wished that she should marry a practising Catholic and she sidelined the fact that her betrothed was a Protestant-agnostic with whom she had been involved in an adulterous relationship. Hemingway insisted that he had been baptised into the Roman Church by a priest who ministered to other wounded men in 1918. He admitted to taking communion irregularly since then but declared his continued dedication to the Church and his love of the Mass. The priest who conducted the Catholic ceremony in Passy, Paris, was thus content that his previous 'marriage' to Hadley, a Protestant, had been invalid from its inception, despite the fact that no one could obtain a certificate of his alleged baptism in Italy. It would be too easy to assume that his fabric of lies was a cold pragmatic strategy because there are indications that Hemingway invented in his own mind a rather colourful fantasy of himself as a tortured Catholic recusant. At the end of March, just over a month before his wedding, Hemingway and Guy Hickok drove to Italy in the latter's old Ford. The ostensible purpose of the visit was to gather material for an article on the accelerating implementation of Mussolini's Fascist policies, but Hickok began to suspect that his companion was anxious to absorb something of the mood of rural communities for which Catholic practice and symbolism had been a feature of life for almost two millennia. He deliberately sought out the priest who he claimed had ministered to his wounded comrades during the war, though Hickok disclosed nothing of their intimate exchanges. The next day, however, Hemingway asked him to stop as they drove towards a shrine that marked a remote road junction. Without further comment he left the car, knelt before the shrine, crossed himself and prayed silently for more than ten minutes. On his return to Paris he composed 'Today is Friday', a playlet that would appear somewhat incongruously among the stories of *Men Without Women*. As a literary work in its own right it is embarrassingly awful. Two Roman soldiers sit in the premises of a Hebrew wineseller, and seem desperate to get drunk as they discuss their recent activities; specifically as part of the team who had crucified Christ. They reflect on how much pain he would have felt as the nails went in and that this would have intensified as the 'weight starts to pull on 'em'. They admire his courage, and as the wine takes effect one of them repeats that he 'feels like hell' and we, better than they, suspect that this indeed might be their destination. Hemingway causes them to sound like working-class US servicemen carousing in a bar kept by a 'kike' with a similar accent, who addresses one of them as 'Lootenant'. Modernising Shakespeare as an exercise in thematic timelessness is bad enough, but Hemingway's piece is the equivalent of rewriting the New Testament in the manner of a *Cheers* screenplay; everything is preposterously incongruous, and not funny at all. One suspects that the true purpose of the work is a private exploration of unfocussed guilt. It is doubtful he felt any remorse for his savage portrayals of friends and acquaintances; his letter to Chard Smith was exemplary in that regard. More likely, he was torn between his new commitment to Pauline and a residual sense of affection for the woman who had indulged without complaint his numerous failings and stood to one side while he made arrangements to exchange her for someone else. One of the Roman soldiers cannot make sense of how he feels about the display of fearless endurance from the fellow human he has recently put to death. Hemingway suspected there was some connection between the iconography of Spanish Catholicism, particularly in gory representations of the crucifixion and the martyrdom of saints, and the equally barbaric culture of bullfighting. It thus seems more than an accident that he chose to locate the story he began immediately after completing 'Today is Friday' in a remote village in the Ebro valley. In 'Hills Like White Elephants' a man – American – and a woman are between trains and the oblique topic of their exchange is referred to only once, as 'an awfully simple operation' which by the end he appears to persuade her to be in both their interests. Nonetheless her misgivings and sense of fear endure: '"I'll scream," the girl said.' It is implied that in rural Spain visceral, elementary religion is compatible with the routine practice of abortion. It is a work of unalloyed genius, combining the quietly nuanced atmospherics of Joyce's *Dubliners* with an effect much less easy to describe, of something immanent, unspoken and terrifying. It deserves praise as literary writing but an autobiographical thread runs through it too. In that Hemingway was at all susceptible to any sense of guilt, his initial response to Hadley's first pregnancy with Bumby was a notable example. He spoke privately to others of abortion and was advised against, but when she lost their second child 18 months later he found it difficult to suppress his relief.

There are eerie parallels between the story and the letter he had written to Hadley five months earlier to thank her for ending the three-month trial period and effectively exempt him from any marital commitments. In each we encounter a man faced with conflicting emotions and attempting to be accountable for his feelings. Throughout the letter he proffers self-condemnatory explanations, and when he has exhausted himself of apologies comes close to admitting that without her he would never have become a writer. *The Sun Also Rises* had already sold 13,000 copies and he vowed to pay all present and forthcoming royalties to her and Bumby, the implication being that his brutish overreaction to the manuscripts being lost from her carriage at the Gare de Lyon would now be repaid in kind. He concludes: 'And I won't tell you how I admire your straight thinking, your head, your heart, and your very lovely hands and I Pray God he will make up to you the very great hurt that I have done you – who are the best and truest and loveliest person I have known' (18 November 1926). Is he sincere? There is no reason to think not, but it is equally possible to discern behind the words a gradual exhalation, an exercise in release by self-exculpation. God, it seems, will 'make up to' her, despite Hemingway's inability to do so.

It is instructive and fascinating to compare his letter to Hadley with the one he wrote exactly two weeks later (3 December) to Pauline, who was then in New York. Less significant than the content of the two pieces is their manner. There is no reason to doubt his earnestness in each but for Hadley he adopts a measured style, by parts composed, elegiac and apologetic, while the letter to Pauline seems to have been written by a different person.

> I know, or anyhow I feel, that I could be faithful to you with my body and my mind and my spirit for as long as I had any of them – and I know now too that because being the same guy and yet a whole something started in my body that had gotten to be an integral part of everything that being alone and just lonesome all sorts of things seem to damn up the balance of it all be thrown off and it attacks the spirit and it isn't good for the head either [...] But I know it will be swell and to let you know that I am feeling swell and that the world is grand and that I feel good inside and not just dry like a piece of cuttle fish bone like they feed canaries but really fine and I'll write you EXCELLENT – and that means you just read this letter as by someone else and know that I'm fine in the head and inside.

He had nothing to prove to Pauline and it is absurd to suspect that he was calculatingly portraying himself as driven insane by love. It is, then, astonishing that he could within two weeks have been transformed from a contrite, lucid individual into someone who is unable to fix upon a rational sense of what he feels, with collateral damage to his syntax. Aside from Hemingway's possibly unstable mental condition, we learn here something of his evolution as a writer during the Paris years. His finest work was spontaneous and unpremeditated and so were many of his quite dreadful pieces. The two letters – bizarre in their differences – show us that behind the bravado was a man for whom words and thoughts were often indistinguishable.

There is no specific point at which he decided to return permanently to America, but by the close of 1927 his departure had become little more than a matter of timing and practical arrangements. The months following his marriage had marked the incessant erosion of his affection for Paris, and his fascination with Spain was mutating into a file of notes and recollections to be revisited for future writing. With a few exceptions, notably Hickok, McLeish and Pound, he had alienated himself from most of his friends. Sylvia Beach remained on amicable terms with him, an attachment underpinned by her fascination with his erratic temperament; he had become more a curiosity than a confidant. Dos Passos was now in New York and had no specific plans to return. He had written to Fitzgerald on 24 November 1926: 'God I wish I could see you. You are the only guy in or out of Europe I can say as much for (or against) but I certainly would like to see you.' The Fitzgeralds were about to leave for the US. Before Christmas 1926 Hemingway had toppled from his skis in Switzerland and sustained painful but mercifully skin-deep cuts when the glass in his goggles shattered. He passed off the accident jokingly but two weeks later Bumby was sent by Hadley to visit his father, now with Pauline, in the same resort. The 3-year-old, involuntarily, drove his fingernail into the pupil of Hemingway's good eye. The wound would heal but for ten days he was almost blind, joking again – this time that his son had proved more dangerous than the mountain. In April, less than a month before the wedding, Hemingway visited the lavatory late one night in the comfortable Paris apartment he now shared with Pauline. Mistaking the cable of the glass skylight for the overhead flush he brought the former down onto his head. McLeish drove him to hospital for multiple stitches. He would wear the scar for the rest of his life. There are photographs taken of him soon afterwards that recall those of the wounded hero from the Italian front – with generous bandaging to head rather than leg – but Hemingway the pseudo-Catholic dissembler was now beginning to wonder if the continent where he had sought fame and excitement was turning into his nemesis. He had treated the man who had introduced him to Europe and established for him a series of influential contacts with utter contempt, but Sherwood Anderson never sought revenge. When Hemingway and Pauline, now pregnant, left for Florida in June 1928 he thought he was beginning a new life, but one person was intent that his recent past would pursue him into it.

The Autobiography of Alice B. Toklas was written in six weeks during 1932 and published the following year. Friends of Stein had for some time urged her to publish a memoir covering her previous three decades in Paris. She had after all been the mentor and confidante of most of those who'd forged a new era of writing and painting, and in basic terms this is what the eventual *Autobiography* amounted to: a series of anecdotes on Picasso, Gide, Joyce, Pound, Fitzgerald and, most pointedly, Hemingway.

The guilelessness of the account suggests no malice, yet enough is given away to suggest that the two of them are laughing at him behind their hands.

> I remember very well the impression I had of Hemingway that first afternoon. He was an extraordinarily good-looking young man twenty-three years old. It was not long after that that everybody was twenty-six. It became the period of being twenty-six. During the next two or three years all the young men were twenty-six years old. It was the right age apparently for that time and place. There were one or two under twenty, for example George Lynes but then did not count as Gertrude Stein carefully explained to them. If they were young men they were twenty-six. Later on, much later on they were twenty-one and twenty-two.

> So Hemingway was twenty-three, rather foreign-looking, with passionately interested, rather than interesting eyes. He sat in front of Gertrude Stein and listened and looked. (p. 214)

The passage on 'everybody was twenty-six' seems whimsical, yet beneath the guise of the rambling narrator is the hand of the merciless satirist. The notion of everyone becoming the same because number 26 has some unexplained portent is preposterous, yet the ruthless, repetitive insistence that something apparently arbitrary has immense significance was a key element of Hemingway's most celebrated prose:

> He and his wife went away on a trip and shortly after Hemingway turned up alone. He came to the house about ten o'clock in the morning and he stayed for lunch, he stayed all afternoon, he stayed for dinner and he stayed until about ten o'clock that night and then all of a sudden he announced that his wife was enceinte and then with great bitterness, and I, I am too young to be a father. We consoled him as best we could and sent him on his way. (p. 216)

By the time the book went to print rumours were already circulating about why this newly celebrated author had abandoned his wife so soon after the birth of their only child. Some of those who knew Hemingway beneath the public persona were aware that he had spoken of an abortion, fearing that the future as a settled family man might erode his image as reckless pioneer. This is bad enough, but even worse was the fact that he had confessed his fears and preferences only to others and never to Hadley herself. Rather, he had advised her that a demanding physical regime – including regular tennis matches, hill walking with rucksacks in Pisa and Siena and downhill and cross-country skiing in the Dolomites – would be good for a woman of her age. To others it seemed as though he was trying to induce a miscarriage. Stein's book is important because it lit the flame of suspicion that would follow Hemingway through the rest of his life, and beyond his death. Few outright accusations are made, but continually Stein chips away at the mythology of Hemingway's Paris years, hinting that the image of him as the genuine outspoken American hard-man among a legion of Ivy League dilettantes is suspect.

Having left the impression of the immature high-school boy now facing fatherhood and lamenting his loss of independence, they turn to his reputation as a sportsman:

Hemingway was teaching some young chap how to box. The boy did not know how, but by accident he knocked Hemingway out. I believe this sometimes happens. At any rate in these days Hemingway although a sportsman was easily tired. He used to get quite worn out walking from his house to ours. But then he had been worn by the war. Even now he is, as Héléne says all men are, fragile. Recently a robust friend of his said to Gertrude Stein, Ernest is very fragile, whenever he does anything sporting something breaks, his arm, his leg, or his head. (p. 220)

When Hemingway's income from journalism was severely reduced, followed shortly afterwards by the mismanagement of Hadley's estate by her uncle, the couple did for a time contemplate the very real and dreadful prospect of an image he had carefully cultivated: they were becoming penniless bohemians. In response Hemingway attempted to market another aspect of his illusory persona. He hired himself out as a sparring partner in some of the gyms where tough members of the Paris proletariat trained to become prize-fighters, and often found the real world of professional boxing very different from that of exchanges with expatriates where he could bully fellow countrymen who had fought only in college bouts.

Alone, these portraits might depict him as a deluded *ingénue*, rather out of his depth among the new acquaintances who will, he hopes, indulge his inflated self-image. The knife begins to turn when Toklas/Stein implies that his illusions about his manhood also inform his writing:

They [Stein and Anderson] admitted that Hemingway was yellow, he is, Gertrude Stein insisted, just like the flat-boat men on the Mississippi river as described by Mark Twain. But what a book, they both agreed, would be the real story of Hemingway, not those he writes but the confessions of the real Ernest Hemingway. It would be for another audience than the audience Hemingway now has but it would be very wonderful.

The following passage is a beautiful example of ridicule by latent whisper:

Gertrude Stein never corrects any detail of anybody's writing, she sticks strictly to general principles, the way of seeing what the writer chooses to see, and the relation between that vision and the way it gets down. When the vision is not complete the words are flat, it is very simple, there can be no mistake about it, so she insists. It was at this time that Hemingway began the short things that afterwards were printed in a volume called In Our Time. (p. 217)

Toklas later recalled Stein's response to Hemingway's early attempts at poetry: 'Gertrude rather liked the poems, they were direct, Kiplingesque'. The poems referred to, particularly 'The Soul of Spain', are embarrassingly bad and Stein's reference to Kipling is by way of a compliment drenched with sarcasm, but her observation would also have struck a private chord. One of the most irredeemable poems ever written is Stein's 'Sacred Emily', published in her collection *Geography and Plays* in 1922. Hemingway produced 'The Soul of Spain' little more than a year later, and were it not for the fact that he did not actually steal phrases verbatim from Stein's piece his own comes very close to an example of unapologetic plagiarism. The most conspicuous difference between the two works is that while Stein is elliptical and completely incomprehensible, Hemingway personalises this same formula with his own intrepid boorishness.

The following is from Stein:

If I was surely if I was surely.
See girl says.
All the same bright.
Brightness.
When a churn say suddenly when a churn say suddenly.
Poor pour per cent.
Little branches.
Pale.
Pale.
Pale.
Pale.
Pale.
Pale.
Pale.

And this is Hemingway:

Come let us fart in the home.
There is no art in a fart.
Still a fart man not be artless.

Let us fart in an artless fart in the home.
Democracy.
Democracy.
Bill says democracy must go.
Go democracy.
Go.
Go.
Go.

One might suspect him of caricature were it not for the fact that when he wrote it he was completely in awe of Stein and hopelessly unclear about where his literary ambitions would lead him. Moreover, he also turns his desperate imitation of Stein into a tribute to the man he would respect for the rest of his life:

Dictators are the shit.
Menken is the shit.
Walso Frank is the shit.
The Broom is the shit.
Dada is the Shit.
Dempsey is the shit.
This is not a complete list.
They say Ezra is the shit.
But Ezra is nice.
Come let us build a monument to Ezra.
Good a very nice monument.
You did that nicely.
Can you do another?

William McGonagall is routinely credited as having blinded himself to his unprepossessing badness as a poet but Hemingway surely matches him here. Stein will always be associated with a particularly enigmatic phrase which comes from 'Scared Emily': 'Rose is a rose is a rose is a rose'. As an exercise in repetitive meaninglessness it is near unchallengeable, but for some reason it has attained a gnomic status of its own. Hemingway's piece opens with a respectful nod of gratitude to Stein, though he manages to blend impenetrability with cliché: 'In the rain in the rain in the rain in the rain in Spain'.

Hemingway was so outraged by the Toklas autobiography that he sent a telegram direct to rue de Fleurus of one line: 'A bitch is a bitch is a bitch is a bitch'. In *For Whom the Bell Tolls* (1940) that phrase, still largely unknown in the public domain, resurfaced once more when the main character Robert Jordan mumbles a version of it: 'A rose is a rose is an onion [...] An onion is an onion is an onion.' And then silently reflects: 'a stone is a stein is a rock is a boulder is a pebble'.

As personalities, Stein and Hemingway were absurdly ill-matched and the fact that he so enthusiastically cultivated her friendship tells us something about what would happen at the end of his Paris years and beyond that. During the 1920s in Europe he was a selfish opportunistic individual, and while these qualities are not uncommon among young writers Hemingway was quite extraordinary in his laissez-faire pursuit of fame. His enduring bitterness regarding Stein was fuelled by two things. He grew to recognise that her writing was hopelessly chaotic and self-absorbed and he loathed the implication that he had been her pupil, that his work epitomised the collective indulgences of the 'lost generation'. He cherished the notion of uniqueness, both as a man and a novelist, and as he and Pauline boarded the liner for America he gave himself over to an exercise of cause and effect. *The Sun Also Rises* had transformed him from non-entity to literary celebrity, and it was a book driven by a manic desire to dissociate, often via vindictiveness. He could, he sensed, become the architect of his reputation as a writer. He could do so by insinuating the explosive, magnetic figure of Ernest Hemingway as the engine of the story, a presence who in life and fiction imposed himself on all who knew him by various means, and his approach enabled him to discard those figures from whom he had once sought patronage and advice.

CHAPTER 3

Key West

When Hemingway and Pauline left France in March 1928, they had no clear destination. They were heading for the US and at some point they would spend time at Pauline's family estate in Piggott, Arkansas. They discussed staying there until the birth of their first child, but beyond that had no plans.

Key West would be the closest that Hemingway could call home for the subsequent 11 years, a period that also marked the duration of his marriage to Pauline and his most prolific period as a writer. But for an accident it is almost certain they would have passed through and hardly noticed the place. Pauline's uncle Gus had arranged for the delivery of a Ford Coupe to await them in Key West after they disembarked from the *Orita* in Havana and sailed for the nondescript island which was linked to the Florida mainland only by ferry. The car was not available; apparently problems at the Ford plant in Miami had delayed the provision of new vehicles by six weeks. The prospect of a rail journey from an island in the Florida Keys to Arkansas, with Pauline five months' pregnant, was not appealing so, with sanguine resignation, they rented rooms above the offices of the Ford agency.

Paris was Hemingway's odyssey of grand ambition. It made him a writer, albeit more by good fortune than design. It is thus appropriate that another twist of fate should have inaugurated his second decade as a novelist and contrary human being.

During the six weeks spent waiting for the car Hemingway discovered something of the US that he had previously neither heard of nor imagined. Some of the island's buildings dated from its pre-Confederacy existence as a trading outpost and navy yard; it had been settled by the British some 20 years before the American War of Independence. There was a stone fort that might have come from the Mediterranean Coast which was full of disused rusting artillery pieces from the Civil War. In the late nineteenth century, another naval dockyard had been constructed and then abandoned. It stood unused and without any apparent future; large steel cranes hung as if a morbid signal to the economic collapse that would engulf the Western industrial world barely four years hence.

The population was a languid mixture of Latin Americans – most from nearby Cuba, others from Mexico and further south – Afro Caribbeans and a rather incongruous group of third-generation white Protestants whose ancestors had first settled further north and who had at various points drifted to Florida in search of new prospects.

It was certainly not the sort of multiracial paradise envisaged by the more optimistic liberals of the 1960s. Yet, perhaps because it was an island, the tensions that informed every other part of America regarding colour and status appeared to have been relaxed, without premeditation or design.

Within a week, and despite the discomfort of their small, rather dingy apartment, Hemingway had grown to love the place. He had no experience of sea fishing, either from shore or boat, but was soon enchanted by the challenges of amberjack, barracuda, tarpon and sailfish. He hooked one of the latter from a dinghy and played it for almost half an hour until it broke his trout rod in half and threw the hook. Equipped with stronger sea tackle he eventually boated a six-foot-long tarpon. The creature, almost his own weight, raged against defeat on the deck of Charles Thompson's fishing boat. Hemingway had met Thompson soon after moving out of the rooms above the Ford agency to the more comfortable and hygienic Overseas Hotel. He and Pauline became regular guests at the Thompsons' house and the friendship, including that between Pauline and Thompson's wife Lorine, would endure until the break-up of the Hemingway's marriage and Ernest's departure from Key West. Thompson's family had been residents on the island since the early nineteenth century. He owned a fish-processing plant, cigar box factory, ship's chandlery and tackle shop, and was of Hemingway's age and from the same decent entrepreneurial stock that Ernest had grown up with in Oak Park. More importantly, Thompson was well-enough acquainted with men in Key West who would not have been welcome in Hemingway's hometown and whose company he craved as an antidote to his past.

Josie Russell would eventually become the official owner of a bar he named Sloppy Joe's in Green Street, but when Hemingway first arrived the manufacture and sale of alcohol was prohibited by Federal Law. In 1928 Joe's Green Street premises had no name, its customers were admitted only when recommended by regulars and its merchandise was made up mostly of rum, vodka and whisky smuggled in from Cuba. There was already a bar called Sloppy Joe's but that was in Havana, and when Prohibition was repealed in 1933 Hemingway, by then a permanent resident of Key West, persuaded Russell that he should borrow the name, as an ironic footnote to his previous history of imports from the island. Russell's long-term chief bartender was an Afro-American called Skinner, Christian name unknown, who mixed with his white and Hispanic clientele without any notable sense of disparity. One of the former was Sully, J.B. Sullivan, who had moved from Brooklyn to work on the railroads built on the mainland Keys during the first decade of the century. It was not until the mid-1930s that Sully found that his regular drinking partner was a novelist of international renown. Hemingway was not entirely secretive about his profession and growing fame. He simply told stories of his previous decade as a freelance journalist in Europe, rough-house boxer and adventurer, the sort who would not seem out of place among men who worked with their hands. Another regular at Joe's illegal bar was Captain Bra Saunders who made money by charging tourists for day trips on his cabin cruiser. When there was no demand for these, he would use the boat to search out the numerous shipwrecks that lay off the dangerous reefs on the eastern shore and loot them. Hemingway wrote to his editor Maxwell Perkins:

Caught the biggest tarpon they've had down here so far this season. Sixty-three pounds [...] We sell the fish we get in the market [...] Have been living on fish too [...] This is a splendid place. Nobody believes me when I say I'm a writer. They think I represent Big Northern Bootleggers or Dope Peddlers – especially with this scar [the one he acquired in Paris following the skylight accident]. They haven't even heard of Scott [Fitzgerald]. Several of the boys I know have just been moved by first reading of Kipling. (21 April 1928)

He had already begun a routine that would endure until he left Key West. After an early breakfast, he would write until lunchtime and then spend the afternoon fishing and drinking with his new circle of friends. There could be hardly a greater contrast between this new environment and his arrival in Paris seven years earlier, but there were perverse resemblances too. On both occasions, he was exploring a new role, a different means of remoulding his personality in relation to individuals who, unlike him, were sure of what they amounted to. Certainly the creative, intellectual cauldron of Paris in 1921 differed greatly from this rather forlorn outpost of the American Caribbean – he had written to Perkins of how the population had fallen by 16,000 over the previous decade and that on the wall of the public lavatory the declaration 'if you don't like this town get out and stay out' had been answered with 'Everybody has'. Key West was the very antithesis of the compulsive intellectualism he attacked in *The Sun Also Rises* and which had caused him to alienate so many of his associates in France. Nonetheless, he invited two of his remaining friends from Europe, John Dos Passos and the painter Waldo Peirce, to visit him in his new playground. Dos Passos, an avid Communist, was thrilled to find dedicated affiliates of Marxist-Leninism among the workers in Key West's largest cigar factory; it seemed as if European radicalism had found an albeit narrow foothold just beyond the US mainland. Peirce, like Hemingway, relished physical danger and confrontation and took pleasure in diving from Saunders' boat onto the wreck of the Spanish liner *Val Banera* that had run aground and sunk in 1919. Once, he swam in through a porthole and brought to the surface jewellery from the skeleton of a woman passenger.

In April 1931, the Hemingways purchased a rather grand neocolonial house at 907 Whitehead Street, but even after he became a permanent resident Ernest drew up boundaries between the various compartments of his life. He invited some from the New York intellectual circuit, the Fitzgeralds and Max Perkins included, but aside from making use of Saunders' yacht for Peirce's macabre dives he made sure that there would be no interaction between the Whitehead Street guests and the bars and boats where he spent his afternoons when he had no visitors.

In the 1928 letter to Perkins he also mentioned his second novel: 'Would like to finish it down here if possible, put it away for a couple or three months and then re-write it.' He hoped that the routine of Key West would enable him to spend a lengthy undisturbed period on the book, but for reasons partly beyond his control his movements over the subsequent nine months would be erratic and indeterminate, something that would have a major impact on the mood of the novel. He had begun *A Farewell to Arms* shortly before he and Pauline left Paris and his promise to finish it was based in part on the fact that he had signed a contract with *Scribner's Magazine* in February. They later offered him $16,000 for the serialisation rights. The magazine was the popular, very profitable arm of his book publisher, Scribner's, and Max Perkins had taken a gamble on the serialisation ensuring a considerable readership for chosen extracts and generating popularity for the eventual novel. Early passages from the work began to appear in the magazine in May 1928 while he was still agonising over revisions of the later chapters; he would not complete the draft until January 1929. It was not that he was giving unusually fastidious attention to style and copy-editing. His irresolution was caused by something far more extraordinary.

When he arrived in Key West, the rough draft was made up of variations on what he had done, experienced and lied about during the previous ten years. The time span of the novel is less than 12 months and the events are related by the first-person narrator Frederic Henry, an American ambulance driver serving in the Italian Army. Like his creator Henry suffers a severe leg injury and falls in love with a nurse. Agnes von Kurowsky appears in the novel as

Catherine Barkley and the former's background in upper middle-class, East Coast America is exchanged for Barkley's roots in the English minor gentry. The story is set in northern Italy more than a year before Hemingway arrived there, which allows Henry to take part in some of the most ferocious and deadly battles between Italian and Austrian troops. It could be argued that this provides a more appropriate setting for a novel that was praised by many as the first brutally realistic representation of World War I. Equally, however, one can see parallels between Hemingway's fabrications and exaggerations regarding his experience of front-line action – especially his involvement with the Arditi at the close of the war – and the retelling of these by his fictional proxy. Moreover, while Catherine can be regarded as an exercise in wish-fulfilment – a woman who commits herself unreservedly to Henry rather than the one who treated Hemingway with affection which mutated into condescension – there is also something of her that enables Hemingway to assuage his conscience regarding Hadley who loved him without any thought for herself; the Hadley he had recently, cold-heartedly exchanged for someone else. Henry is dispassionate, verging on the callous, causing some to regard Hemingway as having discovered post-traumatic stress disorder more than half a century before psychologists recognised the condition as a consequence of modern warfare. A more probable explanation is that he made use of fiction to excuse and explain aspects of his recent past.

Via Henry he could transform his pseudo-adolescent obsession with Agnes into something suffered by her which he heroically endures. His selfish, opportunistic treatment of Hadley becomes a love affair that will be brought to an end by factors that neither party can control, and Pauline's pregnancy and devotion to him is replicated when Catherine finds herself with child and they flee to what they hope will be another life uncontaminated by their recent past. Hemingway and Pauline took a liner from France to America, leaving behind the cadre of writers and intellectuals in Paris he had come to loathe and many of whom now found him distasteful. Henry, due to be arrested by the Italians for treason, escapes, with Catherine, by crossing a waterway, this time in a rowing boat across a lake to Switzerland. So much for the author's past and present reformulated as invention, apology and fantasy. But what happens next? This was the question Hemingway faced as he pored over the drafts of the novel in Key West, wrote to Max Perkins and began his final revisions.

At the end of May 1928 Pauline left Key West by train for Piggott, Arkansas, and Hemingway, joined by Pauline's father Paul, set off by car for the same destination. This was now the Pfeiffer family's hometown with Paul having sold his business interests and bought a spacious property which bore an unnerving resemblance to 600 North Kenilworth Avenue. Pauline was soon due to deliver their child and it was thought best that the final weeks of her pregnancy would be spent as close as possible to her family. As soon as Hemingway arrived, he felt a deep contempt for the district. It was in some respects a replica of Oak Park. The population of almost 3,000 was exclusively white and Protestant, with no black or Hispanic residents, though some Afro-Americans were employed on a part-time basis as servants by wealthier householders. Along with this, it seemed to Hemingway that the environment of his youth had been transplanted to an unbearably humid subtropical location. The average temperature, when he arrived, was well above 30 degrees, vegetation of various damp and threatening forms seemed to encroach upon every building and mosquitoes were a deafening, persistent feature of life. By comparison, the Florida Keys seemed refreshingly airy.

On 13 June, it was decided that Kansas City in the neighbouring state offered the best medical facilities for the birth and Pauline was driven there by Hemingway. Patrick, his second son, was delivered by caesarean section on the 28th following a two-day period of labour which threatened Pauline's life. Indeed, Hemingway was told that a section was the safest option for his wife, irrespective of whether their child would arrive safely and without complications. Catherine's child dies shortly after birth and she expires less than an hour later. In Kansas, he had drafted a number of hypothetical endings for the novel and he had certainly not decided on which one to use. He too faced the prospect of a stillborn baby with potentially fatal consequences for Pauline. Henry's story had reached around 400 longhand pages, roughly three-quarters of the book as it would eventually appear, and Hemingway, assured that his wife and son were well and back in Piggott, decided on a form of escape of his own.

On 25 July he met his old friend Bill Horne in Kansas and picked up his Ford, which he had left in the city after taking Pauline to the maternity hospital. He and Horne drove west towards Wyoming and there is no evidence of his motive for this expedition. Even Baker, his first biographer, who interviewed so many of his friends and family, avoids an attempt to explain Hemingway's sudden wish to deliver himself from everyone closest to him and head towards what remained of the Wild West, a landscape of undisturbed rivers, wolves, grizzly bears, elks and mountains that no one had climbed. We must however be aware that Horne was his closest confidant during his relationship with Agnes and might thus have been deemed a suitable companion when Hemingway redrafted this as fiction.

When Hemingway left Kansas, Henry was still on the run and the narrative had stalled. He was suspected of being a German spy; if captured he would be executed without trial by the Italians and he was cutting himself off from friends and comrades, heading through wild north Italian countryside that might offer him refuge from the pursuers. His author had yet to decide on the final outcome of his flight, and as he too roamed apparently aimlessly across the Midwest he seemed to be willing himself into the desperate state of mind of his character, at once looking over his shoulder and wondering what the future, with Catherine, might involve.

In his letters, Hemingway persistently compared his experiences in Wyoming with what he remembered from those parts of Europe that seemed enchantingly remote and unexplored. At Big Horn, 'Looks like Spain, Big Horn Mountains for the guadaramas only on a bigger scale, same color, same shape' (Hemingway to Waldo Peirce, 9 August 1928). The remainder of the letter turns into an interior monologue with Hemingway shifting the focus from the state of the book ('To hell with novels, I've written 548 pages [. . .] have been in a state of suspended something or other for 3 or 4 months'), to more immediate activities ('have shot 3 marmots (Rock dogs) almost as big as badgers, with the pistol and the head off a water snake, plus catching thirty trout') and continually he drifts to memories of the previous decade: 'Valencia is the best 7 bullfights in 7 days starting July 25. Swim in between in the Mediterranean at Grao. Ride out on the tram [...] That's where I'd rather be now instead of here trying to write.'

In every letter, irrespective of correspondent, he allows the engrossing vacancy of the American West to fill itself with his memories of Europe. To Guy Hickock (18 August): 'Have been here 1 mo[nth] or more – good beer from the brewery – good wine from a wop – a nice French family (bootlegger) where we sit on the vine shaded porch and drink'. The family, in Sheridan, Wyoming, had built a miniature version of their original home in southern France, including a small vineyard. The rented out rooms to guests – mostly those reckless enough to hunt and fish on what was the boundary of settled America, too far from the nearest authorities to worry about the illegality of producing and sharing alcohol. Everyday Hemingway was reminded of something he'd enjoyed in the unprepossessing countryside of Europe. To Peirce again, on 28 August: 'I finished the damn book, first draft and [...] fished, caught 30 [trout] [...] This is a cockeyed wonderful country, looks like Spain, swell people.' Hickok: 'We have driven daily over bloody mountains that make the Appenines look like the back steps to the urinoir – but no vines on their slopes – many a still though' (*circa* early September 1928, JFK). Hickok had been his companion on a journey through Tuscany in 1927 – hence the reference to the Apennines. When he returned to Key West at the end of the year he was undecided on the fate of Henry and Catherine's baby, and Catherine herself. He wrote to Maxwell Perkins that 'this fall [...] in Key West [...] [will] rewrite the book' (*circa* early September 1928)

What is evident is that Hemingway's flight into the American outback was an attempt to reanimate the novel by reliving the previous decade. Aside from his own comparisons between Wyoming and Europe he was receiving letters from those he'd met there who had stayed or returned. Dos Passos reported on his experiences of village life in the newly collectivised Soviet steppe, reminding him of those Americans in Paris – particularly Edmund

Wilson and John Reed – who were captivated by communism in practice. Hadley was still in France and she, more shrewdly than his other correspondents, detects the impulse behind her ex-husband's pursuit of the kind of rural isolation she had shared with him in France and Spain. 'Try and ease up the tired mind and heart in that grand sun dried west and forget all the women and children and the various woes they have bro't you. I have tho't about you a great deal and I am sure you need a place to rest' (Hadley to Hemingway, 4 August 1928, JFK).

Throughout his letters, Hemingway interwove accounts of his progress across an increasingly alien and bewitching landscape with reports on the number of pages he had completed on Henry's journey of escape. What he had not done, however, was to disclose to anyone the autobiographical links between himself and Henry, Agnes and Catherine. Wyoming reminded him of the most remote regions of France, Spain and Bavaria, especially where the civilised world seems to give way to something more untamed. But he systematically avoids any mention of northern Italy, where Henry escapes capture and eventually crosses the border with Catherine. Wyoming was a close replica of this forbidding mountainous region and it clearly lent energy to a story otherwise in a state of inertia, but not once did he tell anyone – including Pauline – that Henry and Catherine were based on his encounter with Agnes and his hunger for what their relationship would lead to. It was not merely that he was withholding from his wife the truth about the novel – that it was moulded by a fantasy about his first love. More disturbingly, he would have felt uneasy about telling of its inspiration because he would also have to admit to being selective about his past. If he told Pauline that Catherine was based on Agnes, he would have had to tell her that Agnes existed; throughout their marriage, and after their divorce, Pauline would remain ignorant of Hemingway's teenage infatuation. From the moment he began the novel Hemingway kept with him, secretly, a file of letters that Agnes had sent him when she was working away from Milan in 1918 and he took this with him when he left Key West for Kansas and thereafter during his excursions through Wyoming. Catherine is an individual who forms an impression on us not from what others say of her but via her spoken presence. She is candid, resigned, philosophical and, when she allows, passionate; read Agnes's letters to Hemingway and any doubts that they are the same person will vanish.

All of this sheds some light on his bizarre decision to head west so soon after his wife had given birth to his second son, Patrick. The caesarean had been successful in that mother and baby survived but, unbeknown to Pauline, he had made notes on the terrifying sequence of options and consequences he'd witnessed and influenced in the maternity ward. This was the real world, a story that concluded well for all concerned, but now, in the novel, he was about to substitute his wife for a version of his first love, Agnes, of whom Pauline new nothing. He was not simply a maker of fictions; he lived them.

At the beginning of December, he arrived in New York to meet Hadley and Bumby who had sailed from France. He was due to spend time with his first son in Key West, but when the train stopped in Philadelphia he received a telegram from Oak Park informing him that his father was dead. Over the next few weeks Hemingway behaved commendably, returning to his home to deal with the funeral arrangements and perform as a steadying presence for his mother and siblings. He did not learn that Clarence had committed suicide until he arrived at Chicago railway station, and in Oak Park everyone seemed in a state of shock or denial. Hemingway took responsibility for inspecting the body to see if the undertakers had properly disguised the bullet wound to Clarence's right temple, and after the funeral he dealt with the remains of the estate, clearing the outstanding mortgage on the family home and arranging for the meagre payout on Clarence's life insurance. He would eventually establish a generous trust fund for this mother based on the advance for the serialisation of *A Farewell to Arms* and royalties from the novel.

At the same time, however, his performance as the senior male sibling was shadowed by something more chilling. When he informed Hadley of what had happened his only comment was that suicide would be his destiny too. A year after the event he contacted the coroner's office and demanded that the weapon used by Clarence must be sent to him. The revolver was carried by his grandfather during his service in the Civil War and was, at least until Clarence put it to his head, a family heirloom, something that embodied the finest, male, American values. Now, however, its status had been contaminated by Clarence's choice to use it in this way. There were, after all, many other more recently manufactured and efficient weapons about the house. The following year Hemingway would drop the gun into one of the deepest lakes in Wyoming, but this ceremony of clearance would not abate the neurotic and troubled history of his thoughts on what Clarence had done. There is a passage intended for *Green Hills of Africa* (1935) which he excised before publication: 'My father was a coward. He shot himself without necessity. At least I thought so. I had gone through it myself until I figured it in my head. I knew what it was to be a coward and what it was to cease being a coward' (JFK). This version of Hemingway would reappear as Robert Jordan in *For Whom the Bell Tolls*, who contrasts his own struggle with cowardice with his grandfather's documented record of courage and his father's weakness: 'I'll never forget how sick it made me the first time I knew he was a cobarde. Go on, say it in English. Coward.'

After the funeral, Hemingway spent three months rewriting the closing chapters of *A Farewell to Arms*. He had already decided that Catherine and the baby would not survive but now he gave special attention to Henry's anguished state and how he would deal with matters that demand inner resolution, the opposite of cowardice.

> I went to the door of the room.
> 'You can't come in now,' one of the nurses said.
> 'Yes I can,' I said.
> 'You can't come in yet.'
> 'You get out,' I said. 'The other one too.'
> But after I had got them out and shut the door and turned off the light it wasn't any good. It was like saying goodbye to a statue. After a while I went out and left the hospital and walked back to the hotel in the rain.

The final pages of the novel involve a well-crafted blend of pathos and tragedy, made all the more effective by a hint at nihilism. Yet when we read through to the circumstances in which they were written we detect something else. The conversation between Henry and the surgeon on the safest as opposed to the most effective treatment to administer – caesarean or deep-forceps delivery – and their relative dangers to the survival of mother and child are an exact replica of the exchange between Hemingway and the obstetrician who performed the caesarean on Pauline. For a while it appears that Henry, Catherine and their newborn son will survive the traumas visited on them by the narrative, yet suddenly and unexpectedly the baby dies and Catherine succumbs to a haemorrhage. The mood of stoicism that informs his description of the person he once loved as a 'statue' must surely also owe something of his recent 'saying goodbye' to the embalmed corpse of Clarence. The imagination is a treasury of terrible scenarios but for a writer to prey on what almost happened to his actual wife and son and what his father had brought upon himself in order to portray his avatar's moving state of resignation verges upon the macabre.

When *A Farewell to Arms* was published in September 1929 the Hemingways, accompanied by Patrick and Bumby, were in Paris. Why exactly Hemingway had decided to sail for Europe in April is unclear. There are numerous if brief records of the details of the visit, ranging from dates of arrival and the practicalities of proofreading the novel during the summer to Hemingway's unease regarding his imminent reacquaintance with Scott and Zelda Fitzgerald. Max Perkins had sent him a telegram asking if he could 'write me soon about how he [Fitzgerald] is'. Fitzgerald was the first of Perkins' literary discoveries, followed shortly by Hemingway and Tom Wolfe; he treated all of them more in a caring, avuncular manner than as a publisher concerned primarily with profit and sales. In 1929 Fitzgerald was troubling him. Stories were told of his excessive drinking and the imminent collapse of his marriage. He and Zelda were the focus of gossip on the literary circuit, particularly in New York, and indeed they were barely a year away from the ineluctable decline which resulted in her hospitalisation for schizophrenia and the beginning of Scott's perpetual alcohol-induced illnesses. Hemingway replied to Perkins: 'Last time he was in Paris he got us kicked out of one apartment and in trouble all the time (insulted the landlord, peed on the front porch – tried to break down the door – 3–4 and 5 AM etc.)' (Hemingway to Perkins, April 1929, PUL). All of this was untrue, but Hemingway knew that it would be made credible by the rumours currently circulating in the US on the Fitzgeralds' behaviour in France. Hemingway's mendacity carries a clue to his motive for retuning to Europe. Reynolds surmises that 'he [had] come back to a good writing place, trusting that the luck will return', a statement based on generous guesswork. There is no evidence that Hemingway returned to Europe to reignite the creative flame of *The Sun Also Rises* and his early short stories. Indeed, most of these had been inspired by his contempt for the US expatriates he had met in the 1920s. Malign triumphalism would be a better description of his impulse to go back. His first novel had turned him into a literary celebrity and he calculated that his second, irrespective of praise or scorn from reviewers, would become a magnet for worldwide controversy in addressing the traumatic consequences of the Great War. He would be right.

Owen Wister, author of *The Virginian* and one of the most popular US novelists of the early twentieth century, provided fulsome cover blurb, but in private voiced his concerns to Perkins. In his view there were discontinuities in the narrative; specifically, a novel that seemed at first to be about the experiences of the effects of war mutated into a tragic love story to which the war had become a burdensome appendage. Perkins agreed and said as much to Hemingway, who ignored him. The irregularities discerned by both men had come about because of Clarence's suicide. In the first of the Switzerland-based drafts Hemingway had allowed Henry to become reflective, comparing the horrors of the conflict he had recently experienced with his private contemplation of Catherine's life-threatening pregnancy. After the suicide he pared down all of these passage so that once they had removed themselves from Italy Henry and Catherine were part of an existential crisis where the past offered no clear sense of what was to come and the future seemed to promise only shock and despair. During the months before his suicide Clarence was unwell and worried about his finances, but showed no inclination to kill himself. Hemingway was shocked but able to steady his emotions – hence his role as the single member of the family capable of dealing with the practicalities of his father's death. His capacity to exchange his grief, such as it was, for detachment was the key factor in his decision on how the novel would end. Once Henry and Catherine reach the Swiss side of the lake the mood alters to one of blissful contentment; for them the war is in the past. However, Hemingway knew that in exchanging the brutal realism of a war novel for melodramatic wish-fulfilment would be disastrous. Suddenly, as he pored over this creative dilemma, he experienced his mother and siblings in a state of numb disbelief, unable to properly comprehend Clarence's decision to blow his brains out, and he had found a solution. Henry is assured that mother and baby are well and returns to his hotel, and we, the reader, feel similarly content on there being a happy ending. Suddenly, without warning, everything changes; Catherine and her child are dead and there is in Henry's spiritless final sentence an echo of his experiences on the front line supplanted by something far worse. Hemingway's real life caused his novel to turn into a work that some found unfathomable and others saw as radical and brilliant.

Asked by Cape to do the cover blurb for the UK edition, J.B. Priestley was one of the first to discern something exceptional in the book. He found that Catherine and Henry are 'curiously lonely, without backgrounds, unsustained by any beliefs'. They had, he felt, transcended the cause-and-effect actions of the war and this added to the 'terrible poignancy and force' of its close. The most telling piece was by Dorothy Parker, part profile of Hemingway as a man, part account of him as the author of the most outstanding *roman-à-clef* in English ('The Artist's Reward', *New Yorker*, 30 November 1929). Given Hemingway's contemptible treatment of Parker in Paris her generosity seems extraordinary, except that when we read the piece closely it is evident that Parker is sowing the seeds for what would soon become a broader mood of hostility towards America's new literary superstar. Aside from her own impression of him, she knew from others of the Paris years that he had an appetite for over-glamourising everything from his personality to his past. She had no evidence of the exact extent to which his boasts about Italy departed from the truth but she was aware that most readers who had any experience of the real Hemingway would see that the hardened, tragic persona of Henry was forged from his author's histrionic tales of the most horrific battles of the conflict, the ones in the novel that had occurred almost two years before Hemingway's arrival at the front line. Her prose carries a superbly nuanced subtext: 'no, I don't believe it either'. She did not expose him as a fraud. Far worse, she presents Henry and his creator as indistinguishable: 'He has the most profound bravery that it has ever been my privilege to see [...] He has had pain, ill health, and the kind of poverty you don't believe [...] He has never turned off on an easier path than the one he staked himself. It takes courage.' The article trembles with hyperbole, and wonderfully feigned credulity. This critic, she announces, is convinced that the novel is a brilliant distillation of its author's roughened grief and his 'courage', yet one senses a wry smile forming as she tells of 'the kind of poverty you don't believe'. Parker knew well of his performances in Paris as an indigent bohemian. She was helping to create a myth so grandiose that its disintegration was virtually inevitable.

This would come later, but in the interim Hemingway returned to Paris as he had hoped; triumphant and contemptuous of all those who had questioned his ambitions. He took an uncomfortable lunch with Gertrude Stein and Alice Toklas, arranged by Sylvia Beach and held in the neutral environment of a cafe. Politeness prevailed but mutual contempt hurried the meal to an early conclusion. He would meet Stein and Toklas only once again and felt he had indicated that he no longer required their advice or sufferance.

With weary determination he and Pauline dined with Fitzgerald and Zelda in their apartment. According to later accounts by Hemingway, Zelda slipped into a state of drunken incoherence by the time the first course was served, and from various recollections – Pauline's included – he treated Scott with condescension. The dinner seemed to involve the ceremonial exchange of a franchise. Hemingway could not be certain that Fitzgerald would produce only one more novel but he suspected from what Perkins had said and what he witnessed in person that he would now replace his friend as the preeminent young American novelist of the early twentieth century. Following their return to the US there would be a discernible change in their relationship, with Hemingway offering advice that often came close to mockery and vilification, implying that Fitzgerald's plight was well deserved.

In Paris events took on an air of farce. Extracts from US reviews published during the weekend of 19 and 20 October were being pored over by all in the city with an interest in the arts, particularly those who had witnessed the discomfiting presence of Hemingway earlier in the decade. None of the reviews disliked the book but nor did they seem to agree on what it was, and if a lack of consensus can be treated as testament to originality then this was indeed a radical work.

In short, commentators seemed to be writing about different novels. *The Nation* called it an 'occasion for Patriotic rejoicing'. Percy Hutchins, in the *New York Times*, compared it with *Romeo and Juliet*, 'a high achievement in what might be termed the new romanticism'. Others saw it as a different departure from the general project of modernism, most preposterously the *Tribune* reviewer who proclaimed that 'Hemingway is the direct blossoming of Gertrude Stein's art [...] whole pages in the new book [...] might have been written by Gertrude Stein herself'. While stifling outright laughter one might compare this with a claim that Raymond Chandler's hardcore manner had been inspired by Virginia Woolf.

Despite such slipshod interpretations, enthusiasm was the prevailing mood and Gertrude Stein made the most of this with one final attempt to re-establish the de Fleurus apartment as the fulcrum for a new generation of artists and writers. On the Tuesday after the reviews came out she sent an enigmatic note to Hemingway, asking him to bring Fitzgerald and the promising newcomer Allen Tate to an evening at her apartment. She did not comment on what lay ahead and Hemingway took it upon himself to extend the invitation, summoning Ford Madox Ford, John Bishop and Tate's wife Caroline Gordon, and Stein behaved in much the way he had anticipated. The only account of the evening is contained in an unpublished interview between Carlos Baker and Allen Tate (19 April 1963, PUL). Apparently Stein held court with a brief lecture on the 'Greats' of American literature, beginning with Emerson and Hawthorne. As she evaluated the figures of the later nineteenth century she gave credit to all, with not quite unqualified praise, even for Henry James, and it became clear to all present that she was working towards the equivalent of a coronation, the announcement of a writer who had both inherited and transcended this legacy. It was also evident that there were only two contenders for the crown, Hemingway and Fitzgerald.

Stein's estimation on the merits of the two writers was consummately ambiguous, designed to feed on the vulnerability of one and the ambitions of the other. From Hemingway's letter to Fitzgerald, dispatched a few days after the event (date unclear, 24 or 31 October) it is evident he is convinced he had been declared the victor but he attempts, disingenuously, to reassure Fitzgerald that Stein's sotto voce asides were as important as what she seemed to be saying: 'Gertrude wanted to organise a hare and tortoise race and picked me to tortoise and you to hare and naturally, like a modest man and classicist you wanted to be the tortoise – all right tortoise all you want – it's all tripe anyway.' Stein loathed Hemingway, the feeling was mutual, and the former's status as the impresario of Parisian modernism had faded. Beyond those present at the Fleurus gathering no one would have cared or known of her pronouncement, yet the night prompted in Hemingway a new and maniacal appetite for delusion, provocation and role-playing.

Allen Tate, novitiate to the expatriate scene and unapologetic fan of Hemingway, was treated to the great man's explanation of Ford Madox Ford's recent separation from his wife Stella Bowen. He was, declared Hemingway, impotent, and when Tate confessed his ignorance of this condition Hemingway went on to expand his general thesis on sexuality, including his conviction that there were parallels between a man's sexual practices and the Calvinist model of predestination. There were, he told Tate, a fixed number of orgasms available to every man and each of us should be careful not to squander our allocation too early. Ford, evidently, had done just this and was now bankrupt. Tate was uncertain as to whether his tutor was drunk, roguish or inspired by a deep loathing for Ford. He seemed, Tate recalled, completely sane.

Hemingway had briefly left Paris for the bull-run in Pamplona and soon after the Stein melodrama he visited Spain once more to witness the last bullfights of the autumn. For some time he had been planning a book on bullfighting but had not formally proposed this to Perkins. He made notes for what would, three years hence, become *Death in the Afternoon*, but the more immediate effects of the *corrida* were private and rather disturbing. In between his two periods in Spain he ran into Morley Callaghan, a fellow journalist from the Toronto years. Callaghan was a keen amateur boxer, who had sparred with Hemingway and the two men did so again in Paris. According to Callaghan in his memoir, *That Summer in Paris* (1964), before, during and after the fight in the American Club, Hemingway seemed to be seriously unstable. The fight certainly took place because in Hemingway's letter to Fitzgerald (12 December 1929) he assures his friend that he does not hold him responsible for the outcome. Fitzgerald had been appointed timekeeper and unofficial referee. He was unsuited to both roles because he knew little about boxing and on the day in question was exceedingly drunk. Hemingway had asked him beforehand to keep the rounds shorter than the conventional two minutes; he outweighed his opponent by around 50 pounds but Callaghan was much fitter and faster of hand. According to various witnesses Callaghan soon had Hemingway on the canvas and while some of Hemingway's biographers have questioned Callaghan's probity the true reason for their unease was his account of what happened next. Hemingway, according to Callaghan, approached him and spat a mixture of phlegm and blood into his face, announcing that 'that's a way of showing contempt [...] that's what bullfighters do when they're wounded', adding 'It's a way of showing contempt'. Callaghan was left 'wondering out of what strange nocturnal depths' this 'barbarous gesture' had come.

It is probable that it came from Hemingway's recent association in Spain with Sidney Franklin. Franklin was the son of orthodox Russian Jews and brought up in Brooklyn, New York, by his parents who retained the original family name of Frumpkin. His father, a policeman, visited regular beatings on Sidney who left home, never to return, in 1922. He was 19, the same age as Hemingway when he departed for Italy. Franklin went to Mexico, learned Spanish and became an amateur bullfighter. By the time Hemingway met him he was making his name as a matador on the Spanish circuit and he would feature prominently in *Death in the Afternoon*: '[Franklin] has the ability in languages, the cold courage and the ability to command of the typical soldier of fortune, he is a charming companion, one of the best story tellers I have ever heard [...] brave with a cold, serene, and intelligent valor but instead of being awkward and ignorant he is one of the most skilful, graceful, and slow manipulators of a cape fighting today' (pp. 505, 503). If we give any credit to accounts by others who knew Franklin, fellow matadors included, this is an utterly false representation. He was a crude, unsophisticated fighter and he made up for his lack of balletic skill with hurried brutality. Hemingway later reported that during their first meetings in Spain Franklin knew nothing of his career, and now burgeoning reputation, as a writer. Implicitly, he seems to commend his new friend for this, but it could also be seen as a calculated gesture of condescension on Hemingway's part. Why, one might wonder, did he not tell Franklin what he did for a living? Again, he was role-playing, feeding Franklin snippets of information about his experiences in Italy and suggesting parallels between each of them as Americans who had exchanged their stifling home environment for adventures abroad. He was projecting onto Franklin a fantasised image of himself. The Franklin of *Death in the Afternoon* bears no resemblance to the real man because Hemingway was cultivating a myth. He turns Franklin into an American who has mastered a uniquely Spanish ritual, because he himself wanted to enter this exclusive arena, if not literally then via a convenient proxy.

In the light of this we can offer a belated answer to Callaghan's question of what 'strange nocturnal depths' had been plumbed by his opponent for such a 'barbarous gesture'. He was already rehearsing the role of the feral, savage bullfighter he would confer on Franklin.

The Paris of the 1920s was disintegrating. Pound was spending most of his time in Rapallo, Italy, becoming more and more preoccupied with Mussolini's Fascism, and Joyce had involuntarily withdrawn from previous social and intellectual circles, having to endure and recover from regular eye operations. As Hemingway and Pauline boarded the liner for New York on 9 January 1930, he would have felt he had both transcended and vanquished his past. The reviews of *A Farewell to Arms* were unanimously enthusiastic, despite there being no consensus regarding why exactly the novel was so extraordinary. An offer from *Fortune* magazine to pay him 2,000 dollars in advance for an article on bullfighting testified to the esteem earned by his second work of fiction. This came several weeks after the New York Stock Exchange collapse and in the midst of the financial domino effect that would spark the global depression of the 1930s. Few at the time were willing to gamble 2,000 dollars on anything, but *Fortune* were taking note of the weekly sales figures for Hemingway's novel, which were soaring. On 24 October 1929, the day of the Wall Street Crash, *A Farewell to Arms* had already sold 28,000 copies and despite the widespread fear of an economic apocalypse the reading public remained willing to purchase novels. By the beginning of November sales had passed the 30,000 mark.

It thus seems odd that over the subsequent five years he would give up entirely on novels. Shortly after his return to Key West he began early drafts of what would become *Death in the Afternoon* (1932), and following its publication he devoted most of his time to *The Green Hills of Africa* (1935). He produced a number of worthy short stories but the best of these were offshoots from his non-fiction. 'The Capital of the World' is macabre and farcical, telling of how a waiter in a matadors' *pension* bleeds to death after staging a make-believe bullfight against a fellow worker who brandishes a chair with two meat knives strapped to its legs. 'The Snows of Kilimanjaro' and 'The Short Happy Life of Francis Macomber' are distilled from the autobiographical material of *The Green Hills of Africa*.

Throughout this same period Hemingway displayed an obsessive vagrancy, never allowing himself to be bound to a particular location for more than five or six months. He had returned to Key West in February 1930 and by late spring was already planning to spend time at the L-Bar-T ranch owned by Lawrence Nordquist, in Wyoming. A car accident in Wyoming in November caused him to postpone his plans for another trip to France and Spain. He had hoped to leave before the end of the year but his broken arm and other injuries meant that he and Pauline, then two months pregnant with their second child, would sail for Europe in May 1931.

On 30 April the *Key West Citizen* announced that Mr and Mrs Hemingway had filed deeds 'transferring ownership of the fine home in Whitehead'. It was indeed fine, if a little dishevelled; a pre-Civil War property of great style which reflected the architectural taste of its first owners, members of the Spanish gentry. The purchase indicated permanence and stability, which would soon be belied by Hemingway's habits and inclinations.

Pauline, accompanied by Patrick, took the train to New York, where she collected Bumby and disembarked for France. Hemingway stayed on for a few days in the new house and then took the ferry to Havana, and from there boarded the *Volemdam* en route for Spain, eager to see the earliest bullfights of the season and talk to spectators and participants. On 26 June, Pauline, Patrick and Bumby joined him in Madrid, and on 6 July the three of them met up with Sidney Franklin in Pamplona.

For the rest of July and August the Hemingways commuted between the major bullfights in Valencia, Santiago de Compostela and Madrid, with Ernest treating Franklin as his intermediary for introductions to the more illustrious matadors on the circuit. Constantly he was recording anecdotes and supplementing these with intensive, albeit random, research into the cultural history of bullfighting from books he came across in hotels and libraries.

They sailed for New York on 23 September. Pauline was then seven months' pregnant and once more she had to undergo caesarean section. Gregory, Hemingway's third child, was born in Kansas City on 12 November. A month later, in mid-December, the family were back in Key West. Builders had begun work on the property, Hemingway supervising the conversion of the first-floor servants' quarters into what would be his spacious study, opening on to a balcony on one side and joined to the rest of the house by an elegant mezzanine walkway on the other. Key West suited Hemingway not because of its character; quite the opposite. He relished it as indeterminate, on the edge of other places. Technically it was part of the US, but its only physical link was an artificial causeway. He could drive west, sometimes travelling overnight, and disappear into the untamed emptiness of Wyoming, Idaho or South Dakota, and in the other direction Cuba was little more than an hour away by boat. From there, three times a week, steamers would maintain a link between the island and its colonial ancestor, Spain. Hemingway preferred this route; it seemed to him to cut out his American background and connect him more directly with the Hispanic/Iberian culture that first energised him in the 1920s. Also, Key West's air of multi-ethnic dissoluteness, including villainy, set it apart from the cultural elitism of the upper East Coast and the largely Protestant morality that still prevailed in American small towns and urban suburbs, at least on the face of things. Today, his house offers tourists everything from crockery bearing representations of Papa to the opportunity to get married in the garden. But even in the early 1930s when the US, assisted by the New Deal, began to recover from the Depression and northerners started to take cheap holidays in Florida and the Keys, many were drawn to the charismatic inhabitant of Whitehead Street. Hemingway earned himself various titles, including 'The Old Master'. Despite the fact that he was still in his thirties he would gladly offer visitors sagacious insights into matters literary or quasi-philosophical. He was also referred to as 'Mahatma': while retailing bespoke wisdom he often wore a towel around his head to keep off the sun. Katy Dos Passos reported to Sara and Gerald Murphy of how he could hold the attention of American visitors with his 'tendency to be an Oracle' while at the same time, on his way out to a bar in the afternoon, he would be followed by 'a crowd of Cuban Zombies' who regarded him as a 'conquistador' (12 December 1934). It is difficult to imagine another region of America where such behaviour would be treated as routine, but Key West seemed perfectly suited to the outlandish and exotic.

Often enough he would be absent, particularly after 1932 when he bought his own boat, the *Pilar*, and discovered the virtually uninhabited island of Bimini. On the one hand Bimini was another example of the primitive remoteness that Hemingway craved, with a seven-mile white sand beach and guaranteed sunshine. Yet at the same time that he began to visit it regularly it had also come to the attention of wealthy Americans who had survived the Crash, notably the stockbroker Kip Farrington, Mike Lerner (owner of a chain of women's clothing stores) and Tommy Shevlin, who had used some of his considerable inheritance to found the

International Game Fish Association. All built properties on the
island and treated it as their private estate. This upper-middle-class
version of peasant-free feudalism seemed to Hemingway to bear a
perverse resemblance to Spain and he soon promoted himself to a
senior role in it, putting down a challenge that he could dispose of
any man on the island who dared to take him on by the third
round. Most of all he enjoyed creating an image for himself as
something similar to a bullfighter, with fish sometimes three times
his weight, shark included, replacing bulls. He and his long-term
fishing friend Mike Strater had for years attempted to solve the
dilemma of competing predators. Specifically, if they had hooked a
giant tuna or marlin and played the fish, weakened it, and
gradually reeled it towards the boat, its vulnerable state would
attract sharks and often the magnificent specimen would be little
more than head, gnawed flesh and bone by the time they brought it
aboard. Hemingway borrowed and eventually kept a Thompson
sub-machine gun. Sometimes he or a companion would use it
against the sharks while someone else struggled with the game fish,
but after a few months he mastered a technique of playing the fish
with one hand while shooting at the sharks with the other. Katy
Dos Passos sent a vivid report to Gerald Murphy (20 June 1935):
'They come like express trains and hit the fish like a planing mill
[...] Ernest shoots them with a machine gun, *rrr* [...] It's terrific to
see the bullets ripping into them – the shark thrashing in blood
and foam – the white bellies and fearful jaws – the pale cold eyes –
I was really aghast but it's very exciting.' The parallels between her
account and Hemingway's descriptions of bullfights are extraordinary. He enjoyed relaxing with a drink in the comfortably
appointed beach houses to which his friends would welcome
him after his expeditions, his clothes still spattered with drying
blood. He would entertain them with lurid accounts of how
the water turned red around the boat as he machine-gunned
the sharks while managing to bring home black marlin or tuna
of up to 500 pounds, demonstrating with body language the
balance between gun hand and rod hand. He presented himself as
matador and toreador rolled into one, with his boat replacing the
latter's horse.

Like many writers Hemingway disliked writing: not the finished product and certainly not the experiences that inspired it, but rather the activity. His correspondence, published and unpublished, is littered with descriptions of his profession as the cause of agitation and disquiet. Typically, to Ivan Kashkin:

> A life of action is much easier to me than writing. I have greater facility for action than for writing. In action I do not worry anymore. Once it is bad enough you get a sort of elation because there is nothing you can do except what you are doing and you have no responsibility. But writing is something you can never do as well as it can be done. It is a perpetual challenge and it is more difficult than anything else that I have ever done. (19 August 1935)

When he was away from Key West he was constantly collecting material for his writing and when he returned he would subject himself to an activity that seemed a masochistic necessity. Tellingly, Hemingway showed his most amicable, tender characteristics, particularly for his wives, when he was away from home. When he returned to face the 'perpetual challenge' of pen and typewriter he became someone else. In the early 1950s he confessed to Bernard Berenson that his dreadful treatment of Pauline, his excessive drinking and his general state of irresponsibility and malice had all coalesced as escape routes from the painful responsibility of putting words on the page.

Eventually the fund of wars, natural dangers and locations offered by the world beyond his study in Whitehead Street and then Havana would be used up – and so would the opportunity to reinvent himself, the inspiration for his work. Following *The Old Man and the Sea* he would continue to produce fiction, prodigiously and obsessively, but it was unpublishable. It would go into print after his death, flatteringly modified – a languorous confection of half-formed narratives would be rewritten as separate novels. In its original state it is by parts unreadable and fascinating. It tells us, albeit unintentionally, the story of an author who cannot stop writing but who has run out of things to write about. As he laboured over these incomplete – in truth unfinishable – fictions he attempted to relive the adventures of his past, revisiting key parts of Europe and Africa that had formed his profile as a writer from

Paris onwards. Inevitably, the work that resulted from this was a self-absorbed, directionless repetition of what he had produced in his heyday. But at the beginning of the 1930s the fascinating spectacle of the man who needed excess in order to write about it was still unfolding. *Death in the Afternoon* is intriguing as much for what it does not say as for its effusions and ardency. Before he set off from Havana, Spain was entering the period of political conflict and division – sometimes involving street violence – that would lead to the Civil War. A few days before his liner docked in Vigo a Spanish army 'death squad' had garrotted several left-wing activists, resulting in the arrest of two officers from the unit. Hemingway wrote to Waldo Peirce that he hoped to get to Madrid (14 May 1931, JFK) 'before they set up the guillotine in the Plaza Major', presumably for the execution of the two army majors. Three months later in a letter to Max Perkins he wrote: 'Wish there were some market for what I know about the present Spanish situation. Have followed it as closely as though I were working for a paper' (1 August 1931, PUL).

At the end of May Hemingway was at the Madrid *corrida* when the star fighter, Gitanillo, was tossed by the bull into the *barrera*, the animal hooking him through the thigh with one horn and lifting him backwards. The bull returned and pinned him to the wood with a horn through his lower back. The crowd were gripped with horror and exhilaration and subsequently local newspapers carried regular, macabre reports on his condition. Astonishingly, he survived for ten painful weeks before eventually succumbing to meningitis. Three days before the goring on 27 May, 31 strikers and activists had been shot in various parts of Spain by the Guardia Civil, a prelude to almost daily outbreaks of violence during June in the run-up to the general election of the 28th of that month. Two days before that Hemingway reported to John Dos Passos that the governance of the country was riven by extreme and incompatible factions: 'the Gallegos are proclaiming the Social Republic of Galicia [...] and are striking on election day [...] Andalucia is coming to the boil [...] the workers committees have gotten all harvesting machinery banned [...] it is no uncommon thing for a prelate to shoot down a good republican from the top of an autobus or for a Carmelite to destroy with kicks an agitator.' The facetiousness of the last part should not cause us to doubt his acute awareness of Spain's condition, but the fact that he resorts to it reveals his equal determination to separate politics, indeed reality, from his own ongoing preoccupation.

When he arrived in Madrid in May he had taken a balcony room in the Hotel Biarritz where in the evening he could follow the street violence of a city where political affiliation was too disparate to classify. Monarchists, Carlists, Fascists, Jesuits and members of the military often had as little in common as the Socialists, Communists, Republicans, Anarchists and Anarcho-Syndicalists. It would have seemed that madness was abroad but Hemingway was more interested in how his first son's namesake, Nicanor Villata, had progressed since the mid-1920s. He was disappointed in his erstwhile hero's performances, and a month later when he had brought Bumby over from France to see his first bullfight, involving Nicanor, he was equally upset by his son's disquiet and disgust at the spectacle as a whole.

In his letter to Dos Passos of 26 June there is an unintentionally revealing passage: '23,000 Navarros in Pamplona bull ring 2 weeks ago. Enthusiastic for Don Jaime who has promised to cross the Pireneos [Pyrenees] with the sword in one hand, the cross in the other and the Sacred Heart of Jesus on his chest.' Jon Jaime de Bourbon was not a matador but rather a descendent of the branch of the Bourbon House which had maintained its claim to the crown of Spain since the early nineteenth century. Another set of Bourbons, rather more content with the notion of things having changed since the absolutist monarchy of the sixteenth century, had occupied the throne since then and its final scion, Alphonso XIII, had abdicated in early May 1931. Don Jaime was a pretender to the throne and a time traveller who believed that Spain could be returned to the golden age of the 1500s, when the monarchy, the aristocracy and the church supervised an inflexible feudal society.

It was evident that the '23,000 Navarros' felt it appropriate that a bullfight was a suitable location for a political celebration of Spain's glorious past and its re-establishment in the form of the ludicrous Carlist Don Jaime, but neither in the letter nor in the book does Hemingway even hint at some connection between bullfighting and the various ideological groupings that would soon form an alliance with Franco's Fascists. During his summer in Spain, the farmers who raised bulls for fights were being subjected to attacks by left-wing insurgents but not because the latter were concerned with animal rights; rather they treated the minor gentry who owned these farms as the natural allies of authoritarian Spanish conservatism, figures who revered the culture of the bull ring as a throwback to the Spain of the Conquest. During the war Republican soldiers would storm the ranches of bull breeders, shoot the farmers and proclaim their manifesto: 'one less torero, one less fascist'.

All that Hemingway had to say to Dos Passos was that 'Present republic all for bulls', an ignorant misreading of the state of the nation and of the political significance of bullfighting. He added that the 'ganaderos [breeders] have just about ruined the bloody bulls'. Irrespective of the accuracy of his judgement on the competence of the breeders, the statement shows him to be oblivious to the aspect of Spanish culture epitomised by these *ganaderos*, and the consequent degree of loathing felt against them among dissenting political groups.

Before taking the train from Madrid for Navarre and witnessing the Plaza de Toros filled with Carlists chanting 'Viva Cristo Rey', the battle cry of the sect, Hemingway had met up with the artist and socialist activist Luis Quintanilla, whom he had known during the 1920s. Quintanilla told him that revolution in Spain was a 'necessity' in that the conservative elements of the establishment were even more retrogressive and stultified than those of Tsarist Russia. Thus, he explained, Spain would experience something more brutal than the events of 1917 and the subsequent Civil War; there would be an explosive conflict with forces gathering at each end of the political spectrum. He added that Pamplona, to which Hemingway would set off the following day, exemplified intransigent conservatism, a city thus chosen by the supporters of Don Jaime for a re-enactment of Carlist wars of a century before. The crowds that had gathered for the political rally disguised as a bullfight on 14 June soon dispersed, but during the following few days there endured in the city an atmosphere electrified by something more violent than the *corrida*, something that would soon cause a frenzied collision between those who longed for a return to the past and others hungry for a radically different future. Hemingway stayed on for almost a week and was absorbed exclusively with the compilation of a glossary of bullfighting terms to ensure that when he drafted the book his unprepossessing command of the idiom of the ring would announce him as an insider. He had become the equivalent of an anthropologist whose preoccupation with a circumscribed cultural ritual had blinded him to its broader nuances and associations.

Imagine, if you can, a writer touring Bavaria during the mid-1930s and collecting impressions of folk festivals, beer and sausage fairs, and maypole dancing, while ignoring that fact that Nazism had recently found hospitable parallels between this largely innocuous rural subculture and its notions of healthy Aryanism. It might seem a ludicrous hypothesis but it prompts comparison with Hemingway's fixation with bullfighting, at the expense of the real state of Spain in 1931. He too was constantly gathering apparently random images and anecdotes. He was magnetised by anything and everything, from cuisine and wines, clothes worn and discarded, practices of marrying and burial, the colour and smell of the landscape and the towns. He skillfully accommodated this collage of impressions in the book:

> the noise in the streets in Madrid after midnight [...] and the fair that goes on all night [...] Valencia in the dusk on a train holding a rooster for a woman who was bringing it to her sister [...] twilight at Miro's; vines as far as you can see cut by the hedges and the road [...] In front of the barn a woman held the duck whose throat she had cut and stroked him gently while a little girl held up a cup to catch the blood for making gravy.

The all-informing Catholic religiosity of the place and an obsession with ritual and devotion are, Hemingway hints heavy-handedly, re-enacted in the bullfight, a uniquely Spanish and faintly pagan Mass. Indeed the random parts of Spain, adoringly apprehended in the prose, only become a whole when he transports us to the ceremony of courage and death in the ring. This was also a country on the brink of Civil War but from Hemingway's account one wouldn't suspect it.

Many reviewers inferred with gleeful vindictiveness that the book was really a projection of Hemingway and his masochist fantasies. Most famously, Max Eastman in *The New Republic* (7 June 1933) asks why 'does our iron advocate of straight talk about what things are, our full-sized man, our ferocious realist, go blind and wrap himself in clouds of juvenile romanticism the moment he crosses the border on his way to a Spanish bullfight?' Eastman answers his own question, by implying that Hemingway had telescoped a phenomenon which also involved swathes of Spanish history and culture into a book-length exercise in narcissism and self-delusion. There is some truth in this, but Eastman and similarly hostile reviewers were not fully alert to quite how bad the book really was. Hemingway had been given the opportunity to produce a piece of work that would have been unparalleled in the years leading up World War II. Everyone in Europe was aware that parts of the continent were drifting towards something far more tumultuous than 1914 and 1917. In the summer of 1931 Hemingway witnessed a chiaroscuro of factions and affiliations that seemed to involve history stuck both in fast forward and rewind. Champions of Spain's past were finding sympathetic parallels in the doctrines of Fascism while others saw the new Soviet state as the model for its future. True, his self-imposed objective was to research bullfighting alone, but it was evident to him that this ritual had now also become the nexus for violently opposed perceptions of what Spain used to be and what it might soon become, all of which he ignored.

During the two years following the publication of *Death in the Afternoon* it was not so much the book itself as the critical disputes it prompted which cultivated the mythology of Hemingway, in which the real author often became indistinguishable from the persona he created. Letters to various editors and other published correspondence involved lurid accusations – including suggestions that an author so obsessed with virile toughness must be compensating for his own impotence – and threatening counterclaims, also published, by Hemingway. The prose hinted at violent intent, and when Hemingway punched Eastman in Max Perkins's office in 1934 newspaper hacks were ecstatic. The *Herald Tribune* interviewed both men, whose contrasting accounts of what actually occurred five floors above Fifth Avenue were turned into a piece that resembled James M. Cain's hard-boiled crime fiction.

Edmund Wilson, in *The Wound and the Bow* (1941), was the first to portray Hemingway as a self-cultivated literary celebrity. By 1939, ventured Wilson, he had

> passed into a phase where he is occupied with building up his public personality [...] Hemingway has created a Hemingway who is not only incredible but obnoxious. He is certainly his own worst inward character. [...] A man is essentially what he hides. The real and most important of the many Hemingways was the reflective man who wrote the books and conceded his innate sensitivity under the mask of a man of action. (p. 241)

He goes on to quote Thurber and Stein, who presented him as essentially gentle, compassionate and vulnerably shy. On the face of things Wilson holds that he projected the less agreeable characteristics of his inventions on to his rough-house public image. Much later Meyers contends that the latter was a protective shield behind which dwelt a far more sensitive presence. Their seemingly antithetical arguments are based on a shared premise, that Hemingway was a perpetual fraud, constantly choreographing alternate personae and sometimes outright lies as substitutes for his private self. A correlate requirement is that we accept that he could, consciously and premeditatedly, distinguish between fabrication and truth. Meyers is more outspoken on this than the other biographers but all base their presentations of him on the rationale – with which I disagree – that behind the stories and the bluster was a man alert to who he really was, the actual Ernest Hemingway.

Hemingway was certainly flesh and blood but we must ask whether this living presence was reflected in the fables that bolstered his public image, tales he told to friends and family about how he felt and what he had done, and stories he sold to publishers; or if, without them, he would all but cease to exist. It seems likely that the 'real' Hemingway was an individual whose sense of himself and his fictional accounts of this were frighteningly interdependent because when this relationship began to fragment, so did the man and the writer.

No one is sure of when Hemingway met Jane Mason. Acquaintances of both have testified to having seen them together in Key West during the spring and summer of 1932. She was aboard

Joe Russell's boat *Anita* in May that year. Hemingway taught her to fish for marlin and Ernest, Pauline, Jane and her husband Grant took drinks and dined as a foursome during that same month. In 1932 and early 1933 Hemingway spent an inordinate amount of time fishing with Jane on Russell's boat or staying at the Ambos Mundos hotel in Havana, 20 minutes from Jaimanitas, the Mason's grand estate. Grant co-owned Pan American Airways and held substantial shares in Cubana Airlines, the main carrier between Cuba and the US. He was a scion of the East Coast WASP (White Anglo-Saxon Protestant) upper classes. Tall, handsome and with the cultivated manner of an English gentleman, Grant was a replica of the kind of American whom Hemingway had come to loathe in France during the 1920s, except that he was unapologetically concerned with money and cared little for the arts. During parties at Jaimanitas dozens of servants would be on hand for as long as guests could endure their hosts' exercises in excess, sometimes lasting 36 hours, providing all kinds of conspicuously rare and expensive foodstuffs and alcohol. Twenty years later those who knew Jane would claim that Hemingway's favourite blonde, Grace Kelly, was her replica, and indeed the world of the Masons was the equal of something contrived by a Hollywood producer with a taste for meretricious fantasy.

Pauline's letters from her family home in Arkansas during this period disclose her anxiety. She does not openly accuse him of anything but it is evident that his journeys to Havana immediately following her departures for Piggott seemed to her to be more than coincidental. She wrote of her hair, now trimmed, her certainty that she too will play giant marlins for two hours – as he and Jane had done – and throughout a sense of alarm and desperation seemed to tarnish affirmations of love or commitment: 'I'm not going to leave you again for a long, long time [...] I miss you very much and all the time [...] I miss you all the time and will follow you around like a little dog'. In spring 1933 she wrote, promising to have her ears, lips, nose and moles dealt with by a cosmetic surgeon so that she might compete with 'Mrs Mason and those Cuban women'. She did not have the operations but she certainly enquired about costs and likely side-effects. For those who give credence to natural justice the parallels between the effect upon Hadley of Pauline's predatory regime of the 1920s and her state of desperation five years later are difficult to ignore.

Biographers are uncertain as to whether Hemingway and Jane had a sexual relationship. Reynolds assumes the role of Hemingway's moral advocate and claims they did not, while Meyers insists with prurient glee that they did. The rest – Baker, Mellow and Lynn – insinuate all manner of things without openly accusing either party. They all face the same problem: none can locate convincing evidence of what happened.

Does it matter? It does, because, as I will show, the true nature of their relationship provides an invaluable insight into the way that Hemingway dealt with truth and invention.

The Fitzgeralds' life of excess and indulgence in France seemed modestly restrained when compared with what the Masons got up to in Jaimanitas. Her car, a Packard, was a customised, supercharged model which she drove at preposterously high speeds along the narrow Cuban roads with Hemingway as a passenger, tempting fate, and death, at every corner.

Bumby, Patrick and her own adopted son Antony were in the same car when she played a game of chicken – that is, who would swerve first – against a bus on a road near Havana airport. The car tumbled down a 40-foot embankment but, miraculously, none of the occupants was seriously injured. Several days later Jane jumped from a balcony of the Jaimanitas house and broke her back. She was not permanently disabled and the fact that she had fallen from the first floor into a dense cushion of bushes raises the question of whether suicide – which she later denied – or drink-fuelled carelessness was the cause.

She spent almost a year in a back-brace along with periods of psychoanalytic treatment with Dr Lawrence Kubie, a man who dispensed Freudian wisdom with all the depth and subtlety of a fairground clairvoyant. Whatever went on between Jane and Hemingway endured until 1936. In 1934–5 she spent a good deal of time with him on *Pilar*, and Hemingway amused his barroom acolytes with stories of how when he stayed in the Amber Mundos in Havana Jane would climb in through the window to avoid the

attentions of staff and other guests in the lobby, and to add some
extra thrill to their liaisons.

The Masons, Jane especially, featured in Hemingway's fiction far
more frequently and disconcertingly than did any other people he
knew during this period. They are Heléne and Tommy Bradley in *To
Have and Have Not* (1937), and most explicitly Jane is Mrs Macomber
in 'The Short and Happy Life of Francis Macomber' (1936) who
shoots her eponymous husband at the end of the tale. Her
encounters with Kubie were recycled as Nick Adams' head injury
trauma in 'A Way You'll Never Be'. These incessant reinventions of
Jane and her marriage were neither tributes to her as a lover nor
triumphant rebukes to the ever-suffering Grant. Rather, Jane
provided him with something far more addictive than sex or
romantic subterfuge. Like him, she seemed able to ignore the
difference between the lived-in world and an existence that defied
credibility. In a letter to MacLeish (27 July 1933, Library of
Congress), he wrote:

> All women married to a wrong husband are bad luck for themselves
> and all their friends [...] Mr M. is a man of great wealth and will have
> more [...] people seem to put up with each other beyond our
> understanding [...] I tried to write a very short story about it by saying
> every spring Mrs M. wanted to marry someone else but in the spring of
> 1933 she broke her back.

The story he had tried to write would eventually become 'The Short
and Happy Life of Francis Macomber', which he completed shortly
after the Masons had returned from an African hunting safari, a
replica of the journey that Hemingway and Pauline had taken six
months before. The most bizarre feature of this courtship between
life and fiction was that Hemingway seemed unclear about the exact
nature of the distinctions between the two. In the MacLeish letter he
implies that Jane's fall from the window and subsequent disability
had caused him to suspend his relationship with her fictional
counterpart. It is as though he cannot invent Mr and Mrs Macomber
before Mrs Mason is fully recovered and creating mayhem. In letters
to his friends he always refers to the Masons as Mr and Mrs M or Mr
and Mrs Mason, even though his correspondents had met the former
and knew her as Jane. He gives the impression that he is not friendly

with them; rather that he knows a great deal about them but prefers to maintain an omniscient distance. He wrote to Dos Passos (12 April 1936) that: 'Mrs Mason, I believe is also crossing with us. Mrs Mason is almost as apt at going places without her husband as Mr Josie [Russell] is without his wife. But then Mrs Mason has also had her husband for a long time too although Mr Josie I believe there is no doubt has had his much much much oftener than as longer than Mr Mason.' Substitute 'Macomber' for 'Mason' and the passage could have been lifted from the short story.

The letter to MacLeish is freakish and extraordinary, and we can only guess at what MacLeish made of it. He knew that 'Mrs M' was Jane but he must surely have been puzzled by Hemingway's drifts between her as a particular individual and his general observations on the kind of women who marry rich husbands. It is prescient – a prototype for what Jane would become in Hemingway's writing.

As Mrs Macomber she is 'an extremely handsome and well kept woman of the beauty and social position which had, five years before, commanded five thousand dollars as the price of endorsing, with photographs, a beauty product which she had never used'. She is a fraud. In the file clipped to the later draft of the story is a photograph from *Ladies Home Journal* of Jane, the stunningly beautiful 'Mrs George Grant Mason' who endorses 'the creams [that] take care of your skin more easily than others'.

Hemingway's prediction in the MacLeish letter that Mrs M wanted to marry someone else comes to pass in the story. Mrs Macomber dispatches her husband, whom Hemingway refers to in the letter as a 'poor twerp', with a single shot from a 6.5 mm Mannlicher. The story would be completed shortly after the Masons had returned from their African trip. Jane had had an affair with the retired British army officer who had co-hosted the Hemingways' safari. She seemed to be encroaching on Hemingway's imagined empire and he got his own back in *To Have and Have Not* where Jane resurfaces as Heléne, a ruthless, unfaithful sexual predator. Hemingway seems to be in a grotesque hinterland between erotic-noir fantasy and private grievance. Connoisseurs of the very eerie should go to the exchange between the real Hemingway and Pauline in the non-fictional *Green Hills of Africa* (1935). The former asks, 'who's a beautiful woman?', and before Pauline has time to answer replies to himself, 'Margot is'. Pauline adds 'I know I'm not' but he reassures her: 'You're lovely.' Margot is Mrs Macomber, a character discussed by two people, one of whom invented her and based her on a very real woman who both attracted and frightened him. Later commentators might call this kind of thing post-modern; madness seems more appropriate, and even then something of an understatement.

The reason why Jane seemed to haunt Hemingway is straight-forward. Scour through correspondence – outgoing from him to her, incoming from her to him – and you will encounter a dialogue between two people that is in truth a superbly rehearsed performance. There is a good deal of candour and humour, but certainly no indication that they were anything other than individuals with well-suited dispositions. One does not need to be a callous sceptic to wonder why Jane gives disproportionate attention to Pauline and Hemingway's children, asking how they are, sending good wishes, enquiring about their ongoing activities and so on. This was their code, based on an assurance that Hemingway would show the letters to his family, especially Pauline, or at least leave them around to be read by any of them who cared to do so. The subtext was, 'see, nothing to hide, because nothing is going on', but the truth was quite different from what these apparently innocuous and candid exchanges indicated. One letter that Hemingway did hide eventually found its way into the JFK archive.

Following the car crash involving Jane and the children, Hemingway drafted two letters to Pauline. Both tell versions of the same story but each undergoes heavy revisions; he even gives them different titles – 'Letter I' and 'Letter II' (JFK, 1935). He is determined that the finished draft, an amalgam of the two, will not give too much away. The air of blithe geniality is self-evidently false: 'I can at present, despite protestations verging on hysteria, ensconced in the oft-maligned hospital and, I may say, consider myself fortunate.' He did not need to convince Pauline of his ability to endure pain and deal with life-threatening incidents. So why the enforced joie de vivre? 'The Stretcher bearers Union have devised rules which would induce fear in the breast of a robot.' It is clear that he is trying to hide something or at least find some way of obscuring a particular aspect of the accident beneath an abundance of jollity. In 'Letter I' he mentions that 'Bumbie piped up in his plaintive 9-year-old voice and said "It's quite all right Mrs M. I am not hurt and Patrick isn't either; he's just frightened"'. In 'Letter II' this single reference to 'Mrs M' is excised. Obviously, Hemingway knew that he would not be able to keep from Pauline the fact that Jane was driving the car but it appears that his, and Jane's, deeply embedded habit of writing in code had influenced this strange exercise in evasion in Letters I and II.

One assumes that Hemingway and Jane destroyed letters between each other in which they were candid about their affair and there is sufficient proof that such a correspondence took place in the survival of the only one they overlooked. It begins 'Most Honored Darling' and is signed 'The Cuckoo', cuckoo in the nest being the commonplace term for someone having an affair with a person already in a relationship. It seems to have been mistakenly retained by Hemingway among unrelated carbons of correspondence to others and it eventually found its way into the JFK archive; it is dated by archivists as '1935?'.

'Your letters entranced, enchanted, enthralled and pleased me immensely', she writes. Because of him,

> life is once again a splendid exciting thing [...] For which I thank you again, bobbing a curtsey [...] Take a look at me darling, portrait of a woman in three combined colors, portrait of a too loving spirit tied down to a fraudulent feminine carcass [...] and a good many, too many miles away from the, may we say, object of her love, perhaps not love exactly – something a little below and little above it, but whatever it is something pretty damned strong.

She also refers to herself on several occasions as 'Lone Wolf', and it is evident that she refers here to having lived undercover, beyond the attention of those who might otherwise condemn her. A lot of care has gone into hiding any absolute proof of the identity of writer and recipient – all we know of the date is that it was begun at '2 AM Thursday 16th' and completed on 'Friday AM' – but there are sufficient clues to disclose them as, respectively, Jane and Hemingway.

She sometimes refers to the activities of 'Ernest', but this was not unusual. In the fake correspondence they frequently allow themselves to drift into a strange third-person mode as if they are aware of who they are but have taken a step back. If confirmation were needed that her addressee is also 'Ernest' then her references to Dr Lawrence Kubie provide it, he being the New York psychologist who had treated her from 1933 to 1934. Kubie was planning to publish an article claiming that much of Hemingway's writing involved attempts to distance himself from classic symptoms of sexual neurosis, including the Oedipal struggle against his father for the possession of his mother and his fears of his own recent homosexual inclinations. Before the publication of this Hemingway had threatened to sue Kubie for libel and the essay did not appear until 1984. At the time of the private letter from Jane to Hemingway only five people knew of it: Hemingway himself, Kubie, Hemingway's lawyer, Charles Scribner and Jane. Certainly she had informed her therapist that Hemingway had confessed that much of his work was autobiographical. She had done so on the assumption that the rule of doctor–patient confidentiality would be maintained, but in the letter she refers disdainfully to how Kubie had broken that trust.

It is an extraordinary letter, given that it discloses the amount of effort, from each, that lay behind the composition of the rest of their correspondence in which their relationship appears entirely non-sexual. This exhausting exercise in subterfuge testifies to the fact that their affair was something more than an extra-marital fling and to Hemingway's predisposition towards protean shifts. Throughout, Jane rejoices in the irony of how having to deceive others has enabled her to embody her long-repressed true self. She has struggled to 'tame the really rebellious child which was me' but now because of 'Ernest' this spirit has been 'released'. The letter is informed by a tangible thrill at being part of their clandestine arrangement, of being two different people, and it is clear that she sees Hemingway as having cast the spell for this. As we have seen he also made use of this facility to cause their life to inform his fiction. She closes the letter: 'Good night, may I kiss you quite gently, quite tenderly – go!' It is a poignant document. Her sincerity is transparent but so is a sense of weary resignation. She loves him yet she is aware that, probably quite soon, what they had will be no more. By early 1936 their relationship would be over, but this letter should cause us to reconsider his subsequent reinventions of Jane in his fiction. In each instance she disappears or mutates into someone else, but there is always a touch of regret, of loss.

In his Foreword to *The Green Hills of Africa* Hemingway proclaims that 'unlike many novels none of the characters or incidents in this book is imaginary [...] The writer has attempted to write an absolutely true book to see whether the shape of a country and the pattern of a month's action can, if truly presented, compete with a work of the imagination.' One might treat this as a thought-provoking observation on the differences, if any, between fiction and non-fiction, but such a reading would be generous.

Hemingway's declaration is irrational and it mirrors the extended strangeness of the book. The prose descriptions of the landscape might have come from *A Farewell to Arms*: 'It was green, pleasant country, with hills below the forest that grew thick on the side of a mountain, and it was cut by the valleys of several watercourses that came down out of the thick timber of the mountain' – and on and on, with 'forest' (three times), watercourses (twice) and mountains (twice) recurring in the two subsequent sentences. This is Hemingway from *The Sun Also Rises* onwards, his signature manner, which raises questions: does he think that verbal repetition will sooth the reader into an empathetic sharing of the author's experience, or is he too lazily self-assured to care about such old-fashioned notions as sentences that stand alone as respectable components of good prose? Most significantly: if this is neither fiction nor non-fiction then why does it replicate the manner of his earlier novels?

His claim that the book is based on what happened when he and Pauline visited British East Africa in 1934 is authentic enough: it concentrates largely on the stalking and killing of an astonishing variety of wild animals. But it is an expurgated version of what actually occurred. Pauline's 'safari journal' (Stanford University Library) reads as an anxious, apologetic subtext to the book. When she wrote it she was not certain of how, if at all, her husband would make use of the safari for his writing, let alone if her own notes would be open for public scrutiny. But once the scholarly industry began to consume Hemingway and his world it gradually became evident that Pauline was, albeit inadvertently, exposing Hemingway as delusional.

To summarise, she tells of how she, as a poor shot, subjected various creatures to a tortured, lengthy demise; in a number of cases Philip Percival would have to follow trails of blood until he could mercifully dispatch the animals. She also confesses to feelings of disgust with the ceremonial temper of the killings. In her account the hunters impose on their victims a class structure, with lions, tigers and other wildcats as the aristocracy, and accorded a collateral ranking when killed: dispatched as swiftly as possible and treated with according respect as noble carcasses. When these haute monde beasts were not available rifles were turned towards reedbucks, impala, gazelle, roan, waterbuck, buffalo, rhino, zebra, warthogs and anything else that seemed conveniently alive. In her journal she presents hunters as figures whose sense of power and esteem is embarrassingly incongruous with insanitary day-to-day existence and messy cruelty. They lived in tents and huts that rarely offered access to clean water, disease-bearing insects were an incessant feature of life, night and day, and within two weeks Hemingway was beset by a particularly foul bout of dysentery. One of Pauline's most vivid recollections was of being driven to witness the corpses of two giant buffaloes which her husband expected her to treat as evidence of his superiority as a marksman. All she remembered was that the bodies of these creatures were seemingly still alive, an effect created by the enormous variety of insects feeding upon and apparently mobilising their flesh.

None of this appears in the book. Instead we are presented with resonant disquisitions on the purity of slaughter. 'I did not mind killing anything, any animal', he writes, 'if I killed it cleanly, they all had to die and my interference in the nightly and seasonal killing that went on all the time was very minute and I had no guilty feeling at all'. As Pauline's journal reveals, one of the reasons why the wounded animals would spend days dying in excruciating pain was Hemingway's inability to control his bowel movements. Despite his being unable to chase the dying creatures his self-image as warrior-in-chief made him forbid Percival and his native helpers from doing this on his behalf, at least until even the most hardened of the group could no longer condone such cruelty.

The book's best-known passage has nothing to do with hunting or Africa. The narrator digresses, and speaks to an Austrian, Kandisky – based on the Austrian, East Africa trader, Hans Koritschoner – on the destructive pressures of being a modern writer. It is an assembly of high-minded tautologies and platitudes, in which the cultural establishment is accused of destroying great writers and great writers are blamed for colluding in this (p. 17).

One can only explain its presence by considering the almost comic history of the book itself. By 1934 Max Perkins felt reassured that his star writer's work in progress was a welcome return to fiction and Hemingway had not misled him in this, at least not deliberately. On 28 November 1934 (PUL), Perkins wrote to him that 'I see that you regard this as a story, not a novel', meaning that Hemingway had given him the impression that it was more like an extended short story or a novella than a long piece of fiction. He added that the length of *In the Highlands of Africa*, its provisional title, 'makes no difference'. When the typescript arrived Perkins initially believed that the work was indeed fiction; the first-person narrator was anonymous, his wife was referred to as P.O.M. (Poor Old Moma) and the rest of the figures who had been on the safari all carried pseudonyms. It was only during the production process that it became evident to him, mainly via accounts from mutual friends, that the 'African story' was an extension of *Death in the Afternoon*, with Hemingway starring as a unique presence, a hunter whose courageous facing down of lions testified to his equally dauntless revolt against the literary establishment.

The prefatory note that it was an 'absolutely true autobiography' was added at the insistence of Perkins shortly before the book went into print. Hemingway was not attempting mendacity or evasion, at least not deliberately. Aged 35 he dwelt in the same hinterland between truth and fiction that had plagued him since his teens. He was apparently oblivious to the ways that the book broke down the division between stories he had made up and what had actually occurred, and one cannot ignore the parallels between *The Green Hills of Africa* and the bizarre world of evasion and subterfuge he shared with Jane Mason. The correspondence between them that was not hidden from Pauline and others was a masterpiece of epistolary novel-writing; authentic, in that it was convincing, and all the more impressive in its capacity to appear a reflection of the truth. The single letter that revealed the actual nature of their relationship points up the labours and craftsmanship that under-pinned the ones that hid it. In the book something very similar occurred, and one can only wonder at the nature of Perkins' thoughts when it dawned on him that his star author was delusional.

CHAPTER 4

Conflicts

By the end of the 1930s Hemingway's marriage with Pauline was over. She was replaced by the alluring novelist and journalist Martha Gellhorn, almost ten years Hemingway's junior. Superficially it seemed an ideal partnership in that she shared his taste for dangerous enterprises and equally unbridled writing. In truth, it was disastrous from the outset and as their incompatibility began to dawn on Hemingway he sought further refuge in excess and self-deception.

Hemingway's first encounter with Martha is one of the myths of modern literary celebrity, by equal parts engrossing and suspect. In December 1936 three tourists walked into Sloppy Joe's bar just as Hemingway was paying his bill and preparing to leave. According to Lynn the youngest woman's 'beautiful mane of tawny gold shoulder length hair, high cheekbones, and full-lipped mouth caused him to do a double take. His eyes followed the simple lines of her black cotton dress down to her long and shapely golden-brown legs' (p. 464). Lynn does not provide a convincing source for this, hinting only that much later the black bartender, Skinner, gave various accounts of the evening to journalists. He omits to explain how Skinner could have witnessed the rest of the story he peddled to the press, with Pauline hosting a crayfish dinner for friends, sending Charles Thompson to the bar to see what was delaying her husband and becoming distressed when Thompson returned to inform her that he was seemingly captivated by a young blonde woman.

Skinner's account and its numerous permutations began to gain currency after the film version of *To Have and Have Not* was released in 1944. In this, Humphrey Bogart, as Harry Morgan, comes across Lauren Bacall, playing Marie 'Slim' Browning, in a hotel bar in Martinique. Audiences revelled in the electricity generated by the most popular tough-guy star of the 1940s and the beautiful blonde newcomer, 20 years his junior, and this on-screen scenario seemed to all to be a mischievous dramatisation of what happened between Hemingway and Martha when he was completing the novel.

It is certain that Martha, her mother and younger brother were on holiday in Key West in late 1936, but it is likely that her first encounter with Hemingway was rather more conventional than the louche tale of strangers in a bar. Hemingway held court not only for his retinue of friends from the upper East Coast. Whitehead Street was an open house for any visitors to the district remotely connected with writing and publishing, and it is likely that Martha and her mother Edna would have encountered the Hemingways socially in Key West, irrespective of what occurred during the subsequent three years.

Her novel *What Mad Pursuit* (1933) was about three young women who drop out of college and embark on unorthodox lifestyles and was a minor sensation. One of the cover blurbs heartily recommending it was by Mr Ernest Hemingway. She worked for *Vogue* in Paris, for the *New Republic* and the *St Louis Post-Despatch*, writing articles on the enduring effects of the Depression. Following this, the government employed her as a researcher to provide accounts for the best deployment of federal financial relief. She became a close friend of Eleanor Roosevelt, a regular guest at the White House and her collection *The Trouble I've Seen* was based on her reports on the dire conditions still endured by many blue-collar Americans. The political and cultural establishment were stunned by a radical left-leaning polemic which received a glowing tribute from the First Lady. It was published and very favourably reviewed three months before Martha arrived in Key West. Hemingway might not have met her in person before December but he certainly knew a great deal about her.

Martha left Key West on 10 January 1937 and Hemingway departed the following day for New York. He stopped over for an evening in Miami and Martha joined him and his friend the boxer Tom Heeney for dinner. There is no evidence that either had pretended that the encounter was accidental and Hemingway was honest enough, before his departure, about the possibility that he would meet Martha in Miami. His wife knew that he and Martha were concerned with and had spoken about the rise of Fascism in Europe and the political crisis in Spain. Hemingway had contacted Heeney well in advance and arranged to dine with him during his journey north and the trip to New York had been arranged before he met Martha in Key West. He was due to meet Perkins to discuss his ongoing novel, *To Have and Have Not*, and to make arrangements regarding his imminent departure for Spain. The North American News Alliance (NANA) had contracted him to cover the Civil War which had begun six months earlier. From Miami he took the train to New York and Martha left for St Louis. He would return to Key West before travelling north once more in late February to sail for France. He spent almost two weeks in Paris, flew to Valencia on 16 March and then went by car to Madrid. Martha sailed from New York roughly two weeks after Hemingway and arrived in Madrid only a few days later than him. Both booked into the Hotel Florida in the centre of the city, but this can hardly be treated as evidence of a calculated romantic liaison. Virtually all foreign correspondents stayed there.

Lynn presents her as an eerie replica of the Pauline of almost ten year earlier, suggesting that a letter Martha sent to Pauline from Missouri thanking her for her hospitality and stating that she greatly admired Hemingway's work was cruelly disingenuous, designed to remind Pauline of what she had done in France, befriending both Hemingway and Hadley while quietly contriving to become the latter's replacement (p. 467). To believe that she premeditatedly re-enacted Pauline's behaviour we must also accept that Hemingway himself had told her of what happened a decade earlier. When she wrote the letter she had known him for less than a month and he never spoke of his break-up with Hadley; he would remain remorseful about his treatment of first wife for the rest of his life.

True, Martha refers to Hemingway as 'Ernesto', but so did most others who had met him and talked to him of his passion for Spain.

Something happened between them in Spain later that year but who courted whom will remain a matter for speculation. Before he left she wrote to him in Key West, and it was clear they had already talked of meeting up in Madrid:

> We are conspirators and I have personally already gotten myself a beard and a pair of dark glasses. We will both say nothing and look strong [...] Angel, I have so much to tell you, but suddenly I feel there is no time even to think straight [...] please, please leave word in Paris [where she would arrive after him] [...] write if you can. Please don't disappear. Are we or are we not members of the same union? Hemingstein, I am very fond of you. Marty. (Gellhorn to Hemingway, 8 February 1937, JFK)

Some might treat this as evidence that they intended to use Spain as the opportunity for an affair, irrespective of what might endure beyond that. Yet the sense of furtive urgency ('We are conspirators'; 'beard and dark glasses'; 'say nothing and look strong'; 'no time [...] to think straight'; 'members of the same union') amounts almost to self-caricature and evinces her excitement at the prospect of an adventure close to the front lines of a struggle between good and evil, accompanied by a man who, she believed, shared her political convictions. It was fuelled as much by their passion for the Republican cause as by an amorous kinship. She also asked him to 'Give my love to Pauline', which in a letter fired by such urgent transparency could hardly be regarded as sarcasm. Also, if Spain was part of some secret plan to cuckold Pauline, it seems odd that on 17 March the *St Louis Post-Despatch,* after contacting Martha, reported that 'Miss Gellhorn, as a journalist, has made arrangements to join Ernest Hemingway and other Americans seeking entrance to that country [Spain]'.

Martha has long been portrayed as an ambitious interloper, using Hemingway as a route to eminence, but the opposite was the case. He was using her. She had published fiction, and though she was certainly his junior as a literary celebrity, it was clear to him that she was acutely alert to the conflicting trajectories of politics in the US and Europe during the 1930s. To put it bluntly, she was better informed than him on these matters. But it is evident from the letter of 8 February that he had convinced her that they were of the same cause, advocates of the left who would play a significant part in the defence of Europe against Fascism during the years to come. Much later, when she spoke to Kert of her first conversations with Hemingway in Key West, she makes it clear that it was she who advised him on forthcoming dangers to the Spanish Republic. In a letter to Eleanor Roosevelt (5 January 1937) written during her visit, she comments only that he is 'an odd bird [...] a marvellous story teller' and that he had shown her the 'mss of his new book' (*To Have and Have Not*), seemingly to demonstrate his shift towards politically resonant fiction. He was, she implied, keen to join the coterie of radical, ideologically engaged writers, of which she was already a signed-up member.

Martha was as glamorous and attractive as Jane Mason but the latter was, at best, a disposable asset: inherently unstable and certainly not worth the potential dangers of a long-term relationship. While we have come to treat Hemingway's trip to Spain as the beginning of a whirlwind romance, with a shared experience of warfare as an extra quotient of excitement, it is evidence that for him this war was as much a calculated exercise in self-advancement as a romantic adventure. He wanted Martha as a woman, but more significantly as a courtier with impressive credentials as an activist and ideologue. She would, he planned, always remain secondary to Ernest Hemingway but he would find her useful, as his partner and confidante, in the transformation of his profile as a writer, in which he would evolve into the author of political novels, often written from the front line. The beginning of his relationship with Martha would coincide with his ruthless detachment of himself from friendships that had survived from Paris, notably that with Dos Passos.

Perkins was desperate for him to complete his next novel. His chief author had pioneered a tough naturalistic style which, Perkins insisted, was perfect for a piece of fiction on the enduring effects of the Depression. What Perkins expected from Hemingway was something that was as controversial and relevant as the work of Dos Passos but which, crucially, would be far more reader-friendly. Two parts of Dos Passos's *USA* trilogy were already in print and they reflected the writer's greatness and incongruities. When he wrote *USA* he openly advocated communism as a solution to the frightful iniquities of a world experiencing what seemed to be the death throes of capitalism. He researched his fiction thoroughly, living among the lower classes in various parts of the US. The problem was that the beloved raw material of his fiction, the oppressed, were those least likely to read it. His techniques were self-consciously experimental, often involving stream of consciousness and the erratic juxtaposition of 'found' writings, including newspaper clippings, autobiographical reflections, blunt unadorned realism and hollow documentation. It was celebrated by the literati but largely ignored by the kind of people who were its supposed inspiration. When he met Martha, Hemingway was close to completing the first draft of *To Have and Have Not*, a novel that pointed up the essential differences between the two authors, and in a bizarre way their similarities as men attempting to harmonise their private inclinations with their writing. It is based in Havana and the Florida Keys, and the financial inequalities and social and ethnic tensions of the region feature as an uncomfortable but dutifully appended subtext; one senses Hemingway laying down the thematic foundation for a novel about politics and then struggling to subdue a more powerful urge to write a thriller. The result is a hybrid that resembles the books produced by Dashiell Hammett at the beginning of the 1930s, with *Red Harvest* and most notably *The Glass Key* (1931), noirish crime novels shot through with portraits of political corruption and labour exploitation. Hammett was, daringly, making use of the conventions of crime writing as an appropriate frame for the moral hypocrisies of American capitalism, but Hemingway was struggling to reconcile otherwise incompatible aspects of his personality. He was aspiring for recognition as a novelist who could combine storytelling with social and ideological insight but his addiction to fantasy, risk and self-aggrandisement would always prove more powerful than genuine political affiliation. Hemingway's problem would eventually lead to the ugly termination of his friendship with Dos Passos.

Their relationship is exemplified by an episode on May Day 1934. They took the ferry from Key West to Havana, and found the island in a state of political turmoil. The dictator, Gerardo Machado, had recently abdicated, but Colonel Fulgencio Batista was marshalling the army against protesting workers, labour leaders and Communist agitators. On the day they arrived 25,000 protesters marched towards the Cristal Stadium where speakers were due to denounce the continuation of what amounted to a military dictatorship backed, as most saw it, by America. Army fighter planes dived towards the rally without opening fire but government snipers did so from roof-tops causing the marchers to disperse. Eleven were wounded. The following morning transport workers held a political strike and paralysed the city, and soldiers fired at random upon a group of high-school students who had gathered to protest against what had happened the day before: one died and six more were wounded.

The ostensible reason for the visit was to enable Hemingway to secure and pay for a permanent docking site for his recently acquired boat, *Pilar*. Both men were aware of the political situation on the island but their reactions to it on arrival prefigured the gradual cessation of their friendship. Hemingway divided his time between negotiating agreements for the docking site and socialising with the Masons, who treated the widespread violence much as the Roman nobility had enjoyed the gruesome spectacles offered at the Colosseum. On the second day their chauffeur drove them into the centre of Havana where they took drinks on the balcony of a friend's apartment as the high-school students were picked off by the army. Hemingway joined them. Dos Passos also observed these events, but he mixed with protesters and strikers, and took notes. He saw parallels between what was happening in Cuba and the political situation in Spain, except that the latter would, he predicted, lead to something far more turbulent and momentous. He enjoyed the company of Hemingway, but he was much closer to the Spanish intellectual and political activist José Robles. Thanks to Dos Passos, Robles had secured a post at Johns Hopkins University and returned to Spain every summer. He had translated Dos Passos's celebrated novel *Manhattan Transfer* (1925) into Spanish, but the most significant aspect of their friendship was Robles's role as oracle. Both men were Communists and the latter advised Dos Passos that Spain would soon emulate the Russia of 1917: it was, he believed, a society unaffected by the Industrial Revolution and the Enlightenment, still dominated by the aristocracy and the church – Robles was himself a scion of the Spanish nobility – and destined for an imminent conflict with the revolutionary left. Most significantly, Robles distrusted the standard Marxist notion of history as a predetermined narrative. He advised his friend that Spain, his native country, was so conflicted, so caught in a time warp as to ensure that the outcome of the forthcoming war would not be a socialist utopia. This contributed to Dos Passos's shift towards humanist scepticism regarding the ultimate benefits of communism. When Robles became the victim of the intransigent Soviet-sponsored Spanish Communists Hemingway would make use of his connections with them to visit his bitterness upon Dos Passos.

Hemingway's Spain was the idealised fantasy of *Death in the Afternoon*, the one that Robles and Dos Passos predicted would soon be swept into a turmoil of revolutionary ideology and medievalist Fascism. Hemingway never met Robles, but his gradual realisation during the mid-1930s that he and his friend were far more alert than he was to the complexities of society and politics in Spain infuriated him: they exposed his perception of the country he espoused to love as embarrassingly naive. In a letter to Pauline from Madrid in 1933 he tells of how he had spoken to the brother of two waitresses at his hotel, and that by various means this young man had introduced him to a minor aristocrat whose estate held abundant stocks of partridge and wild boar. He would, he announced, be spending some time there hunting. Not once does he indicate that Spain was on the brink of a political crisis. Six months earlier members of the Civil Guard had massacred 24 people who they believed had anarchistic sympathies. In a letter to Pauline's parents he reported that 'All the idealists now have their fingers in the pie and they have got down to where the plums are very small. When they run out pie there will be another revolution' (16 October 1933).

At the time he wrote this the government was made up of an unstable coalition of conservatives and liberal socialists, but which among these he sees as the 'idealists' is unclear. He was happily ignorant of the politics of Spain in 1933 but three years later he became an unrelenting advocate of the Soviet-backed Communists of the Civil War. This was not due to some ideological epiphany; he had not suddenly found a cause. It was an act of vengeance against Dos Passos, who had inadvertently caused him to confront his political apathy and callowness. In 1936, when Dos Passos began to disavow Soviet communism as a form of tyranny, Hemingway embraced it for the same reason, as a means of provoking and alienating his erstwhile friend.

Soon after their journey to Havana Hemingway began *To Have and Have Not*, basing it on a short story, 'One Trip Across', that had appeared in *Cosmopolitan* earlier in 1934. On the surface their relationship remained transparent and cordial, yet Hemingway was already making plans for the character Richard Gordon, a novelist and outspoken Communist sympathiser. He is also an unmanly dilettante, loathed by his wife as a hypocrite and sycophant, a man who uses his political allegiances as a route to personal betterment. The finished product would bear conspicuous resemblances to Dos Passos, with a great deal of vindictive distortion thrown in.

The infamous conclusion of their friendship did not occur until Hemingway's first visit to Spain in 1937 when he was completing the final draft of the novel, but it is evident that Hemingway had already decided to eliminate him from the steadily diminishing group of acquaintances from his years in Paris.

The residents of the Hotel Florida in spring 1937 were transfixed in equal degrees by the sheer thrill of their experience and the prospect of recording a landmark in modern history. It was a charming, sumptuously appointed nineteenth-century building, its guests well served by uniformed staff bearing all manner of wines, spirits and cocktails and by Fascist forces based just outside the capital who were just as generous in the provision of high-explosive shells. Henry Buckley of the *Daily Telegraph* was there, along with Sefton Delmer of the *Daily Express*. From the US there were George Seldes of the *New York Post*, Heb Matthews of the *New York Times* and Virginia Cowles of Hearst Papers. Dos Passos was writing freelance articles, as was Josephine Herbst and Martha Gellhorn. Joris Ivens was directing the documentary film *The Spanish Earth*, sponsored by Contemporary Historians Inc. of New York, which involved Lillian Hellman, Dos Passos, Dorothy Parker and Archibald MacLeish.

The hotel was shelled every day by Franco's guns and the journalist George Seldes recalled that 'there was never a secret about Hemingway living with Martha at the Florida Hotel [...] when the hotel was straffed [*sic*] our great fun, Helen and I, was to stand at the foot of the stairway to see who was running out of what room with what woman.' He adds that 'I don't need to tell you who came out of Hemingway's room'. Hemingway had booked a room on the eighth floor, but by the time he arrived the seventh and eighth floors had been destroyed by artillery fire. He moved to the sixth, boasting that it felt most like the front line of the siege.

Hemingway and Gellhorn would visit Spain during the Civil War on two further occasions, but 1937 galvanised their relationship. Later, in 1972, she spoke of her life alongside men on the front line: 'I accompanied men and was accompanied in action [...] I plunged into that [...] but [...] sex, that seemed to be their delight and all I got was the pleasure of being wanted.' On Hemingway, including their time in Spain: 'I provided sex only after all excuses failed and with the hope that it would be over quickly' (quoted by Moorhead, p. 408). In Madrid he wrote his only play, *The Fifth Column*. As drama it is woeful but it is intriguing because Rowlings is Hemingway and Dorothy is Martha, portrayed, as he saw things, at the beginning of their relationship. She is sexually alluring, with 'the longest, smoothest, straightest legs and the loveliest damn body in the world'. Dorothy says of him – Rowlings/Hemingway – that 'he's full of life and good spirits [...] so lovely and so sort of vital and so gay'. He tempers this narcissism with her opinion that he is also a 'conceited drunkard', a 'braggart'. As usual he takes control, as author of an alternative reality, and reshapes it according to his wishes: she has her doubts but she is fascinated and beguiled by him nonetheless.

Another perspective is provided by the reports they delivered during this period. Martha was a superb writer and her article for *Collier's* (17 July 1937) is engrossing. She tells of a square in Madrid:

> An old woman, with a shawl over her shoulders, holding a terrified thin little boy by the hand, runs out into the square [...] A small piece of twisted steel, hot and very sharp, sprays off from the shell and takes the little boy by the throat. The woman stands there, holding the hand of the dead child, looking at him stupidly, not saying anything.

Compare it with one of Hemingway's NANA dispatches (22 March) on the corpses of Italian volunteers left behind by their retreating Francoist comrades:

> They did not look like men, but where a shell burst caught three, like curiously broken toys. One doll had lost its feet and lay with no expression on its waxy stubbed face. Another doll had lost half of its head. The third doll was simply broken as a bar of chocolate breaks in your pocket.

Hemingway's trope involving childhood and innocence contrasts with Martha's unforced naturalism, but given that they read each other's dispatches one has the sense of two people working together and maintaining their separateness. She confessed to Kert that when they visited the front line in April she listened carefully to his advice on when to fall flat and how to find cover from machine-gun fire. Much later Hemingway reflected, wryly, that she was more courageous and fetchingly irresponsible than most men with whom he had shared battlefield experience. In this respect we can begin to appreciate her remark that sex was something they dealt with 'quickly'. That year in Spain they shared experiences far more elemental than then sensual gratification. To Kert she admitted that these months were the best of their relationship. 'I think it was the only time in his life [...] when he was not the most important thing there was. He really cared about the Republic and he cared about that war. I believe I never would've got hooked otherwise' (Kert, p. 299).

When she joined him in the Hotel Florida Hemingway did his best to shape and control her, but over the subsequent weeks she responded by becoming as intransigently independent as him. She would leave Spain as a confident reporter and a brave woman, and while Hemingway played a part in this he also ensured that she would escape him. Their partnership in Spain was the beginning of their relationship and the guarantee of its failure. The reckless, outspoken woman who had enchanted him in Key West would, through her collision with an equally impassioned presence, find that she no longer needed it.

Hemingway was aware that Pauline would eventually learn of what was going on and would not be able to dismiss it as an aberration, albeit infuriating, as she had with Jane Mason. He and Martha had already made plans to meet briefly in the US in early summer and then to spend another month together in Spain in August 1937. His marriage to Pauline would last until 1940 but in name only; when away from Key West he spent as much time with Martha as he did with his wife. They moved in together, permanently, in Havana in May 1939.

The other significant event in Madrid involved Dos Passos and was enacted by Hemingway in a sadistic, melodramatic manner. José Robles had been held in detention by the Communist-controlled Popular Front since December 1936. There were no specific charges against him and no date for a trial had been set. No one knew where he had been detained, and the nature of his 'arrest' by figures who had no official sanction for their activities showed, for many, that the Russian contingent of the Republican coalition was intent on an authoritarian outcome to the war – one that did not indulge dissent. Dos Passos made persistent enquiries regarding the location and possible fate of his friend. Regularly he visited the Gaylord Hotel, more luxuriously appointed than the Florida and better stocked with food and drink, despite the shortages brought about by the siege. The hotel had effectively become the headquarters of Stalin's representatives in the city and the three most senior commanders of the Spanish Communist faction – Enrique Lister, Juan Modesto and Valentín González – were the nominal heads of Madrid's version of the Kremlin.

The hotel was also frequented by Pepe Quintanilla, brother of Hemingway's friend, the painter Luis, and also known as the 'Executioner of Madrid'. He was responsible for implementing the

1   Grace Hall Hemingway, photographed in 1905 when Ernest was six years old.

2   Hemingway in an American Red Cross Ambulance in Italy, 1918.

3   Hemingway in uniform, Milan, 1918.

4   Hemingway recuperating in the Milan hospital where he met
Agnes Von Kurovsky.

5   Hemingway in uniform in Oak Park, 1919.

6   Hemingway and Hadley's wedding day, 1921. To the left of the couple are his sisters Carol and Marcelline, and to the right his mother Grace, his younger brother Leicester, and his father Clarence, 'Ed'.

7 Hemingway and Hadley with their son John Hadley Nicanor (aka 'Jack' and 'Bumby'), Schruns, Austria, Spring, 1926.

8 Ticket stub saved by Hemingway from a bullfight he attended in Pamplona, 1926.

9 Hemingway with his second wife Pauline (nee Pfeiffer) at their home in Key West, circa early 1930s.

10 John Dos Passos reads aloud to his wife Katy when the couple were visiting the Hemingways in Key West, 1932. They are on board the *Anita*, a boat used by Hemingway for sailing and fishing.

11 Hemingway on his own boat the *Pilar*, 1935. Before the war he sometimes used the tommy gun against sharks. Later, when he turned *Pilar* into a 'U-Boat hunter', more powerful weapons were added to its armoury.

12 Hemingway with his third wife Martha Gellhorn in Chunking, China, 1941, accompanied by various Chinese military officers and men.

13   Hemingway with his friend Colonel Charles T "Buck" Lanham, with captured German artillery piece, 18 September, 1944.

14   Hemingway aboard the *Pilar*, 1950.

15   Hemingway and his fourth wife Mary on safari in Africa, shortly before their near-fatal plane crashes, 1954.

16   Bullfighter Antonio Ordonez and Hemingway, by the pool at La Consula, the Davis estate, near Malaga, 1959. The Davis's had recently hosted Hemingway's extravagant sixtieth birthday party.

Stalinist policy of seeking out figures who were suspected of going against the party line, officiating at show trials where the verdict was predictable and ruthlessly enforcing the death penalty. Hemingway ingratiated himself with most of these figures and became a regular guest at the Gaylord. He was not conversant with the ideologies of post-Marxist communism but he was attracted to men who were tough and fanatical. The three Spaniards spoke fluent Russian; two of them – Lister and Modesto – had spent time in the Soviet Union, organised workers' uprisings in Spain during the years before the outbreak of the Civil War and had been joined shortly before Hemingway's arrival by a Hungarian, Emilio Kléber – originally known as Manfred Stern – a Soviet intelligence agent who liaised directly between the Spanish Communists and Moscow. Despite the fact that the Republican/Loyalist forces and factions involved a collage of political affiliations – including anarchists, moderate socialists and what we now refer to as democratic liberals – the Communists effectively had a controlling hand. The principal source of foreign arms was the Soviet Union, with smaller amounts supplied by Mexico, and the Kremlin had made detailed plans to suppress all other branches of Republicanism following the expected victory over the Francoists. Spain would be a province of the Soviet Union. It was for this reason that they were neurotically concerned with eradicating open-minded, or as they saw it treacherous, figures such as Robles.

Throughout late March and early April Dos Passos made despairing enquiries to those who were willing to speak to him at the Gaylord and on each occasion nothing was disclosed. Hemingway played the role of an intermediary between his friend and the Communist hierarchy but this was largely a pretence; he reassured Dos Passos that he had influence with the Communists while making sure he did nothing to unsettle his Soviet-backed associates. He enjoyed being conferred with power by association but displayed nefarious cowardice at the same time. On one occasion he asked another Communist supporter, the writer Josephine Herbst, to tell Dos Passos to desist because 'everybody', including the US journalists, would be 'in trouble, if he continued', while insisting that Herbst must not disclose that he was the true source of this warning.

Herbst was probably the first to learn that Robles had been executed without trial. She advised Hemingway to keep this from Dos Passos but not because she wished to spare the latter the painful effect of the news; rather she feared Dos Passos might turn against the Communists and make use of his profile as a left-leaning intellectual, albeit now a dissident, to damage the support base of the Russians in Europe and America. Alongside this she was pursuing a private exercise in vindictiveness. She had published four novels in the 1920s and early 1930s, which some compared with Dos Passos's *USA* trilogy. Her fiction charted the history of her country from the nineteenth century onwards, was realist in manner, underpinned by a solidly Marxist model of social development and was accorded far less acclaim by the literary establishment. Dos Passos, Hemingway and indeed Martha had stolen the attention of the reading public as literary celebrities and an entry in Herbst's journal made at the time that she postponed the disclosure of Robles' fate is revealing. She had watched Martha leave the Florida after drinks with Hemingway and Dos Passos: 'Pushing whore like M gets pretty much around on what she's got. Don't mean in the head. The pants. Plays all. Takes all. Never speaks of anyone not a name. Glib stupid tongue.' We will never know if envy or Stalinesque zealotry was her prevailing motive, but it is evident that Hemingway colluded in her exercise in cruel subterfuge with an equally wicked agenda of his own. He fed his friend troubling details of how Quintanilla had assured him that Robles would receive a 'fair trial', the equivalent of informing him that the guilty verdict had already been delivered. Herbst told Hemingway that Robles was dead in March but for three weeks he continuously fed Dos Passos false information on progress of the trial and allowed his friend to continue his campaign for Robles' release.

In February 1937 the XVth International Brigade – made up mainly of British and American volunteers – suffered severe losses and during March it was effectively reconstituted with the addition of further foreign recruits. A luncheon was held to celebrate its new manifestation in Madrid in the second week of April. At the gathering and in the presence of others Hemingway informed Dos Passos that his friend had been shot and went on to deliver an impromptu contra-obituary, stating that the Communists' decision to execute him was itself proof that he was spying for the Francoists and therefore fully deserving of his fate, adding that Dos Passos himself, in defending Robles, was effectively conniving in his treachery. Herbst later wrote that Hemingway was unable to properly understand the 'new realms of experience' that existed in Madrid in 1937. She meant that the Communists had found him a willing dupe, easily seduced by their imperious, ruthless presence. He was, as she put it, hinting at his ingenuousness, their 'fair-haired boy'. Her assessment was generous to say the least. Hemingway knew exactly what was going on and exalted in witnessing the pain and humiliation endured by Dos Passos. This was worse than arbitrary vindictiveness. Hemingway had successfully dethroned and supplanted Dos Passos as the predominant literary apologist for global revolution, irrespective of the fact that this had involved the murder of the latter's closest friend.

Karkov of *For Whom the Bell Tolls* is based on Mikhail Koltsov, the senior *Pravda* representative at Gaylord's who provided Hemingway with the party line on recent events, such as the 'fact' that Andres Nin, head of the anti-Stalin Communist faction the POUM (Partit Obrer d'Unificació Marxista), was a Falangist informer, and was currently being questioned, as indeed was Nin's friend and fellow traitor Robles. To ensure Hemingway's trust and gullibility Koltsov drew him further into this web of confidences. Did he know, for example, that Robles had served as an interpreter for Jan Antonovich Berzin, one of the senior figures in the Soviet Military Mission in Madrid? Well, Berzin was also under suspicion and would soon be recalled to Moscow. Nin was being tortured and died from his injuries shortly after Hemingway left Madrid, and Berzin would be executed in the Russian capital in 1938. Being entrusted with these secrets caused Hemingway to see himself as an instrument of the only party, the Stalin-backed Communists, who could rescue Spain from Franco. In *For Whom the Bell Tolls* Jordan adores Karkov and follows his wisdom unreservedly. Martha knew Dos Passos but astonishingly she never learned of what her lover was doing to him during the first months of their relationship. She too had become disillusioned by the authoritarianism of the Soviet Communists in

Spain and one has to wonder whether they would have stayed together after that spring in Madrid if she could have seen Hemingway as he really was.

Hemingway and Dos Passos did not speak again during their time in Spain, and on 18 May the former delivered another blow. Disembarking from the *Normandie* in New York he was greeted by a dozen news reporters and a photographer from *Life*. Knowing that his brief statement would be quoted verbatim in the US and Europe he declared that all of his 'friends' in Madrid were still alive and in good humour, and predicted that this presaged the eventual victory of the Loyalists. It was the equivalent of the Stalinist practice of removing images of culled party members from official photographs, and there is no record of whether Dos Passos responded to what he had said.

Little more than two weeks later, on 4 June, Hemingway addressed the Second American Writers' Congress at Carnegie Hall, nominally a politically neutral event but sponsored by the radically Communist League of American Writers and intended as a forum for supporters of the left-wing factions in Spain. There were no specific references to Dos Passos in his speech, but what he said goes some way to explain his systematic campaign of vindictiveness against him. Hemingway divides writers into two categories; those who feel 'comfortable' spending their time 'disputing learnedly on points of doctrine', and for whom there will 'always be new schisms and new fallings off and marvellous exotic doctrines and romantic lost leaders [Robles?], for those who do not want to work at what they profess to believe in, but only to discuss and maintain positions [...] [via] typewriter [...] and fountain pen'. For other writers – and as he heavy-handedly implies, proper writers – 'there will be from now on for a long time war for any writer to go to who wants to study it'. He raises the question of why writers who actually experience wars first hand will in some way be cleansed of the self-righteous inclination to contemplate 'fallings off', 'schisms' and 'marvellous exotic doctrines'. Leaving that aside, it is obvious that Dos Passos, and Robles, fell into this last category. True, they did not avoid direct experience of conflict – and this cost Robles his life – but neither were content with inflexibly doctrinaire political formulae. After

Robles's death Dos Passos treated Stalinist communism as Fascism rebranded but before that, from 1934 onwards, he had regularly found cause to regard the Soviet regime as increasingly despotic and had shared his doubts with Hemingway. However, during the same period Hemingway had become temperamentally averse to thinking. As he disclosed in the speech he preferred action and involvement, irrespective of the shortcomings of the cause or the eventual outcome.

Hemingway's original screenplay for *The Spanish Earth* echoes much of his speech, at least in terms of vehemence and bombast. Its content was largely a Marxist manifesto on the war and the future of Spain, and in this regard Hemingway was mouthpiece rather than author; it had been supplied by the Gaylord's Comintern. Hemingway had initially been taken on as the narrator but Ivens suggested that a professional actor might do proper justice to his words, and in late June Orson Welles arrived in New York to record it for a wireless broadcast. The Hollywood star made it clear the text was a curious mixture of ideological jargon and grandiloquence and suggested substantial revisions. MacLeish, Ivens and Hemingway were present at the recording, and Welles claimed that Hemingway responded to his proposals with 'You fucking effeminate boys of the theatre, what do you know about real war' and threatened to hit him with a chair. Welles turned the incident into a comic anecdote 30 years later in *Cahiers du Cinema* (1966), claiming that things concluded with the two of them convivially sharing a bottle of whisky, but it is evident from the account that Hemingway seemed to him to be a strange kind of despot, dedicated to extreme leftism for the sake of it.

Aside from his bouts of rhetoric, bolstered by detail supplied by the party, it is impossible to detect in print, correspondence or reported exchanges any evidence that Hemingway had familiarised himself with the philosophy or political programmes of communism. His sudden affiliation to the cause is comparable with his attachment to the modernist aesthetic of Paris in the 1920s. He was the gate-crasher at the party, pretending to be an acquaintance for no other reason that he wanted Ernest Hemingway to be the unavoidable presence in the room.

Some hosts welcomed him, did their best to familiarise him with the conventions of his new territory and were rewarded with utter contempt. Stein in Paris is notable in this respect, and there were many others, but during his Communist phase Dos Passos stands out not only as a victim but also as the motive for his obsession with extreme left-wing politics. Hemingway's aggressive radicalism, and his unthinking support for Stalinism, enabled him to invoke the sanction of the left-leaning cultural elite to undermine the reputation of Dos Passos who was courageous enough to question such ideas and who by implication threatened to outrank him as a writer with a more humane intellectual compass.

The fall out between the two men continued in various forms for the next 25 years. They met on only one further occasion at Gerald Murphy's apartment in New York later during that summer of 1937. Hemingway accused him of treachery, made quasi-racist remarks about his Portuguese ancestry and called Katy, his wife, a thief, stating that she was responsible for the couple's failure to pay back to Hemingway a modest loan from the 1920s. Dos Passos and Katy left the building without commenting on what had occurred.

Most novels are dominated by a singular presence who carries the story and the rest of the fictional populace in his or her wake. Sometimes two or three figures might compete for prominence but once we've closed the book one of them will live on in our memory with more bearing than the rest. *To Have and Have Not* (1937) is an exception to this formula. Harry Morgan, Hemingway's alter ego, is a fishing boat captain caught between his own desperate lack of funds and his conscience, and forced to set aside the latter when smuggling illegal immigrants from Havana to Key West. The first two sections of the novel are largely about Harry but when we move to the third something quite extraordinary occurs. It is not that Richard Gordon takes over from Harry; more that we become aware of the effort involved in creating a fictional character that is so pitiful, ludicrous and repulsive. Other things and other individuals feature in the narrative of the concluding section but they do so as slightly infuriating distractions. We want to encounter Gordon yet again, not because we sympathise with him or, God-forbid, find something in him remotely endearing. No. We are fascinated by

Hemingway's energy in incubating someone who is so ghastly in so many different ways. If he were a criminal or in some other way calculatedly evil we could treat him as one of literature's better insights into the macabre or the Grand Guignol, but instead he is offered as a crowded incarnation of pretension, embarrassing self-absorption, political hypocrisy and sexual unfulfilment. It took some skill for Hemingway to invent a man so outstandingly unreal yet who bears such a close resemblance to Dos Passos, and the novel must be credited as literature's most accomplished act of sadistic misrepresentation.

Even when the book was at draft stage, and Hemingway was speaking to Perkins on what form it should take, there is clear evidence that Dos Passos was perpetually on his mind. In July 1937 he proposed that the novel as it then was, essentially Harry Morgan's story and Richard Gordon's verbal crucifixion, should be published alongside some of Hemingway's dispatches from Spain, the Carnegie Hall speech and an article he had written in 1935 on how destitute World War I veterans, sent to Key West as cheap labour, had lost their lives in a tropical storm. The last of these was called 'Who Murdered the Vets?' and draws a stark contrast between the existences, and deaths, of these men and the lifestyles of enormously wealthy Americans who treated the island as their playground. The parallels with Harry Morgan's story were self-evident but underlying them was Hemingway's desperate wish to overtake Dos Passos as the social, and socialist, conscience of American fiction, despite the fact that he now spent most of his time in the company of the wealthiest residents of Key West, Bimini and Havana. He offered his proposal to Perkins as a 'living omnibus', a montage of fiction, polemic and reportage. It was an attempt to replicate the hybrid of invention, documentary prose and 'found' material that Dos Passos had perfected in the *USA* trilogy, and the fact that he included in it perhaps the most vindictive caricature in literary history – of his friend – offers an uncomfortable insight into his state of mind.

By 1937 Scott Fitzgerald had become afraid of spending any time in the presence of Hemingway. The latter criticised and patronisingly praised *Tender is the Night* (1934) but he had also dropped hints with associates and friends that in his opinion Fitzgerald was now finished as a writer. In late June 1937 Dorothy Parker hosted an informal drinks party mainly for those involved with the Spanish Loyalist cause. Hemingway was the star guest, despite the fact that Parker thought him by parts unpleasant and ludicrous. Fitzgerald was also due to attend and insisted on driving his own car with Lillian Hellman as passenger; she later related that he was so terrified at the prospect of seeing Hemingway that he was barely able to hold the steering wheel and went no faster than 12 miles per hour. When they arrived Hemingway was holding court, telling stories of Spain and his commitment to communism and hurling glasses into the stone fire place. Fitzgerald fled to the kitchen and left soon afterwards. Another guest, Dashiell Hammett, recalled that the event offered him a vivid example of unalloyed fear, on Fitzgerald's part, one that influenced his later crime noir inventions.

The day after the party Fitzgerald wrote Hemingway a note which appears to have been delivered by hand. It is unpublished and is worth quoting in full (JFK, June 1937):

> It was fine to see you so well and full of life, Ernest, I hope you'll make your book fat – I knew some of that *Esquire* work was too good to leave out. All best wishes to your Spanish trip [planned for Autumn] – I wish we could meet more often. I don't feel I know you at all.
> Ever yours
> Scott

He adds a postscript, which effectively closes their relationship. He will never again visit Key West or the Caribbean, a region that seems to him to exemplify the more unsettling aspects of Hemingway's personality. 'Going South always seems to me rather desolate and fatal and uneasy [...] Going North is a safe dull feeling.'

Hemingway's decision to alienate his two closest friends at the same time was not coincidental. He had begun to cultivate a private hatred for both men in the mid-1920s because each had dared to question the merits of his writing.

The horrible cruelty of *The Torrents of Spring* remains a mystery. Sherwood Anderson had introduced him to the literary elite of the early twentieth century. Why should he, in return, ridicule his mentor and patron? In an unpublished letter Anderson discloses his feelings.

About the book – your letter – and your letters to me these last two or three years – it's like this. Damn it man you are so final – so patronizing. You always do speak to me like a master to a pupil. It must be Paris – the literary life. You did not seem like that when I knew you. (July 1926, JFK)

Anderson is not so much angry as bemused and he goes on to raise questions, for himself and Hemingway, on how he had come to deserve such treatment. At one point he asks 'About the little play?' No record exists of the draft but it is evident that Hemingway had given it to Anderson for comment and that the latter was not impressed. 'I'm sorry I even mentioned it', says Anderson.

Hemingway bore grudges. Even before he had made his name as a writer he would respond with intense bitterness towards anyone who questioned the quality of his work. Archibald MacLeish recalled one evening with him in El Pilar, Spain, four months after *The Sun Also Rises* had been published. MacLeish commented to his companion that Joyce and Picasso had evolved new ways of perceiving and understanding the world, implying that Hemingway's first novel was indebted to the pioneers of modernism. Despite the fact that four years earlier he had praised *Ulysses* as the finest novel of the new époque Hemingway now subjected MacLeish to a rant against it, and Joyce, peppered with obscenities. MacLeish was shocked both by the sudden alteration in Hemingway's manner and what appeared to be a threat of violence. He advised him to 'relax a little bit and give Joyce more credit' but, without replying, Hemingway retired to their shared bedroom and did not speak to him until the following day.

Reynolds quotes from Scott Fitzgerald's letter to Hemingway on *The Sun Also Rises* but does not comment on the former's lengthy observations on the novel's failings. Fitzgerald knew that Cohn was based on Loeb, and he was unsettled by his friend's arbitrary cruelty: 'Why not cut out the inessentials of Cohen's [Cohn's] biography? His first marriage is of no importance. When so many people can write well and the competition is so heavy I can't imagine how you could have done these […] pages so casually. You can't play with people's attention' (June 1926, JFK). By the time Fitzgerald wrote this it was too late for Hemingway to revise the novel, but the impact of these and other comments would endure. Fitzgerald judges the work 'careless and ineffectual' and goes on for four pages picking at passages that are '*embalm*[ed] in mere wordiness', that give a 'feeling of condescending casualness', full of perverse and wilful non-essentials', 'shop-worn', 'utterly immaterial', 'somehow [its] not good', 'doesn't seem to make sense'. At that point Hemingway did not remonstrate against his friend, which seems odd given his largely unprovoked vilification of Anderson, but he was biding his time. Dos Passos too had reservations about *The Sun Also Rises*. His review, praising its style while suspending judgement on its significance as a work of art, is widely quoted. More significant is Dos Passos's unpublished letter sent to Hemingway before the review came out: 'I've written a dense, priggish mealy-mouthed review of it that makes me sick' (20 November 1926, JFK). Regret segues into candour: 'The book makes me sick anyway, besides making me anxious to all you are'. Two days later Dos Passos sent him a draft of the review, and the typescript is intriguing because Hemingway turned it into a dialogue, offering in the margins responses to Dos Passos's judgements, beginning: 'I've sworn off writing reviews, after this'. Later: 'How well the boy closes his affections'. After the final paragraph of the review: 'Some sentence!'

Over the subsequent decade Hemingway remained on amicable terms with Fitzgerald and Dos Passos but he had a long memory. He recorded his thoughts in the margins of both of his friends' letters but he would postpone direct responses until the mid-1930s.

On 14 January 1932 Dos Passos sent Hemingway a letter, unpublished, on the manuscript of *Death in the Afternoon*. He praises it as 'absolutely the best thing that can be done on the subject', and his implication that 'the subject', bullfighting, is a self-serving preoccupation – its fans oblivious to all other elements of 1930s Spain – informs the rest of the letter. There is something about it that Hemingway would have recognised from previous letters on his work by Dos Passos and Fitzgerald. Persistently both men praise his inherent talent, his style, in a manner that seems overenthusiastic, as if they are preparing him for a 'but'. In this case Dos Passos is unhappy with Hemingway's tendency to sentimentalise Spain: 'the parts where old Hem straps on the long white whiskers' and then serves the reader with an abundance of portraits of the country in ancient primitivist glory: 'it would be a shame to leave in any unnecessary tripe – damn it I think there's always enough tripe even after you've cut it out' (14 January 1932, JFK).

A day later Hemingway replied with a simple sentence. 'Have just finished cutting out all you objected to'. This was an outright lie. He did not revise the draft but he made his opinions clear on how he felt about Dos Passos daring to give him advice: 'and may God damn your soul to hell [. . .] – seemed like the best of the book to me' (JFK, undated). He did not sign the note and said nothing more of the matter because he was waiting for a better opportunity to exact revenge on the man who had accused him of misrepresenting Spain, which would eventually be provided by the country itself and the unfortunate Robles. Hemingway's infamous final letter to him (26 March 1938) is a rant made up of allegations that Dos Passos had told lies about the military involvement of Russia in the war, and that his insistence that the Soviet Communists intended to turn the country into a totalitarian outpost of Russia reflected his perverse sense of victimhood. The piece is largely incoherent, Hemingway's twisted logic counterpointed against his expressions of loathing for a man who, less than two years before, had been his closest friend.

The letter is revealing not just as evidence of how Hemingway could summon up previously unfathomable degrees of hatred. Its style features in other correspondence with fellow writers.

In an unpublished letter in the JFK archive Fitzgerald inadvertently tells us something about Hemingway's shifts from conviviality to outraged delirium. Fitzgerald refers to Hemingway's 'troubles with the very end of *A Farewell to Arms*':

> I remember that your first draft – or at least the first one I saw – gave a sort of old-fashioned Alger book summary of the future lives of the characters. 'The priest became a priest under fascism' etc., and you may remember my suggestion to take a burst of eloquence from anywhere in the book that you could find it and tag off with that; you were against this idea because you felt that the true line of work of fiction was to take a reader up to a high emotional pitch but then let him down or ease him off. You gave no aesthetic reason for this – never the less you convinced me. (1 June 1934, JFK)

Aside from comparing Hemingway with Horatio Alger – an untalanted, sensationalist writer of the nineteenth century – Fitzgerald maintains the restrained temper of this passage. A year later Hemingway showed how unwholesome he'd become. He opens with comments on Fitzgerald's decline as a writer and on how, in his opinion, Zelda was the principal cause of this. Fitzgerald had tolerated such insults since the 1920s – they were part of their hard-man/sophisticate double act – but now it was evident that Hemingway was impatient with anything resembling laconic dialogue.

After three paragraphs the banter gives way to something far more unnerving. He invites Fitzgerald down to witness the revolution in Cuba promising that 'I'll see you get killed', adding, 'I'll write you a fine obituary that Malcolm Cowley will cut the best part out of for the new republic, and we can take your liver out and give it to the Princeton Museum, your heart to the Plaza Hotel, one lung to Max Perkins [. . .] If we can still find your balls I will take them via the Ile de France to Paris and down to Antibes and have them cast into the sea of Eda Roc' (21 December 1935). He then proposes that MacLeish should compose a poem which will be read as the Mediterranean receives his testicles, and offers a sample of the kind of elegy he has in mind:

> Fling flang them two two finally his one
> Spherical, colloid, interstitial
> uprising lost to sight
> in fright
> natural
> not artificial
> no ripple make as sinking sanking soaking sunk

Impressionistic mood swings often feature in Hemingway's letters but he reserves his most bizarre shifts between rationality and mania for fellow writers. The first example was his unbalanced letter to Anderson (21 May 1926) in which he contradicts himself in every subsequent sentence and appears unable, or unwilling, to explain why he has caused him such distress. With Dos Passos and Fitzgerald, the more each of them displayed indulgence, even encouragement – especially regarding their opinions on his work –

the more demonic he became. Caustic letters between writers are engaging supplements to their books: if you can write well then you can usually turn your hand to equally accomplished, private displays of venom and satire. But one can scour archives and published collections of literary correspondence without coming upon anything resembling Hemingway's tirades. If they possess an endemic feature it is his tendency to place seemingly random recollections of the past he shared with his correspondent – usually refashioned and exaggerated – alongside bursts of vitriol that one might expect from a detainee in a mental institution.

To locate a cause for this we should, I think, consider the fact that Hemingway's fiction was indistinguishable from his life and his sense of who he was. To comment, even constructively, on his work, was to trespass on and compromise his identity.

On 6 July 1937, Hemingway, Martha and Joris Ivans, the director, were invited to dinner at the White House for a screening of *The Spanish Earth*. The Roosevelts treated Martha almost as a niece. She was seated next to Hemingway at dinner and no thought was given to including Pauline, who was in New York, on the guest list. Aside from the event's significance in the history of Hemingway's personal life it was quite momentous with regard to the state of American politics in the late 1930s. Even before they saw it the Roosevelts were aware that the film was avidly pro-socialist, and that its message involved a scathing attack on capitalism and political conservatism that extended beyond the Spanish conflict. Fifteen years later, when the neurotic Senator McCarthy and his acolytes monitored the political and intellectual infrastructure of America, this scenario would have been utterly preposterous. Extraordinary, unprecedented things were happening in Europe and America and Hemingway wanted to be at the centre of this maelstrom. Part of Martha's attraction was her ability to open doors for him, such as those to the White House. He was looking for contacts – highly placed figures who might help him present himself as a writer finely attuned to the tension that would soon engulf Europe and Asia.

Soon after Hemingway returned from Spain in spring 1937 Pauline had become aware of the affair, but its progress would be marked less by his ambivalence and fear of ruining his marriage than by Martha's independent lifestyle. Hadley and Pauline had been effectively spinsters waiting for the right man. Neither had a career and the latter had shaped her future around a strategy of patience and subterfuge during the year in which she lured Hemingway away from his first wife. Jinny, her sister and accomplice in this, was the most outspoken of Pauline's friends and acquaintances in warning her against what was likely to happen with Martha. She had already been part of the anti-Hadley campaign and she suspected that Martha was involved in a similar undertaking. She was wrong. Martha enjoyed Hemingway's company and was happy enough to conduct an extra-marital affair but there is no evidence that she would have been overly upset if he had decided to end things. She was concerned primarily with her life as a writer and political activist, and not at all interested in becoming a wife. Hemingway returned to Spain in Autumn 1937 and asked Martha to join him. She declined, not because she didn't want to go but because she was busy writing articles on the war and attending public events in the US. She eventually joined him in Barcelona in December where they took a double room for the weekend in the Hotel Majestic. She then sailed from New York to Le Havre, while Hemingway went to Paris after discovering that Pauline had crossed the Atlantic without informing him and was booked into a spacious suite in the Hotel Elysée Park. There, for the first time, she accused him outright of infidelity and a horrible argument ensued, with Pauline threatening to jump out of the window, comparing her suicidal threat with the act of his previous 'mistress', Jane Mason.

The next time Hemingway and Martha spent a lengthy period of time together was in April 1938 when he took the train for Perpignan from Paris, along with two other US journalists, Vincent Sheen and Jim Lardner; he met Martha in the southern French city, travelled across the Pyrenees and they based themselves in Barcelona and small hotels in surrounding regions. Catalonia was the most rebellious and fractious of the Spanish regions, enthusiastic about devolution from Spain itself and the hotbed of various anarchist groups. Even its own leftist faction, the POUM, bluntly refused to follow the line of the Soviet Madrid-based branch, basing its programme on the sharing of wealth, land and property and libertarian individualism. The Fascists loathed them even more than they did the Stalinists, and when Hemingway and Martha arrived Barcelona had become, like Madrid a year earlier, a city besieged by the Francoist forces. This time Hemingway asked his fellow scribes to avoid mentioning Martha in letters to friends or in their reports because he wanted to eliminate circumstantial evidence and avoid a repeat of what had happened in Paris four months earlier. As a result she exists in surviving documents as a ghostly presence, sometimes warily referred to yet never fully acknowledged as being there. The only specific proof of her presence is her own voice in articles from the region for *Collier's*.

Flying to Key West from New York in May, Pauline greeted him at the airport and he drove the Ford back towards Whitehead Street, colliding with a vehicle of unrecorded make but apparently dating from the 1920s, driven by Samuel Smart. Smart and Hemingway began a fist fight, which was broken up by officer John Nelson. The policeman took them to Police Court to face Judge Cara who eventually dismissed any charges against either man. Pauline had taken Patrick, Gregory and Toby Bruce in the car to meet him at the airport, attempting to create the impression of them sharing an idyllic family environment, but the pretence was shattered once he arrived home from the court. He was fuming at being accused by Smart, a mere WPA (Works Progress Administration) worker, of causing the accident and his rant prompted Pauline to attack him again for using Spain as the opportunity for trysts with Martha, though this time she had little reliable evidence. Meanwhile, Martha had gone to Czechoslovakia to report on the recent Nazi annexation of the country, moved south, in August, to Corsica, to work on her new novel and at the end of the month had taken local trains along the France–Germany border to take notes on how Hitler had begun to reinforce the region with infantry regiments, artillery and armour, while everyone else pretended that war might be avoided. She would spend the remainder of the summer of 1938 in Europe reporting, mainly for *Collier's*, on what she regarded as a prelude to the outbreak of a conflict far more devastating than 1914–18.

For the Hemingways the summer was a protracted series of attempts to spare their children from the arguments that seemed to spring up regarding otherwise innocuous matters, but were under-pinned by Pauline's knowledge that he would by various means arrange to meet Martha again and his unwillingness to decide on whether to terminate the marriage or the affair, or attempt to sustain both by convincing Pauline that the latter had ended. They moved listlessly between Key West, Piggott and the L-Bar-T ranch in Wyoming and Hemingway kept up his standard rituals of writing, fishing and hunting. But he was drinking more, putting on weight and behaving much as he had during the transitional period in Paris between his break-up with Hadley and his marriage to Pauline. In mid-July he wrote to Archie MacLeish and accused him of cheating him out of money invested in *The Spanish Earth* (*circa* mid-July 1938, JFK), a letter that echoed the even more scathing one to Dos Passos (28 March) where he implies that the latter's attacks on the true Communists, and his defence of Robles, were symptomatic of his obsession with money. In Key West during June and July he spent time helping to train the boxer Mario Perez, and when interviewed by the local newspaper told a ludicrous story of how he'd been the amateur heavyweight champion of Illinois in his youth and had considered turning professional before deciding to become a writer instead (*Citizen*, 18 June and 13 July 1938). As in Paris he was creating worlds of his own, at once delusional and horribly vindictive, and once more it is evident that his inclination to make things up was as much an index to his perpetually unsettled state of mind as a reflection of his vocation as a writer.

Further evidence of this is provided by two works written in 1937–8 that would soon go into print, the aforementioned play *The Fifth Column* and a short story called 'The Denunciation'. It was not until much later, after his death, when critics began to pore over Hemingway's work for autobiographical resonances, that it was put to Martha that she was the model for Dorothy in the play, and she said that it was like being shown a portrait of herself she'd previously known nothing of – one that was perversely distorted. In the third act, Philip/Hemingway explains to Comrade Max, a sanitised version of the murderous Seguridad chief Pepe Quintanilla, that his girlfriend is typical of 'American girls [who] come to Europe with a certain amount of money. They're all the same'. Camps, college, money in the family, sometimes affairs to show their rebellious side but finally they'll marry and settle down or not marry and settle down. At the best, they might open shops, play instruments, even write. 'This one', Dorothy, writes. 'Quite well too, when she's not too lazy'. 'Ask her all about it', he adds, in case Max suspects Dorothy of being a political liability, and assures him that 'It's all very dull though, I tell you'. Martha was unconcerned with the image she presented to others and it was understandable that she did not find a trace of herself in Dorothy: she was a superb writer, ferociously astute politically and dedicated to her profession. It was not that Hemingway was obscuring parallels for his girlfriend's protection and he was certainly not caricaturing her. Dorothy is Martha as Hemingway saw her, albeit in his characteristically self-delusional manner. Unlike Philip/Hemingway, Dorothy treats writing as a hobby. In the end Philip abandons her and commits himself to the cause, joining Max to clear out an artillery post manned by half a dozen Fascists. In truth, Quintanilla only 'saw action' when he captured, tortured and executed those who his counter-espionage department found suspect, but once again Hemingway was entertaining his private delusions regarding heroism; in this case putting his commitment to purist communism above his involvement with Martha. As Edmund Wilson astutely put it in his review, it is 'in the nature of a small boy's fantasy, and would probably be considered extravagant by most writers of books for boys' (p. 111).

It was not until they became a couple that Hemingway suddenly realised that Martha was his equal, both intellectually and with regard to being prepared to put her personal safety at risk when reporting from the front line. During the period of their extra-marital affair she was, while physically present, in all other respects his invention, in just the same way that Philip and Dorothy were projections of his self-serving conception of the world in which he lived.

'The Denunciation' is narrated by the principal character Henry Emmunds, who hands the waiter at Chicote's bar in Madrid the telephone number of the Seguridad, instructing him to report that

Luis Delgado, a Fascist sympathiser, has been using the bar. Delgado is arrested and sentenced to death but Emmunds asks his friend Pepe and the Seguridad to inform Delgado that he, not the waiter, made the phone call. The twisted motives of false honesty, compassion and remorse are thrown into a short narrative that, as literature, is imperfect yet engrossing. Beyond its status as a short story it discloses Hemingway's need to turn personal dilemmas he would rather avoid into ones that can, on paper, remain unresolved. His sense of guilt regarding Dos Passos and Robles is certainly evident, without him openly admitting to anything, and buried even deeper is a hint at regret about his treatment of Pauline and Martha, though we remain uncertain about what exactly he felt about either of them.

In mid-August Martha was in Paris. She knew Hemingway was due to arrive soon and on 6 September they met. As far as we know they did not agree on anything specific for their next assignation let alone plan a permanent relationship.

Pauline rented an apartment in New York, promising to provide him, on his arrival, with a 'golden key' to it. The lease was for two months and in November they returned to Key West for what would be their final Christmas together, a season ruined by his ill-concealed bitterness towards everyone and everything.

Again Martha was in Europe, making notes on the Italian preparations for the invasion of Albania and then crossing France to witness units of the International Brigade retreating from Spain over the French border. Foreign combatants had been withdrawn from the front line in late September and their departure seemed to her a prelude to the first military victory for Fascism. Hemingway never publically acknowledged his soon-to-be permanent partner's role as a commentator on this crucial point in the history of Europe. He was too concerned with his catastrophic private life – a web of anxiety, anger and fabrication.

Soon after the New Year Hemingway flew to New York to work on revisions of *The Fifth Column* and the stories he planned to include in the volume containing the play, or at least this was his claim. He could have had the material posted to Key West and worked on it there; Martha arrived in New York from St Louis on 14 January.

Bumby, now referred to as Jack, visited his father unannounced from his Hudson River boarding school and was greeted at the hotel room door by a stunning blonde barely 12 years older than him. He was precociously sanguine. After all, his father had abandoned his mother for Pauline roughly a decade earlier.

At the end of the month Hemingway returned to Key West and the charade of contented family life continued. Uncle Gus, Pauline's most generous relative, arrived soon afterwards, followed shortly by Sara Murphy and then, unannounced, by Hemingway's mother Grace. Nothing specific was said but all were uncomfortably aware of the subject of the forbidden discourse, and this weird state of collective denial continued for the subsequent seven months. Hemingway began to retreat from it, but without daring to state that he was doing so, at least to those he would soon leave behind.

Grace left on 14 February and the following day Hemingway took the P&O ferry to Havana. He offered no explanation to his family for this sudden departure but during the next five weeks he exchanged letters with Pauline that carry every indication of shared love and commitment. He returned to Key West in early March to greet Jack, who disclosed nothing of his encounter with Martha in New York, and on 5 April he set off again for Havana. This time he packed more clothes and, alone, piloted *Pilar* rather than taking the ferry.

A week later Martha joined him at the Hotel Sevilla-Biltmore. She alone knew he was staying there. He had told everyone else to write to him at his usual hostelry, the Ambos Mundos, who happily accepted and forwarded his mail. In outgoing letters he indicated that Ambos Mundos was his location even when he was living elsewhere with Martha. It was as though he wanted to provide himself with alternate versions of the truth.

On her arrival Martha was horrified. He had stocked the room with hams and cured meats, bottles of rum, whisky and wine, and seemed not to have changed his clothes for several weeks. It was, she later reflected, a replica of the room they had shared in the Hotel Florida in Madrid during the siege. He was typing and had put together the first two draft chapters of what would become *For Whom the Bell Tolls*, his novel on the Spanish Civil War.

Immediately she began searching for a self-contained property which could be made hygienic and would, more significantly, signal their status as a couple. La Vigía – 'The Lookout' – was a Spanish colonial farmhouse some ten miles from the city. It had been occupied by middle-class Cubans who had installed a pool, but when Martha found it it was close to being derelict – overgrown with vegetation that had crept through doors and windows into the interior, alive with rodents and infested by mosquitoes and other disagreeable insects. The pool was polluted and the 15 acres of grounds a virtual jungle. She hired people to make it habitable and in mid-May she and Hemingway moved in, he working on *For Whom the Bell Tolls* and she on her next novel, *A Stricken Field*. Both would be published in 1940.

Until July he was still writing to Pauline from Havana as a devoted, loving husband and it would not be until early autumn 1939 that she forced him to accept that this was a sham. He could no longer pretend to be her beloved spouse when he was living, apparently permanently, with another woman. Perhaps this was the moment of termination that he had hoped to provoke but we have to compare the real-life Hemingway – shifty, nefarious and unable to admit the truth to himself or anyone else – with a similar exercise in falsehood that informed the novel he began a few days after moving to Havana.

For Whom the Bell Tolls is still regarded by many as the archetypal 'Great American Novel', mainly because its principal character, Robert Jordan, is the US hero abroad – a man willing to sacrifice himself for feckless foreigners engaged in conflicts that might spread to something horribly global. Several of the Kennedy brothers expressed an affinity for Jordan, as did the presidential candidate Senator John McCain who regarded Jordan's exploits in Spain as comparable with his own experiences as a fighter pilot in Vietnam. Even Barack Obama has admitted to empathising with him, as an American who feels accountable for a world in crisis. The film adaptation, starring Gary Cooper as Jordan and Ingrid Bergman as his lover Maria, was the top box office hit of 1943, earning 7.1 million dollars. It might have been about Spain but it attracted mass audiences because it came out during the year that hundreds of thousands of young Americans were joining another European campaign against Fascism, opening in North Africa and Italy.

The film does not retain the most curious feature of the novel. Many of its reviewers were puzzled by and often contemptuous of the narrative and the dialogue, the latter almost exclusively involving exchanges between Spanish characters. Expressions are laboured and scattered with terms that might have come from English Renaissance drama. Characters frequently address each other with 'thou', 'thee', 'thus' and 'thy' and in other passages they revert to a variety of twentieth-century idioms, without any clear allegiance to region or context. No one has offered a convincing explanation for this stylistic melange, let alone a justification for it. For about three-quarters of the book Jordan is there, not as the commanding presence but as the figure who in some way distracts the attention of the others from more pressing concerns, principally their struggle to regain control of their country.

The narrative seems caught between the world Jordan shares with the rest of the characters and the language that alienates him from them, and often from us. The most toe-curling passage is Jordan's enquiry to Maria after they've had sex: 'But did thee feel the earth move?' In its own right the phrase is woefully embarrassing and it is not untypical. Jordan often sounds like an individual who has been diminished, even ridiculed, at the hands of a ludicrously incompetent translator. A generous interpretation would see Hemingway as having deliberately turned his character into a figure who appears marginal and incongruous, with Jordan presented as playing a small, if courageous, part in a more significant collective struggle. A more realistic verdict would be to treat the novel as it is: a literary failure. Stylistically it is an abysmal experiment with no discernible objective.

For Whom the Bell Tolls has numerous defects, not least as a vehicle for Hemingway's notion of the Communists as the only true advocates of anti-Fascism, but as an autobiographical work of fiction it is beyond compare. Whether or not this was conscious and calculated will remain a matter for debate. One has to wonder if it reflects his, albeit private, acceptance of Dos Passos's belief that he only half understood Spain, but the novel is certainly not a gesture of repentance. It reflects a man in a state of uneasy transition; he is unclear about why he is exchanging one way of life for another. For Jordan, and by implication his creator, life appears to be an inexorable process over which neither has control. The Spanish characters who surround Jordan are uncertain about who exactly he is and what he will do, and he is detached from the world he shares with them and to which he has committed himself. The story lasts for three days and at its close he dies. Hemingway, as he began the opening chapter in Havana, has Jordan lying on the 'brown, pine-needled floor of the forest' with the wind blowing 'in the tops of the trees'. He doesn't know what will happen next and nor did his author. He had said goodbye to Dos Passos, MacLeish, Fitzgerald and virtually everyone else who had been part of his life in France; Key West was gone, as was Pauline. He was facing the future with a woman who fascinated him and who he had romanticised into the Maria of his new novel. But Martha would turn out to be nothing like his fictional conception of her.

CHAPTER 5

War: With Martha

The shrewdest assessment of Hemingway and Martha's relationship can be found in a passage from her novel *A Stricken Field* (1940), written shortly after they had moved in together at the Figia. '[Marriage] is for living in one place, and tennis with neighbours on Sunday afternoon. We aren't like that [...] Maybe marriage is also for absence'. During the five years of their marriage, which in truth lasted less than four, they spent roughly half of that time in each other's company. Prolonged separation had been a feature of Hemingway's family arrangements since his early years in Paris with Hadley, but these were initiated by him. With Martha he experienced a form of role reversal. She was the writer and foreign correspondent, and even when he joined her on forays into regions in various states of unrest – notably to China following the Japanese invasion – she led and he followed.

Pauline reacted with bitterness to being abandoned and caused as many difficulties as possible with the divorce. Financially she was secure enough through her own family but she employed lawyers to ensure that the final settlement in terms of estate and property would be prolonged, complex and expensive.

Almost a decade after their divorce and four years after he had left Martha for Mary Welsh, Hemingway remained uninhibited in his loathing for her. On money she claimed he owed her for costs, school fees included, involving Patrick. He responded: 'You hand me a fine packet of poison in a letter [then] I hear nothing [...] You write decently twice or three times and then quit from sloth and drunkenness; or perhaps because of the cost of postage stamps [...] am prepared to increase your blood money any time [...] if it will relieve your mental and moral penury.' He closes: 'People are no longer as naive as I was when I married you and believed what you said[...]But you were not beaten by Miss Martha. You were beaten by coitus interruptus imposed by the Church' (Hemingway to Pauline, 26 January 1949, JFK).

Martha took responsibility for restoring the Finca as a modest, elegant colonial house. She hired local craftsmen to modernise the kitchen, repaint the high-ceilinged rooms, remove decades of grime from the finely tiled floors and restore the swimming pool. The 15 acres of grounds were transformed from an overgrown wilderness to an ordered estate, affording views towards Havana and the coast. The building stood almost 500 feet above the city. Before the divorce was finalised he asked friends in Key West to ship over his collection of paintings by Miró, Gris, Masson, Braque and one Picasso, plus his hunting trophies, including heads of lions and tigers, and as much of the private library from his study as could be packed into crates.

We should not, however, regard Martha as a natural homemaker by temperament. She loathed the unhygienic state of his hotel room where they lived in Havana before moving to the Finca, for obvious reasons – most people do not elect to live in filth – but also because Hemingway seemed intent on prolonging aspects of his recent past, recreating the grim situations which both of them had experienced in Spain. Turning their new home into a clean, comfortable residence was an expediency, but quite soon she began to realise that her efforts were at odds with Hemingway's taste for rough-living.

After outings on *Pilar* he would return in smelly, unfitting clothes which hadn't been washed for days and were stained with fish blood, and then sit around the house in them, holding forth for guests. He was, Martha began to realise, re-enacting previous lives in Italy and Spain while she was hungry for experience of the present day. After only three months at the Finca she spent a further three (November 1939 to January 1940) covering the war between Soviet

Russia and the Finns. He felt, he said, like an 'old Indian' who loses 'his squaw with a hard winter coming on'.

His observation becomes all the more compelling when we compare it with his unpublished letter to her during the first year of their time in Cuba. In the late summer and autumn of 1940 Hemingway wrote six letters to Martha and three to Edna, her mother. On August 28 he begins: 'OK, I understand that. Thanks for putting it so clearly' (JFK). What exactly she had put to him becomes evident from his assurances.

> Regret I'd accumulated the baggage before we met. (i.e. the responsibilities) [...] Will find someone to handle the children or ship them back [...] I understand about Finland and that being the only fun you've had. I love the irresponsibility of war I guess as much as any one. Don't ever worry. We will see much war before it is through and after the first time you are hit and know how it feels and you're your nerves and your body and all of you there ever is inside shattered you'll be able to write a good book about it if there is enough left to write it.

There is here an awkward mixture of kindness and condescension. If he were writing to someone he despised, without pretending otherwise, then his implication that her lack of experience of real warfare made her inferior to him as a correspondent would be bad enough, but this was his new partner. Self-evidently he wanted to offer her some licence to live and work independently but at the same time he could not accept that she was his equal.

He goes on to offer advice on her anxieties and to admit that he too sometimes swung between feeling perfectly 'happy' and depressed, and then confesses that his possessiveness might often make her feel 'worthless, enchained as a son of a bitch, a thwarter of your hopes, a sabotageur of your work etc'. They can, he assures her, battle against this together but there is precondition – which would later resonate through a 1943 letter to him on marriage:

> There is only one thing you have to answer in my letter and that is the thing about getting married. I'm awfully sorry but I have to know about that. Whatever you do is ok but that is one thing I have to know, I will never interfere with your career, your friends, nor whatever the other things are that one interferes with. (1943, undated, JFK)

He even promises her that he will turn a blind eye to 'men' she might wish to associate with. To Edna he is even more forthright: 'Well she is going [to Finland] and it isn't just a bad dream in the way I'd hoped it might be. She is going to save her soul because you have to do something that is vital and interesting and important and not settle into boredom and ignorance' (28 September 1940, JFK). He insists that she represents a crossroads in his life: 'she is also doing it to be the sort of person I admire and not to be the dull wife who just forms herself on me like Pauline and Hadley'. So far he appears resolute, convinced that he has faced up to and renounced his earlier preconceptions, but soon he drifts into a dialogue with himself, insisting on something, doubting it and then finding it impossible to accept. He seems to prefer to explore the dilemmas of his new relationship more candidly with Edna than her daughter. 'She [Martha] is doing it [going to Finland] because she has to and she did not tell me because she wanted me to be rested from the book [...] I understood it ok but God knows I can't say I like it [...] You see Marty has gotten kind of confused in her remembering [...] So now I have to let her go because if I try to hold her she will disenjoy everything on purpose'. Given that he was still married to Pauline he had formed a relationship with Edna that involved, on his part, extraordinary candour and intimacy. He signed his letters to her 'love to you dearest Mother', and a year earlier she had written to him (1939, JFK, undated) on how she had been enchanted by 'Hadley and Jack' when the four of them had taken lunch in New York. He was living a double life both in the sense that he had taken on a lover and a proxy mother-in-law long before he admitted anything to Pauline, and also in his belief that he could cast off four decades of ingrained habits regarding women. A letter to Martha from late 1940 (JFK, undated) has him insisting that he has 'not been [...] uncooperative selfish or deprecatory of your work. I tried to be of use to you whenever I could be in any small ways that I could and I tried to take as much of the dirty work off your hands that I could [...] I did not ever try to interfere but only to give the same sort of aid and am grateful to you'. He listens to himself and when he detects intolerance he reverts to his liberal persona: 'And another thing – You can have all the man friends you want and go anywhere with them'.

Their relationship began less with a honeymoon than with 18 months that already indicated its eventual demise. He was drinking a lot more but it was not so much his behaviour and standards of hygiene that caused Martha to suspect that the man she thought she had got to know during their pre-1940 clandestine liaisons was rather different from the resident of the Finca. Once *For Whom the Bell Tolls* was completed and dispatched to Perkins in early 1940, Hemingway began work on another assembly of characters. This time they were very real, and during the next few years he would hold court among them rather like the controlling presence in a novel. It was not simply that he had cut himself away from his life with Pauline; he had also detached himself from the circle of acquaintances who dated back to his Paris years. He remained on good terms with Perkins and Charles Scribner, both of whom could be classed as friends, but if they were not, respectively, his editor and publisher one wonders if these relationships would have endured. He wrote to both regularly from the Finca but despite his issuing numerous invitations to Perkins he did not visit; he had been a regular guest at Key West. Archibald MacLeish was an occasional correspondent but most of his letters were to the Hemingway children and, more frequently during the early 1940s, Hadley, who he addressed in a manner that was authentically affectionate, with a tinge of nostalgia and regret.

There is evidence that Hemingway chose his new group of friends in an attempt to transform his self-image. Mario Menocal, roughly Hemingway's age, came from a distinguished colonial family. His father had fought as a general in the War of Independence against Spain and served as President of Cuba from 1913 to 1931. Born in 1902, Thorwald Sanchez was the grandson of the Danish Consul to the island. His family had purchased a vast amount of real estate, notably sugar cane farms, and became one of the wealthiest dynasties in Cuba. Elicia Arguelles was Menocal's cousin. He had trained as a lawyer but by 1940 was more concerned with managing the family estate, comprising mainly a cattle ranch and a sugar farm. His father had openly supported Franco and served as the principal fundraiser on the island for the Spanish Fascists. Hemingway overlooked this allegiance, shared by Elicia, because his new friend met other criteria. Menocal, Sanchez and Arguelles were fanatical devotees of hunting, shooting and fishing – Menocal's yacht/fishing boat *Delicias* dwarfed *Pilar* – and they wore their intelligence lightly in the sense that none was overly concerned with intellectual and aesthetic issues and all treated literature as a minor recreation. Hemingway was not secretive with them regarding his past and his profession, but he presented himself as, like them, a businessman: an entrepreneur who had become wealthy through producing goods – in his case books – that sold in enormous numbers. They became his inner circle of Cuban upper-class friends, regular guests at the Finca and hosts who welcomed Hemingway into their own luxurious residences and introduced him to other members of the island's ruling elite. Martha, without causing offence to her husband's companions, kept her distance from what she regarded as a pantomime of mutual admiration and hauteur.

Each of his new companions was sufficiently detached from his previous lives and associates to have no reliable means of confirming the truth, or otherwise, of the tales he told about his life before Cuba.

Beyond the past-colonial aristocracy, Hemingway put together a group of less respectable figures who had arrived in Cuba mainly to escape their pasts. Father Andrés Untzáin, known as the 'Black Priest', was a Basque and one of the tiny minority of the Catholic clergy who supported the loyalists. He left Spain in fear of reprisals and lived in Cuba as a kind of clerical–secular hybrid, making no excuses for his hedonistic lifestyle and taste for drink. Roberto Herrera had served in the International Brigades – where his younger brother José Luis had been a surgeon – and would eventually become caretaker of the Finca, and Juan Dunabeitia was a Basque sea captain, another whose Loyalist associations had driven him abroad. All three would involve themselves in raucous drunken evenings at the Finca and often be joined by similarly boozy members of the island's dispossessed. All had an appetite for Hemingway's stories of his involvement with the war, many of which were lies.

Similarly, his wealthy friends were transfixed by accounts of his heroic career in World War I – this time with him giving greater emphasis to his service as an officer with the elite Arditi companies of the Italian Army – his graduation from a follower of bullfighting to a man who had faced beasts in the ring, and his clandestine activities in Spain, working for Communist intelligence agencies while disguised as a war correspondent, and sometimes involved in armed combat on the front line.

Despite his promise to treat her as an equal, especially as a writer, Martha later recalled that while he at first welcomed her comments on the first drafts of *For Whom the Bell Tolls*, he had, by the time they settled in Cuba, come to regard her opinions as impertinent. She tells of how he sought a more credulous audience, telling tales to his new retinue of friends and on one occasion 'reading aloud from the Bell to a bunch of grown-up well-off semi-literate pigeon shooting and fishing pals, they sitting on the floor spellbound' (Gellhorn to Gerry Brenner, 8 March 1976, JFK). He was, she recalled, offering them the book as pure autobiography; Jordan's heroic enterprises were based on his own, he claimed, despite the former's inadvertent death and humiliating imprisonment in language that no sane person would have consciously elected to use. Menocal's son, Mario Junior, was in his late teens and sometimes Menocal allowed him to join others at the court of Papa Hemingway. After the latter's death, and as verifiable facts began to emerge on his life before Cuba, Mario became aware of the ludicrous discrepancies between what he and his father had listened to and the truth. Charitably he allows for Hemingway's ability to dramatise events: 'things became more enjoyable when done with him or looked at through his eyes [...] He managed to imbue the most trivial [...] activity with his own sense of the challenging and the dramatic'. On other occasions, however, 'he began to tell stories that were, quite simply, lies' (Mario Menocal Junior to Jeffrey Meyers, 18 April 1983, quoted in Meyers, p. 331).

The nastier reviews and essays on *For Whom the Bell Tolls*, particularly those that mocked the novel's stylistic archaisms, would come later, but the first wave in late autumn 1940 were unqualified in their praise for it: 'one of the finest and richest novels of the last decade [1930s]' declared the *Saturday Review of Literature*, and the

New York Times acclaimed it as 'the best book Ernest Hemingway has written, the fullest, the deepest, the truest'. Within six months almost half a million copies had been sold and by the end of the year Paramount had paid 110,000 dollars for the film rights. It was at this point, according to Menocal junior, that he began to spin his web of falsehoods.

The author of a work which mixed-up fiction with documentary war-reporting extended this licence to stories he told to friends and admirers. To Gustavo Duran, whom he'd met during the Civil War and who visited Cuba soon after the novel came out, he claimed that, while set in Spain, the novel drew inspiration from several other periods and events, including his time on the front line during the Greco-Turkish conflict in the early 1920s, and his active experience alongside Cuban revolutionaries prior to moving to the island. He added that it also owed something to his genetic inheritance. He was, he stated, directly descended from Major Colquhoun Grant who fought alongside Wellington in the Napoleonic war in Spain and that Grant's experience of the Iberian conflict of a century and a half earlier had fused with his own more recent one. Duran, a celebrated musician, a close friend of the poets Lorca and Alberti, the artist Dali and the director Bunuel, had given up the creative life in 1936 for full-time military service in the Loyalist army, and when Hemingway met him in Madrid in 1937, he was a legend – a charismatic leader who had risen in a year to the rank of colonel commanding a battalion of front-line troops. The Chink Dorman-Smith experience would become for Hemingway something of a ritual, and he repeated the Milan combination of hero worship and self-delusion when he took drinks with Duran in the Florida Hotel. He too, he informed him, had commanded a battalion of the Italian Army in Italy in World War I, aged only 19. In 1937 Duran was 31. At the close of the Spanish War Duran had escaped to England via France and avoided execution by the Falangists by a matter of days. His father, hearing that he had in fact been captured, cut his own throat. He would spend the rest of his life as an exile and when he arrived in Cuba he accepted Hemingway's ludicrous stories unreservedly. Why would he doubt the word of a man with whom in Madrid he'd shared confidences of war and horror? Within a year Duran's gullibility would cause him to be drawn into Hemingway's darkly comic games of espionage.

On 1 February 1941, Hemingway and Martha left San Francisco on the *Matsonia* for Hawaii. They then flew to Hong Kong and spent almost a month in the province. Their eventual destination would be mainland China where interviews were arranged, for Martha, with Chiang Kai-shek, leader of what remained of an independent Chinese state. The Japanese had invaded the country four years earlier, were militarily superior and by 1941 occupied more than three-quarters of it. Martha later wrote that it rekindled some of the excitement of the first months of their relationship in Madrid. Irrespective of their private differences, which were becoming ever more conspicuous, both enjoyed what Martha called 'the sort of blindness and fervour and recklessness' of reporting from war zones. 'I hate being so wise and so careful, so reliable, so denatured, so able to get on', adding that sex was an ingredient in this cocktail (interview with Kert, p. 380). However, it is clear that Hemingway was not quite so exuberant, principally because his role was more as passenger than adventurer.

Collier's was sufficiently impressed by Martha's reports from Spain and other parts of Europe to commission her to do a series of articles on the Sino-Japanese war and the likelihood of Japan having further imperial ambitions in Asia and the Pacific. Hemingway was obliged to find his own sponsor and secured an arrangement to write similar pieces for *PM*, a respected current affairs magazine that was, however, not as generous in its payments to contributors.

Hemingway's articles were shrewd and prescient in that he stated on several occasions that once it had dealt with China, Japan was intent on invading other states in the region, mainly to secure natural resources and to turn itself into the Germany of East Asia. He also predicted, almost a year before the attack on Pearl Harbor, that America would eventually be drawn into the conflict. During their brief stay in Hawaii he commented that the crowded anchorage of battleships that made up the Pacific Fleet presented a sitting target for an air strike. Martha was equally astute, but more intriguing are the pieces later rewritten for her memoir *Travels with Myself and Another* (1979). 'Another', Hemingway, features as a middle-aged adolescent, particularly during their time in Hong Kong, where he involved himself in the cultural fabric by, in a matter of days, picking up 'coolie English' – a mixture of West African, Caribbean and Chinese idiolects grafted on to English sentences. This enabled him to mix with the less respectable colonials who spent most of their time drinking and gambling with the locals. She writes of how his reports of the food served in downtown bars – including various dog-based dishes – made her nauseous, as did his accounts of open-air geisha prostitution. His enthusiasm for snake wine, a misnamed spirit with dead coils of the animals at the bottom of the bottle, which he brought back to their suite in the high-ranking Peninsular Hotel, tested her patience even further. Soon he met General Morris 'Two Gun' Cohen, a Jewish mercenary soldier from the East End of London. He had fought in World War I and had earned his senior rank through association with Sun Yat-sen's army in the 1920s. Married to a Chinese woman, his nickname came from his insistence on wearing two revolvers. In Hong Kong he worked for the recently formed British Special Operations Executive, an annex to MI6, and procured arms for Chinese forces. For Hemingway he was Chink Dorman-Smith reborn as a spy and gunrunner with a cockney accent and a prodigious appetite for alcohol. Martha gives the impression of her husband as a man unsettled by her role – in effect his senior as a journalist – and desperate to become part of the exclusively male subculture of Hong Kong as a way of resurrecting his wild rough-house persona of Europe in the 1920s and 1930s.

In mainland China they travelled as a couple and Hemingway joined his wife in interviews and exchanges with Chiang Kai-shek and other senior figures in the Chinese administration, but according to her account he was always the observer rather than the main participant. The conditions were foul. Hotels were hideously unhygienic, many of the meals served to them caused food poisoning, flights seemed to be destined for crashes on take-off or landing and the whole country presented itself as a dystopian vision of global conflict, with columns of refugees trudging in different directions along the same roads, uncertain of where they were going and from what exactly they were fleeing.

Within a year his attempts to reinvent himself as a man able to respect and tolerate his new partner's independence had proved futile. She chose to stay on in China for several weeks after he left for New York and he wrote to her, supplementing his routine affirmation of eternal, unconditional love with a bizarre account of how he had become his brother; not Leicester, but a facsimile of Ernest, an exact reproduction in all but one respect:

> Oh. They will say. Do you see much of your brother Mr Hemingway? No I will say. No I do not see much of him. And we will leave it at that unless someone brings up the subject of my brother's marriages and I will say that his present wife, Mrs Hemingway, is the most beautiful woman I have ever known and one of the most charming and a great authority on the Orient.

> She just can't live away from the sound of those temple bells I will say. (May 1941, JFK)

Hemingway continues this strange fable, with Martha, the wife of his alter ego, continually absent and sending reports from various war-torn regions of the globe. It might seem fantastic but within eighteen months it would prove to be very prescient. Shortly after the letter she joined him in New York, and they flew back to Havana in mid-June. Nazi Germany launched Operation Barbarossa, its invasion of the Soviet Union, and both saw this as a confirmation of their opinion that quintessentially evil regimes – European Fascism and Japanese Imperialism – had begun to take control of much of the developed world outside the US and that America, then emerging as the globe's most significant economic and military power, was burying its head in the sand.

As Hemingway's articles from Asia began to appear in mid-June, warning of the threat to the US from Japan, Charles Lindbergh embarked on a series of well-publicised lectures telling his fellow Americans that Britain would soon be a Nazi colony and that any form of support from the US was pointless. On campuses throughout the country, student campaigns and meetings were overwhelmingly anti-war, most insisting that the supplying of provisions to Britain by convoy should end, given that they would provoke German attacks against US merchant ships. Hemingway and Martha were horrified by what appeared to be a consensus among their fellow citizens that whatever was happening overseas was no business of theirs. Martha urged her friend, Mrs Roosevelt, to stand by her husband's pro-British policies and Hemingway continued to write articles on the evils of Fascism.

Briefly, the spark that brought them together was reignited, with their commitment to each other matched by their determination to campaign against Japanese imperialism and the military expansion of Fascist states in Europe. Ironically, America's eventual involvement in the war marked the beginning of the inexorable decline of their marriage. Kert suggests that their sex life was problematic, but that their problems were resolved by a doctor who had devised a version of Viagra 50 years before it officially emerged as a solution to male erectile dysfunction. However, this did not offer a solution to the underlying mutual awareness that they were incompatible. Martha regarded sex largely as an obligation, and Hemingway's resurrection as a fully functioning partner was something she put up with rather than celebrated. Oddly, Cuba itself would reinforce Martha's opinion that she had married a man she did not know.

Batista, who became president of the island in 1940, at first seemed ambivalent regarding his international sympathies. Many of his associates and supporters openly supported Franco and sympathised with Hitler and Mussolini, but in 1941 he expelled all German and Italian consular officials from the country and went so far as to suggest to Washington that a joint US-Hispanic force – including a substantial number of Cuban conscripts – should invade Spain and overthrow the Falangist regime. Whether or not Roosevelt took this seriously remains a matter of opinion, but it is likely that Batista was presenting Cuba as America's natural ally. He knew that Roosevelt, irrespective of popular opinion, was resolutely anti-Fascist. The bombing of Pearl Harbor on 7 December 1941 enabled Batista to show his hand. On 8 December Cuba declared war on Japan and the Axis states. Batista's act was based more on pragmatism than conscience or idealism. He was confident that America would bring the conflict to a triumphant conclusion and, as an ally, was keen to reap any potential benefits. In practical terms the island made itself available as a US naval and air force base for the battle against Germany in the Caribbean and the Atlantic, though a small number of lightly armed Cuban craft would see action against U-boats, sinking one in 1943.

All of this provided Hemingway with the opportunity to reinvent himself as the young man who set off for Italy in 1918. He was, he knew, too old and physically unfit for military service but he regarded Cuba's new role as an officially declared ally of the US as an astonishing piece of good fortune. Graham Greene's *Our Man in Havana*, based on the ludicrous antics of the intelligence services in pre-revolutionary Cuba, did not appear until 1958, but 15 years earlier Hemingway enacted a remarkably similar story that was even more darkly comic.

In early 1942 he visited his friend Robert Joyce at the American Embassy and asked him to put a plan to the new Ambassador Spruille Braden. He would, he proposed, recruit and lead a group of locally based counter-intelligence agents, largely men but with some women, who would mix with factions on the island sympathetic to the Axis cause and pass on to Hemingway information on how Fascist insurgents were themselves spying on American forces based in Cuba. Braden approved the proposal and sent a report to J. Edgar Hoover at the FBI asking for his opinion. Hoover too offered provisional support for the plan.

His recruits were made up of the friends he had made when he first settled in Havana. Menocal, Sanchez and a few other upper-class figures promised to report on what was going on among the right-wing community of Falangist sympathisers. Father Untzáin, Roberto Herrera and Juan Donabeitia would gather intelligence and recruit other informers from the lower orders – the groups in the docks that might have been infiltrated by German spies. Soon the Finca became a long-running espionage drama. Figures would arrive in the middle of the night, mostly using the shaded garden approach to the house, to deliver packages to Hemingway who was now the self-appointed head of what had become known as the 'Crook Factory'. There is no record of what the packages contained nor of their value as intelligence material, but Hemingway would make use of these clandestine encounters to hold meetings with his agents, largely in Spanish but sometimes drifting into various Hispanic-English idiolects. It would have been a film director's dream, with the group sitting around a table in one of the six rooms, now requisitioned by Hemingway for special business, dimly lit and sealed off from other residents. Ceiling fans whirred and strained to cool the humidity, the whispered exchanges were accompanied by background hisses as ever-present mosquitoes and flying ants were electrocuted in Martha's traps. She saw it all as a farce. Hemingway's three sons were present for most of the summer and found her a liberating stepmother, at least compared with the rather pious Pauline. She would entertain them with tennis and card games while he was busy with his private intelligence agency, and she allowed herself time away from her writing. Later, she wrote that 'During that terrible year, 1942, I lived in the sun, safe and comfortable and hating it' (Gellhorn, p. 64).

Eventually she persuaded *Collier's* to sponsor her as travelling correspondent in the Caribbean and neighbouring parts of Latin America. She hoped he would understand that this was her job; she was as much concerned as he was with the ongoing U-boat war in this region and the increasing dependence on the US economy of semi-affiliated states such as Venezuela and Columbia. But she had another motive, in that it seemed to her that her husband now existed in a self-deluding bubble, so much so that she now felt uneasy in his presence. As the US Ambassador Braden put it, the Finca had become a magnet day and night for 'a bizarre combination of Spaniards; some bar tenders; a few wharf rats; some down-at-heel pelota players and former bullfighters; two Basque priests; assorted exiled counts and dukes; several Loyalists and Francistas' (Braden, pp. 282–4). He was not exaggerating. Regulars at the Finca would soon become members of a crew for the *Pilar*, dubbed by Hemingway, without irony, as the 'Hooligan Navy'. They would man Hemingway's boat initially as a means of extending intelligence-gathering to sightings of enemy activity in the Caribbean, and within months attempt to turn *Pilar* into a miniature warship. This curious assembly was made up of the American Millionaire Winston Guest, who treated the exercise as recreation with arms and explosives, Dunabeitia, known during the expeditions as 'Sinbad the Sailor', and Herrera; the 'pelota player' referred to by Braden was the playboy Paxtchi Ibarlucia, and the principal 'bartender' was Fernando Mesa, a Catalonian exile, who brought with him a regular barroom customer Don Saxon. Saxon, when not playing war games, was a marine sergeant attached to the American Embassy who supplemented Hemingway's accounts for the ambassador with his own. Braden dutifully assessed Hemingway's reports and then dispatched them to the State Department but there is no evidence that either regarded them as serious contributions to the war effort. His playing spymaster to a group of dispossessed princelings, refugees and desperadoes was bad enough, but what really prompted Martha to look for escape was his plea to Braden that the *Pilar* should become an auxiliary to the small Cuban Navy as a U-boat hunter. His request that it should be equipped with a .50 Browning machine gun, a bazooka, depth charges and sonic detectors was turned down with as much diplomatic restraint as possible. The recoil from such guns might easily destabilize a boat the size of *Pilar*, as would the impact of the launching of depth charges from one side of the deck. Hemingway argued that he planned to patrol the north coast of the island, hoping to lure a U-boat to the surface, without explaining why a German submarine captain would show particular interest in a small fishing vessel. He spun out the fantasy, claiming that a U-boat would be more likely to surface if a vessel as apparently innocuous in appearance as *Pilar* was the only foe sighted by periscope, implying that the Germans would relish the destruction of anything. Once such diabolical cowards reached the surface, he and his crew – most of whom were recruited from the 'Crook Factory' – would surprise them and open fire with the heavy machine gun and the bazooka. If the submarine dived again they would resort to depth charges. In the end he was supplied only with Thompson sub-machine guns, one bazooka and two boxes of grenades. The latter were as much an insult than a concession. Grenades against U-boats, even if they exploded underwater, were the equivalent of fireworks against battle tanks.

During this period he showered Martha with letters – on average one every three days – strewn with coded messages on his activities involving the 'factory'. Typically:

> Burn this letter when you get through reading it and will give you some dope [...] I have to go to dinner at the Embassy on Sat night [...]

for a most important conference [...] otherwise I would have been at sea tomorrow. (7 January 1942, JFK)

She would have been aware that his dealings with the embassy involved the arming and re-equipping of *Pilar*. Usually he gives her information on when they are about to set sail – 'I'm shoving off daylight Thursday morning if nothing turns up to stop it' (12 June 1943, JFK); 'Definitely last letter as we are shoving before daylight tomorrow' (15 January 1943, JFK) – and after his excursions he tells of marlin, shark and tuna 'spotted' or 'seen', but, pointedly, never fished for or caught. They are, in the code they shared, U-boats. In truth, he did not see any enemy vessels but he was attempting to compensate for the fact that his wife was reporting on the war while he appeared to have settled for a blend of self-delusion and early retirement. Martha played along to the extent that she even agreed to give (false) accounts to his sons regarding his frequent absences aboard *Pilar*: 'E is doing a lot of work collecting specimens [for] the Natural History Museum' (Martha to Jack/Bumby, 1943, JFK, undated).

Martha returned to the Finca in autumn 1942 but matters did not improve. She was invited to breakfasts and suppers almost every day with Hemingway, Gustavo Duran – for whom Hemingway had spun false tales of his life before Cuba – and Duran's wife Bonte. Duran was being primed as the new leader of the Crook Factory, which would enable Hemingway to devote more time to turning *Pilar* into a viable warship. Martha was distressed and perplexed by the lies told by her husband to Duran about his experiences in the Spanish War – some of which she, as a witness, knew were pure falsifications –and equally by his self-evident ambition to become a hero of the Atlantic war against submarines, as captain of a fishing boat. In November Hemingway reported to Agent Leddy, an FBI associate with the military authorities in Cuba, that from *Pilar* he had spotted what he believed to be a U-boat trailing the Spanish ship *Marques de Comillas*. His account raised suspicions with Leddy who informed Agent Ladd, Hoover's immediate junior, that their unofficial representative in Havana was at best an unreliable informant, and possibly a man whose affiliation with communism during the

Spanish War might prompt him to deliberately send false evidence to US intelligence agencies, despite the fact that America and the Soviet Union were now allies. By mid-1943 Hoover had instructed his own agents and diplomats to disassociate themselves from Hemingway, gradually but incessantly. In autumn 1943 the American Embassy had begun to refuse to endorse patrols by *Pilar*, and since the vessel was not, officially, assigned either to American or to Cuban forces, Hemingway became enraged by the realisation that he was no longer thought worthy as a combatant. He had been living a lie for the previous 12 months. Every sailing seemed to reinforce the unspoken suspicion that they were following shadows, and in the absence of real enemies Hemingway and his crew used their sub-machine guns and grenades against sharks and marlins.

In an undated letter written to his brother Leicester in 1942 Hemingway describes his actions with *Pilar*.

> We had a bomb with a short fuse and handles. We kept it topside, unleashed and ready to fling. The idea was to keep nosing around where we heard them talking [he does not explain the equipment that would enable them to eavesdrop on U-boat conversations]. Eventually one would surface and order us alongside. Then Patche and his pal would arm the bomb, grab the handles, and, as we came abreast of the sub's conning tower we figured to clear her decks with our guns. (Quoted in Leicester Hemingway, pp. 431–2)

The letter is an extraordinary exercise in smoke-and-mirrors deception that Hemingway rarely matched in his published prose. He shifts elusively between events that he claims have occurred ('we had', 'we kept it'), hypotheses ('The idea was to keep', 'his pal would arm') and planned strategies ('we figured to clear her decks') while never making it clear whether he was recalling an actual encounter with a submarine or describing exercises or strategies devised to prepare them for battles so far only imagined. Through four pages, the actual, the wished for and pure make-believe shift in and out of focus.

Martha looked on as a mood of disillusionment descended on Hemingway and his crew. Following her return from the *Collier's* Caribbean assignment in November 1942 her husband had handed over his intelligence role to Duran, and set off as a self-appointed privateer. However, by spring 1943 she was aware of the futility of his voyages, the withdrawal of official sponsorship and the effects of both on a man whose presiding ambition was to embody a brand of heroism that had, so far, been confined to his fiction.

The first indication that there was something terribly wrong with the marriage comes in a letter to her written on 16 March 1943 (JFK). He opens: 'I can't stick the atmosphere [...] I come back [from one of his patrols] to an atmosphere as though I were some sort of villain of the piece.' He claims that he has 'tried to help you in every way and when I was here I have tried to take every single thing of management etc off your hands and keep your time free for writing. I tip-toe in the mornings, I make the servants be quiet, I tell people who want to bother you that they cannot see you [...] and I have no greater joy than seeing your book develop so amazingly and beautifully.' It is evident that the promises he had made regarding her freedom to live and work as she wishes are becoming conditional.

> There is no need to destroy me because you feel you have to go out into the world again.

> Once you told me when you got that way to insist that you make a small trip first because then you saw things clearly when you were away. Nearly always, when you go away hating me as the nearest and most articulate object because what you hate is not being as free and as young as we both were when we started for Europe.

He does not provide exact details regarding the cause of her apparent unhappiness but much can be inferred. He comments on his 'two hard jobs', one of which is his make-believe role as U-boat hunter: 'But when we are fighting [...] [the] boat is [a] crammed sty of destructive weapons.' Martha, in his view, resents his absences while he has tolerated hers. 'That you were here alone the last ten days was not of my choice [...] last summer it was me in the house and you on the ocean [...] and [earlier] in Finland.' For much of the rest of the sprawling seven-page letter he provides her with a lesson in how writers can survive against the odds, a potted memoir involving the life and work of Ernest Hemingway. She 'would turn on the gas or take an overdose of sleeping pills if you had to go back and live in the squalid places that were beautiful to me in Paris because I was young in Paris'. He gives her the impression that destitution was an unsought burden when in truth it was part of his performance as down-at-heel bohemian. He tells of how he had to write *A Farewell to Arms* in 'Paris, Havana, Key West, Piggott, Arkansas, Kansas City, Big Horn Wyoming and back to Paris [...] with a side trip to Chicago just before writing all the last chapter when my father shot himself and I had to pay his debts'. Again, he presents this odyssey as some dreadful misfortune, when in fact he planned these excursions as an escape from family life with Pauline. *Death in the Afternoon*, he reports, was composed in longhand when he had 'a compound fracture of my right humerus with paralysis of the musculo-spiral nerve [...] To Have and Have Not, which God knows has many scars from it was started in Madrid [...] then rewritten with the Spanish War intervening and me in love with you'. *For Whom the Bell Tolls* was 'started [...] under a less than perfect state of mind' and while it was about him and Martha much of it was written was when he was

> with Pauline dureing [*sic*] which time had to sleep in the same bed and be told each night it wasn't true, that you were a jew, that I was mad, that why be sad, that just come home, that just stay home, what about my children, that I'd never be able to work, that you would leave me as soon as you got what you wanted from me, that I could never have a divorce, that why not make love and see if it would not be all right again.

Hemingway's declared concern for her unhappiness soon mutates into a solipsistic monologue, based on his view that a minutely detailed account of his struggles and successes will serve her as an example she should respect and follow. 'Everybody that I know would like to help you. But if you do not settle down and cut out the prima donna business and write your novel [...] then you will never live happily with yourself no matter where you go and there is no land where you can run away from yourself [...] From your loving husband who is evidently being kicked out of your life.' He goes on to accuse her of narcissism:

> no-one that chased their youth ever caught it [...]
>
> Your beauty will go
>
> Your youth will go

> Everything will go except writing well and the only way to write well is to do it in spite of bloody what all.

There is no evidence that Martha was remotely concerned with the consequences of ageing; she was still only 34 and might easily have been mistaken for a woman in her mid-twenties. He was projecting his own anxieties and preoccupations on to her.

Her novel, 'the book', would be published in 1944. *Liana* is about the marriage between Marc Royer, a middle-aged white patriarch who dominates a Caribbean island, and Liana the young mulatto girl he attempts to re-educate as a version of himself. True, Martha was not a mulatto teenager, but she shared with her character a sense of being treated with extraordinary condescension by a man who cared little about who she really was.

The portrait that survives of Hemingway from these years is formed predominately by Martha's memoir and interviews by others, and his own letter seems to confirm this impression, albeit involuntarily. We should not doubt that he treated his wife appallingly but, while in no way excusing this, there was another aspect of his life of which she and most others remained ignorant. The second of the 'two jobs' involved his work for US intelligence. Martha has ridiculed his presentation of himself as a spy and even his most sympathetic biographers regard his version of his role with embarrassed indulgence. However, two weeks after they returned to the Finca from China (20 July 1940, JFK) he wrote a lengthy, detailed letter to Henry Morgenthau which remains unpublished. Morgenthau was Secretary to the Treasury in the Roosevelt Administration but by 1940 he had become the president's principal advisor on the US's ongoing and potential role in World War II, and in this regard he played a major role in establishing the foundations for an a overseas intelligence-gathering network. The Office of the Coordinator of Information was founded by Colonel Robert Donovan after Pearl Harbor in July 1941 and this would mutate into the Office of Strategic Studies (OSS) little more than a year later – the OSS was the forerunner of the postwar CIA. Hemingway's letter was not unsolicited. He was, he writes, asked by 'Mr White [...] to look into the Kuomintang-Communist difficulties and try to find any information which could possibly be of interest to you.' 'White' was actually Donovan who before Pearl Harbor had become, with Roosevelt and Morgenthau's approval, freelance gatherer of overseas intelligence. We cannot be certain of who prompted Donovan to seek Hemingway's assistance but it seems more than coincidental that Hemingway's drinking partner in China was Morris 'Two Gun' Cohen. Cohen's case officer in MI6 was William Stephenson and in early 1940 Stephenson had become British Intelligence's unofficial 'man in New York and Washington', offering advice to Donovan on the pragmatics of gathering intelligence. Hemingway's report to 'White' is an extraordinary document, not least because of the evidence it displays of his intense research. Despite Martha's story of him in China as unfocussed, even dissolute, it shows that he made copious notes of everything he observed and heard, including conversations with Chou En-lai and Chang Kai-shek and interviews he conducted, in confidence, with military officers and officials serving the government and the Communists. Moreover, it becomes evident that there was a version of Hemingway travelling in the Far East very different from the one routinely presented and perceived. He certainly played the role of the irresponsible drunk but it is clear enough from his reports that this was a performance, a means of preventing suspicious observers from presenting an account – to foreign agencies – of him acting as an informant for the US government. He pretended to be the foolish aficionado of snake wine and stewed dog to distract his wife from what he was actually up to. Most importantly his reports are, stylistically, unlike all of his other correspondence. Hemingway's letters are routinely chaotic and unorthodox. Certainly, he improves on this for publishers, lawyers and, usually, the press, but even then a mood of overexuberance and distractedness informs the prose. The six, single-spaced pages to Morgenthau might have been written by someone else, such is his impersonal temper and his attention to detail and clarity. He was working for the government and not allowing for ambiguity or imprecision to cloud his message. His account is remarkably incisive on how the tensions, sometimes outright gun-battles, between the forces of the official Chinese government, under Chiang Kai-shek, and the Communist forces were at the time proving beneficial to the Japanese. He makes comparisons between the dedicated but bitterly divided elements of the Nationalist cause and the united, militarily better-organised Falangists of Spain. The latter were in his view the equivalent of the Japanese invaders, while the former might have prevailed in Spain if the Russia-backed Communists had taken command of the other Nationalist factions. He argued to Morgenthau that the Chinese Communists would find greater support among the peasantry and working classes than the official government and if Roosevelt wanted to prevent China becoming another Spain – albeit as a colony of Imperialist Japan rather than an internally suborned Fascist dictatorship – the US should shift its allegiance to the Communists. He had originally arranged for a meeting in Washington with Morgenthau 'in June' which 'I was sorry not to get to', but this was to have been the second of their encounters: 'there was so much to say when I saw you last'. Hemingway was reporting directly to the third most powerful figure in the Roosevelt government. Further letters between them would follow and, while we now treat his reports to the Havana embassy regarding the activities of *Pilar* as fanciful, there is counter-evidence to show that he was working for two very different branches of US intelligence and presenting two separate personae for each. His FBI contacts treated his reports, especially those founded on his *Pilar* expeditions, as improbable and politically suspect, but a decade before the McCarthy Hearings Hoover was already neurotically suspicious of anti-Nazism, especially evidenced by those who had participated in the Spanish War, as an indication of pro-Soviet communism, and Hemingway was a prime suspect. Under Hoover, and even during World War II, the FBI was preoccupied with internal security to the exclusion of global intelligence. Hoover was unsettled by the fact that the Soviet Union must now be counted as an ally of America. He began to treat Donovan with suspicion and sometimes employed agents to gather information for a file on the latter's private life, particularly his reputation as a womaniser, and in many ways one can detect parallels between his antipathy towards the Internationalist project of the OSS and its extrovert leader (Donovan had won numerous gallantry medals for his near suicidal exploits on the Western Front, earning himself the nickname 'Wild Bill') and his dealings with Hemingway, a man with a similarly dazzling past and, even worse, left-wing sympathies. There is evidence that Hemingway deliberately provoked the antipathy and suspicion of Hoover's representatives in Cuba, sometimes in a darkly farcical manner. On 8 October 1942, Agent Leddy reported to his boss, Hoover, that Hemingway seemed involved in a campaign designed to 'severely criticize the Bureau', adding that 'in attendance at a Jai Alai match with HEMINGWAY, the writer [Leddy] was introduced by him to a friend as a member of the Gestapo. On that occasion, I told HEMINGWAY that I did not appreciate the introduction.' An embassy document, later made public, reports that 'Mr Joyce of the Embassy asked the assistance of the Legal Attache in ascertaining the contents of a tightly wrapped box left by a suspect [an agent of the Crook Factory] at the Bar Basque under conditions suggesting that the box contained espionage information.' On opening it Joyce and Hemingway found themselves staring at a cheap edition of *The Life of St Teresa*. Hemingway sustained his performance as the disappointed spymaster for about five minutes before giving in to laughter. In a letter to Meyers (28 February 1983) Joyce admits that eventually he and his FBI associates eventually realised they'd been fooled. 'Of course their intelligence [to him and the FBI] was completely fabricated. If their reports were sensational they were paid more – \$20 instead of \$10.' He adds that despite the apparent incompetence of Hemingway and his Crook Factory operatives, a major general connected to a branch of the OSS in the Pentagon had insisted that his material, for the OSS, was valid and authentic. He doesn't explain this inconsistency to Meyers and nor does the latter address it. Joyce was being candid enough, but he had worked in the intelligence services and was rationing out facts while withholding elucidation. He became a full-time member of the OSS in September 1943. Previously, he had operated as an intermediary between Hemingway and figures at the embassy, notably, Leddy, who dealt primarily with the FBI. In September he left Cuba for Bari, Italy, and made contact with Martha who was covering the Allied advance. He wanted to discuss with Martha her husband's suitability as a permanent OSS agent. She was honest enough about his personal shortcomings and their marital difficulties but she recommended him unreservedly as a man who would sacrifice anything to defeat Fascism. Joyce informed Whitney Shepardson, the head of Secret Intelligence in Washington, that Hemingway should be recruited. No documents exist – or at least none have been disclosed – which explain why this procedure went no further, but it is clear that Joyce was following orders from his superiors who were aware that the intelligence he had sent to them was meticulously sourced, unlike the nonsense he'd fed to the FBI.

Washington and the OSS always regarded Hemingway as a reliable source of information on figures whom the US might trust, or suspect, as intelligence sources after Pearl Harbor and the declaration of war. For example, on 3 May 1943 (JFK) he delivered a report on the suitability of one Edward Knoblaugh for membership of the newly formed 'Mission in the Investigation of Falangist Activities.' The latter was a euphemism for an OSS sub-department which would track down US based Nazi sympathisers, notably, though not exclusively, those associated with Falangist groups during the Spanish Civil War. Knoblaugh, who had volunteered as a member of the Mission while withholding details of his active involvement with the Falangists in Spain, was treated as a likely double-agent, and Hemingway had been appointed his investigator, a role he undertook with extraordinary scruple. He had encountered Knoblaugh briefly in Madrid and read his anti-Communist book on the war but now he went much further, writing to fellow correspondents for their accounts of Knoblaugh's activities. Typically, he sent a detailed letter to Jay Allen, who worked for the *Chicago Tribune* and had witnessed a number of the events that featured in Knoblaugh's book, including the massacre of more than 400 government sympathisers in Badajoz, which Knoblaugh claimed was a falsehood. Allen replied to Hemingway, promptly and assuredly, Hemingway sent a full report, and Knoblaugh became *persona non grata*.

Accusations made in recent books that Hemingway was a Communist spy, betraying the US, are unfounded. Notably, Nicholas Reynolds, in *Writer, Sailor, Soldier, Spy*, claims that he worked with the Soviet NKVD (People's Commissariat of Internal Affairs) in the 1940s and during the early years of the Cold War.

Reynolds does a remarkable job of creating a 260-page charge sheet from a sequence 'events' based almost exclusively on rumour, speculation and probability. His thesis is founded on the belief that Jacob Golos of the NKVD cultivated Hemingway as a Soviet spy at various times and places, from the latter's visit to the Orient with Martha in 1941 onwards. There is no evidence that the two men ever met, and the story that Hemingway passed information on to the Russian is based entirely on the testimony of Alexander Vassiliev. Himself an ex-KGB operative, Vassiliev was employed during the early 1990s to author books on the activities of the organisation and its agents. This was the period in which post-Soviet Russia decided to address its past, honestly and publically, and Vassiliev had been given access to NKVD files from the 1940s. By 1995–6, however, hardliners within the KGB's successor organisation, the SVR, and in central government began to deny researchers access to files and documents. Vassiliev feared for his safety and fled to the West, taking with him only notes from and recollections of documents he claimed to have seen, such as: 'Throughout the period of his connection with us [the NKVD], "Argo" [Hemingway's codename] did not give us any polit. Information'. We have to trust Vassiliev as to the authenticity of this, and even if we do so it reveals only that the information gained from Hemingway was of no significance. Sometimes during the 1940s he would encounter Communists in Cuba he had known in Spain – certainly Alexander Orlov who had been a senior NKVD figure in Madrid – and it is likely that he spoke to them of his continuing pro-Soviet, anti-Fascist opinions, but if he was an NKVD agent it is bizarre that he said nothing to them of his close connections with the OSS, let alone his dealings with Hoover's rabidly anti-Communist FBI. During the 1940s Hemingway regarded Soviet Russia as the natural ally of Britain and the US against European Fascism and its Japanese counterpart, and so did most of the pro-interventionist supporters of Roosevelt. He did act as the surpassing spy, a figure who could make John le Carré's presentations of duplicity seem laboured, but he was dedicated unswervingly to America. He became two different individuals, one who the pre-Cold War FBI perceived as suspect and sometimes absurd, and another who produced invaluable intelligence for the OSS regarding the very real fear that pro-Fascist fifth-columnists were at work in the US and Latin America. The fact that the Soviet alliance with the West was, post-1945, transformed into a different political/military conflict hardly registered for Hemingway. As we shall see, by 1946 he was living in the past, but for others the past involved the accumulation of damning evidence. Hoover would become Senator Joseph McCarthy's closest ally in the various security agencies, and in 1943 he regarded Hemingway with suspicion because of his previous sympathies. He would search in vain for proof that the writer was in some way colluding with figures from Communist regimes, while spreading rumours that would eventually give credence to the accusations of Vassiliev and Reynolds. Hemingway was certainly playing roles, embodying two different states of mind and affiliations almost simultaneously, but his wartime commitment to the US intelligence agencies was unswerving. He made a fool of himself for Hoover and the FBI but was meticulously sound for the OSS. On this occasion his leaning towards fabrication was premeditated and patriotic.

In April 1959 Hemingway met Graham Greene on the set in Cuba where Carol Reed was filming a version of Greene's novel *Our Man in Havana*, published the previous year. The meeting was a little frosty by all accounts, with Hemingway apparently showing some unease when the plot was explained to him. In it, Wormold is MI6's reluctant representative in Havana. He sends his bosses fabricated reports of espionage networks and on one occasion makes sketches of vacuum cleaner parts (in real life he's a carpet cleaner salesman) and claims they are plans of military bases in the mountains. Sound familiar? It was probably a coincidence but we should remember that Greene based the novel on stories he'd heard during World War II when he was working for MI6, OSS's sister organisation.

In September 1943 Martha left for England to cover the build-up to the invasion of continental Europe, something that was not publically acknowledged but which, via her friendship with Eleanor Roosevelt, she already knew involved a well-advanced military enterprise. Her acute sense of the divide that had opened between them is evident in a letter she wrote on 28 June 1943 (JFK). He was docked with *Pilar* at Caya Confites, an island 60 miles south of Cuba. She wishes they could 'stop it all now, the prestige, the knowledge, the victory'. She goes on, a little enigmatically, to present him as a man so used to being married that 'I do not believe that it [marriage] can touch you where you live and that is your strength. It would be terrible if it did because you are so much more important than the women you happen to be married to.' She adds, 'You have been married so much and so long' and by courteous implication she excuses herself from the subordinate roles of Hadley and Pauline. She knows, without condemning him, that he cannot help regarding marriage as a calming, stable subsidiary to his other lives, lived dangerously and projected into his fiction. The most insightful passage comes when she considers their possible and previous states: 'I would like to be young and poor and in Milan and with you and not married to you.' He had told her of Agnes – the only person to whom he disclosed this – and she had, again with great discernment, picked her out as a blend of the real and the imaginary. Then she takes him back to the time when the two of them did feel compatible: 'it was the first winter in Madrid. There was a sort of blindness and fervour and recklessness about that sort of feeling which one must always want.' Each was addicted to a life on the edge which, when they returned to domestic stability, caused them to recognise that something was missing. 'I hate being so wise and so careful, so reliable, so denatured, so able to get on' (Gellhorn to Hemingway, 28 June 1943, JFK).

Within 12 months they would be married only on paper. She left for Europe in September 1943, again working for *Collier's*, and covered conflicts in North Africa and Italy. Earlier that year US regulations on not allowing women correspondents to report from the front line were revised, but they could still operate only in 'rear zones' behind the front line. Martha had never before been subjected to such restrictions: the US was not directly involved in Spain and other conflicts and thus had no say in what its agencies and their correspondents could do. She felt frustrated and often succeeded in persuading the military authorities to ignore her movements far beyond the designated 'hospital areas' that marked the boundary of women reporters' activities.

Through the winter months of 1943–4, Hemingway and Martha exchanged letters in which neither indicated that they were ready to abandon their relationship. In December 1943 she wrote several times asking him to join her in Europe. They could, she implored, recreate the frantic, dangerous mood of Madrid. Afterwards they would 'write books and see the autumns together and walk around the cornfields waiting for the pheasants' (quoted in Kert, p. 384). A week later she conceded that if he insisted on remaining in Cuba 'I will not speak of it again', but she had not quite given up. She imagines both of them as witnesses 'to the invasion'; they would 'see Paris right at the beginning and watch the peace.' As in the letter of June she does her best to explore their temperamental differences. 'I have to live my way as well as yours or there wouldn't be any me to love you with' (quoted in Kert, p. 388). She adds that 'You really wouldn't want me if I built a fine big stone wall around the Finca and sat inside it.'

Following her unannounced return to Cuba in March 1944, Martha once again presented the invasion of continental Europe as their opportunity to relive Spain.:

> He woke me when I was trying to sleep [...] to bully, snarl, mock – my crime really was to have been at war when he had not, but that was not how he put it. I was supposedly insane, I only wanted excitement and danger. I had no responsibility to anyone, I was selfish beyond belief [...] it never stopped and believe me, it was fierce and ugly. (Interview with Kert, pp. 391–2).

If one has any doubts about the accuracy of her recollection one has only to compare it with a letter he wrote to Edna about her at the same time. 'I thought maybe she has pretty bad paranoia [...] Nothing outside herself interests her very much [...] she seems mentally unbalanced; maybe just borderline' (March, JFK, undated). Once more he was apportioning his own failings and impulses to Martha. His rant was an unnervingly exact description of how he was about to behave in France and Germany, but as well as prompting him to displace his abnormalities on to her, Martha had provoked a more elemental instinct: misogynistic envy. Over the same period that Hemingway was being encouraged by US authorities to wind down the U-boat hunts – by the close of 1943 judged by Agent Leddy as variously ineffectual and embarrassing – Martha was attaining global esteem as the one woman reporter who had access to the events on the front line and who had the capacity to inform hard prose accounts of the events with something almost empathetic. In England in early 1944 she had managed to interview members of Bomber Command on their experiences of night raids over Germany and had sent *Collier's* a beautifully eerie description of watching the Lancaster bombers take off as darkness fell, describing them as 'enormous black birds of prey', some of which would never return. At the end of January 1944 she flew into Naples, via Algiers, hitching rides on supply planes by means that remain fascinatingly undisclosed. The city had been liberated by the Allies three months earlier but their advance towards Rome was stalled in the mountainous regions roughly 80 miles north. Martha was present during the second, infamous assault on Monte Cassino in early February when the medieval Abbey on the mountain was reduced to rubble by American bombers and British artillery. She told of how monks who survived the bombardment were more concerned with the potential suffering of Allied soldiers than their own fate. A week after she delivered her report *Collier's* advertised her as standing out 'among gal correspondents not only for her writing but for her good looks. Blonde, tall, dashing – she comes pretty close to living up to what a big league woman reporter should be.'

In April 1944 Hemingway signed a contract with *Collier's* as a correspondent on what press insiders knew was the imminent invasion of northern France. He knew that they were pleased with the reports delivered by their rule-breaking woman reporter from the front line from which she was, supposedly, forbidden. But he was equally aware that they would relish the services of the man who had since 1918 combined bestselling fictional accounts of the century's turmoils with biting news reports on the same events. He could easily have found well-paid positions with other high-profile magazines or agencies, but he chose *Collier's* to force them to decide on whether dispatches from him or Martha would be given precedence.

Later in April the couple flew to New York, ostensibly to continue together across the Atlantic to cover the war, much as Martha had envisaged in her plea that they should revive the spirit of Madrid. She assumed, understandably, that he would use his influence to secure a seat for each of them on the same Pan Am flight to London whose other passengers were senior military personnel and officially designated correspondents, but when she asked him, two days before departure, if her booking was secure he replied, 'oh no […] I couldn't do that. They only fly men'. His lie was self-evident and cruel. She knew, and he knew she knew, that the actresses Gertrude Lawrence and Beatrice Lillie and at least two other women with jobs in military administration would be on the aeroplane. Three weeks earlier he had written a piece in *Collier's* praising his wife's inclination to break the rules: 'When she is at the front or getting there, she will get up earlier, travel longer and faster and go where no other woman can get and where few would stick it out if they did […] She gets to the place, gets the story, writes it and comes home. That last is the best part' (*Collier's*, 4 March 1944). The short closing sentence carries a bitterly ironic sting; as he wrote it he was planning to exclude her from the Pan Am flight.

A day before he boarded the plane and amid what Martha recalled as his 'hideous and insane reviling' of her, he stated that he was 'going to be killed' and that he hoped she'd be satisfied 'with what she had done'. In her memoirs she reports this without comment, seemingly baffled. He was providing her with a chilling forecast of his reckless, almost suicidal behaviour over the coming months.

He arrived in London three weeks before Martha's ship docked in Liverpool, and set himself up in the Dorchester Hotel as a man who had no time for the privations of rationing and the shortages of luxury goods endured by the rest of Britain over the previous five years. Where exactly the lobsters, prime steak, pre-war bottles of Champagne and grand cru Burgundy reds came from goes unrecorded, but guests, particularly the British, were captivated by his largesse. Many Americans holding senior ranks in the military and diplomatic corps might find themselves with modest quantities of rare drink and foodstuffs flown over from the US, but Hemingway appeared to have persuaded the hotel that he was the equivalent of royalty. His lifestyle was shamelessly bacchanalian; he often had wine and spirits with breakfast and continued all day with various types and strengths of drink. Martha does not comment on why she did not join him in London but his behaviour indicates that communication between them had ceased. In early April he decided to take lunch at the White Tower restaurant in Soho, known for its cellar of wines, gin and Scotch whisky kept in reserve mainly for American journalists and servicemen willing to pay over the odds. Hemingway found himself distracted by a woman taking lunch with a uniformed infantryman. Irwin Shaw had had short stories published and plays performed but at the time he was enlisted as a warrant officer in the regular army. Hemingway pushed a chair between the couple and introduced himself to the slight, sharp-featured young woman rather in the manner of someone whose fame precludes such incidentals as politeness. Next, he invited Mary Welsh to have dinner with him; she accepted, and he left without acknowledging the presence of Shaw. He knew of him without knowing him personally, and later commented on his satisfaction of having stolen a 'Jew's date'. He met Mary again two days later at a party in the Dorchester, before having arranged their dinner date, and opened the conversation with, 'I don't know you Mary, but I want to marry you.' She thought he was joking but, twice married herself and with no respect for middle-class morality, she began an affair with him before he left London for France.

On 24 May he went to a party at the photographer Robert Capa's flat in Belgravia. Much alcohol was taken by all and Hemingway was offered a lift back to the Dorchester by the English doctor Peter Gorer, who, as drunk as everyone else, crashed his car into a steel water tank in a blacked-out street. Hemingway was severely concussed, required 57 stitches to repair his windscreen-battered forehead and suffered horrible bruising to his abdomen and legs. Prone to accidents, especially to his head, this was his worst yet. Martha visited him in hospital and, without asking what exactly had happened, assumed that he had, drunkenly, brought it all on himself. The weeks spent in London by Hemingway and Martha before D-Day pointed up their incompatibility. Her stability, normality and most of all her success caused him to become embittered. He was not a misogynist in terms of harbouring all-inclusive prejudices; his were targeted specifically against the woman to whom he was married. They were a couple who lived in different parts of the city. He sometimes invited her to parties at the Dorchester where he insisted that all guests would drink more than they wished for or could endure, in the full knowledge that she loathed his drunken extravagances. Once, he arranged to meet her for dinner, as a couple, at a central London restaurant, then failed to arrive at her at her hotel room and made sure that mutual acquaintances would tell Martha that they'd seen him out with Mary Welsh.

He wanted to be part of the invasion and the ensuing conflict, but only senior officers in the armed services knew the location and details of the seaborne assault and even for them the schedule was revised on a daily basis, according to ongoing and predicted weather conditions. Junior officers, non-commissioned officers and private soldiers were aware, from their training, that beaches somewhere on the northern French coast were likely, but apart from being told to await further directions they had no information on their destination. The military command had decided that just over 500 journalists would be allowed to report as direct witnesses, most accompanying the seaborne landings and a smaller number allowed in bombers. Hemingway, like everyone else, was in a state of frustrated anticipation, knowing that an event that would alter the history of the rest of the century was imminent, but nothing else. He busied himself, when sober, by seeking assurances from *Collier's* that he alone would be their official correspondent for the invasion. Women reporters were in any event forbidden from covering it but he took particular satisfaction from knowing that *Collier's* office would inform Martha of whom they had chosen as their single representative.

He reported his involvement in D-Day, 6 June 1944, for *Collier's* readers in 'Voyage to Victory'. 'As the boat rose to the sea, the green water turned white and came slamming in over the men, the guns and the cases of explosives'. This is his eyewitness account of what it felt like to be in an infantry landing craft as it approached Omaha beach and it is authentic, to an extent. What he does not state is that the landing craft's commander, Lieutenant Robert Anderson, put the troops ashore and returned to the transport ship *Dorothea L Dix* from which the craft had been dispatched around half an hour before, taking with him his single civilian passenger, Ernest

Hemingway. Hemingway goes on to indicate that he too had gone ashore and had assisted Lieutenant Anderson in locating key landmarks, such as the church tower of Colleville, which he had memorised from his study of Ordnance Survey maps. These, he claimed, would provide vital information for infantry movements and artillery aiming. The myth of his D-Day landing was sustained by Hemingway himself throughout his life. On 15 September he wrote to his son Patrick of his 'landing on Omaha beach', enquiring, 'Suppose you saw that piece in Colliers[?]'. After his return from Europe he repeated the account for his brother Leicester who documented it in his memoirs. In 1962, William Van Dusen published an article in *True* magazine called 'Hemingway's Longest Day' invoking the title of the soon-to-be released, star-studded film about the Normandy landings. In it he tells of how Hemingway had taken command of a rifle team that was pinned down on the beach by German fire, led it to safety and delivered a report on enemy gun emplacements to the beach commander. Van Dusen was a former naval officer and he gives the impression that the story had been authenticated by others who saw action on D-Day. In fact, its single source was Hemingway, who had first met Van Dusen on the Pan Am flight from New York and mesmerised him with his tales of combat in Italy and Spain. Thereafter Van Dusen treated everything the author told him as irrefutably true. Hemingway's addiction to self-glorification was by 1944 well embedded, but his enduring preoccupation with the D-Day myth had a particular cause – Martha. She befriended a medical officer serving on a US hospital ship, found where the vessel was docked and stowed away below decks among the network of lavatories and storage rooms. She remained hidden until the ship docked just beyond the beachhead and began to receive injured servicemen. After stealing a spare medical auxiliary's uniform she went ashore as a stretcher-bearer, without anyone noticing she was a woman. She helped evacuate several injured men, and she also took notes. She was the only woman, and certainly the only woman reporter, to land on the D-Day beaches on the morning of 6 June. Hemingway learned of this on his return to London, and when he eventually joined Allied forces on the European mainland he was subjected to endless reports on the exploits of his wife. She had stolen his persona.

Hemingway did not reach France until late July but in the interim he did his best to see action, from the air. Before D-Day he had tried several times to persuade his Royal Air Force (RAF) contact, the poet and public relations officer John Pudney, to secure him a seat as passenger on one of the raids being conducted on German military sites in France. Why he did not pursue this goal with the presumably more partisan and accessible United States Army Air Forces (USAAF) remains a mystery, but we should bear in mind the fact that Martha had already impressed readers of *Collier's* with her stories about RAF Bomber Command. Aside from this, his choice of the British resulted in some revealing disclosures about his state of mind.

Nigel Hamilton, biographer of Field Marshall Montgomery, reports a story told to him by Pudney of Hemingway's performance in the officers' mess at an RAF base in Hampshire. Apparently Hemingway 'held court' at the bar and 'to John's disgust' began a rant on the flaws of the current RAF strategy, claiming that senior officers, from squadron leader upwards, were 'cowards'. In fact they had been forbidden from flying over enemy territory because they knew a great deal more about plans for the invasion than did flight lieutenants and flying officers, and it was assumed that Germans would use torture on them to obtain as much intelligence as possible about imminent events. Pudney does not say if Hemingway knew anything of why the senior airmen were 'grounded' but, according to Hamilton, his friend was 'ashamed of him'. 'That Hemingway should boast and brag at the bar about his own bravery and exploits [involving stories of Italy and Spain] in front of innocent but brave pilots [...] was to John a typical case of the egotism, vanity and shameful bragging of a certain kind of writer' (interview, Nigel Hamilton to Jeffrey Meyers, 8 March 1983). One of the 'grounded' senior officers present was Peter Wykeham, who later served as Air Chief Marshall. He wrote in *The Times* ('Hair Raising', 5 August 1969) that Pudney seemed like a 'gentleman who's accidentally found himself leading a rampaging bull', telling of Pudney's disgust at having to follow Hemingway to 'more and more drunken parties, fights and wrangles, being thrown into fountains, ejected from hotels and locked in people's rooms' while everyone else was concentrating on an imminent military operation which would determine the history of the continent and end the lives of many involved in it.

This notion of him as faintly deranged is echoed by other reports of his behaviour between D-Day and his eventual departure for France more than a month later. One afternoon he, Mary Welsh, Cyril Connolly, Desmond McCarthy and the novelist Frederic Prokosch took tea as guests of Lady Emerald Cunard in her luxurious suite in the Dorchester. According to later accounts Hemingway seemed like a caged animal. He complained that the West End of London gave off a leaden dreariness, and offered an example: 'Look at Eaton Square, for instance', he pronounced. Many had, given that it contained probably the most celebrated neoclassical terrace in London. 'The houses are all identical. It makes for monotony.' 'That it does', Lady Cunard responded, rather in the manner of a grandee from a play by Wilde; 'there is doubtless a certain monotony'. The exchange was joined by others, including Connolly and Prokosch, and all pretended to regard Hemingway's increasingly scabrous opinions on London's dreariness as discerning and sagacious, without his being aware of the unintendedly farcical contrast between his perceptions of them and theirs of him. Prokosch later commented that 'there was a sheen of criminal stealth and carnivorous stupidity' about him (Prokosch, pp. 24–5).

The only occasions on which his pressurised mood of rage and confinement was relieved was when he was granted his wish to fly missions with the RAF. He went twice, first as a passenger in an American-manufactured Mitchell bomber and then he took the seat normally occupied by the navigator in the revolutionary British fighter bomber, the twin-engined Mosquito. With a fuselage of timber, plywood and fabric the Mosquito was much faster than any aircraft of comparable size, with stripped down versions reaching 425 mph. The Mitchell bombers were attacking launch bases for V1 rockets which at the time were subjecting central London to another version of the blitz. Group Captain Wykeham Barnes was the pilot of the Mosquito and in an interview with Carl Baker he told of how his innate notion of responsibility and common sense was eroded by the very presence of Hemingway as his only companion in the cramped cockpit. The Mosquitoes were not mounting direct attacks on the V1 launch-pads. They were lightly armed to reduce weight and increase speed so that they could intercept the rockets and report on their height and direction. Barnes tells Baker that when they came upon a V1 'I was acting against my better judgement [...] I know there were proper night fighters after them and I was getting in the way [...] If you did blow one up, particularly at night, it was touch and go for yourself also.' But he followed the rocket through exploding flack and search lights and opened fire several times, 'and the aeroplane danced around like a leaf in a whirlwind.' Why, one asks, had he acted against his better judgement? 'I knew I was supposed to keep Ernest out of trouble [but] [...] Ernest seemed to love the fireworks bursting all around us, and urged me to press on and make sure of the V1' (interview with Barnes in Baker, p. 474). Barnes, with nuanced admiration, adds that after they landed, 'Ernest seemed to have loved every moment'.

The pilot tells of how he, exhausted, slept for eight hours, to find Hemingway 'looking terrible' next morning having spent the night distilling his experience of the flight into an electrifying story for readers of *Collier's*. The fact that Martha had landed on the Normandy beaches on 6 June, via subterfuge and disguise, caused him great distress and goes some way to explain why he spent the second half of June and the first weeks of July trying to replicate her exploits; her accounts of Bomber Command had become legendary in the US and Britain, but she had not flown with the Lancaster crews. He wanted to tell her, via *Collier's*, that he'd done more than she could.

Eventually, on 18 July, he was delivered by troopship to the Normandy coast. For several days he watched with frustration as General Bradley's First Army attempted with only occasional success to break through a line of German armour at St Lo and he looked on with rage as the USAAF dropped fragmentation bombs on Bradley's troops rather than their intended German targets. His anger would eventually be voiced by his Colonel Cantwell in *Across the River and into the Trees* (1950), but in July 1944 it became the trigger for his subsequent behaviour. He decided that if senior military officers were demonstrably ineffectual and incompetent, a self-appointed part-timer, one Ernest Hemingway, ought to set an example.

His opportunity to do so came soon afterwards when he joined Colonel Charles 'Buck' Lanham's 22nd Infantry Regiment. Lanham and Hemingway would soon become close and lifelong friends, but initially the soldier treated the journalist with amused curiosity, indulging his insistence on carrying arms and dressing in full combat uniform.

On 30 July, Lanham allocated him a jeep and a driver, Archie Pelkey, who would accompany him through numerous hair-raising escapades over the next five months. Hemingway stocked the jeep with road maps, a box of hand grenades, two rifles and a Thompson sub-machine gun, and had Zeiss binoculars permanently hung around his neck. North of Villedieu-les-Poêles he and Pelkey came upon an eighteenth-century chateau recently abandoned by its German occupiers who had left the wine cellar intact. He found bottles of Châteauneuf-du-Pape and Champagne of late nineteenth-century vintage and invited other journalists, including Ira Wolfert and Duke Shoop, to an impromptu evening in which the American liberators re-enacted the lifestyle of the French aristocracy, albeit with tinned rations.

The next day he drove with Pelkey into the village of Villedieu where rifle and sniper exchanges were still taking place between both sides. Without authorisation they became combat troops, with Hemingway hurling two grenades into a basement occupied by armed Germans. Six emerged and surrendered; others, apparently, died. We have no reason to doubt the authenticity of these events. Reuters correspondents offered reports on them, based on accounts by journalists and soldiers. Pelkey later insisted that he had witnessed first hand what others might dismiss as rumour or grandstanding.

Three days later Pelkey, Hemingway and Robert Capa navigated dirt tracks to get beyond the US front line. Capa wanted photographs of the Wehrmacht in action. Hemingway was turning himself into a soldier of the Seventh Cavalry style, at least as depicted in pulp fiction and films, and Pelkey seemed laconically content with his role as sidekick. Soon they were blasted off the road by shells and machine-gun fire. The most famous quote from the incident is of Hemingway berating Capa for 'wanting a photograph of America's greatest writer, dead'. All three men spent a day in ditches next to the road attempting to avoid bullets from machine guns and shrapnel from 88 mm shells. The Germans withdrew and the Americans survived, but despite the feelings of relief expressed by his companions Hemingway was determined to hurl himself once more into the vortex of the conflict.

Lanham recalled, for Baker, the vivid image of his friend standing on a street corner in a village north of Paris that was being defended ferociously by German snipers and machine gunners dug into the rubble of shelled buildings. He was holding a Thompson machine gun 'poised on the balls of his feet. Like a fighter. Like a great cat. Easy. Relaxed. Absorbed. Intent. Watchful' (Baker Collection, PUL).

During a brief respite at Mont St Michel, he met up with an officer of the OSS and asked if he could be introduced to members of the Maquis, the French Resistance, who were working alongside Allied troops, involving themselves in direct combat and providing information and intelligence. He claimed that he intended to write an article on how these guerrillas had established themselves as independent from the official Free French forces. He was lying about the article. Instead, he wanted to see if the OSS man could provide him with contacts via whom he would introduce himself to the underground groups. He knew that the Maquis were armed and sanctioned as combatants by the Allied military establishment but were not subject to anything resembling an official framework of command. They could do as they wished, and he too wanted to become an unaccountable combatant. Gary Cooper, playing Robert Jordan in the 1940 film adaptation of *For Whom the Bell Tolls*, had become the embodiment of the heroic rebel. Hemingway had been on the front line during firefights between Falangist and Nationalist forces in the Spanish War, but in France he wanted to close the gap between observation and active service and in Chartres in August he made contact the man who would enable him to fulfil his ambition. He had liaised with David Bruce when the latter was gathering intelligence in Havana for Donovan's Office of the Coordinator of Information, later to become the OSS, and Bruce was now a colonel in the latter and an intermediary between the Maquis and the US Army. The willingness of a member of the secret service to cooperate with a non-serving journalist testifies to Hemingway's effectiveness as an intelligence gatherer and as the Cuba-based cut-out against the FBI's attempts to stifle the growth and significance of the OSS. Bruce put him in touch with Resistance fighters in Rambouillet, a small town 30 miles west of Paris. Hemingway summoned Pelkey, travelled there by jeep and with no authorisation established himself as commander-in-chief of the Resistance fighters who effectively controlled the region. Bruce visited the town a few days after Hemingway's arrival and later reported on what he found, with astonishment.

> Ernest's bedroom was the nerve centre of these [intelligence] operations. There, in his shirt sleeves he gave audience to intelligence couriers, to refugees from Paris, to deserters from the German army, to local officials and to allcomers. (David Bruce, letter to unnamed war correspondent, JFK)

He was surrounded by men who obeyed his orders without question, most equipped with an abundance of arms: machine pistols taken from Germans, various rifles supplied by the Americans and ample numbers of hand grenades strapped to belts. By a weird coincidence, Irving Shaw, Mary's date in London when Hemingway first met her, arrived with a regular army unit after Hemingway had taken control of the town. He later informed Meyers that Hemingway was particularly concerned with supplying his new Maquis contingent with dynamite and fuses to disrupt the German retreat to Paris. Again, he seemed to be blending present-day reality with invention: in *For Whom the Bell Tolls* Jordan, the explosives expert, had worked behind enemy lines to disrupt the supply chain of Franco's forces.

David Bruce soon became Hemingway's buttress against figures in the regular army who complained about his apparent creation and command of a private militia. His later accounts carry some deadpan fellow-feeling, given that he too was an irregular, albeit one sanctioned by the high command, and he tells of how '"Red" Pelkey [...] carried an arsenal of weapons on his person' and became Hemingway's adjutant, and that within two days of their arrival in the town a 'truckload' of Resistance men were 'in attendance on Ernest [...] accepted his leadership without question and called him "Le Grand Capitaine" or sometimes "Le Chef"' (Bruce's letter, JFK).

We have no record of how regular soldiers felt about being overtaken by Hemingway in the advance towards Paris – he and his private brigade had occupied Rambouillet before the army – but his role as self-appointed military commander of the town certainly caused a good deal of rancour among the group of war correspondents who arrived next. Hemingway had taken over the only hotel as his headquarters and all of its rooms were in use as stores for arms and equipment or makeshift barracks for his devoted irregulars. Most reporters complained among themselves but Bruce Grant, a veteran Chicago newsman, held forth in the dining room and mocked the grandstanding 'General Hemingway' and his 'Maquis army'. The former, seated at the other side of the room, strode towards Grant in a seemingly calm, self-composed manner and then flattened him with a punch to the jaw.

It was a poorly kept secret, at least among senior officers, that General Jacques Leclerc, commander of the largest Free French armoured brigade, would enter Paris first. The city had not been abandoned. Units of German artillery were dug-in at key points on roads towards the centre and snipers were in place in the upper storeys of buildings overlooking the lengthy Haussmann-designed thoroughfares. Tanks were a necessity, as David Bruce explained to his friend, and Hemingway became even more determined not only to reach central Paris before Leclerc but to do so as the leader of a motley group of guerrillas who would enter the city without the protection of armour. Hemingway told Bruce that these Frenchmen – his new command – who had fought against their Nazi occupiers for four years had a natural right to liberate their capital. Bruce's opinion is unrecorded but he used his OSS rank to provide Hemingway and his men with transport, better firearms and authorisation to move towards Paris in their jeeps alongside the French armour.

On 25 August, Leclerc's column of tanks and other armoured vehicles crossed the Seine from the south, entered Paris and was swamped by cheering crowds, despite the fact that pockets of

German troops were still embedded in the upper floors of some buildings. According to several other war correspondents who had interviewed Parisian civilian observers (see S.L.A. Marshall's account), Hemingway and his men had reached the city centre 24 hours earlier and been involved in a firefight with German rearguard infantry around the Arc de Triomphe. Leclerc, according to Marshall, was led to a church door on which a handwritten notice was nailed: 'Property of Ernest Hemingway'. Several other witnesses later testified that on the morning of the 25th, before Leclerc crossed the Seine, Hemingway and several Maquis fighters had, with grenades and sub-machine guns, cleared Germans from an apartment building on the Bois de Boulogne.

He was certainly at the Ritz Hotel before the building was reached by French, British and US forces. In his memoir, *Slightly out of Focus* (1947), Robert Capa states that he arrived at the Ritz on the officially recorded evening of liberation, the 25th, and found Hemingway in the restaurant with Pelkey. Hemingway's occasional, Maquis, driver announced that yesterday 'Papa took good hotel. Plenty stuff in cellar'.

A curious consequence of these exploits was the, albeit brief, transformation of Hemingway from relentless falsifier to modest denier. For example, as he and his Maquis command approached Paris on 24 August, accompanying the vanguard of Leclerc's Sherman tanks, they came upon dug-in 88 mm artillery pieces in the grounds of Versailles, roughly ten miles from the centre of Paris. A brief artillery battle ensued and the German guns were knocked out. Hemingway led his men on foot towards the German emplacements while the Shermans battered them with 75 mm shells – an act of maniacal foolhardiness or heroism, depending on your opinion. In his report for *Collier's* he did not tell the truth, stating that when the exchange of shellfire began he ordered his men to dive for cover and joined them. The authentic version – with Hemingway leading the charge towards the German guns – is recorded in Bruce's JFK account. Bruce enjoyed the company of Hemingway, was fascinated by his recklessness, but he certainly did not idolise him and he showed no inclination to publish his recollections. He was a man of commendable integrity, later serving as US Ambassador to France and the United Kingdom, and there is no reason to doubt the veracity of his report.

Hemingway had lied persistently, about his seeing action with the Arditi in 1918 and about a number of his experiences in Spain, and he had habitually reformulated episodes from his past according to the image he wished to present. Now, he played down his role in these much more terrifying and reckless acts of heroism, sometimes to the point of making himself invisible. To Maxwell Perkins he said only that he 'entered Paris with the first troops' (15 October 1944) without mentioning that, against the rules for correspondents, he had carried arms and fought. For *Collier's* he stated that 'I took cover in the street fighting – the solidest cover available – and sometimes with someone covering the stairs behind me after we were in houses or the entrance to apartment houses' (*By Line*, p. 381). This was his account of the clearing of the apartments in the Bois de Boulogne which as Bruce, truthfully, reported he led, with a Thompson sub-machine gun and grenades. For the readers of *Collier's* he began his report on 25 August with: 'I had a funny choke in my throat and I had to clear my glasses [...] because there now, below us, gray and always beautiful, was spread the city I love best in all the world'. Suddenly the real Hemingway had managed to subdue his fantasist counterpart. It was indeed the city that forged him as a writer and the day after he celebrated the liberation at the Ritz he set out for Shakespeare and Co. Sylvia Beech was still there. They embraced, drank the wine he had brought and enjoyed an hour of quiet contentment.

On 7 September Hemingway, driven again by Pelkey, left Paris to join Lanham's 22nd Infantry Regiment. Lanham was moving towards the Belgian border and by 22 September the regiment had crossed into Germany and established itself in the small hillside village of Buchet. Hemingway, Lanham, the battlefield artist John Groth and a few of Lanham's senior officers settled in a farmhouse which, that evening, came under shellfire from German artillery. The first shell entered through one wall and departed through that opposite before exploding, and the next hit the exterior of the building without detonating. Lanham ordered his friend to put on his helmet. Hemingway ignored him and busied himself at the dining table with his steak and schnapps. A hoarse buzz gained in volume, signalling the approach of another warhead, and all but Lanham and Hemingway, who remained seated at the table, took cover on the floor or behind pieces of furniture. This shell missed the building and Hemingway went on to explain his somewhat capricious theory that if you can hear the shell in transit it is probably destined for somewhere else. The scene carries the air of a barroom shot directed by John Ford, with John Wayne maintaining a nonchalant unconcern as bullets fly past. Few if any treated Ford's films as anything more than skilfully executed fantasies but the story of that evening in the Buchet farmhouse is entirely authentic. Lanham found himself drawn into Hemingway's version of Russian roulette. As shells continued to explode outside he too removed his helmet, poured himself a schnapps and joined Hemingway in a quasi-philosophical debate on whether it was pointless to attempt to protect oneself from artillery bombardment by using furniture as shelter or lying flat. The night cemented a lifelong friendship between them.

Later commentators have sneered at his reports during this period, particularly 'War in the Siegfried Line' (*Collier's*, 18 November 1944), in which he gives a vivid account of how the 22nd Infantry had broken through Germany's most formidable defences. The substance of the report was provided by Lanham himself and by one Captain Blazzard, who had led several attacks. He had drafted the article, honestly, as made up of interviews with both men but editors at *Collier's* rewrote it in the first person so that Hemingway comes across as the front-line observer, directly involved in the action. He was there but he had been decent enough to allow the soldiers he respected to tell their own stories. If he was set on creating a myth for himself as the superman reporter, why did he not send an article to *Collier's* on the night in the Buchet farmhouse? It would have made an extraordinarily gripping true-life short story, involving a narrator and principal character who was a master of the genre. But he said nothing of it. We know of it only via Lanham's recollection, now in his Princeton archive, backed up by interviews given by Groth. Hemingway did not even refer to it in his regular letters to Mary.

At the end of September he returned to Paris and reoccupied rooms kept for him at the Ritz. He had arranged for Mary to join him there and she did, sleeping in his room, but their encounter soon became exceedingly bizarre. Another guest was Marlene Dietrich and Mary was perplexed. She was sleeping with a man she hardly knew, an individual who had proposed marriage to her when they first met, despite the fact that each of them was married to someone else, and he seemed intent on seducing the world's most glamorous film actress, often sharing a bottle of Champagne with her while she lay in the bath. Two days after Mary's arrival in Paris, Hemingway hosted a private dinner party for five of the 22nd Regiment's most senior officers. The only others present were Mary and Dietrich. The latter sang regularly for groups of Allied soldiers and often reprised her sexy role of *The Blue Angel* as a boost for morale. She did so at Hemingway's dinner party which encouraged the otherwise respectable battalion commanders to consume extraordinary amounts of the wine, brandy and vodka. After the guests had left, Hemingway accused Mary of treating his friends with disdain and she replied that she had dealt obligingly enough with 'drunks and slobs', several of whom had vomited in the bathroom, adding that 'they may be heroes in Germany but they stink, stink, stink here' (*HIW*, p. 131). He slapped her across her cheek with her hairbrush and she called him a 'poor fat featherheaded coward [...] [a] woman hitter'. The story of the evening was first told by Mary herself in her 1977 memoir. It might carry an air of retrospective contempt but the prevailing mood is confusion. These were their first weeks as a 'couple'. During the assault on Paris and when he served with the 22nd he had sent her daily letters averaging four pages in length and abundant with the kind of love-struck hyperbole one might expect of a teenager, but he had cautiously avoided any reference to his marriage with Martha. Mary was in a state of limbo, unclear of whether his passionate imprecations were born of the illicit nature of their affair or whether she was expected to take seriously his opening proposal of marriage in London. We can thus appreciate her uncertainty about how she was expected to behave on the evening of the party.

So far Hemingway's affair with Mary bore some resemblance to his previous exchanges of one partner for another: he would keep as much from his wife as possible until it seemed like fate had replaced her by someone else. Yet his disagreeable treatment of Mary in Paris was also symptomatic of displaced bitterness. During the months in which he saw action in 1944 he wrote not only to Mary but also to Martha and Edna. For the Gellhorns he is angry and distraught. From the Ritz, while he was flirting with Dietrich and humiliating Mary, he sent a letter to 'Dearest Mother', asking:

> Could [you] write me anything you know about Martha? Where she is? Her address? What she has been doing? I haven't heard from her since the end of June, or early July. I think the letter was written then. I got it in early August. I hear she came in on the Southern Landing [of France]. But have not heard. Nobody seems to know. If she has been in the Southern Landing it is fine and she will have had a wonderful time and a wonderful story.

He knew from Lanham and others that Martha had landed on D-Day, been arrested, released and then allowed to proceed through northern France, but he pretended to Edna – and probably to himself – that he did not, and he continued with his rewriting of her activities: 'as a result [of her landing in the south] she missed the great campaign and the taking of Paris and a truly wonderful page of history she was better fitted to handle than anyone'. He was in liberated Paris, was now with Mary, but he seemed to regret that Martha had not been able to cover him entering the city with his private militia. The letter is discursive, drifting, sometimes defensive, often apologetic. He tells Edna of his adventures with the RAF, indicating that his head injury in England was due to a plane crash and remonstrating against Martha for not spending enough time with him in the hospital. 'She was [...] coming back to the hospital [...] [but] next day she [had] forgotten [...] because she was busy'. Then he reflects on their life together:

> Everyone worked for her [...] we all helped every way we could and she had flashes of politeness but never any kindness. The hell with all that. She is lovely to you, for which I love her...] [But] Marty was just a bad joke that was played on me in the fall of 1936 and the point of the joke

was that I had to give up my children and 500 dollars a month for life to be the point of a bad joke. I used to laugh about it while we lived in that strange country where she was a close friend [...] She was gone by then. She loves to leave people. It is the bad scene she plays best[...] Martha is a mystery – How anyone could change so – or lie so – or does she just lie for expediency and is it all a lie? (21 September 1944, JFK)

He did not want to leave Martha but he could not cope with who she was. Mary was a manageable alternative and the anger spurred by his inability to deal with his wife emerged in his treatment of her replacement in the Ritz within days of his writing this letter to Edna.

If there are any doubts that Hemingway had come close to madness during these months then one only has to consider what happened two days before he wrote the letter. Martha arrived in Paris and sought him out at the Ritz. He asked her to take dinner with him the following night at a nearby restaurant. She agreed, and found that they would share a table with officers from Lanham's regiment, the same men who had dined with Hemingway and Mary, though at the time she knew nothing of this. He talked, as she put it, 'like a cobra' meaning that every sentence he uttered was strewn with obscenities, 'until the boys [officers] melted away with embarrassment'. Part of their unease was due to the spectacle of a man subjecting first his mistress and then his wife to a performance of thuggish coarseness. It was a rerun of the night with Mary but Martha treated his behaviour with cool indifference, except that, when leaving, she asked him for a divorce. He threatened her with violence but as she collected her coat a feeling of pity overruled anything resembling fear. Alcohol and obesity seemed to have immobilised him in his chair.

The following day she reported the night's events to Robert Capa, who told her that her husband's affair with Mary Welsh, in London, which Martha thought was a brief fling, had now become a louche variation on a ménage à trois, from which his wife was excluded. It was taking place at the Ritz and involved Mary and Marlene Dietrich. Martha thought he was joking but Capa instructed her to 'Telephone the hotel, ask for Mrs Monks [Mary's married name], if she answers ask for Mr Hemingway, and when you speak to him say you'd like to talk with Marlene Dietrich.' Martha followed his directions and it was not until her husband took the receiver that her voice was recognised, a moment followed by a tirade of abuse from Hemingway. Capa had come to regard Hemingway with contempt during the previous months. The photographer was himself prepared to endanger his life but he treated his associate's near suicidal behaviour as a kind of nihilistic egotism. Capa's prank was an act of revenge but it also confirmed for Martha that her husband was close to becoming an individual very different from the man she had thought she knew. The fact that he had written to her mother claiming to know nothing of her location and activities after their encounters in Paris shows him to be a figure who all but defies comprehension.

Two days after the phone call Hemingway set off with the officers he had invited to join Mary and Martha to rejoin the 22nd Regiment, but was recalled to Nancy on 3 October to face a military tribunal. He was arraigned to answer charges that he had flouted regulations governing the behaviour of war correspondents, specifically that he had, in Rambouillet, dressed as a colonel, taken up arms and assumed command of an assembly of unconscripted men. The details of the hearing, recorded in a transcript in the JFK archive, are hilarious. It was evident to all that the prosecuting officers were angry at being removed from active service to hear a case based on complaints by other journalists who resented Hemingway's audaciousness and, more significantly, his fame. Asked if he had had mines in his room Hemingway answered, obliquely, that he 'would greatly prefer not to have mines in my room', and throughout the exchange the accused deflected questions with a mixture of evasion and nuanced mockery, which seemed to amuse his prosecutors. It was found that there was no case to answer and Hemingway immediately rejoined Lanham's regiment. He would stay with Lanham and the 22nd for almost two months, until early December 1944, remaining on the front line during one of the most bloody and ferocious conflicts of the Allies' advance on Germany. Hürtgen Forest reminded Hemingway of his excursion with Hadley and friends from Paris into the wilder parts of western Germany in the 1920s, to fish for trout. Now, the Germans had made use of the unrecovered, primitive landscape as a deadly obstacle course. The hardwood and pine trees were closely packed and gaps between them were filled by undergrowth and bushes. Advancing infantry were obliged to cut their way through, noisily, and the Wehrmacht had built machine gun and artillery emplacements into clearings so that infantry would announce their arrival well before their actual appearance. During Hemingway's two months with the regiment it sustained 2,700 casualties, almost half its number, while advancing little more than six kilometres. Those involved renamed the Hürtgen Forest 'the Valley of Death'. Hemingway, throughout, became a strange combination of the man he wanted to be and the one he had invented. Lanham later reported that he saw Hemingway 'standing bolt upright watching the fight with intense interest. He was moving with the moving wave but I never saw him hit the ground. And this time there was no question that he was armed and using those arms' (Lanham, PUL). Lanham is transfixed by his friend's disregard for his own safety but he gives the impression also that Hemingway has become a near-supernatural figure. 'Men', he adds, 'were firing and advancing and stopping and firing', many dying and others struggling to get close enough to the German positions to shoot or throw grenades. But Hemingway, in Lanham's account, treats the machine-gun fire and exploding shells with disregard, strolling forward like he is taking a walk in the park while discharging rounds from his automatic rifle. He wrote to Mary: 'I was spooked by it [...] before it [the exchange of fire] started [...] But then yesterday and the day before it was just like a gift [...] I get the old feeling of immortality back I used to have when I was 19' (privately held letter published in Fuentes, p. 361). He had also told Mary of his equally heroic exploits with the elite Italian infantry against the Austrians at the close of World War I. His experiences in the 'Valley of Death' were horrific and real but it is bizarre, to say the least, that he should claim that they reignited memories of events that were pure invention.

On two occasions, when the 22nd was advancing beyond the Belgium border and during the Hürtgen battle, he and Lanham had exchanged intimate details of their lives, including their feelings about their families, their relationships and their experiences of warfare. It seemed to each that since they faced the imminent prospect of oblivion they should seize the opportunity to share memories that might die with them. Later, Lanham offered respectful accounts of how his friend's heroism in World War I had inspired him, without once suspecting that much of it was make-believe. Why would he doubt Hemingway's story of serving with the crack troops of the Arditi when what he had recently witnessed testified to a man whose courage was beyond question? Hemingway appeared to be, simultaneously, in two different worlds.

At the end of November Lanham ordered him to return to Paris. He was dizzy and suffering from a persistent ringing sensation in his ears, standard symptoms of shell-shock but in Hemingway's case compounded by a virus, including a fever and throat infection. He was, Lanham told him, unfit even to observe the battle let alone continue in his self-appointed role as maverick infantryman. Back at the Ritz he insulted Mary after a party attended by Jean Paul Sartre and Simone de Beauvoir – both of whom he treated with a mixture of disdain and indifference – and she entered a query in her diary: could she seriously consider a long-term relationship with someone so blind to the offence he caused to others, herself included? A doctor summoned by the hotel management reported that he appeared to be suffering from pneumonia. His symptoms worsened, but on 16 December when the Battle of the Bulge began he managed to secure a jeep and driver and set off the following day for Luxembourg where Lanham's group had joined the First American Army in an attempt to throw back the counter-offensive by Von Rundstedt's division, the final significant assault on the advancing Allies by German forces. Lanham found him in an even worse condition than when he had dispatched him to Paris weeks before – disorientated, perspiring and unsteady on his feet – and begged him to leave the front line. Hemingway refused but three days later, as if in a dream, he found himself sharing a Jeep with Lanham, and Martha, bouncing over rough ground between dug-in infantry units.

At one point a V2 rocket soared overhead towards London and Lanham remembers her taking notes in longhand, pausing only to lean forward and inform her husband that 'this is my article'. Hemingway, recalls Lanham, replied with some bruising monosyllables. The bitter atmosphere endured and segued into farce on New Year's Eve when almost all war correspondents were staying in adjacent hotels in the old city of Luxembourg. Bill Walton was drinking with Martha on the afternoon of 31 January and asked, jokingly, if she would care to dine with him that night, given that her marriage was, he had heard, in a precarious state. She laughed and agreed. Walton, later that afternoon, told Hemingway that he had a date with his wife, and asked if he would care to join them.

Few would dispute what actually took place during the rest of the evening but it is easy to misinterpret the nature of the events. Drink flowed and Hemingway and Martha continued to exchange unflattering comments on each other's intellectual abilities, liberally peppered with obscenities. Walton, tongue-in-cheek, upbraided Hemingway for addressing a woman in such a manner and the latter replied that he 'couldn't hunt an elephant with a bow and arrow'. The three of them returned to the hotel for more drinks and afterwards Martha went to her room. In the corridor Hemingway, stripped down to his vest and undershorts, placed a cleaner's bucket on his head, seized a mop and, using the latter as a blunt lance, charged Martha's door demanding that she allow him in. Was all of this, as most treat it, symptomatic of an incurably ailing relationship? Walton later reported that she shouted through the door, 'Go away, you drunk'. The unspoken subtext might have been, 'forever', were it not for Walton's recollection that her declaration was followed by laughter, which Hemingway joined.

Martha's appearance in Lanham's headquarters at the same time as her husband was not coincidental. She had found his location from other correspondents. The first night the three shared rations and a bottle of whisky, and according to Lanham the mood was equable and the barbed exchanges during the jeep ride the following day could be treated as a form of off-the-cuff gallows humour. Why bother being polite and affable when machine-gun fire or a shell might suddenly end the conversation for good? Similarly, on New Year's Eve all those involved could plausibly have been playing out a kind of farce-noir. Walton was not seriously attempting to seduce Martha – why would he invite her husband if he was? – and what happened between Hemingway and Martha might have been as much reckless misbehaviour as an expression of mutual contempt. They had, days earlier, witnessed ferocious acts of mechanised slaughter and to have become absorbed by their private concerns, let alone any notions of propriety, would have seemed ludicrously conceited. Was it the grotesque conclusion of a marriage or a shared evening of self-caricature by people who knew that their own preoccupations were insignificant compared with what was going on around them? Conclusive evidence that she had deliberately joined him at the Battle of the Bulge is provided in an unpublished letter sent by him a week earlier (5 December 1955, JFK) to an address provided either by Edna or another figure from whom he had sought information on her whereabouts: 'Just got your letter of the 28th Nov', he writes. 'It was bad luck I did not see you.' He does not mention Mary; rather, it is a plea for reconciliation. He confesses that he has subjected her to his 'worst of my worst bad time', and he acknowledges that she had 'written me what you wanted me to do, you wanted complete freedom of all sort' and not a 'daily periodical on where I, formerly we, was going'. This was a version of the exchange between them of four years earlier when he was attempting to arrive at an agreement on what exactly her degree of autonomy and freedom would involve – as far as he was concerned this was limitless. They were still arguing over what might happen between them, despite his secret acquisition of Mary as a fall-back.

Martha was tough, intellectually and verbally. She could give as good as she got and perhaps Luxembourg was a further enactment, albeit a perverse one, of what had drawn them together in the first place: they were versions of each other. He had insulted Mary continually over the previous months, but she had behaved as the poor woman scorned and sought to comfort in self-pity, unlike Martha.

A week later he returned to Paris and, as Walton recalled, 'sported' Mary as 'this cute little girl on his arm as he swept into the Ritz dining room'. Within a few days Lanham had joined him and presented his friend with two fully loaded Luger sidearms, in velvet cases, taken from senior German officers. After a night of heavy drinking Hemingway invited several servicemen and journalists back to Mary's room, discharged several shots into a framed photograph of Mary and her husband, which he had ceremonially removed from her luggage, and emptied the rest of the magazine into the en-suite toilet bowl, which collapsed and flooded the bathroom. Mary, distraught, burst into tears, fled from her room and begged Walton to allow her to spend the night on the couch in his. In the light of what happened in Hürtgen and Luxembourg one might suspect that Hemingway was, once more, conducting a compare and contrast exercise with his wife and his mistress. By anyone's standard's Martha was by far the more turbulent, stalwart woman but did this recommend her to Hemingway?

For the next two months his relationship with Mary was by parts fractious and uncertain. She did not know if he wanted her as his lover or if he had long-term commitment in mind. He had not, so far, even discussed her possible divorce from her husband or his from Martha.

In January 1945 he returned to Cuba and wrote to Edna (31 January 1945, JFK):

> No word from Martha but then her last letter was started on one day and finished 8 days later. Had written before left saying how thrilled she was I was coming over. One thrill more.
>
> Am very discouraged about the whole business.

He reassures her that royalties from *For Whom the Bell Tolls* and 'motion picture' advances will provide them with 'all the money we need to live on through 1945–46'.

To this day we cannot be certain if by 'we' and 'live on' he has in mind the prospect of remaining with and supporting Martha for at least the subsequent 12 months or if he envisages being able to offer her enough money to cover the separation. He adds that her

> Excuse of doing journalism in order to make needed money is not valid. Martha is doing exactly what she wants to do. There is no monetary necessity for it. She evidently thinks a wife has no duties at all of any kind to her husband; neither to ever to be with him and help him so he, also, can write; neither to take any responsibility or share in taking care of common property, not to help with any of our common interests.

It is a litany of complaints, but is he grumbling about the cause of their ongoing problems, which might be remedied, or explaining an irreversible breakdown? Not once does he indicate an imminent separation, let alone his involvement with someone else. In March 1945 he travelled to London and sought out Martha at the Dorchester. According to her interview with Kert 'though he had previously refused even to talk of divorce [...] he then came to say Yes, he would get the divorce in Cuba'. Aside from his agreement to arrange the divorce she leaves it unclear as to which of them wanted it. It was only much later, in another interview, that she affirmed that she wished to be rid of him. She was his most significant partner, the one who faced him down, challenged him and caused him to question himself, and there is no reason to believe that she did not enjoy their time together. A letter from her (13 August 1945, JFK) reveals that the possibility of a permanent break-up had over the summer mutated into a formality: 'A notice has come that my clothes are in customs; Mother will pick them up today.' She goes on to instruct him on what else should be shipped to her at the Dorchester Hotel, Park Lane, London, W1. There would only be one box, containing presents from her family 'papers, and typewriter'. It is 'scarcely a job for a healthy man' and she advises him to use one of the servants and send her the bill for packaging and postage. The temper of the letter is resigned and she closes with a regretful eulogy to what might have been:

My dear Bug,

I may not have been the best wife you ever had, but at any rate I am surely the least expensive, don't you think? That's some virtue. As for the rest, whatever I had a share in is yours (the ceiba tree because I found it and even when, at the beginning you said 'Well if this is where you live, I guess this is where you live'. I did know it was lovely – do you remember what a stinker the house was, fresh from the D'Orn's [the previous owners] and painted poison green? I give it to you as a wedding present and hope you are always happy there and that this marriage is everything you have been looking for and everything you needed. And I hope you go on writing wonderful books there, and if you do the Finca will one day become a national monument and tended by a grateful and admiring government. And meantime it also makes a fine place for Mousie to paint: I think often of the colors and the African view over the hills and the palm trees and I think he must be doing lovely things. It is a sorrow not to see Bumbi, not to see Mousie's work, not to hear Gigi: I really expect I will never see any of them again.

However, I think I have learned all there is to know about amputations; one has to learn all the time doesn't one? I never want to learn again; it seems to me a terribly enduring kind of knowledge.

Take care of yourself and good luck.

Love,

Mook

Only a resolute misanthrope would find insincerity here, and it goes some way to explain Hemingway's obsession with the ceiba tree, which throughout the 1950s would expand vastly and cover the entrance to the house. After Martha's departure he insisted, without explanation, that he alone should prune and trim it. One thus has to wonder why he conducted such a vile campaign of defamation against her during the subsequent years. He composed a letter of reply which he returned to and revised continually during the 12 months after he received hers. If the final version, dated 5 August 1946 (JFK), is anything to go by he could not quite make up his mind on which of these drafts would cause her the most pain. He opens with an accusation about her wartime activities which he would repeat to others many times during the 1950s. While he'd 'hand-carried the wounded' to safety, she'd ridden in 'captured jeeps', securing lifts by offering sex to drivers. Regarding her fiction, she is guilty of 'over-writing [which] comes from your always being your own heroine which, since you are not terribly sound about yourself makes your characters sooner or later quite silly unless someone corrects them'. Having warmed up on her as a war correspondent and novelist he turns his fully sharpened malice towards Martha as a woman. She is now an 'aging prima donna', a 'product of beauticians', her faded physical attractions all that remain of 'a career bulldozer' with a 'phony accent: much more phony each year'. He reflects, decently, that he 'won't put anything in about your physical make' and goes on to do precisely that, providing a meticulous account of the various devices she employed to postpone the effects of ageing: 'your thousands of rubbers, pots, pans, jars capsules, greased guns, mud packs, bust lifters, mustache removers, flat foot aids, pessories, or other aids to beauty. Congratulations on your thatched roof cottage in the country. Why don't you try thatching the roof with yourself?' He closes. 'Good night, Marty. Sleep well my beloved phony and pretentious bitch.' He did not post the copy of 5 August but that does not mean that it was not his final rehearsal for the one he did send. His reference to her 'thatched roof' might seem a somewhat cryptic, incongruous conclusion to the list of her 'aids to beauty', were it not for his use of the same image in a letter to Lanham a year later (November 1947) where he claims that he had only recently learned that she was Jewish, that she had denied any Judaic family links during their time together (both outright lies, she was not religious but had been open about her ethnic background to everyone), but that his suspicions had sometimes been raised by her abundance of pubic hair: 'thatch' as a description of the latter had been a rough vernacular common-place in American English since the 1930s. Generously, he goes on to state that had he known of her background when they'd first met, he'd still have married her, given that 'the Virgin Mary was Jewish'.

In the early 1950s the internationally renowned art historian and dealer, Bernard Berenson, became Hemingway's closest confidant. It was a strange friendship given that they never met, and Hemingway regularly entrusted to Berenson secrets and profound reflections. In one letter he advises Berenson that for him fiction writing and lying were indivisible: 'Writers of fiction are only super-liars who if they know enough and are disciplined can make their lies truer than the truth [...] That is all a fiction writer is' (14 October 1952). Despite knowing nothing of each other, beyond their public reputations, perhaps they intuited empathies; Berenson would later be exposed as a habitual fraudster.

Hemingway's letter to him of May 1953 (JFK) is largely an account of his relationship with Martha, blending artless candour with fabrication:

> I can say M. was the most ambitious girl I ever met that doesn't mean
> much because I have not met many ambitious girls as they frighten me
> and I dislike them [...] She loved politics and that nastiest of all things
> war and finally got to love even the trappings of it [...] I always like the

irresponsibility of war and the nomadic life and the fact that you do not have to think about your work because you may not have to go on and write it. But Martha got to like war as a means of making money; for its spurious glamour; and for the attention a beautiful girl receives when she moves around among 2 million men who have left their women.

Following his biased generalisations on her opportunism he begins to make things up, accusing her of persuading her friends in the military, by offering them sex, to steal jeeps so that she could witness, first hand, the horrible aftermath of battles in which, he, Hemingway, had fought, a more detailed version of the lies he'd told her about herself, in the letter to her of 1946: 'She was in at the death or the wiping up and the horrors of the places like Belsen etc. She probably made more tax free money writing about our dead [...] than any female author made since Harriet Beecher Stowe wrote Uncle Tom's Cabin.' She performed 'acts of useless valor in wartime London, flattering and seeking favours from the English upper classes, a worthless crowd' with whom she 'degenerated very much'. 'She was', he adds, 'not built for bed but few nice people are'. In his opinion Martha – like most educated middle-class women, 'nice people' – had a narrow vagina which made her sexually unresponsive. Respectfully he kept from Berenson the story – unconfirmed but spread by Hemingway – that she'd had an operation which expanded her vagina. This, or so he informed his son Gregory, his friend Gustavo Duran and several others, did not greatly improve their sex life. It felt, he reported, 'like coming into Penn Station'. Nor did he treat Berenson with a transcription of the poem 'To Martha Gellhorn's Vagina', which he wrote during their break-up and recited to the general amusement of GI troops before his return to Europe. It is as foul as the piece he did on Dorothy Parker almost 20 years earlier: in it he compares her newly expanded vagina with the neck of a hot water bottle.

He asks Berenson to 'Please never show her this [letter]', cautiously avoiding any request that his correspondent should keep it from anyone else.

CHAPTER 6

Secrets and Lies

Mary arrived at the Finca in early Mary 1945. Her husband had agreed to a divorce and Hemingway had spent most of April preparing his Havana estate for its new mistress. There is no evidence that either had read Daphne du Maurier's *Rebecca* (1938) or seen the 1940 film adaptation, but the parallels between this gothic tale and what happened at the Finca are unnerving. Hemingway demanded that his staff should refresh the place completely. Three gardeners, a houseboy, a chauffeur, a cook, a carpenter and utility builder and three maids worked beyond their designated roles to redecorate parts of the main house, clean the pool, kitchen and bathroom and restore the acres of vegetable pastures, lawns and orchards to something like the order of a domestic garden. He wanted Mary to see the house as a blank page, a place without a past, and his reasons were clear enough. Each of his previous marriages had involved, voluntarily or otherwise, a cleaning of the slate. When he and Pauline left France it was if they were casting off the decade he had spent with Hadley, mostly in Paris. Similarly when he exchanged Pauline for Martha he abandoned Key West for Cuba. But his plan to erase the preceding five years from the Finca failed. Hemingway's sons had perceived Martha less as a stepmother than as an elder sister, their escort to adulthood. She had treated them as equals, was indeed the first woman they had known who could match their father intellectually and in terms of the sheer strength of her will. During the clean-out they insisted that the furniture, pottery, light fittings and other items that she had brought into the house should remain; in her goodbye letter she had asked for no more than a few personal belongings to be sent to her in London. They accepted she was gone but saw their father's attempt to hide the fact she was there at all as furtive and self-deluding.

Hemingway wrote to Lanham (9 June 1945) that after a month in Havana Mary was content, was already on good terms with his sons and that he and she were enjoying enthusiastic sex – 55 times since her arrived in May, he added triumphantly. It was true that Jack, Gregory and Patrick were pleased enough that she appeared to make their father happy, but by July Mary's journal entries showed that the place unsettled her greatly. 'Nothing is mine', she wrote, 'the room belongs to Marty'. It is not clear exactly which room she is referring to but it is evident from other entries that she felt threatened by the almost ghostly presence of her predecessor. The bed, on which she and Hemingway performed, virtually twice a day according to him, was of a Spanish colonial design and purchased by Martha. Even the cats and the servants seemed to Mary somehow redolent of her, but worst of all was a framed photograph which hung on the wall in the dining room in which her expression seemed proprietary. Soon Mary and Hemingway had taken to exchanging letters on matters that might in spoken exchanges ignite bitterness or enmity. They would leave notes at agreed points and collect replies later during the same day. In October 1945 she wrote that she accepted that some remembrance of Martha, for his children, was understandable, but 'I cannot help but wonder or not [if] you kept pictures of Pauline around for the sake of your children when Marty was here' (October and November, 1945, Mary Hemingway Papers, JFK)

It is usually the case that hastily formed relationships begin to fray after a gradual awareness that reality does not correspond with eager anticipation. For Mary, however, the horrible nature her new commitment came within weeks of her arrival in Havana. In June/July 1945 she regularly entered statements in her private journal, such as: 'I'd be an idiot to stay here and marry Papa'; 'He puts a premium on bad manners, on violence, on killing [...] on toughness, on death'; 'I'd better go while the going is possible and can be without too much bitterness' (JFK). On 20 June Ernest drove her to the airport. She was to fly to Chicago to finalise her divorce from Noel Monks, but there is sufficient evidence from her diary that she would have taken the opportunity to contemplate going 'while the going is possible'. Hemingway crashed the car and she was confined to hospital for almost a month after he arranged for a plastic surgeon to repair her severely damaged cheek. During the rest of the summer he was solicitous, and listened to her suggestions for redecorating parts of the house, a means of making her presence felt. In September she made the journey to Chicago and returned on 1 October, with the divorce finalised. Seven days later she wrote of how his critics are 'right about him and women – he wants them like Indian girls – completely obedient and sexually loose'. She went on to complain about his autocratic manner, particularly regarding expenses, and this observation would become a constant refrain in the journal thereafter: the subtext being that whereas Hadley, Pauline and Martha could rely on family, wealth or their careers as a get-out mechanism, she was effectively his servant. 'I wish the hell I were out of here and running my own household and my own life – with no dictatorship [...] this is like being a high priced whore.' For the next 15 years, until Hemingway's mental instability had drained him of outright vindictiveness, Mary continued to fluctuate between periods of weary contentment and desperation. Her marriage had begun in much the same way that it would continue. On their wedding day, 13 March 1946, she wrote: 'He came out with only a few of the nasty ironic resentfulness he usually accords me [...] [He is] so phony, so cheap, so chickenshit [...] making jokes as we went to the Florida [hotel] about "Have a glass of hemlock" [...] Tonight he has made the concession of allowing me to sleep alone – which is a relief' (Mary Hemingway's journal, 13 March 1946, JFK). Two weeks later she wrote to Connie Bessie of her 'simple-minded happiness' (27 March 1946, JFK). Bessie was not a close friend and it is almost certain that she was lying. Rarely did she confide to anyone her true feelings for Hemingway.

During a visit to the Finca in October 1949 Lanham found himself confronted by a man who appeared utterly different from the one with whom he'd forged such a close attachment over the previous five years. He confessed to his surprise at 'Mary's increasing submission to Ernest's exhibitionism. Ernest would sit around the pool or at meals and brag about his sexual conquests (real or imagined), and Mary, covering her embarrassment, would act as though she was proud of his manliness.' He was speaking to Kert almost 30 years later (Kert, p. 444), and while his account was honest enough he thought it appropriate to edit out the exact nature of his friend's disclosed 'sexual conquests' and their effect on Mary. These included at least two Havana-based prostitutes who he paid for sex when Mary was visiting her family. One should probably regard Lanham's exercise in censorship as commendable given that Mary was still alive when he spoke to Kert in 1980.

On 15 October 1944 Hemingway had written to Max Perkins, from Paris:

> Have stuff for a wonderful book. Have been with every action of the Div since just before the break through and if have good luck a little longer want to lay off and get to work on the book. Want to write novel – not war book. It should have the sea and the air and the ground in it.

As usual he was allowing the words on the page to overtake anything resembling logic or coherence. He did want to write a 'war book' but one that transcended documentary realism, and blended armed conflict with sublime, epic notions of the 'sea' 'air' and 'ground'. He added that he 'Had the sea ready to write when I came over', meaning that he could rewrite his farcical U-boat excursions as heroic naval conflicts. 'Then that time with the R.A.F.': the 'air' narrative would draw on his pre-D-Day RAF flights, imaginatively embroidered. The 'ground' was, when he wrote the letter, an unfolding narrative. 'Now have the rest of this', he adds: he was about to join Lanham and his troops in the Hürtgen Forest.

His attempt to transplant war stories into an all-encompassing reflection on the nature of existence occupied his time, exclusively, from 1945 until 1948. The vast, sprawling manuscript – at one point coming to almost 2,000 pages – would be returned to during the 1950s. Several times he thought about making savage cuts and sending it to Scribner's, but the manuscript would only go into print, generously and misleadingly edited, after his death.

The book became such an unmanageable enterprise because Hemingway decided that there was some symbolic affinity between nature, particularly the sea, at its most untameable and merciless and the horrors of mechanised warfare. It was an interesting aesthetic conceit but problems emerged when he attempted to shoe-horn his own firsthand experiences of World War II, based almost exclusively on what happened in France and Germany, into the world of the main character, Thomas Hudson, who, for the duration of the novel, spends his time largely in the islands of the Caribbean, mostly Bimini and Cuba. Hudson experiences the European conflict first by proxy, losing his eldest son in action, and then appears to exact some revenge by pursuing and killing members of a shipwrecked U-boat crew who had massacred the population of a village. Hemingway transfers to Cuba a combination of his *Pilar* submarine-hunting fantasy and his now regular claim to have shot more than a hundred German troops.

Hemingway's dedication to the book during the three years following his marriage to Mary was relentless, and in other circumstances might in some way have stabilised his moods. He had produced nothing substantial since *For Whom the Bell Tolls* (1940) and now he could at least commit himself to an objective. In fact, as the manuscript became more and more formless in design and elastic in content its author began to spiral away from a clear sense of who he was and the effects that his unstable personality had on others, Mary in particular.

The question of whether the book was the cause of his erratic behaviour or if the former was a reflection of an unsettled state of mind will remain a matter for speculation. What cannot be denied is that the two were inextricably linked. *Islands in the Stream*, as it would eventually be known, was a literary Leviathan, doomed from its outset because Hemingway was attempting to address funda-mental existential issues via an act of hubris. As the words spread restlessly across the pages Hemingway himself became a manic fabulist, seemingly unable to stop telling stories about his own past, virtually all of them untrue.

Three months after he married Mary, Hemingway invited Slim Hawks to the Finca. He had become a friend of Slim's husband

Howard when the latter had directed the film adaptation of *To Have and Have Not* (1944). They had co-written the screenplay and the verbatim inclusion of Hemingway's original, sharp dialogue had ensured the film's success as a romantic thriller. Slim was a Hollywood beauty who her host enchanted with tales of his heroic exploits in World War I, in Spain and in World War II while Mary looked on, aghast. She too had been treated to these stories but now she listened as he enthralled Slim but included exaggerations that caused her to question everything she knew, or thought she knew, about his alleged past. By late summer 1946 Mary was confirmed as pregnant and, for a while, Hemingway seemed to relent from his apparent campaign of loathing against her. When they were travelling to Ketchum, Idaho, on 19 August she suffered acute stomach pains. Her fallopian tubes had burst, the baby was stillborn and she came close to losing her life.

On the operating table Mary lost so much blood that the surgeon informed Hemingway that she was a hopeless case; a major transfusion would cause her to die from shock. Hemingway ordered the physician to open her vein and transfuse blood. Without quite laying a hand on him, Hemingway thrust his 16-stone frame to within inches of the surgeon and insisted that he follow his instructions. Against all odds, she sustained signs of life and Hemingway – now directing procedure from the door of the operating theatre – demanded that the obstetrician must operate to remove the ruptured fallopian tube. In his quintessentially brutish manner Hemingway had ensured Mary's survival.

For other couples, such an experience of loss, trauma and, from Hemingway, rough kindness, might have ameliorated their troubles, but once they returned to Cuba he exchanged his attachment to Mary for the macabre relationship between who he thought he was and his expanding fictional universe.

Visitors to the Finca were treated to even more histrionic accounts of his experiences in Italy, Spain, France and Germany. The same hardcore of associates and admirers had endured from the years when Martha was mistress of the house: notably Tommy Shevlin, Winston Guest, Father Andres, Herrera, Dunabeitia and Menocal. In 1943 the FBI agent Raymond Leddy had summed them up as 'a clique of celebrity-minded hero worshippers' who took Hemingway's stories and opinions 'as gospel'. But now even the most credulous of his devoted fans and friends found it hard to believe his claims that he had personally dispatched more than 150 members of the Wehrmacht and SS using a machine gun that he had carried from the beaches of Normandy to the Hürtgen Forest. It is not uncommon for writers to use novels as a means of projecting themselves into versions of their existence they prefer to those they have to put up with, but few, if any, told stories to their friends and acquaintances just as fantastic as the ones unfolding on the page.

What we know of this period comes from third-party recollections and Mary's journals, which she revised after Hemingway's death. A single exception is a three-page note from him to her, an example of his half of the silent dialogue they conducted via scripts left on pieces of furniture. It is undated but the JFK archivists believe that it comes from late 1945 or early 1946. Its subject seems to be an altercation from the night before, involving a sequence of misunderstandings resulting in him waking her, apparently for sex, after an evening out in Havana, and a subsequent argument on what each of them had said: 'In Paris [...] one time I told you [...] I couldn't stand to be called a liar. Now we can take that as a defect that has to be cured and why should I mind being called a liar?' What began as his objection to her personal affront against him segues into a reflection on the nature of lying; specifically on how, for him, lying and writing fiction are interdependent. The note is the closest that we have to his statement of principle, a unique account of who he is and why he writes:

> All writers are liars I know; all invention is a lie, imagination is a lie. I lie all the time in that way. We romanticise; we make up. None of our lives are as we think nor as we have convinced ourselves they are. Call me a liar on that basis and it is ok though would still rather you didn't. Because I know about that. All fiction is just lies made truer than the truth; or as near as we can get to that.

He is particularly angered by her having questioned him, in private, on what he had said to an audience of guests some days earlier regarding his wartime experiences:

Did I see them? Yes or No. I would die before I would give you anything but what I believed to be the absolute truth.

Did I go up the hill? What was there? Was I really there? (Bristles begin to come up along the back). Am I sure I was there?

(You've been really angry in your time. Insert your own sensation). You lie. You weren't there. (Explosion)

Apparently, none of his guests was willing to question him on his recollections let alone suggest he was making things up, with the exception it seems, of his wife, which brings to mind a grotesque re-enactment of Hans Christian Anderson's 'The Emperor's New Clothes', with Mary standing in for the inquisitive child. He responds by appearing to conduct an interrogative exchange with himself, disputing his recollections and then subtly shifting towards a kind of existential dialogue; asking himself specific questions while expressing doubts about his, or by implication anyone's, grasp of indisputable certainty. It is a fascinating document, in which he goes on to present himself, to his wife, as the alchemist of untruth, even asking her if she is certain of her recollections; if not, how can she question his?

There is no record of her response, but soon afterwards he was obliged to deal with enquiries from beyond the Finca and Havana from individuals who were at once fascinated and perturbed by the relationship between Hemingway's fiction and his life, beginning with Lillian Ross and Malcolm Cowley.

He had agreed to speak to Ross for her forthcoming profile of him for the *New Yorker*. Ross interviewed him in Sun Valley in December 1947 and listened to the same stories about his childhood and war experiences as those with which had captivated his guests at the Finca. After she returned to New York he telegraphed her and demanded she send him the first draft so that he could check her references to events, dates and locations. In truth, he had suddenly realised that the world he had created for himself might raise suspicions when published as biographical fact, particularly for those readers whose lives had intersected with his.

He had known Cowley in Paris during the 1920s and initially the latter planned to do an article for *Life* on Hemingway in France. But as they talked, this time in Havana in March 1948, Hemingway's garrulous candour caused Cowley to suggest a longer piece, a 10,000-word biography on his life from Oak Park to the present day. Hemingway agreed and this time his fabrications were even more extraordinary than those he had provided for Ross. He presented himself as a noir version of Huck Finn, an anarchistic teenager whose armed escapades around Walloon Lake meant that he had to go on the run from the local sheriff's officers. It was a gross exaggeration of the largely inconsequential events that followed his shooting of the heron. In Italy, his heroism earned him five medals for gallantry and bravery and during World War II he had, he told Cowley, gone from the D-Day Normandy landings, via Paris, to Hürtgenwald in the same jeep with a Browning heavy machine gun welded to the chassis, pausing only at Rambouillet to take command of the local Maquis and rid the town of all German snipers. Much of this was authentic but he had grossly distorted the narrative, much as a novelist would refine the untidy raw material of actuality into a seamlessly engrossing story. Commanding *Pilar*, he informed Cowley, he had brought one U-boat to the surface and depth-charged others. He suspected that his recklessness was due to the Cheyenne Indian blood in his family, an inheritance that might also have instilled in one of his sisters an incestuous love for him.

Cowley never questioned these accounts but his assiduous attention to detail caused Hemingway to regret his exaggerations. For example, on 20 March 1948 (JFK) Cowley wrote to Michael Lerner asking for his version of Hemingway's legendary fight with Willard Saunders in 1935: 'How did the fight happen to be arranged and how big was Saunders, and was there much of a crowd and how did the fight come out[?]' He explains to Lerner that 'The trouble with getting stories [...] from Ernest is that he has a streak of modesty a mile wide – he'll start a story but if it is something in which he played a leading part, he'll stop before the climax, so I have to learn the rest of the story elsewhere.' One has to commend Cowley for his artless gullibility, given that what he interprets as 'mile wide' modesty was in truth Hemingway's tendency to lose coherence during stories he made up as he went along.

As Cowley's enthusiasm for firsthand supplements to Hemingway's fables grew so the author became more and more anxious about what exactly he had told him. On 11 July 1948 (JFK) Cowley wrote to him: 'Look, I'm still in a state of profound confusion about your wounds in Italy, after reading pretty near everything that was published about them. Here's the story that I've got pieced together'. He asks about: (1) the 'Bad wound' received two weeks before his nineteenth birthday; (2) 'more serious wounds suffered before Armistice Day'; (3) 'The night on the Piave, when you carried the guy up the ditch away from the river, with the searchlight playing on you; that might have been when you got machine gunned. At the time you were a lieutenant in the Arditi'; (4) 'In several hospitals – number unspecified, but with dates overlapping – for some time after the Armistice'. 'That's how I piece the stories together, but Bill Smith [whom he had just interviewed, without informing Hemingway] thinks that (1) and (3) were the same occasion and that you carried the guy back after the trench mortar burst.'

Cowley treats the contradictions and inconsistencies as the consequence of poor reporting by others and regards Hemingway as the ultimate source of probity. Instead of responding to Cowley's enquiries on the particulars of his life – Cowley had also interviewed people from Oak Park on his alleged career as a star footballer – Hemingway first demanded that he should preface the article with a statement that he, Hemingway, had not asked to read it in advance of publication (he had) and a request, by Cowley on his behalf, that anyone who doubted the authenticity of the events reported should provide inviolable proof of their inaccuracy (9 June 1948, privately held by the Cowley estate).

It was bizarre gesture and he recognised it as such once Cowley had returned to New York. He sent him a letter each day, on every occasion picking up on particulars of Cowley's draft and requesting that points should either be left out or revised in a manner that rendered them vague or ambiguous. The exercise was both revealing and ludicrous. He was not correcting Cowley's errors but, rather belatedly, attempting to cover up his homespun web of fantasies. To what can we attribute his shifts between lying and neurotic concealment? It was almost eight years since he had published a novel. His 'big book', as he called it, was out of control, becoming ever more sprawling and directionless. There appears to be a causal relationship between his loss of security regarding a work of fiction that seemed likely to go on endlessly and his tendency to visit upon those closest to him – including Cowley – utterly perverse variations on the truth. His lies about who he was amounted to a desperate attempt to compensate for his sense of being hopelessly adrift between a novel that was going nowhere and an equally unaccomplished existence involving little more than fishing, drinking and behaving appallingly towards his wife.

In June 1948, John Huston visited the Hemingways in Havana, bringing with him the screenwriter and author Peter Viertel. Viertel had lived in Dresden until 1928 when, aged six, he moved with his parents to Santa Monica. A Jewish family, they did not return to Germany, but Viertel remained fluent in German, a skill which led to his recruitment as an OSS intelligence officer during World War II. Following Viertel's departure from Havana Hemingway wrote to him suggesting that they co-author a story, which might then form the basis for a screenplay. It would involve, he explained, the crew of a disabled U-boat who would take over the Cayo Lobos lighthouse and then be pursued by the outnumbered crewmen from the *Pilar*; all of this was, he explained, based on fact. He argued that Viertel's knowledge of how German servicemen behaved – their mindset, tactics and moral compass – would add vital authenticity to the piece. The story would eventually become part of *Islands in the Stream* and it seems likely that his attempt to persuade Viertel to cooperate was a further symptom of his being caught between a novel he seemed unable to finish and a fanatical impulse to tell ever more bizarre stories to anyone who would listen to them, or in Viertel's case collaborate in their telling. During the summer he bombarded Viertel with letters in an attempt to bring him on board, even offering to pay his fare so that they could work on the piece together in Europe during a trip that he and Mary planned to take later that year. In one of these he informed Viertel, for no apparent reason, of how during the Spanish Civil War he had spent a whole night, along with others from the Communist-backed militia, executing prisoners of war. He had, he added, pulled the trigger so many times that blisters had formed on his index finger (Hemingway to Viertel, 28 June 1948, JFK). It was a lie but Hemingway believed it to be the truth. In Baker's archive of interviews deposited in Princeton the biographer records a conversation with Buck Lanham in which the latter recalls that Hemingway, at around the same time he wrote the letter to Viertel, told him of how he had been appointed as official executioner for the Republicans, shooting captured Moors who were regarded as the most inhumanly brutal of the Falangist troops and therefore deemed to merit no mercy. Lanham did not state to Baker that he disbelieved Hemingway but he was puzzled by the question of why he had not before shared this with him before during their seemingly exhaustive exchanges on their respective pasts.

Viertel was unsettled by the mood of desperation that informed Hemingway's appeals. He turned him down, politely citing an abundance of other commitments. Since his return to Havana after the war Hemingway was constantly in search of someone sufficiently credulous to steady his accounts of his past. Guests at the Finca were useful but transient gulls, and he needed a more steadfast figure whose belief in his stories would provide them with a ring of truth. Only this could have motivated the dangerous games of fabrication and candour he played with Ross and Cowley. He subjected Mary to a similar exercise, as is evident in his note to her on the nature of indisputable fact, and Viertel was another of his attempted recruits. He was looking for a real-world fulcrum, a listener who would lend confidence and energy to the story he was telling on the page – a *roman-à-clef* based on his experiences of war that was growing daily, page by page, and going nowhere. Such an individual would soon become part of his life and enable him to produce a very different novel. She was called Adriana Ivancich and they would meet in December 1948.

On 7 September he and Mary boarded the *Jagiello* in Havana, for Italy. For the first month they would tour various parts of the north that formed the topography for his increasingly fluid notion of what he had experienced in 1918 and the early 1920s, including his injury and various acts of heroism, and his journeys through the region as a journalist, though he said nothing of Agnes von Kurowsky. Such calls from the past inspired him to treat Mary to other accounts of the early life of Ernest Hemingway. He presented his mother as by parts narcissistic and demonic, in one instance spending so much on clothes that Clarence was brought close to insolvency and forced to sack his secretary. Mercifully, Mary never learned that his father neither employed a secretary nor that Grace's private income made her largely self-sufficient. In October they took rooms in the Gritti Palace, which as its name indicates was once the palatial residence of the Doge of Venice, Andrea Gritti. Converted into a hotel in the nineteenth century it was the most luxurious and expensive in the city. As a surprise he drove Mary to Fossalta di Piave, just outside Venice. Here, he announced, he had suffered injuries while defending the city against Austrian forces which were launching an attack across the marshes and chose to augment the well-known story of his wartime experiences with one that carried an air of romantic gallantry – defending Venice. It seems clear that he was once more looking to shore up the inchoate autobiographical 'big book'. If, as he was beginning to suspect, the latter would outlive him, uncompleted, then at least his wife's version of his private memoir would be regarded as a dependable alternative.

On 1 November the Hemingways moved into an inn on the remote island of Torcello, a place with a rich medieval past but now reduced to a population of a few hundred. After a few days Mary set off on a tour of sites of historical interest while Hemingway settled down to write an article on the delights of Cuba and the Caribbean for *Holiday* magazine, which provided him with a welcome release from the prospect of returning to the novel. This ended at the beginning of December when he exchanged letters with Charles Scribner. While the latter was, as usual, diplomatic regarding Hemingway's long-standing promise of a war novel his hints caused the author to launch into a rant against the dismal quality of books about the recent conflict that seemed to be appearing every month. He was particularly infuriated by Ira Wolfert's *An Act of Love* (1948) which dealt with the war from D-Day onwards – Wolfert had also been a news correspondent in London, France and Germany and had shared with Hemingway and others rare wines from the

Normandy chateau recently abandoned by the Germans. Norman
Mailer, previously unheard of, was becoming the magnet for critical
attention with his *The Naked and the Dead* (1948). Worst of all were
Irwin Shaw's *The Young Lions* (1948), which contained unflattering
portraits of Hemingway, Mary and his brother Leicester, and Martha
Gellhorn's *The Wine of Astonishment* (1948). To Mary he claimed that
Martha had plagiarised his ongoing novel before it was finished,
stealing stories he had told her about Hürtgenwald. He knew that
everyone from readers of his *Collier's* wartime reports to members of
the American literary establishment were perplexed by his absence
from this new sub-genre. No other journalist had been so
conspicuously involved in front-line conflict, but neither Scribner
nor Hemingway himself had advertised a forthcoming book. Within
days something, or rather someone, would offer a solution to this
dilemma. On 13 December he went to lunch in Venice with the
Duke of Aosta and the aristocrat's distant relative, the 18-year-old
Adriana Ivancich. He had met her, briefly, two days before when
duck shooting at the Franchetti estate north of Venice. Now he had
the opportunity to talk with her.

Hemingway left Italy on 30 April 1949, little more than four
months after his first encounter with Adriana. He took with him
early drafts of a novel that was utterly different from his stalled 'big
book' on the war, the earth, the sea and the air. It tells the story of a
few weeks in the life of one Colonel Cantwell, actually the final few
weeks, spent in Venice largely in the company of Renata, or as the
Colonel and the narrator more often refer to her, 'the girl'. Aside
from the change of name Renata is an almost exact replica of
Adriana and her experiences with the Colonel are Hemingway's
fantasised version of his four months in Venice. For three-quarters
of the novel Cantwell and the girl have effectively exorcised the
rest of the world. Writers, barmen, gondoliers and his driver dwell
on the margins but exist mainly as necessary props; like the city,
they are the setting for an intimate dialogue, sometimes
punctuated by sex.

Hemingway was rarely alone with Adriana in Venice and they did
not have sex. Yet the novel reflects a rather chilling exercise in wish-
fulfilment. He talked with her in restaurants, in bars, walked with her

beside the canals, behaving as if the people who often accompanied them did not exist. Adriana's mother, Dora, was often present, along with her brother Gianfranco, and of course Mary, but he pretended that they weren't, monopolising conversations with her and making demonstrable attempts to exclude everyone else from their private exchanges. Within a week of meeting her he began to enact on the page what he yearned for in life.

Between the 1948–9 visit and his completion of the novel in September 1950 he and Mary returned to Europe once more, in March 1950. This second trip was prompted entirely by his desire to see Adriana again. He was revising the final draft and he was desperate for another injection of her presence. In Paris he strolled with her along the banks of the Seine and declared that he loved her and wished to marry her, despite the conspicuous problem of their age difference and his marriage to someone else. Three decades later she recalls his repeated pleas that they should become a couple. 'Every male that passes by' he told her, 'would come over and ask to marry you if he knew you and were not stupid … I am not stupid … I love you!' (*La Torre Bianca*, pp. 101–2). Some have questioned the veracity of Adriana's account but there is another document, written at the time, which lends it plausibility. Hemingway and Adriana had begun the draft of a short story called 'The Horse' when they were in Venice and had returned to it the day after he had taken her to the races at Auteuil outside Paris. The completed draft, ten pages long, is in the JFK archive. Called 'The Great Black Horse' it is made up of typed passages by Hemingway and longhand sections in crude English from Adriana. The eponymous black horse is her – her hair was silkily black – and her suitor is one 'Hemingstein'. The following is a typical piece of dialogue.

> 'Let's go to Cuba, horse', he said
> 'Good', said the horse.
> 'I like the Ritz but I think Cuba is better for us both,' …
> 'Will you tell me, can a man love a black horse truly and be faithful?'
> 'Yes – truly.'
> 'Alright – let us go … to Cuba.'
> 'Good – An excellent program … I love you, horse.'
> 'Oh – Please say it again. (JFK Archive)

As an example of rhapsodic bestiality the story is probably unique, but its weirdness prefigures aspects of the novel that would soon go into print. On his return to Havana he wrote to Charles Scribner that *Across the River and into the Trees* was autobiographical and declared that his love for Adriana/Renata was profound and enduring. (Hemingway to Scribner, 22 March, 1950, PUL)

The majority of reviewers treated it with a mixture of astonishment and contempt, but a common feature of their evaluations is that no one appeared willing or able to describe the exact nature of Hemingway's failure. The book was, they implied, self-evidently bad, and no specification of its dreadfulness was required. The most frequently quoted review is the exception to the consensus by John O'Hara in the *New York Times*, a masterpiece of unfocussed hyperbole. Hemingway, he declared, was as great a writer as Shakespeare; no one since 1616 had come close to equalling his achievements. Hemingway was as angered by O'Hara – who offered no justification for his ludicrous claims – as he was by his detractors.

Across the River and Into the Trees is Hemingway's most extraordinary, embarrassing and revealing piece of work. The reviewers knew nothing of its origins in Hemingway's private universe of fantasy and self-delusion. If they had, they would probably have been no more sympathetic, but for us such knowledge offers an insight into an author for whom the boundaries between fiction and actuality had ceased to exist.

During his exchanges with Renata, Colonel Cantwell repeats versions of the accounts of heroism in Italy, Spain, France and Germany that Hemingway had visited upon his friends and guests, Mary included. Renata, however, is adoringly credulous, as was Adriana when he contrived to separate her from others in Venice and offer her intimate confidences.

The worst parts of the novel are the descriptions of sex. The passage in chapter 13 where he brings her to a climax using his war-damaged hand is by parts revolting and hilarious. It is a dreadful piece of prose, compounded by our knowledge that he had distilled his desire for a real 18-year-old into a fictional moment of satisfaction. Writing can project and displace all manner of unresolved longings but this is the closest that anyone has come to literary masturbation. It has a magnificent scion in *Lolita*, but while Nabokov's novel forces us, with caustic, razor-sharp elegance, to confront our worst inclinations, Hemingway's is sad and pitiable.

Adriana was undoubtedly very attractive: tall, slim, with shining black hair and the kind of eloquently aquiline nose that would seem, particularly to an American, the quintessence of European high breeding. Her family were of the minor nobility who had lived in the Venice region since the Renaissance and were now graciously penurious. Their estate had been poorly managed since the end of the nineteenth century and its decline was assisted by Allied bombers; the house was barely habitable.

She enabled Hemingway to revisit the Europe he had known between the wars, a continent that was once the foundation for American culture and politics but now its despondent junior partner. The Colonel never ceases to inform 'the girl' of his supreme heroism in rescuing Europe from the horrors of Fascism. She, in return, adores him, and as they have sex – three times in the novel – she pleads with him not to be 'too rough'.

It is interesting that after he returned to Havana from Venice with the early drafts of the novel he began to make regular visits to a young prostitute in the city whom he referred to only as 'Xenophobia'. He had made use of local prostitutes before but Xenophobia became something more than his paid sex-worker. She was, he hinted in letters to friends – male friends – something of an apprentice at her trade. To Charles Scribner he described her as 'beautiful' and gave particular attention to her age. At '17' she was, he remarked, very precocious (Hemingway to Scribner, 1 October 1949, PUL). She was a year younger than Adriana and there were many other, rather eerie, parallels. In a letter to Viertel (29 September 1949, privately held) he confessed that he had written only 708 words that day, as a consequence of spending most of it with Xenophobia and downing several bottles of Roederer Brut Champagne. His reference to postponing the progress of the book containing Adriana to spend more time with her debauched counterpart is not inconsequential. He informed Scribner (4 October 1949, PUL) of what had recently occurred when Mary returned from a visit to her family. In her absence he had invited Xenophobia to the Finca on several occasions, and Roberto Herrera, his general assistant, had photographed her in several different dresses, indicating that she had been a regular visitor to the house. It was a curious thing to do, even more so when he was deliberately careless in attempts to hide the pictures from Mary. She found them and he was, he proudly informed Scribner, in the 'doghouse'. There seems no obvious motive for his behaviour, which served only to distress his wife and, for him, guarantee his deserved retribution. Mary was aware of his ongoing obsession with Adriana and this goes some way to explain his disclosure of Xenophobia to her, by design disguised as accident. He was creating a double-life which he yoked together for the novel. Renata is able to switch roles from Cantwell's angelic muse to an erotic temptress. Xenophobia, the beautiful, sexually extrovert teenager, enters the novel to make up for what Adriana had denied its author.

In early May 1950, after he and Mary had returned from Europe, he arranged a lunch for his wife and friends on *Pilar*. He arrived with Xenophobia on his arm, without explanation or apology. Mary was aghast and confused. She knew of Xenophobia, had seen pictures of the girl in her own home, and now her husband seemed to be subjecting her to an arbitrary form of torture. She wrote to him, leaving the letter in the Finca: 'Both privately and in public you have insulted me and my dignity as a human being and a woman devoted to you and have debased my pride in you in front of friends' (6 May 1950, JFK). She threatened to leave him, and while Xenophobia was the apparent subject of her anger it is clear from the rest of the letter that she is as much distressed by something she feels difficult to describe. The cause of her despair is as much Hemingway's desperate fixation for Adriana as his flaunting of Xenophobia.

In Paris, Hemingway had invited Adriana and her mother Dora to visit Havana and stay at the Finca. He hoped they would arrive while he was still revising the proofs for *Across the River and Into the Trees*. He had already decided that the novel would close with the Colonel's death; throughout, he was resigned to his fate as a heart attack waiting to happen. It was a matter of how long the dialogue between Cantwell and Renata would persist. By its nature it seems perpetual and unceasing, with only the intervention of external factors – specifically Cantwell's illness – capable of bringing it to a close. Had Adriana and Dora arrived in early summer, as Hemingway hoped, or if Scribner had not demanded corrected galley proofs by the end of July, the novel would not have been particularly different but it would certainly have been much longer. The central, most substantial, part is made up exclusively of Cantwell and Renata in each other's company but there is nothing resembling a narrative.

All we have are his seemingly inexhaustible stories of his past and her declarations of love for him, which were inspired by the effect of Adriana on Hemingway. A few further months of her physical presence – this time in his home environment – would have postponed Cantwell's death by a commensurate number of new chapters, each as directionless as those that went into print.

After leaving Le Havre in March 1950, Hemingway began to bombard Adriana with letters declaring his love for her and representing her as the one figure on whom he depended as a writer and a thinker. Often he used the third person, as if they were part of a narrative beyond the transient world. 'She is', he put it, 'his reference point, his direction [...] the northern point on his compass' (Hemingway to Adriana, 9 August 1950, University of Texas, Harry Ransom Archive). She replied, affectionately if hesitantly – at least if we take her later account of these matters on trust – but even though their correspondence continued he was robbed of the intimacy of the exchanges that fuelled those between Renata and Cantwell. The effect of her absence was bizarre, in that he displaced the confessional outpourings to which he had subjected Adriana/Renata on to others, particularly those he thought would give credence to the imaginings he claimed as facts.

In New York, shortly after his return from Europe, he ran into Chink Dorman-Smith, who had now changed his name to Dorman O'Gowan. Chink had served with distinction as a senior officer in the British Army in World War II, at one point attaining the rank of major general, but he was a reckless, unorthodox commander and as a consequence earned the wrath of his superior officers, notably Montgomery. His military career was stymied and by the time he met Hemingway he was campaigning in the US for a united Ireland while at home in his estate in Co Cavan using his military experience to train Irish Republican Army recruits for their forthcoming campaign in the north: 'The overall intention is to get the British out of our last Six Counties and having taken Belfast, to march on Dublin and purge that of the neo-Georgian takers' (Dorman-Smith to Hemingway, 15 May 1950, JFK).

Chink embodied memories of World War I and the early 1920s and his ongoing activities as an armed rebel inspired Hemingway to invent yet another outrageous and fictitious story of his own. As he was revising the novel, Chink became a proxy for Adriana; one of many. He informed Chink that he had personally dispatched 122 combatants in the Spanish Civil War, and was the captain of one of only four of the 11 'Q Ships' to survive the campaign against U-boats in World War II in the Caribbean. *Pilar*, he reported, remained afloat but of the nine-man crew just four were still alive; the rest being lost during firefights with U-boats. He had seen active service against the Japanese in China before Pearl Harbor, flown as a co-pilot with RAF missions over Europe and been given full officer status by Lanham with the 22nd Regiment during the advance into Germany. Hence, he added, he had been recommended, twice, for the Distinguished Service Cross, a medal that could be awarded only to soldiers on active service (Hemingway to O'Gowan, 2 May 1950; Hemingway to O'Gowan, 21 May, 10 July, 15 July and 8 August 1950, PUL). In normal circumstances these reinventions would have been reprehensible – Chink had shown great courage in both world wars and Hemingway's stories amounted to an insult – but they carried a pretext which, while not excusing them, discloses in Hemingway, once more, an inclination to blur the difference between writing novels and making things up. When they met in New York, Hemingway told his old friend about his ongoing 'war novel' based on the experiences of Colonel Cantwell. He was coy about the exact nature of his character but during the spring and summer of 1950 he sent Chink extracts from the draft along with his letters about his own exploits. Chink did not comment on this after Hemingway's death but the letters he wrote to him during 1950–1 after the book was published (archived in JFK) are fascinating. It is evident that he treated the novel as autofiction, with Hemingway speaking of his own experiences through Cantwell. Convinced that Hemingway had turned his life into a novel Chink also treated Renata, the 'girl', as real, while not, politely, asking about who she really was. In short, Chink had believed Hemingway's lies about himself and, after being allowed to see the parallels with Cantwell's exploits in extracts from the draft, treated the novel as the truth.

During the same period, while he was in Havana and Adriana in Venice, he repeated this exercise in falsehood for Buck Lanham. He gave a vivid account of charging across mountainous territory against Austrian forces in World War I, as part of the elite Arditi regiment in the Italian Army (Hemingway to Lanham, 15 April 1950), elaborating on a story he'd already told him during the war. They had faced mortal danger together and seen comrades die on numerous occasions: why would he lie to a friend and confidant with whom he'd demonstrated his foolhardy courage? Arthur Mizener, an academic, and Robert Cantwell, a fellow novelist, were treated to vivid descriptions of his injuries in World War I, including the long-term effects of being shot twice through the scrotum (Mizener, 12 May 1950) and 22 times in virtually all parts of his body (Cantwell, 25 August 1950). During 1949 he had subjected Charles Scribner to ludicrous accounts of how his Cheyenne grandmother was the genetic source of his inclination towards quixotic brutality. This last involved his story of how he had demanded from a captured 'snotty SS kraut' information on escape routes for German forces. When the prisoner refused to disclose this he 'shot him three times in the belly [...] when he went down on his knees shot him on the topside so that his brains came out of his mouth or I guess it was his nose' (Hemingway to Scribner, 27 August 1949). Once more, he seemed to believe his own fabrications, having told a similar version of the story in a letter to Archie MacLeish less than a year earlier. This time he stated that the 'young Kraut' was 17 years old, though he does not say how he obtained this information; German army identification tags did not contain the date of birth. MacLeish was so appalled at Hemingway's apparent delight in his description of what amounted to a war crime he insisted that the letter should be sealed for 50 years when he bequeathed his papers to the Library of Congress. Further evidence that he regarded his falsehoods as the truth can be found in letters he sent at the same time in which he becomes a present-day manifestation of the brutal combatant of the two world wars. He wrote to Senator Joe McCarthy demanding that he should come to Cuba where Hemingway would 'knock you on your ass' (8 May 1950) and he promised to end any ambition for the Vatican harboured by Cardinal Francis Spellman with violence (28 July 1950). Spellman, the most senior Catholic cleric in the US, was a vehement supporter of McCarthy's anti-Communist purge. He explained in cold clinical terms, for Ingrid Bergman, that he intended to murder Roberto Rosselini (20 June 1950) who had had a much publicised affair with the actress. There is no sense that these are exaggerated threats. He was convinced that he could do all of these things and remain unaccountable, rather like the Hemingway who had visited fury on his Austrian and German foes.

Hemingway had, throughout his life, lied about who he was and what he'd done, but as he wrote *Across the River and Into the Trees* he constantly adjusted the extravagance of his inventions according to the presence and absence of Adriana. When she was not there he visited his fantasies upon a number of his closest friends and he did so to sustain the equally fabulous stories told by Cantwell to Renata. When Adriana arrived in Cuba in October 1950 his letters to friends and acquaintances in which he told quite ludicrous lies about his past ceased abruptly. The novel was finished but the woman who had inspired it was back. He no longer felt the need to pretend in his letters to be a version of Cantwell. Instead he could bring his inventions back to life, irrespective of the effects on those who witnessed this bizarre ritual. Somewhere in his overwrought psyche he had cultivated the illusion that his private universe – the Finca, Havana and the atmosphere of living in the Caribbean – would cause Adriana to see him anew, that she would suddenly submit to his love-struck entreaties. He acted much as he had in Venice and Paris, treating her almost as his prized possession, despite the presence of her mother and his wife. Herrera, others who worked at the house, crewmen from *Pilar*, local friends, occasional guests and, during Christmas and New Year, his three sons were bewildered, sometimes horrified, by his behaviour. On one occasion, during a day fishing on *Pilar*, Adriana cut her finger quite severely on the dorsal fin of a tuna. Hemingway came immediately to her rescue but instead of using antiseptic and a bandage from the first-aid kit, he knelt before her and sucked the blood from the wound. The faintly macabre spectacle of the overweight 51-year-old behaving as if transformed into a medieval knight was greeted by others aboard, Mary included, with embarrassed silence. At the Floridita Hotel the barmen were struck by Adriana's beauty and perplexed by the sight of Hemingway leading her to a reserved table while ignoring all others in the room, including those who had arrived with this 'couple'. He seemed unsteady because he now refused to wear his glasses in public, fearing that press cameramen might have been alerted to what was happening – rumours had already spread in Venice regarding the inspiration for Renata – and he did not wish to appear too old. He had previously treated regulars and visitors to the Floridita public bar to various acts of grandstanding and showman-ship, challenging allcomers to drinking contests and sharing stories of his past, in wars and anecdotes involving figures such as Joyce, Picasso, Pound and Scott Fitzgerald. Now he was inexplicably modest and retiring, reserving himself for the company of this young Italian. He had also earned a questionable reputation in the Floridita bar as the loudest and most enduringly odorous 'farter' on the island, a practice he suspended during Adriana's stay.

One night he enacted a ceremony of unifying Adriana with her fictional counterpart, presenting her with a signed copy of the novel and directing her to passages he assumed would provoke recognition. She read them and declared that she found the character Renata preposterous. She was, declared Adriana, 'boring' and she could not understand how on the one hand a girl who is 'lovely and from a good family and goes to Mass' would also 'drink all day like a sponge and be in bed [with Cantwell] at the hotel'. She added, 'A girl like that does not exist.' Many years later Mario Menocal Junior recalled that Adriana, ran

> rings around him [...] she managed to make it quite clear that she knew exactly what was going on, and that it seemed as ludicrous to her as it did to the rest of us [...] I find it hard to condone both Ernest's fawning self-deceiving attitude and Adriana's acceptance of his attentions [...] Perhaps if Adriana had had the slightest spark of feeling for him as a man, they would have had an affair [...] She

accepted his hospitality, kindness, generosity towards herself and her family – and gave nothing in return. (Menocal to Kert, 9 February 1979; Menocal to Meyers 18 April 1983)

Menocal's presentation of Hemingway as a captive of his own delusions, oblivious to the impressions and activities of others, Adriana in particular, seems generous, given subsequent disclosures. Rene Villareal wrote a memoir, assisted by his son Raul, on his years as a handyman at the Finca and claimed that he – at the time a tall, handsome, dark-skinned young man with a well-sculpted physique – held more appeal for the Venetian aristocrat than her lumbering, drunken host and suitor. He tells vividly and convincingly of how he and Adriana conducted an affair, meeting at night near the pool after Hemingway had retired to his room to argue noisily with Mary, before collapsing. Villareal was an old man when he told of this and was certainly not motivated by the likelihood of any financial remit, and as we shall see Adriana was temperamentally predisposed towards stealth and duplicity. In Baker's unpublished Princeton papers there is a handwritten note from Mary to Adriana's brother Gianfranco who had arrived at the Finca shortly after his sister and their mother.

Bunney-Binney-

It is curious how it does not get any better – the hurting and the longing in the bones and blood and skin and eyes and ears and nose. Sometimes, hurting strong, I ask myself 'Was it worth this – that joy, this misery?' And the answer is always 'yes', *Dearest Huomino*. (PUL)

Baker did not refer to this in his biography and added his own notation: 'Not to be read by scholars until after Mary Hemingway's death'. Unless Mary had composed it as a fabrication to seek long-term vengeance against her husband we must assume that she had entered into an extra-marital relationship with Gianfranco as a more immediate means of satisfying her bitterness against him. His obsession with Adriana seems to have blinded Hemingway to the bizarre sex comedy being conducted at the Finca by those he regarded as his audience.

Adriana and her mother were installed at the 'White Tower' annex, designed, ironically, by Mary, but two days into the New Year

Dora decided that they would move to a hotel in Havana. They would leave the island on 7 February and during the interim all involved maintained a polite sociability.

The story of Adriana's horrified response to his readings of passages from the novel evoking the sexual magnetism between Cantwell and Renata is unquestioned by biographers largely because it is her own, told in her memoir, *La Torre Bianca* (1980), and repeated in an interview with Kert three years later. For the latter she also presents herself as oblivious to Hemingway's fantasies and innocent of the charge that she might have encouraged them. She also insists that after she and Dora left the White Tower – the *Torre Bianca* of her book – she was so appalled by his behaviour that she discouraged further communications between them, despite his frequent entreaties. As her unpublished letters demonstrate, however, she was as compulsive a liar as Hemingway.

On 21 March 1950 (JFK) she wrote, addressing him as 'Hemingstein – Papa – Adam [...] Prince of Greece [...] Great man who just left Europe':

> It is seven hours since your boat ran away from me – and I have to say it makes me sad [...] I would have so many things to say that I prefer to skip them all – you understand – don't you? Let's forget about 'literature and poetry' and come to a simple description of what happened afterwards.

She continues in this teasingly enigmatic manner, telling him, 'Papa',

> I am sorry [...] but I can't stop writing tonight. I will mail [you] letters one by one each day [...] You know all young people have many many good and bad things in themselves. But they don't realise which one they and why they have them – And if it comes from God or the Devil.

She then drifts into verse-form.

> Papa – you know how to look at
> People ...
> Look at me
> At me ... Papa
> Forget my name
> I would love it –

It is the last favour I am asking
you (– until next time of, of course! –)
A Kiss
Adriana

Much of the novel involves dialogue between Cantwell and Renata, and while we cannot be certain of how well Hemingway recalled his exchanges with Adriana it is clear enough that her letters served him well as an aide memoire. The Colonel and the girl usually prepare for their sexual encounters with suggestively nuanced exchanges, such as:

'Oh please let's not talk'
'Is it right?'
'You know.'
'You're sure?'
'Oh please not talk. Please ...'
'You are making the discovery, I am only the
unknown country ... ' (chapter 11)

From her first letters to him in 1949 she adopted a habit of addressing him directly using inverted commas to enhance the impression of spoken immediacy.

'Your voice from Cuba ... Oh Papa ... '
'Sometimes I think it has been better I didn't talk to you ... but sometimes I think it would have been nice ... '

'Remember my long dream?'

'I am thinking about it, in these days. It was too important and clear a dream not to mean something'. (Adriana to Hemingway, 21 June 1950, JFK)

Her creepily erotic declarations are placed in inverted commas, leaving gaps for her anticipations of his replies, which he provided in the novel.

When preparing the first draft Hemingway began corresponding with the New York poet and critic Harvey Breit. They were certainly not close friends and there is no record of them ever having met, and one must assume from their exchanges that Hemingway's single motive was to communicate with someone who could not know if he was telling the truth or making things up.

On 14 August 1950 (JFK), shortly after the book came out, he thanks him for a decent review, complains that others have accused him of failing to 'understand soldiers nor how they talk', and then:

> There aren't any such girls as Renata (and I hope she's sleeping well in Venice tonight). There never was any such girls as Brett Ashley, Catherine Barkley, Miss Marie, nor the bitch in the short Happy Life, nor the nice woman in the Snows, nor the girl in Sea Charge, nor the girl in Hills Like [White] Elephants, Nor Trudy Bolton in Fathers and Sons.

He is offering what amounts to a perverse confession, in that Breit had no reason to suspect that all of these fictitious characters were based on women who had played a significant role in Hemingway's life. He is, in effect, disclosing these secrets to himself, a gesture made all the more bizarre by his simultaneous denial of them.

Two months later he disavows rumours that had been circulating in New York:

> I'll tell you a funny story. Maybe I told it to you before. In Venice there is a girl who is a nice child but has two defects; she makes up stories; like Little Girls fantasies and she makes them up in such detail that part of them always sticks. I have never written her a letter in my life but all last summer on the Lido she told the story about how I wrote her every day etc. (6 October 1950, JFK)

The girl in Venice who did not exist now takes the form of a teenaged fantasist, about whom he seems to know a great deal, and he assumes, correctly, that Breit has heard something of a recent radio broadcast by the Hollywood gossip columnist Louella Parsons, who suggested that Renata was inspired by his infatuation with an aristocratic teenager in Venice: 'Lolly Parsons goes on the air with this hot poop' he writes:

> Nobody in Venice buys them [the girl's stories] but all the tourists, movie people, producers etc take them for the Gods truth and the Axis Fantasist – Selznick – Louella Parsons enters the action.

> Well to shorten it: this girl now has had a book written about her by me; we had a wonderful time in Paris raceing [*sic*] where we won millions.

He began writing to Breit as if he were entering his thoughts and recollections in a diary. He could say what he liked and deal with the truth or make-believe unaccountably, but when other voices started to offer Breit accounts that differed radically from Hemingway's he became slightly unhinged, to the extent that he was no longer able to make sense of what he was putting on the page. He tells Breit of his war service in Italy and France, gross exaggerations included. *Plus ça change*, it seems, except that when we scrutinise these stories closely we find them almost identical to the ones Cantwell told to Renata.

It is almost as though the composite hallucination of Adriana as he wanted her to be and Renata as her extrapolation had finally taken its toll on his mental stability. 'In the meantime', he comments in the same letter, 'I love a good straight, beautiful girl in Venice to die of it', which is incomprehensible enough, but it is followed by a passage utterly devoid of coherence, or even a recognisable subject:

> So take over, Gentleman. The problem is quite simple, as I explained, and you can see the various hills quite clearly from here [...] They are fighting throughout the perimeter and our sectors are no worse than any others. They just seem worse sometimes because they are ours.

There is no record of what Breit made of this.

On 25 October 1950 (JFK) he wrote to Evelyn Waugh, who had produced an enthusiastic review, and once again it seems as though Cantwell has stepped out of the novel. Hemingway gives firsthand accounts of his front-line experiences in France and Germany, some based on fact and some fictitious, and his friends from the first war, Count Greppi and the Duke of Bronte, crop up once more. He repeats, in gruesome detail, how he had dispatched wounded soldiers during the advance to Paris, an almost exact replica of the tale Cantwell told to Renata and the letters he wrote to Scribner and MacLeish. He had, he assured Waugh, 'served as an irregular Colonel'. Of Italy, 'it is all quite complicated – one has to invent from what one knows', and his knowledge of the city of Venice, and its manifestation in the book, Renata included, comes from 'when I was a boy there' in 1919. Five days earlier he had written to 'Mr Tom', Mary's father, who had also heard Parson's broadcast:

> The origin of the Parson's libel is the young sister of friends [...] who makes up fantasies. Like little girl fairy tales; not knowing what damage they can do and, by her complete egotism and love of attention and publicity [...] I have never written her a letter in my life; nor has she been in Cuba; ever. (20 October 1950, JFK)

She had not been 'in Cuba', yet, but neither Parsons nor anyone else said that she had and the fact that Adriana and her mother were due to arrive six days after Hemingway dispatched the letter provides further evidence that he was no longer certain of whether he was affirming the truth or denying accusations. Cyril Connolly had implied, in print, that there was an unsavoury air of frustrated middle-aged craving about the novel and Hemingway's letter to Connolly (21 September 1950 JFK) shows him, as Cantwell, at his most exuberantly unbalanced. He ascribes most of Connolly's churlishness to cowardice, due to his own deliberate avoidance of military service: 'I was both sorry and proud about you not being in the war. But now I am ashamed of you and your lack of knowledge and of courage.' He goes on to recall how in London in 1944 Connolly had seated 'his mistress apart at a table' while he entertained his true constituency, a 'group of hardy homo-sexuals'. He is, in Hemingway's opinion, 'an afterbirth', 'a well nourished abortion; actually an over-nourished abortion', one which had apparently survived to become 'lamentable since birth with the snobbery of the ill-born, your grossness, gluttony and basic cheapness'. He closes, memorably, with a promise that 'if there is a corage [*sic*] shortage where you live [...] I will send you a nice bit of rope and tie the knot myself, so that you will be comfortable, and let us all hope that you will have a good erection when you swing.'

Hemingway was equally enraged when, three months after this letter, James Jones' novel on the war in the Pacific, *From Here To Eternity*, shot to the top of the bestseller list, leaving *Across the River* in its wake. Jones had witnessed the raid on Pearl Harbor, seen active service in Guadalcanal and been invalided out after being wounded by Japanese mortar fire. This parallel with Hemingway's own experience in Italy caused him to become deranged. Scribner was Jones' publisher and when Charles asked his established star writer to do a promotional article or even a cover blurb Hemingway answered that Jones was a coward, a 'psycho' whose novel 'will do great damage to our country', admitting that he could bring himself to read only a few pages of it: 'I do not have to eat an entire bowl of scabs to know they are scabs; nor suck a boil to know it is a boil [...] If you give [Jones] a literary tea you might ask him to drain a bucket of snot and then suck the piss out of a dead nigger's ear' (4 May 1951, JFK). Be assured that this is the most becoming passage in his colourful diatribe.

Western culture has humoured writerly peculiarity for more than two millennia. From the Greek notion of inspiration or 'enthusiasm' as the engine for literary invention, through the Renaissance concept of *furor poeticus* and Romantic celebrations of natural association, to Freud's theory of the wounded subconscious, writers have been portrayed as endearingly odd; not dangerous to themselves or others but rather as the strange, creative branch of the human family. Irrespective of one's opinion on these concepts of artists as acceptably unsound – and most seem to me to be ludicrous – we should be clear that each of them treats artistic lunacy as a figurative concept; writers aren't *really* mad, just idiosyncratically significant. Hemingway, in *Across the River and Into the Trees*, causes us to revise this formula. The novel is a literary work in its own right but it is also a symptom of a man whose world has become a melange of his writing and his perception of who he was. He *had* gone mad.

Across the River and Into the Trees owes its unfortunate existence to Adriana but by disappearing she also played a significant, albeit unintentional, part in his brief return to sanity, in the genesis of what would be his final novel to go into print before his death, the one that most see as earning him the Nobel Prize in Literature. *The Old Man and the Sea* is unlike anything he had written before. It is the story of an aged Cuban fisherman, Santiago, attempting to dispel his 'salao', a cursed period in which he has caught nothing. The narrative, such as it is, focuses on his struggle with a giant marlin, a battle between man and nature, or so critics devoted to symbolism proclaimed. Certainly Hemingway used his knowledge of sport angling and the lives of local commercial fishermen to reinforce Santiago's story with naturalistic detail. But aside from that, the book was his first attempt to draw a line between the words on the page and the world – variously loathed, exaggerated and escaped from – of Ernest Hemingway.

He began the first draft within days of Adriana and Dora's move from the Finca and completed it six weeks later on 17 February. Mary had accompanied the Ivancichs on their journey from Havana to Florida and once she returned he started to read her passages from the manuscript. She declared it beautiful, but one has to question her objectivity given that she had heaped equally unqualified acclaim on everything he had shown her. More significantly, once he started to write the book he underwent a character transformation: he began to treat his wife with kindness and respect. Three months before, just as the Ivancichs were due to land in Cuba, he had, at a Finca dinner party, called Mary a 'camp follower' and 'scavenger'. For those present he seemed to be preparing a case for her replacement at the 'camp' by a new arrival. One night when his wife danced with him he hurled a glass of wine at the wall, and throughout the period of the Ivancich's stay he openly insulted her. Once, when she had prepared dinner for their guests, he put his plate of food on the floor, indicating that it was suitable only for the cats. Mary does not record in her journal anything resembling an outright apology let alone an indication of remorse, but as he drafted his new novel he ceased to mention Adriana to his friends and he appeared to expect his wife to collude in this wilful erasure of the recent past. She did so. She had tolerated his erratic, often abusive behaviour since their first encounter in London seven years earlier, and she would put up with his increasingly alarming acts and states of mind until he killed himself ten years later.

From the early months of 1951 he had drawn Mary towards him as a protective blanket and the early drafts of *The Old Man and the Sea* served a similar purpose, a strategy of camouflage and obfuscation. He was frightened because he felt surrounded by figures seemingly determined to question his lifelong testimony as to who he really was and what he had done.

In 1951 the anxieties prompted by Ross and Cowley had increased considerably. Three men – Carlos Baker, Charles Fenton and Philip Young, all academics in prestigious US universities – were writing books about him, and each wanted to venture beyond a critical evaluation of his writing towards a biographical portrait. On 21 February 1951 (Stanford archive) he wrote a bizarre letter to Baker, opening with an enquiry. Had Baker received an advance from a 'publisher'? If so, he, Hemingway, would enable him to pay it back, with interest, if he closed down the project. He went on to explain why he didn't want a critical biography. He had no wish to offer the reading public details of his father's suicide, his affair with Pauline, his abandonment of Hadley, and his later problems with Pauline, particularly her demands, as a Catholic, that they practise coitus interruptus rather than conventional methods of contraception. Baker was dumfounded, given that he had never posed questions on these matters and had no previous knowledge of them. To his credit he did not mention this in his eventual biography, but more significantly we should note that when Hemingway wrote the letter he was spending virtually every hour of his waking existence working on a novel that, for the first time, would involve nothing of the world and experiences of Ernest Hemingway. His mother, Grace, died on 28 June 1951 and three months after that Pauline succumbed to a combination of blocked arteries and hypertension and expired in the emergency ward in St Vincent Hospital, Los Angeles. In a letter of 6 March 1952 he tells of a single year in which he had found it difficult to retain his 'peace of mind'. Over 12 months he had lost his 'first grandson in Berlin' where Jack 'was stationed as Captain of Infantry', his mother and his former wife, and had learned of 'the death of my last old friend in Africa, and my very dear friend and publisher Charles Scribner', plus the serious illness of his 'father-in-law with cancer' and 'the suicide of the maid servant of this house'.

This might be treated as a melancholic disclosure to a close friend were it not for the unsettling fact that the letter was to Philip Young, one of the three academics who were intent on advancing their careers as literary biographers of the most controversial American writer of the era. By the mid-1950s Carlos Baker had become his authorised biographer in all but name, but in the early years of the decade Hemingway found himself continually dismayed and infuriated by the activities of Young and Fenton. He grew to regard each with contempt, mainly because of Young's preoccupation with psychoanalysis and Fenton's activities as an amateur private investigator; in 1951, shortly after the death of Grace, the latter followed Cowley's example and spent time in Oak Park attempting to track down and interview members of Hemingway's family and people who knew him during his youth. It thus seems bizarre that after berating Young at length for attempting to discern in his work some neurotic condition, he volunteers, unprompted and without ever having met him, a version of the 'talking cure'.

He wrote to Charles Scribner Junior: 'the wave of remembering has finally risen so that it has broken over the jetty that I built to protect the roadstead of my heart and I have the full sorrow of Pauline's death with all the harbor scum of what caused it' (2 October 1951). This mixture of sorrow and guilt was a close replica of his feelings for his mother. Eighteen months before she died he was receiving reports from his sister Madelaine that Grace could no longer recognise her, and while conscious and clinically alive she was effectively absent from the world. He wrote to Scribner: 'I hate her guts and she hates mine. She forced my father to suicide' (27 August 1949). Days after her death he informed Baker that the news of it took him back to his happy home life in Oak Park 'before everything went to hell', without giving details of the cause or nature of the subsequent catastrophe.

He did not attend Grace's funeral, but ten months after her death he revisited Oak Park in a piece of short fiction that would appear after his death as 'The Last Good Country'. It is based on the episode when he shot the protected heron and was obliged to flee wardens and take refuge with friends of the family on the shore of the Walloon Lake. In the story he embellished the largely innocuous truth of his adolescent adventure by turning himself into a criminal fugitive, Nick, forced to go into hiding with his sister Littless. They seem on the verge of an incestuous relationship but the story remains incomplete. Equally uncertain is Nick's relationship with his mother, who appears at first to sympathise with him. But like all of his later unpublished fiction irresolution is the keynote. He began the story only months after Fenton's arrival in Oak Park to conduct investigations into his past. In his letters to Fenton during 1951 and

1952 he resembles a police suspect responding to interrogations. On 18 June 1952 (JFK) he states that he 'had a wonderful novel to write about Oak Park' but that 'he would never do it because I did not want to hurt living people'. His bizarre relationship with the truth, lies and fiction is further complicated by the fact that 'The Last Good Country' is a near exact replica of a story he told to Ross more than a year earlier, assuring her that it was an authentic example of his teenaged recklessness.

Next, for Fenton, he gives a brief remorseful history of his early career as a writer in Paris. He begins: 'I wrote some short stories about actual things and two of them hurt people.' One of these was, without doubt, 'Mrs and Mrs Elliot' (1924), originally entitled 'Mrs and Mrs Smith', the name of the couple, Olive and Chad Smith, whose attempts and tragic failure to have a child he cruelly satirises (see Chapter 2). He adds, 'I felt bad about it', which could not be further from the truth; rather he had mocked and insulted Chad Smith after the latter wrote to ask why he had done such a horrible thing. This can hardly be treated as an act of remorse given that Fenton knew nothing of the biographical aspect of the story.

Hemingway then launches into a lengthy defence of his treatment of Harold Loeb in *The Sun Also Rises*:

> if I used actual people I used only those for whom I had completely lost respect [...] The man [Loeb, whom he does not name] who identifies himself as Cohn in the Sun Also Rises once said to me, 'But why did you make me cry all the time?' I said, 'Listen, if that is you then the narrator must be me. Do you think that I had my prick shot off or that if you and I had ever had a fight I would not have knocked the shit out of you? We boxed often enough so you know that. And I'll tell you a secret: you do cry an awful lot for a man.'

Fenton had some half-formed theories on the novel's groundings in actual events and people but he had not made specific enquiries; Loeb would not mention his portrayal as Cohn until his 1959 memoir. Again, it appears that Hemingway is rerunning his exchanges with Breit, talking to himself, at once admitting to and defending transgressions that his correspondent had never dreamt of. *The Old Man and the Sea* was his only piece of pure fiction; no one in it resembled either Ernest Hemingway or individuals he'd known.

Simultaneously, he was conducting dialogues with individuals who seemed, to him, determined to separate fact from invention in their sense of who he was and what he had done. The two activities were interdependent. Convincing his biographers that the lies he told them of his past were true gave him space to write a book that was, for the first and last time in his career, undiluted fiction.

The novel is short. *Life* magazine found enough space to publish it in one issue before it came out in hardback in early September 1952. Early reviews were largely ecstatic in their praise and some commentators have since treated its reception as an exaggerated gasp of relief by the literary establishment. *Across the River and Into the Trees* was unspeakably bad but the great man had demonstrated that he was not in irreversible decline.

Most justified their eulogies by claiming it revisited themes from classical literature and the Bible, specifically the notion of the individual pitted against insurmountable forces. This kind of critical response testified to a consensus, shared by academia and the cultural establishment, that the fundamental concerns of the Christian and pre-Christian epic were the only true guarantees of literary quality. Some noted that at the opening, Santiago is mocked by fellow fishermen but acquires a faithful young disciple, and that by the close he is forced to carry his mast on his shoulders against the storm and eventually finds himself lying in the boat palms up, as if crucified. They paid minimal attention to Santiago's non-Christ-like preoccupation with those baseball stars able to triumph against the odds as his private assurance against despair.

These general murmurings on Hemingway as the Homer of the mid-twentieth century would probably have influenced the Nobel Committee, always anxious to avoid the promotion of literature as a form of recreation or entertainment. They would have seen it as an expression of heroic grandeur, knowing nothing of what really compelled Hemingway to write it: frailty, a sense of himself as no longer strong enough to act out his fantasies and vindictiveness.

CHAPTER 7

Everywhere and Nowhere

The period between *The Old Man and the Sea* (1952) and Hemingway's death in 1961 has been dealt with by his biographers in the manner of a tactful eulogy to a life unlived. There were events, notably the two potentially fatal plane crashes in Africa, the award of the Nobel Prize in Literature and his descent at the close of the 1950s into what appeared to be a blend of schizophrenia and manic depression. But he published hardly any fiction. The popular press was hungry for more reports of the exploits and travels of Papa, and the cultural establishment were busily evaluating him as one of the formative presences in modern writing. Yet he seemed to have given up completely on the activity that earned him global esteem. No major figure has brought their career so abruptly to a close. He committed a vast number of words to the page during the mid to late 1950s, often at a rate which exceeded that of any earlier period, but it is evident that he never intended to send this material to his publisher. He was writing but he was writing to himself, and this is why the closing decade of his life is so fascinating and unfathomable.

On 23 June 1953, Hemingway and Mary boarded the SS *Flandre* in New York to be met on the 30th at Le Havre by Gianfranco Ivancich. Despite the mutually embarrassing departure of Dora and Adriana from Havana more than two years earlier, Gianfranco was tolerated among the Hemingway entourage as a kind of uninvited courtier. He had no regular employment and welcomed his albeit brief role as travel agent and supervisor for the Hemingways' three-month stay in Europe, prior to their African safari. Hemingway and Mary would be driven through Normandy, staying over in Saumur in the Loire Valley, and then spend a few days at the Ritz in Paris. After this they would go to Pamplona and then to Madrid; they would remain in Spain for most of the summer. In August they travelled to the Côte D'Azur, staying over at spots chosen by Hemingway as memorials to his past, visited by him, Fitzgerald, Zelda and Hadley in the 1920s, before boarding the *Donnotar Castle* in Marseilles for Mombasa on the Horn of Africa. The itinerary was a history of Hemingway's most affective recollections, particularly his time in northern and southern France with Hadley, Pauline and the Fitzgeralds, his first experience of bullfighting and experiences in the Spanish Civil War. It would conclude with a return to the parts of Africa he had visited with Pauline. It was a strange exercise in time travel, enabling Hemingway to indicate that he preferred the past to whatever the present or the future might involve.

Gianfranco greeted them with an enormous, luxuriously appointed Lancia saloon, large enough to accommodate the three of them in comfort and to carry their luggage, hunting rifles included, which weighed in at more than 560 pounds. He was efficient and scrupulous, but his ignorance of the eerie undertones of the trip caused an unintended episode of dark comedy when he introduced them to the man he had hired as the chauffeur, a polite but rather lugubrious individual, Adamo Simon, who had taken the summer off from his usual job as undertaker. Gigantic cars such as this were familiar to him, Gianfranco added, given his experience with motorised hearses.

Paris depressed Hemingway. The locations he had known were undergoing a postwar revival, but the personnel of his 1920s apprenticeship had either left the city or were gone forever. Stein, Joyce and the Fitzgeralds were dead, Pound was in prison in the US for colluding with the Italian Fascists, Dos Passos might well have ceased to exist, Pauline had died in October 1951 and while Sylvia Beech still lived in the city she had closed down the original 'Shakespeare and Company' shop. It seemed to him like a mausoleum, and while he had intended to stay for at least a week he ordered Adamo and Gianfranco to load the car and set off for Spain after only two days.

The border guard knew his face from newspaper photographs and with a wry smile waved the car through. For the subsequent six weeks Hemingway attended *corridas* and bull-runs with desperate frequency, as though he was attempting to ignite a flame that had died 15 years before. He began in San Sebastian, went on to Pamplona and Madrid, then to Valencia and back to Madrid, followed by Burgos and again to San Sebastian. He was replaying his past at high speed and finding that much had changed. In Pamplona he went first to the hotel kept by his friend Juanito Quintana, a building charged with memories. He had stayed there with Hadley and their friends from Paris. That visit was the spark for the novel that launched his career as a writer, *The Sun Also Rises*, and he had returned, with Martha, a decade later during the Civil War. Now, he found, Quintana was a non-person, dispossessed of his property. He had been a vocal anti-Franco activist and no one seemed to know where he had gone. The new proprietor informed Hemingway and his party that no rooms were available, though it was evident to all present that the hotel was not full. Hemingway, Mary, Gianfranco and Viertel, who had recently joined them, found accommodation in a village several miles outside the town.

Even Catalonia, the home of anarchists and various left-wing factions, always treated bullfighting as the one thing that united it with the rest of Spain, and when Hemingway returned to his spiritual and creative homeland he was relieved to find that whatever else had changed, thousands of spectators still flocked to a ritual that transcended the divisions of the Civil War. Matadors continued to be treated like movie stars and when *corridas* were underway the cityscapes were just as he remembered them. In cafes, customers shared jugs of red wine from breakfast onwards, stews made of everything from pork through seafood to snails simmered throughout the day, gaudily clad *raiu* dancers performed in the streets, bands played and fireworks lit the night skies. He was even acclaimed as the apologist, in *Death in the Afternoon*, for a ceremony in bloodletting that Spain saw as uniquely its own. Spaniards had in the 1930s killed each other, but a different brand of killing allowed them to effect a macabre form of togetherness. Matadors went so far as to dedicate bulls to Hemingway at the beginning of fights. His history as a combatant for the Republicans and vocal supporter of the Communist Party – now banned, with many activists still in prison – seemed to have been politely forgotten. In return he appeared to have blinded himself to the fact that, beyond the festivities and the *corridas*, Franco's regime was rigorously authoritarian, placing the enforcement of moral and behavioural rectitude in the hands of the Church and enabling members of the Guardia Civil and Policía Armada to arrest and detain without charge anyone they suspected of political dissent. Hemingway wrote to his friends and family only of his beloved bullfighting, of young men such as the matador Antonio Ordonez, born after his last visit, who were maintaining this legacy.

In letters and conversations he avoided any reference to the anomaly of his joy in reminders of the Spain he loved and the horrible fact that the country was now in the hands of the Fascists he had despised and fought against.

They left Marseilles for Mombasa on 4 August and were greeted at the docks by Philip Percival, now in retirement, but persuaded by Hemingway to join him in this next stage of reliving the past. Percival had been the guide on Hemingway and Pauline's safari in the same district two decades before.

They would remain in Africa for nine months, and as 1953 closed Hemingway did his best to demonstrate to Mary his enduring skill and courage as a big-game hunter. Using his heavy calibre .577 rifle he found that his eyesight had deteriorated so severely that he needed to wear locally purchased extra-thick glasses, which the recoil of the gun often dislodged. He was writing an article on the trip for *Look* magazine, with Earl Thiessen along to take photographs. Three were published with Hemingway standing, gun in hand, next to a dead rhino, a leopard and a lion. In all instances the fatal shot had been discharged by Denis Zaphiro a 27-year-old game ranger, though the captions said nothing of this. Hemingway had wounded the animals and Zaphiro followed their blood trails into the bush to finish them off.

Eventually Hemingway and Mary exchanged shooting for observing and Zaphiro later recalled how he had driven through the night with Hemingway, carefully weaving between giraffes and avoiding collisions with other animals, until 'Papa [...] fell out of the jeep and sat in the brush, his great shoulders shaking with silent laughter' (Zaphiro to Mary Hemingway, 6 January 1955, JFK). It seemed as though the hunter no longer sought trophies for the walls of the Finca and now accepted a more benign relationship with creatures variously dangerous and wild. Yet this prefiguring of the Adamsons' *Born Free* was misleading.

By November Hemingway was associating more frequently with members of the Masai and Wakamba, attempting to learn their language and joining them in tribal customs. Mary returned after a shopping trip to Nairobi to find that her husband had shaved his head, dyed his clothes to match the rusty ochre of Masai garments and was practising, with the assistance of tribesmen, how to kill a lion with a spear, an instrument he now carried with him continuously. He was attempting to go native and become an indigenous warrior.

Since his teens he had shown a desire to insinuate himself into cultures and factions that held the promise of reinvention, a way of casting off some disappointment with what he was. In World War I he acted out the role of a regular Italian infantryman; in Paris he tried desperately to absorb the mantras of modernism and join the burgeoning clubland of the avant-garde. Spain, with it legacies and ongoing conflicts, was epitomised in bullfighting, a ritual that few outsiders enjoyed or pretended to tolerate. Hemingway's preoccupation with the *corrida* went beyond the role of spectator; he wanted to be part of it. When he went to Key West he attempted to mix seamlessly with the rough-house sailors and fishermen of the local bars, make himself one of them. His chameleonesque tendency to disappear from his past and re-emerge as someone else is mirrored in all of his novels; in each he rewrote what he had been as something he would prefer to be.

The relationship between wishful thinking and egregious fantasy became unbalanced when he met Adriana and wrote *Across the River and Into the Trees*. *The Old Man and the Sea* offered a welcome hiatus, given that the novel relied almost exclusively on his imagination rather than his projection of unsatisfactory truth into delusion, but in 1953–4 his addiction to private cravings at the expense of the world shared with others spiralled out of control.

Mary indulged his decision to masquerade as a Masai warrior. Even the shaved head and dyed clothes could, she thought, be tolerated as counter-cultural escapism. But then there was Debba. She was a young Wakamba woman of whom there is no reliable record, either in terms of documents as to who she was or testaments from her to researchers and biographers. We cannot even be certain that she spoke English, but she most certainly existed. Zaphiro told Baker in an interview that she 'hung around the staff encampment [...] She was a slovenly looking brat with a primitive greedy face. She was also none too clean' (Baker, p. 659). Others referred to her, including Mary in her journal. Tribal custom allowed for men to be polygamous, and while there is no evidence that Hemingway and Debba ever had sex he began to refer to her routinely as his 'other' wife. Debba was thought to be in her late teens, about the same age as Adriana when Hemingway met her in Venice, but in other respects they were complete opposites. Adriana embodied the gentrified aristocratic allure of the old continent which many Americans craved but few admitted to, while Debba had more in common with Prudy, the half-Indian girl with whom Hemingway claimed to have had sex in the woods near Walloon four decades earlier. He was drawing himself backwards towards desires variously unrealised and relished, memories that compensated for an unsatisfactory present.

Languorous time travel would soon be interrupted by events too improbable for fiction. Roy Marsh made a good living flying wealthy Westerners in his single-engine Cessna between safari lodges. During January 1954 Hemingway and Mary hired him to take them on airborne tours of the Congo river basin, the northern lakes of Kenya and areas of wild bushland unreachable by motorised vehicles. He flew low partly to thrill his passengers with the experience and partly to show them wild animals being chased from above by the shadow and noise of the aircraft. On 23 January he was diving towards the spectacular Murchison Falls when a flock of Ibis took off from the lake. A collision with these massive wading birds damaged and partially blocked the air intake around the propeller, and he dived beneath them only to make contact with a disused telegraph line. Losing power and with his tail rudder jammed, Marsh warned his passengers of an imminent crash-landing and did a superb job of grounding the Cessna on a stretch of flat grassland surrounded by dense bush. Marsh and Hemingway were bruised and disorientated but Mary suffered the worst injuries, with a weak pulse and rapid heartbeat later diagnosed as the side-effects of two cracked ribs. After limping to the river they attracted the attention of a charter boat which took them to Butiaba. There they were met by another pilot, Reggie Cartwright, who had been patrolling the region in his 12-seater De Havilland during the 36 hours since messages from Marsh's plane had ceased. Butiaba did not have an airfield but Cartwright had landed on surrounding dirt land. Within two hours he and his three passengers were bouncing along this same improvised strip en route for Nairobi. Worried that the rough ground might damage his undercarriage Cartwright reduced his speed to the minimum and when he took off he managed only about 50 feet before the De Havilland nose-dived and crashed, with the right engine catching fire and igniting leaking fuel from the tanks. The wrecked fuselage was about to become an inferno. Marsh forced Mary through one of the windows while Hemingway, courageously, shoulder-charged the jammed passenger-door until it sprang open to release the rest of them from the aircraft.

The four of them went by car to Masandi, the closest town with medical facilities, and the following day, the 25th, they arrived in Entebbe. Thereafter several narratives unfolded. Journalists who had gathered in Entebbe to report the death of one of America's greatest writers were suddenly confronted by the living Hemingway. Before Cartwright had picked them up, every news agency on the globe had reported that Hemingway had been killed in a plane crash. On 24 January an Associated Press bulletin pronounced: 'Hemingway and his wife are feared to have perished in the crash of a chartered plane yesterday in Northwest Uganda'. The following day the *New York Daily Mirror*'s headline was less equivocal: 'HEMINGWAY, WIFE, KILLED IN AIR CRASH'. Reports that

Hemingway had survived only reached the US after the obituaries had gone to press.

At the end of January, Hemingway was receiving specialist medical attention in Nairobi and it became evident that his injuries were much worse than first feared. He had damaged a kidney, and his liver, already strained by alcoholic excess, was heavily bruised. His dislocated shoulder, of which he had not complained, was discovered a week after the crash, as was a collapsed lower intestine; he was now almost blind in his left eye, and hearing in his left ear was blurred almost to the point of extinction. Worst of all he had numerous head injuries. The first air crash had caused him concussion but now he was suffering from delirium. The two crashes brought the total of serious head injuries since 1918 to 11, and alongside this we should take into account the numerous minor accidents, again many involving his head, suffered when skiing or climbing, and most significantly the regular pummellings that came with his addiction to boxing. It would have been astonishing if, in his fifty-fourth year, he had managed to avoid the long-term consequences of regular brain trauma, symptoms of which are now demonstrated to resemble those of Parkinson's disease, Alzheimer's and various forms of neuropsychiatric disturbance. Add to all of this his drinking and we have a recipe for severe mental illness.

In Nairobi Hemingway drifted between relief – given that he and Mary had avoided death twice in three days – and perplexed introversion. He could speak clearly enough but he seemed to all who met him distracted and self-absorbed. He became obsessed with his own obituaries, reading every one, making notes and keeping copies in a scrapbook bound with zebra hide and lion skin. Routinely he had avoided Charles Fenton's enquiries, hoping that the hungry researcher would eventually be discouraged, but on 15 February, barely three weeks after the second crash, he sent him, unprompted, an extraordinarily candid letter. He wrote to him as if he were an intimate friend – despite the fact that they had never met – telling him he felt as that his life was being rewritten for him in the obituaries by individuals who know nothing of it. It was, he confessed, as if he had become the property of other people. He no longer existed, but there was something worse: 'In all obituaries, or

almost all, it was emphasised that I had sought death all my life –
can one imagine that if a man sought death all of his life he could
not have found her before the age of 54?' (21 February 1954, JFK).

He offers no explanation to Fenton as to why he had chosen him
as the recipient of this piece of unbalanced stream of consciousness,
but he sent several other similar letters during the same period.
On 8 February, for example, he provided Leland Hayward with a
meticulously detailed three-page account of the crashes. Most of
what he says is authentic but the puzzling element of the letter is the
apparent premise on which the description is based. The second
sentence runs: 'Since you are in the business this is how it was.' The
'business' was movies. Hayward was a well-known Broadway agent
and film producer and throughout the letter Hemingway inter-
weaves his story of the events with how these could best be adapted
for the filmed version. At one point he informs Hayward that the
'boat' that rescued them 'was that used in the motion picture made
here called the "African Queen"'. It was certainly not, but
somewhere in Hemingway's warped consciousness the real world
and cinematic fantasy had begun to overlap, perhaps as a
consequence of his having to read the equivalent of screen-plays
of his life produced by various obituarists. He goes so far as to
recommend Peter Viertel as a screenwriter: 'The scenes of these
various incidents have been described in a book by a young man
called Peter Viertel', he states. Viertel's novel, *White Hunter, Black
Heart* (1953), was a thinly disguised retelling of his partnership with
John Huston in the making of *The African Queen* and once again
Hemingway seems unable to distinguish properly between the
incidents he experienced less than a month earlier and his fixation
with Huston's film. He ends the letter with an affirmation that he
will not be deterred from flying in the future, including a bizarre
statement of his preference for the Cessna 180: 'I would like to
continue and will continue flying in the aircraft, preferably single
engine and with plenty of ponies.' He makes it clear that as a general
principle, 'twin engine or multiple engine aircraft I regard as
untrustworthy [...] too many gadgets and people are liable to
confuse them and lock things that should not be locked'. He closes,
in longhand, with an assurance that 'It [the film] looks like a smash

hit.' (Hemingway to Hayward, 8 February 1954, JFK). Hayward might have been puzzled. A year earlier he had all but agreed to produce a movie version of *The Old Man and the Sea*, but in the letter Hemingway seems unable to fully distinguish between that project and one entirely of his own making, involving a film version of what had recently happened to him. These shifts between the actual and self-delusion are slight compared with a letter he wrote to Hotchner a month later (14 April 1954, JFK). He opens where he left off with Hayward, insisting that his fear of flying was a pre-war phobia, and reporting that in 1944 he had 'flown' a B-25, a Hurricane, a Mosquito and all manner of other 'kites'. Did he mean 'flown *in*'? Such would be a generous reading; for one thing the Hurricane is a single-seater. He then boasts of having buzzed the 'shamba' (African term for cultivated land) and clipped the flag flying from the local police station with his propeller. He closes the piece with an intimate account of his 'engagement' to Debba. Had his injuries sent him insane? More likely, he had become, albeit briefly, an exaggerated version of the essential Hemingway, no longer merely telling lies but embodying them.

Seven weeks after the second crash the Hemingways left Africa for Europe, and on 23 March arrived in Venice. Once more they stayed in the Gritti Palace and his first visitor was Adriana, whom he had not seen for more than three years. He had written to her regularly since she and her mother had left Cuba in 1951 and what occurred during their meeting, their last, remains a matter for speculation. Reynolds reports that he confessed 'it would have been better if I had never met you that day in the rain' (Reynolds, p. 278). The quote comes verbatim from Adriana's report to Kert (p. 479), who implies that Adriana had confided in her that she was both surprised and embarrassed by the visit. This is suspect given that she had visited him.

Adriana was laying a trail of false clues and the truth comes from her unpublished letters. She had written to him regularly since she and her mother left Cuba three years earlier, despite her later claims that she had discouraged further contact. In 1952, for example, she had sent him a batch of her poems asking if he would use his influence to get them published. He replied that they were 'very good', adding that 'I wish you were here being a good poet in the top of the tower right now. Then after that we could go to the pool and swim ...' (Harry Ransom Archive, 12 April 1952). A month later he professes that his love for her 'goes very fast and travels faster than all rockets and guided missiles and you can have it now already before I finish typing this sentence' (Harry Ransom Archive, 8 May 1952). Shortly after the crash he received a four-page letter, sent by air mail from Venice via his publisher to Africa:

> Well, I really didn't know I loved you so much, until I knew you were dead [...] I read and read, and it was like reading the story of someone else. Then I started crying and my heart was heavy like a stone. And I cried and cried [...] And I read the newspaper again, and of course, I began to cry again [...] the only thing I could do is lie in my bed all morning, as I was too weak to get up [...] I looked my face in the mirror, and it wasn't any more my face. (1954, JFK, no other date)

Then she tells of how she felt when she read of the miracle of his survival.

> I was nothing, just nothing. I was like a stone in the middle of the Ocean. But these are thing's you can't explain [...] You will receive millions and millions of letters from all the world [...] but don't forget, my very dear, that this is the most loving one, because it come from your
>
> Adriana

His Adriana, who goes on to ask him to see her 'one more' time in Venice. He replied 'Both times I died ... I had only one thought ... I had never loved you more than the hour of my death' (Harry Ransom Archive, 1 February 1954). Mary was shocked when he showed her this note: apparently his near-death experience had made him forget that his verbal love affair with Adriana was clandestine and he repeated this act of inadvertent candour when Marlene Dietrich wrote to express her relief that he had survived and declared that she regretted turning down his proposal of marriage in Paris, during the war. He replied that 'I miss you too damned much [...] I used to be happier than ever to hold you close in your damned waking clothes', their code for the fact that she would not be wearing clothes when they woke together, naked. He continued: 'I would like to ask you formally if anything would ever happen with Miss Mary if you would marry me [...] I know I can be a fucking bore and perhaps a bore fucking you.' The journalist Nathanial Bentley was researching an article for *Newsweek* and had asked her if she and Hemingway had had an affair in France: 'Tell him how we left Jack Whitney's dinner and locked the door when he knocked and were good children because I had slept too recently with the worthless Miss Martha and you were in love with the equally worthless Remarque' (1954, JFK, undated). He had, three sentences before, instructed her that this was the account she should offer Bentley despite it being a complete fabrication, the opposite of what really happened. It is clear enough from her letters to him throughout the 1950s that Paris meant something more to her than a one-night stand. 'I think of you all the time and each day I think I will have to call you' (Dietrich to Hemingway, 1952, JFK, undated). 'I want to put my arms around you and my heart. I want to kiss you forever for the beauty that is in you and the purity and the master' (Dietrich to Hemingway, 31 August 1952, JFK). 'I love you and you are always in my thoughts. I look at your picture every morning and say Hello to you' (Dietrich to Hemingway, 9 August 1953, JFK). She admitted to him that she had begun her secret liaisons with Yul Brynner as a compensation for losing him to Mary. Indeed, he was the only person to whom she confided her thoughts, and doubts, about Brynner, who refused to consider leaving his wife and family.

He had arranged, months before the crashes, for Aaron Hotchner to travel with them back to Spain, again in the Lancia with Adamo at the wheel. First they passed through locations in northern Italy that resonated with his experiences in 1918. He told stories to Hotchner and Adamo in a desperate manner, as if his private history would evaporate were he not to refashion it again and again, for the benefit of his indulgent witnesses. This continued after Peter Viertel joined the party in Provence. Hemingway guided Adamo along a four-day tour of the Riviera that took in places where he had stayed with Hadley in the 1920s, holidayed and quarrelled with Scott and Zelda Fitzgerald, and involved himself in a *ménage à trois* with Hadley and Pauline. According to Viertel he spoke of Pauline in the present tense, despite the fact that she had died in 1951.

When they reached Madrid his companions feared that he was close to a breakdown. The newspaper *ABC* ran a brief article on how an 'enemy of Spain' was back in the capital. It was a lighthearted report – Hemingway, as a cultural celebrity and living advertisement for Spanish tourism, was now immune from any form of retribution – but he became neurotic, insisting that figures standing in streets or seated in bars were members of Franco's secret police, following him and looking for evidence that he was consorting with ex-Communists.

In mid-May he and his companions travelled to San Isidro, staying as guests at the country Villa of Luis Miguel Dominguin, then the most celebrated matador in Spain. He was 28 years old, and the scion of a well-established line of minor nobility who regarded bullfighting as a patriotic investment. Hemingway had known his father in the 1920s, and he continued to ignore the self-contradictory relationship between his Communist affiliations of the Civil War and his obsession with Spain as an historical anomaly, involving a relationship between peasants and aristocrats that seemed to have endured for four centuries. Shortly after the Hemingway party arrived they were joined at Dominguin's house by Ava Gardner, one of the most glamorous Hollywood actresses of the era, with whom the matador was having an ill-disguised affair.

Apart from Dominguin himself the rest of the party either tolerated bullfighting – Gardner did so for obvious reasons – or found it variously primitive and abhorrent, but Hemingway forced them to accompany him to the San Isidro *corridas*. He was reliving the weeks in Spain that inspired *The Sun Also Rises*, with Ernest Hemingway as avatar of a primordial substitute for the lazy intellectualism of his friends from Paris. Viertel later commented that what struck him most about Hemingway was 'Papa's duplicity'. Not only did he lie to those in the current party about each other, his recollections of Spain and Paris in the 1920s and 1930s became an exercise in 'bellitl[ing] his old friends' (Viertel, pp. 229–30). Yet again the long excursion to Europe and Africa involved a turning back of the clock.

In Genoa, on 6 June, Hemingway and Mary boarded the *Francesco Morosini* for Havana. They were seen off at the dock by Adriana and her mother. There is no record of whether the Ivancichs volunteered to do so or if they responded to a plea from Hemingway, but it certainly involved a considerable effort for the two women to travel almost 400 kilometres from Venice to the port, simply to say goodbye. Viertel, Hotchner and Adamo had parted company with Hemingway some days earlier, and the moment of farewell between the now rather frail writer and the girl he had many times professed to love might have carried an air of tragedy but for the fact that Mary and Dora were present as uncomfortable chaperones. They would never meet again.

On their arrival in Havana, Hemingway began what he would casually refer to as his 'Africa book'. The manuscript eventually ran to more than 200,000 words, but was reduced by two-thirds and heavily revised for publication as *True at First Light*, going into print in 1999 to coincide with the centenary of his birth. It was, and is, an extraordinarily bad piece of writing. Hemingway purists lamented its appearance as evidence that remaining members of his family had turned the writer's legacy into a vulgar brand franchise. His son, Patrick, edited the volume and in the same year he, and other relatives, licensed the family name to launch an array of products, including 'the Pamplona sofa and the Kilimanjaro bed', enabling fans to relax on well-cushioned extrapolations of the Papa mythology. Fishing rods, safari clothing and even shotguns were put on the market bearing the Hemingway escutcheon, a version of Burberry or Dior for those with cultural aspirations, and a gun licence. *True at First Light* formed the final part of a trio of posthumously published fictional works, alongside *Islands in the Stream* and *The Garden of Eden*. Each has been treated as an unworthy successor to the books that appeared during his lifetime, but a more significant factor has been overlooked. Their publication as separate works is grossly misleading. Some of the manuscript that would eventually become *The Garden of Eden* dates from the late 1940s, around the time that he was giving less attention to what would be called *Islands in the Stream*, but their present status as different novels is due mainly to the fact that many of Hemingway's posthumous editors were scholars and academics, figures inclined to impose order where chaos might otherwise, more honestly, prevail. For example, the three-part structure of *Islands in the Stream* is a falsification of the original manuscript. It would have been more legitimate to publish it as these novellas, given that the parts have little in common aside from the presence of Thomas Hudson, an inconstant figure as mutable and shifting as the narrative itself. It is true that *The Garden of Eden* was begun shortly after the third part of *Islands in the Stream*, but the editors' decision to give it a different title and, more significantly, classify it as a separate literary project distorts our perception of Hemingway, both as a man and a writer, during the last decades of his life. It is certainly the case that the principal character, Hudson, is replaced by one David Bourne, but the name change becomes inconsequential when we consider the continuities. Hudson, the painter, is shadowed without explanation by a character called Davis, a young, successful writer, while in *The Garden of Eden* a painter called Nick Sheldon hovers mysteriously behind the principal figure, Bourne, a writer. The location shifts from the Caribbean to Europe, mostly the French Riviera, and the editors might have seen this as justification for treating them as different enterprises, except that, once again, continuities prevail. Throughout, Hemingway is ransacking his past, using fiction as an intermediary between recollection and uncertainty, and in this respect France and Spain were as significant as Cuba, Florida and adjacent islands.

The main pretext for publishing *The Garden of Eden* as a separate novel is its exploration of sexuality. David's wife Catherine appears to metamorphosise into a figure who is neither female or male. She cuts her hair very short, causing her to appear boyish, something that Pauline had done in the 1930s. At one point, during David's failed attempt to have sex with her, she states that 'Now you can't tell who is who, can you?' and suggests that he has become a version of her: 'Yes you are and you're my girl Catherine.'

The episode has been treated as, variously, proof of Hemingway's doubts regarding his own sexuality, and evidence that one of the most aggressively heterosexual authors of recent years was a closeted sympathiser with gay, lesbian and transgender states of mind. None of these interpretations is entirely valid. When he wrote these passages – which in the draft are utterly incoherent, but improved considerably by the editors – he had only just returned to the manuscript after his 1953–4 safari. The section in the novel is an extrapolation of his entry in Mary's journal on 20 December 1953. He opens with 'Mary is espace [a species of] prince of devils and almost any place you touch her it can kill both you and her.' The rest is an exact echo of the parts of the novel in which David and Catherine exchange sexual roles and gendered identities:

> She has always wanted to be a boy and thinks as a boy without ever losing any femininity. If you should become confused on this you should retire. She loves me to be her girls, which I love to be [...] In return she makes me awards and at night we do every sort of thing which pleases her and which pleases me [...] Mary has never had one lesbian impulse but has always wanted to be a boy [...] I loved the feeling the embrace of Mary which came to me as something quite new and outside tribal law. (*HIW*, pp. 380–1)

The most striking feature of the entry is its shifts between confession and denial, amounting almost to dialogue between conflicting dimensions of Hemingway's personality. In a single sentence – 'She loves me to be her girls, which I love to be, not being absolutely stupid' – we find him disclosing a secret yet looking over his shoulder for some kind of explanation. Mary, he assures us, had wanted to be a boy but had never favoured lesbianism, and though he has 'never cared for any men and dislike any tactile contact between men' he admits to loving the 'embrace' of the boylike Mary.

There is no evidence that Hemingway wished the journal entry to remain a secret – otherwise, one assumes, Mary would not have included a version of it in her published memoir – and despite his continuous revisions of the manuscript of the novel up to the end of the 1950s he showed no inclination to delete references to David and Catherine's transsexual acts and inclinations. In the JFK collection of unpublished correspondence there is an undated anonymous letter classified by the archivists as 'Outgoing Correspondence'. 'You', the recipient, becomes part of a story in which a 'laidy' explains why 'you had never taken a wife'; the 'creatures' with whom he had been associated had be excluded from 'the family' on the instruction of 'the elders', and 'sometimes there are moments when I look on my own femininity with nausea'. The handwriting is Hemingway's and it seems clear that the author of the letter and its recipient are the same person. The parallels between it and the entries in Mary's journal are striking, as are its echoes of the confused sexual 'duality' of *The Garden of Eden*. In unpublished in-house letters to him Mary addresses him as 'you wonder boy-girl' (25 November 1948, JFK) and refers to herself as 'half a woman – or half a boy' (JFK, undated).

In 2007 Hemingway's grandson, John, published *Strange Tribe*, a memoir that purports to offer a unique insight into the relationship between Hemingway and John's father Gregory. The latter suffered from a variety of mental illnesses, compounded by bouts of alcoholism, and met his end, apparently from a heart attack, in a Women's Correction Institution. During the closing decade of his life he 'came out' as transgendered and eventually underwent a sex-change operation. John's claim to having conclusive evidence of the cause of the enmity between his father and grandfather is doubtful. Certainly he has access to previously undisclosed correspondence between the two men but this offers proof only of a growing bitterness between them involving financial matters following the death of Gregory's mother Pauline. His contention that his grandfather and father shared a guilty preoccupation with androgyny is based largely on wish-fulfilment – specifically a desire to explain his father's tormented life. John treats *The Garden of Eden* as a subliminal confession on Hemingway's part, though of what remains unclear: was he extrapolating what he knew of his son into the book or disclosing related inclinations of his own? A more convincing narrative was offered by Jeffrey Meyers in a 1999 *Virginia Quarterly Review* article, entitled 'The Hemingways: An American Tragedy', which John completely ignores, mainly because it casts his father in a less than sympathetic light. Meyers tells of how, 16 years earlier, he had interviewed Gregory and a number of others who had witnessed his break-up with his father in the 1940s and 1950s. He was at the time researching his forthcoming biography of Hemingway but was informed by his publisher, Harper and Row, that the draft had been read by their lawyers and that all material relating to Gregory must be cut; they feared a libel action. One assumes that Meyers chose to tell the story in 1999 because Gregory, the person likeliest to pursue an action, was, as Meyers puts it, 'wander[ing] between Montana and Florida,' too unstable to notice what was said about him in print, let alone seek legal advice on it. In 1946, when Mary had only recently moved into the Finca, she found that some of her exotic French underwear had been removed from her bedroom. Her Cuban maid, whom she first accused, swore her innocence after Gregory, then 14, returned to boarding school. The lingerie was found hidden under the mattress of his bed. Things worsened when, the following year in Key West, Gregory stole some drink and crashed a car, seriously injuring his elder brother, Patrick. Hemingway sent Pauline a letter blaming her for failing to bring up the teenager properly. In 1951, aged 19, Gregory was arrested for loitering in the women's toilet of a Los Angeles cinema, wearing a dress, high heels, stockings, a wig and make-up. Again, Hemingway blamed Pauline for their son's behaviour, telephoning her the night after his arrest to accuse her of neglecting him and turning him into a pervert. She had phoned from Los Angeles; she had flown there from San Francisco to arrange for her son's release. Pauline died 24 hours later of a previously undiagnosed case of abdominal bleeding. It is likely that she had been suffering from this for some time and equally likely that stress would have suddenly worsened it.

Meyers tells us more than John Hemingway about Gregory's miseries, yet he does not provide documented proof that the mutual antipathy between Gregory and his father was rooted in a shared transsexual predisposition. Hemingway's brief letter-to-himself should cause us to think again about that.

In 1954, while he was revising *The Garden of Eden*, he began another semi-autobiographical work, *True at First Light*. Debba appears in it, as does Mary, and the principal character and narrator is Ernest Hemingway, a writer who rediscovers himself in Africa where tribal customs enable him to enjoy a polygamous existence with his American wife along with her African counterpart, Debba. It is a bizarre, almost grotesque extrapolation of fantasies he had entertained during his trip to Africa with Mary.

Two versions exist. *Under Kilimanjaro* (2005), edited by two academics, R. W. Lewis and R. E. Fleming, purports to be more faithful to the original manuscript. Its predecessor, *True at First Light*, edited by Hemingway's son Patrick, is the more famous and marginally the worst, largely because the editor, in cutting the book so severely in length, makes even more conspicuous the raw unedited prose. Some writers, for various reasons, not least age and drink, become poor practitioners of the craft at which they once excelled. But something else happens to Hemingway in what would be his final work to go into print, albeit posthumously. The narrator's manner reminds us of Hemingway's first novel, *The Sun Also Rises*, where he evolved a style that has left a significant imprint on the history of twentieth-century fiction. Figurative language is minimised, sometimes eradicated, and in exchange we find ourselves with staccato sentences conveying brief packages of information and little else. His rationing of verbal extravagance is counterbalanced by self-conscious pithiness in that no one before his debut novel had repeated single units of sense so frequently and arbitrarily. His return to this in *True at First Light* is unbearable. Sometimes he appears to be parodying his former self: 'It was very good snuff, not as powerful as that of Asop Meina but enough snuff to let you know you had snuff when you tucked it under your lower lip.' Sentences wind desperately towards a conclusion as if tortured by their very existence.

A sentimental longing for what maleness ought to be lurks in all of his earlier books, as does a refusal to think or care about such inessentials as the feelings of others beyond the greedy sadness of the main character and his retinue of victims and lovers. In *True at First Light* these disagreeable aspects of Hemingway are projected into the foreground. He can have everything he wishes for. In the novel he turns himself into a man able to hunt and kill with spears, a figure who would become an elder of the tribe. During the 1953–4 trip he had acted out these ambitions, embarrassingly, and later he fictionalised them. Mary is his link with America and Europe while Debba, his other wife, is the kind of woman he always wanted, a subservient accessory to the clever ones he married. Debba is illiterate, knows nothing of his fame as a writer and loves him in a primordial uncultured way, perhaps as he expected women in general to behave. Throughout *Across the River and Into the Trees* we suspect that had the relationship between Renata and the Colonel endured she would, in her sophisticated maturity, come to recognise him as the fantasist he is. Debba, as her replacement, forestalls such a denouement by being unable to grow up.

The writer of the letter-to-himself and of the novels published in his lifetime played games with who he was and who he wanted to be, and by the time he wrote *True at First Light* he existed only on the page, a preferred alternative to the world of the actual Ernest Hemingway. During the 1950s he returned continually to the sprawling, expansive novels he would never properly finish: *Islands in the Stream*, *The Garden of Eden*, and *True at First Light*. The editors who prepared them for posthumous publication blurred our understanding of what happened to Hemingway as he wrote them. They thought they were, respectfully, completing the tasks that he had set for himself, but this assumption arose from the premise that writers treat fiction as a journey with a foreseeable destination. For the vast majority this is indeed an essential working principle and one that Hemingway followed for most of his career. However, after *The Old Man and the Sea* he underwent a transformation that had nothing to do with his sense of himself as a literary artist or his opinions on literature in general. The deaths of individuals who had played key roles in his existence from childhood onwards, the permanent absence of others whom he had excised from his world, combined with a coterie of interrogators and investigators set on excavating truths buried in the past, made him feel as though the present, let alone the future, had been suspended.

It is no accident that during the final ten years of his life Hemingway habitually revisited his past both in his writing and during ceremonial excursions to parts of Europe, Africa and the American Midwest that held a store of memories of everything he had been and done before 1950. Each was a bizarre exercise in time travel, as were the novels that they inspired. He was returning to the location of his past but not so much to resurrect it as to rewrite it. Sentimental recollection, a silly post-Romantic concept, rests on the assumption that diligently improved memories will enable us to cope with the less agreeable present. For the reassuring fantasy to work we need to be able to contrast now with then, even if the latter is an investment in wish-fulfilment. But for Hemingway such a contrast was ruled out by his eradication of the present day. His stories – eventually his posthumously published novels – would never reach conclusions because they were perpetual revisitations of what had gone before. They would only be brought to a close, unfinished, by the death of their creator.

Epilogue

On 5 October 1954 the *New York Times* reported that 'sources close to the Swedish Academy' had disclosed that only two candidates were being taken seriously for the forthcoming Nobel Prize in Literature: Haldor Laxness, an Icelandic novelist, and Hemingway. Shortly afterwards the newspaper supplemented the rumour with further news from their 'source', who now hinted that Hemingway was slightly ahead because of his recent near-fatal air crash: if the Academy did not act now they might not have the chance again, given Hemingway's well-publicised taste for jeopardy. None of this endeared Hemingway to the Nobel Committee. That his perishability had given him the edge over an obscure figure who adapted Icelandic sagas to the present day was not greatly flattering.

When he was announced as the winner on 28 October his comments to the press were sparing and reserved. He began with a response to the *New York Times* stating that he was 'very pleased and very proud' to receive the award, and nothing else (16 October 1954). For the *New York Times Book Review* (7 November 1954) he expanded on this, but only by regretting that the prize had not been given to 'my own countrymen' Mark Twain and Henry James. His most revealing comments were made privately to General Buck Lanham. During a long letter (10 November 1954) he seems reluctant to speak of the prize at all, digressing continually until he can no longer avoid addressing his feelings to his old friend:

> You know when I called [you] up I was trying to decide whether to
> accept the thing or not. There were a lot of good reasons not to. But
> no-one would understand them except your friends.

He had spoken of one of these 'reasons' in their earlier phone call:
that the prize was, for many, an epitaph, a memorial to past
greatness and a signal that nothing of significance would follow.
He declined the invitation to attend the ceremony in Stockholm,
claiming that he was still suffering from the effects of the air crashes
and unable to travel long distances, which was an exaggeration.

When the prize was announced, and during the subsequent
months as he was swamped with requests for interviews from
journalists and academics, he was preoccupied with matters that
testify to his having given up on producing another significant work
of fiction. Throughout September and October he spoke openly in
letters, and to Mary, of how he wished to transform himself into the
character, also called Ernest Hemingway, in the rapidly evolving
manuscript of what would become *The Garden of Eden*. Robert
Morgan Brown was a graduate student at New York University
planning a dissertation on Hemingway, and despite the latter's
anger over Fenton and Young he replied candidly to Brown's
enquiries on his ongoing work. He explains that in Africa 'You did
not have to be a literary character', meaning that he found in the
spirit of the place something which eroded the distinction between
what he invented and who he was. Despite the fact that he was
replying to Brown from Havana he refers to Africa and his
experiences there in the present tense. 'I can', he announces, 'pray
to the Mountain'. 'There is an illegal shamba at its [the Mountain's]
foot, and [we pray] to the trees, the special trees.' 'Miss Mary', he
adds, 'can't have children [but] can have Debba to help her as a
second wife. Debba can have the children' (Harry Ransom Archive).
Brown might be forgiven for being confused as to whether
Hemingway was discussing his plans for a novel or his projected
future among the Wakamba with 'Miss Mary' and Debba. In truth,
Hemingway himself had disregarded the distinction, which perhaps
goes some way to explain why he treated the Nobel Prize as in turn
an irritation and a distraction. In early October 1954, when
journalists were speculating on who the likely winner would be, he

wrote to Harvey Breit and showed the letter to Mary before posting it. 'It does not seem so stupid to me', he reflected, 'to have five wives if you can afford them [...] I am very faithful. But I can be faithful easier to your good wives than to one' (quoted by Mary Hemingway in *HIW*, p. 422). He appeared more preoccupied with the fantasy existence he was projecting into the novel than the prospect of the most prestigious of all international literary prizes.

Five months after the award was announced, four of Baker's Princeton students arrived at the Finca to savour the observations of the world's most celebrated writer. Hemingway amused his young guests with stories of Paris and insisted that they join him for strong drinks before lunch. What he did not mention was his double life as the creator and subject of a novel, specifically his rolling disagreement with Mary regarding his determination to have his ears pierced. He would, he insisted, wear sets of Wakamba earrings brought back from Africa and thus move his Westernised presence a little closer to the one with whom he shared several hours a day on the pages that covered his writing desk.

Professor Fraser Drew of Buffalo University was received two weeks later on the morning of Good Friday with equally hospitable insouciance. As Drew later noted, his host was 'kind, modest and unassuming'. Hemingway volunteered to him that 'I'm a Catholic, as far as I can be. I can still go to Mass', but said nothing of how he reconciled this with his alter ego who prayed to the 'Mountain' and the 'Special trees'. He expanded, telling him of how Father Andre, the priest in a nearby Cuba village 'prays for me every day', adding: 'I can't pray for myself anymore, perhaps it's because the self has become less important and others become more important' (Drew, pp. 108–16). Drew does not attempt to decode this cryptic observation, but with benefit of hindsight it seems likely that Hemingway was disclosing, albeit half-consciously, his sense of having become two people, the physical inhabitant of the Finca alongside his fantasised replica in the novel. Mary, meanwhile, was still attempting to persuade him that wearing earrings in photographs of the laureate demanded by every news agency would have a 'deleterious effect' on his profile as 'a writer and a man'. Almost exactly a year after the *New York Times* had announced that he was a close contender for the Nobel Prize (4 October 1955) Mary left him an interhouse letter imploring him that 'the fiction of having your ears pierced [to] make you a Kamba' would be 'an evasion of reality': she was aware that he was 'writing about them' (the Wakamba) as a substitute for 'the mystery and excitement of becoming one of them' (Mary to Hemingway, 4 October 1955, JFK). Reluctantly he agreed and cancelled his appointment with a tattooist and ear-piercer in Havana city, but for the next five years he continued with the private fantasy of the book, extrapolating who he was and had been into a spectrum of pure delusion.

Hemingway would make three more visits to Europe. In 1956–7 he and Mary spent more than six months in France and Spain, and in 1959 the same amount of time in the two countries. He went to Spain, without Mary, for a month in late summer 1960.

Hemingway had been restlessly nomadic since his teens. He rarely spent more than 12 months in the same place without being drawn elsewhere, yet we should note that he was quite the opposite of the adventurous traveller. By the mid-1930s he had a selection of sites that were predictably magnetic. He rarely stopped moving but his menu of Havana, Key West, Sun Valley, France, Spain, Italy and Africa was largely unvaried. Despite his performance as a peripatetic irregular he was addicted to revisiting places that enabled him to relive key moments of his life. He behaved like King Lear, jealously guarding what has gone before and fearful of what the future might bring.

Hemingway and Mary disembarked in France on 6 September 1956 and began what had become almost a ritual. They had a new driver but Hemingway insisted on a Lancia almost identical to the one that had collected them at Le Havre more than three years earlier. Their first destination was, as usual, Paris and the Ritz, where they stayed for more than a week. On several evenings they were joined by friends from Hollywood. Gary Cooper and Hemingway had been close since the early 1940s when the former starred in the film adaptation of *For Whom the Bell Tolls* (1942), and he had also played Frederic Henry in the movie version of *A Farewell to Arms* (1932). The roles were, respectively, based on Hemingway's fictional accounts of his exploits in the Spanish Civil War and World War I, and though on the surface the two men seemed to have little in common – Cooper was a reserved, mild-mannered conservative – Hemingway enjoyed the actor's company, not least because he was fascinated by the hall-of-mirrors effect created when they talked. Cooper's on-screen persona – cool, laconic, indomitably brave against the odds, epitomised in *High Noon* – was an extrapolation of his private mannerisms. With Cooper, Hemingway felt he was talking with a version of himself, or rather the version he had projected into the novels. Also present were Mel Ferrer, Rita Hayworth, Audrey Hepburn and Pete Viertel, who was hoping that he would be commissioned as the screenwriter if *The Old Man and the Sea* was to be filmed. As had been his habit since leaving Paris at the close of the 1920s he had assembled a coterie of friends who he would entertain with stories of his past exploits. This time he supplemented the tales with an actual presence, a teenage girl, attractive and seemingly well educated, whom he introduced to the others only as 'La Comtesse'. Not even Mary knew her real name and he withheld any information on her background, but his wife and Viertel were aware that he was re-enacting the events of Venice seven years earlier. 'La Comtesse' enabled him to return to his courtship of Adriana Ivancich. Viertel later remarked that Hemingway had 'once again embarked on one of his imaginary romances', a polite way of describing a fantasy based on a delusion. Verbal recollections that survive emphasise the fact that the girl seemed both amused by and contemptuous of Hemingway's insistence that she should be referred to by her noble title.

In mid-September he and Mary were driven across the border into Spain and on the 17th arrived at the Gran Hotel Felipe II in El Escorial, 40 kilometres from Madrid. Their destination had been recommended by doctors because, at almost 4,000 feet above sea level, it might provide some relief from the constant anaemia from which both had suffered for the past 10 years, a condition aggravated by the humidity of Havana. However, on the way there Hemingway insisted that they should spend two days at Logrono where Antonio Ordonez, one of the most celebrated bullfighters of the era, was the star of the *corrida*. Hemingway wanted to watch and talk to Ordonez not merely because of his skills. He was the son of the bullfighter who fought under the name of Nino de la Palma, the model for the gifted, courageous Pedro Romero of *The Sun Also Rises*. Yet again the present day was being exchanged for what had gone before.

Ten days later in Madrid the Spanish journalist José Luis Castillo-Puche arranged a meeting, at Hemingway's behest, between the American and the Spanish-Basque novelist Pío Baroja. Castillo-Puche later recalled that Hemingway had referred to the Spanish writer as 'Don Pío', thanked him for 'how much I owe you', commended him as 'our master' and proclaimed that Baroja was far more deserving of the Nobel Prize than its most recent recipient, Hemingway (Castillo-Puche, p. 73). We have no reason to question his account, but it should be noted that the only evidence that Hemingway had read Baroja's work, let alone been influenced by it, comes from Castillo-Puche's record of the exchange. They had certainly never met prior to this. He knew something of his past, specifically his anarchist sympathies and his opposition to Franco during the Civil War, though Baroja was too old for front-line involvement. He was the scion of minor gentry who managed to reconcile privilege with artistic endeavour and political radicalism.

Baroja died almost three weeks after their meeting. Hemingway wrote to Harvey Breit: 'We buried Don Pío Baroja last Tuesday', and as if in anticipation of Breit's 'who?' expands on how he was 'a hell of a good writer you know', and complains that Knopf had dropped him 'when he did not sell'. Then he offers a lyrical portrait of the 'very moving and beautiful' funeral. 'The day was misty with the sun breaking through and burning off over the bare hills and on the way out to the un-consecrated ground cemetery through the country he wrote about [...] There were not many of us [...] Thought Dos Passos or *some* Americans could have sent a word' (5 November 1956). His account of the funeral is as skilfully executed as some of his earliest short stories. He gradually narrows the focus, treating the few other mourners with respect but making it clear that there is a special bond between him and the deceased. He was reinventing himself as the one American who remained heroically faithful to the Republican cause, unlike, he implies, his erstwhile friend Dos Passos. It was an impressive performance, in the sense that it was certainly an exercise in showmanship. Hemingway knew that Baroja was seriously ill and, despite the fact that he suggested to Breit that he was saying goodbye to an old friend, they had never met before he descended, vulture-like, on him. Hemingway was making use of Baroja as part of his own legend, implying that he was paying due respect to an embodiment of the idealistic, sometimes fantastic, notion of the Spain he knew in the 1930s.

Their next destination was supposed to be Kenya, turning the expedition into an almost exact replica of 1953–4, with both involving a compendium of narratives from Hemingway's memories of Europe and Africa from the 1920s and 1930s. The reckless, and doomed, attempt by Britain, France and Israel to seize both banks of the Suez Canal from Egypt caused them to cancel the trip. He would not visit Africa again, at least in person, but the Ernest Hemingway of the perpetually revised 'Africa novel' would never leave it.

They returned to Paris, to the Ritz. If Hemingway had doubted such notions as serendipity he would suddenly have been caused to abandon his scepticism. The manager announced that staff had discovered boxes and suitcases filled with typescripts and longhand manuscripts, all by Hemingway and dating from his time in Paris during the 1920s. He and Pauline had stayed at the hotel shortly before their departure from France and, clearly, the anxiety and turmoil of the period had caused him to forget that he had stowed in the basement of the hotel samples of his writing and notes on his life covering the previous decade. As he read the fragments and impressions it was a though the young man of the 1920s had returned to speak to his 57-year-old incarnation. The experience would energise his determination to go back in time, and enable him to add a new element to his habitual rewritings of his life as he wanted it to appear: *A Moveable Feast* was born.

From 1957 to 1959 Hemingway preyed hungrily on these archives for his memoir of the Paris years, but week by week he would switch his attention between this project and *The Garden of Eden*, his fictional representation of the same period. The manuscripts offered him raw material for both but we should hesitate before reading them as, respectively, an autobiography and a novel, at least in our conventional perception of these genres. As his younger self spoke to him from the papers his memories of his exchange of Hadley for Pauline became more vivid, specifically his reluctance to leave his wife for his lover, which resulted in the *ménage à trois* conducted mainly on the Côte D'Azur. This was not born out of a shared taste for deviancy; rather it was a result of Hemingway's cowardly indecisiveness. In the novel he protects himself from these painful recollections, via David, by turning Catherine into a woman able to shift persona and with an inclination to androgyny. Towards the end of the draft, written when he was reading the pieces from the Ritz, David exchanges the faintly grotesque demands on Catherine (who seemed to combine aspects of Hadley, Pauline and even Martha) for a continued existence with Marita (little Mary; obviously his current wife). Fiction is by its nature a brand of lying, but this is one of the few cases in which it became a form of involuntary self-delusion.

A Moveable Feast masquerades as a memoir, and while it is assembled from actual events and individuals, these are informed by malicious distortions and fabrications. Sometimes he was vengeful – particularly with Stein, Toklas and Anderson – and on other occasions he exaggerated the part he played in the artistic cauldron of 1920s Paris. His character sketches of Sylvia Beach, Dos Passos, Scott Fitzgerald, Ford Madox Ford and Joyce give the impression that they saw him as their mentor. With Fitzgerald one comes close to admiring Hemingway's deftness in conflating facts with savage misrepresentation. His description of their car trip from Lyon to Paris is acutely detailed as indeed are his accounts of the excellent food and wine consumed in the south-eastern city. In the late 1950s hardly anything had been written about the minutiae of expatriate writers' lives in 1920s France and no one would find reason to dispute the story of the two men in Lyon and their trip back to the capital, but Hemingway knew that within a generation meticulously researched biographies would give credence to his testimonies, at least in terms of such largely inconsequential details. When this abundance of circumstantial evidence was verified then greater credence would be lent to his characterisation of his old friends. Fitzgerald is portrayed as a compound of timid xenophobia, especially regarding the French, sexual and psychological naivety, and a talent wasted by gauche overambition. Zelda, the self-obsessed, alcoholic cuckold, is largely to blame for her sad husband's failings. Dos Passos is dealt with more concisely if no less brutally. Hemingway opens with the time they spent in the Austrian ski resort of Schruns in 1925 – again, authentic – but he spins this into a trope that presents Dos Passos as what he terms the 'pilot fish', followed and trusted by 'the rich'. This enigma is easily decoded in terms of a phrase supposedly coined by Lenin, the 'useful idiot': typically a Communist sympathiser based outside the Soviet Union who is by equal degrees the dupe of the Soviets and their enemies. The 'rich', who are allegedly led by Dos Passos the 'pilot fish', are those educated, comfortably off figures who espouse left-wing causes as a salve to their conscience. We are, of course, now in Spain during the Civil War: 'He enters and leaves politics or the theatre in the same way that he enters and leaves countries and people's lives [...] Nothing ever catches him and it is only those who trust him who are caught and killed' (*A Moveable Feast*, p. 188) – specifically Dos Passos's friend Robles, executed by the Madrid-based Communists, with Hemingway's connivance. His most fascinating reversal of actuality involves the true cause of his loathing for and alienation of his two friends – his bitter resentment at their albeit well-meant temerity in acting as advisers and critics of his work in progress, particularly *The Sun Also Rises*. He states that Fitzgerald was 'upset because I would not show him the manuscript of [...] *The Sun Also Rises*' (*A Moveable Feast*, p. 167) when in fact it was Fitzgerald's lengthy commentary on the first draft that prompted Hemingway's protracted, venomous campaign against him. He reports that Dos Passos enthused that 'It's great Ernest. Truly it's great. You cannot know the thing it has.' 'I wagged my tail in pleasure', Hemingway recalls, 'and plunged into the fiesta concept of life to see if I could not bring some fine attractive stick back, instead of thinking, "if these bastards like it what is wrong with it?"' (*A Moveable Feast*, p. 190). Once more, he alters the past. Dos Passos had offered constructive comments rather than hyperbolic praise, but Hemingway's anger that his inferior had dared to offer an opinion at all endures in the revised version. An inclination to return to the scene of the crime in order to falsify the evidence is proof enough of guilt. *A Moveable Feast* is as delusional as *The Garden of Eden*, but while the latter protected him from the truth the former appropriated and distorted it.

Shortly after he first looked through the old manuscripts he spent a day in Paris with the journalist Leonard Lyons, who was writing an article on him for the *New York Post*. Hemingway showed Lyons some of the buildings where he had lived 30 years earlier and took him to bars on the Left Bank in which he had eaten and taken drink with others who had altered the landscape of twentieth-century writing and art. He also informed his interviewer that after his front-line service in Italy he had postponed his return to America for a year and worked in Paris as a taxi driver. He had, he explained to Lyons, gained a special knowledge of the real city, of its rough ordinary citizens, with whom he drank and boxed, long before his arrival with Hadley in 1921. He implied that the distinguished expatriates who crowded the metropolis during the 1920s had a somewhat etiolated relationship with the place, at least compared with his own. It was one of his more ludicrous remodellings of fact and it offers an insight into his mindset as he began work on his account of the 1920s.

Between his return to Havana in February 1957 and his departure for Spain in April 1959 he slipped precariously between the past and the present, attempting to remain equally faithful to the memoir and the novel; the former, however, proved much more addictive. Within two years he had sent a draft to Scribner's who were delighted by what they found, oblivious to it being largely a catalogue of distortions. In the real world, history seemed to be taking revenge. During most of 1957 his legal representative and accountant Alfred Rice reported on apparently intractable problems with the costs and upkeep of the Key West property. Hemingway was not too concerned with the money but it seemed as though a place that held so many memories had refused to become one. Between Pauline's death in 1951 and Hemingway's in 1961 the property was left uninhabited. Hemingway employed Toby Bruce as caretaker and instructed him to employ gardeners, builders and painters as, in effect, preservationists. On several occasions he stayed over when travelling by car and ferry from Cuba to Ketchum but he was reluctant to remain for longer than a night. He would deal with Bruce on practicalities, and according to the latter he was always keen to leave as soon as possible. There was no reason why he could not have put it on the market. It was a very desirable residence in an area that had recently undergone an economic revival, and its associations with a Nobel Prize winner added considerably to its value, but Hemingway left it empty and well maintained, effectively a mausoleum. Rice's enquiries about accruing debts testify to Hemingway's perverse obsession with his past: he could not release himself from it, even when it unsettled him, as Key West certainly did. In the same period he became the most outspoken campaigner for the release of Ezra Pound, who since 1945 had been detained in St Elizabeth's Hospital for psychiatric patients. His letters on Pound to the US authorities and others are heart-wrenchingly ambivalent. He is caught between treating his old friend as a deluded fool – and therefore excusing his apparent support for Mussolini as a symptom of mental instability, which was the argument that after the war saved Pound from a charge of treason, and possible execution – and arguing that a literary genius has a licence to champion ideas that others find obnoxious. His letters to Pound echo the mildly surreal bonhomie of their exchanges 30 years earlier. Previously undisclosed, but striking and illuminating, are Pound's replies. They are lost gems of literary history, often resembling drafts of his *Cantos*, involving random line breaks, syntactic discontinuities and a haphazard collage of private and literary allusions. While the personnel of the *Cantos* are drawn from a philosophical and cultural net cast as far back as ancient Greece, the figures who appear in the Cantoesque letters to Hemingway come almost exclusively from their Paris years. For example, he weaves references to Bill Bird into reflections on the alliance between Britain, the US and the Soviet Union against Nazi Germany.

> 'Russian an ally that sticks in
> my throat[...]'

> quote from 1914

I see how Mr Baron (B) looks a bit like Bill Bird, who used to
look a little like Groucho/

I don't spos the cantoneros have
Anyway of knowin when B.B. woke (partially) up.

He almost closes:

AND so on,
But yr/letters lighten captivity

And then allows himself space for a further pseudo-poetic
observation:

Mr Zulu wants to disembowel all priests (cat) and kikes, I take
it this is Nietzchean. Did I tell you about Zulu and the King of Fall
River?

(Pound to Hemingway, 14 April 1952, JFK)

He complains of receiving no word from 'The Revd Eliot'. T.S. Eliot
had by this time become an advocate of High Church Anglicanism,
and Pound, for Hemingway, mocks him:

Possum [Eliot] more relaxed this year, last year rather edgy/
he had got over annoyance at adjective applied to his religion
in private correspondence. Of course cdn't get him to define point
at which the mot juste is: lowsy

The buzzard who 'received him' has since walked out and taken
Refuge with 'Romans'

(7 August 1955, JFK)

On 13 September 1957 (JFK) he urges the 'Admired author of the
Torrents of Sprint' to 'turn yr/satiric talents' against several
journalists who had recently interviewed him, misrepresented
'What [he] said to Adolf' and presented a 'TOTALLY lying account
of interview with Muss [Mussolini]/and the old gag to offened yr/
self/as from Jew Park [one assumes 'New York'] 1939 etc.'

The incarcerated Pound of the 1950s tells us much about the
literary artist who broke down the border between unfocussed
rambling and literary art, and he also discloses a figure whose Fascist
sympathies and antisemitism were not dissipated by his imprisonment. He was far more guarded in his exchanges with others. The

letters might have been written in the 1920s when the two men were drawn to each other by their intellectual egotism. For each, politics, and its consequences for human beings, was subservient to the adoration of aesthetic dissent. Hemingway was ambitious but hopelessly out of his depth among the group of thinkers and writers who invented modernism. He was enchanted by Pound, finding much of what he said and wrote utterly impenetrable but staying faithful to him as the high priest of radicalism. By the 1950s their roles seemed reversed, with the Nobel Prize winner the principal campaigner for the release of his old friend. While we will never know what Hemingway thought of Pound's letters to him it is clear that the latter regarded their relationship much as it was 30 years earlier, constantly projecting each of them into a shared past.

> She [Sylvia Beach] wuz a nice girl in 1910 even if
> she was a bit vague as to
> costume historique.

> It has been reported that 19 Poundanistas assembled in
> one room in Chelsea s.w.3 (Sodom on Thames)
> without mayhem or even bloodshed, but that was some months ago.

> The presence of my friends and acquaints in confrontation/has
> allus been one of my special diversions

> ANTHropologic research

> did you ever see Jim J [Joyce] and Wyndham assembled?

> Demme I don't believe I ever saw you and the Possum [Eliot]
> simult???

> (9 August 1956, JFK)

Even the most indulgent reader would have to accept that Pound was off his head, but Hemingway did not treat his friend's replies to his letters as unusual because they were not unlike the utterances and correspondence of the man he knew in Paris. Pound was released on 7 May 1958 and Hemingway sent him a charming letter of congratulation:

> During P Harbor to A Bomb war which I actively participated in I wrote
> A Tate the Poet that if there should arrive any questions of you being
> hanged I would get up onto the gallows and make clear that I would be

hanged with you [...] I stayed with you within the limits of my ability intelligence as well as I could. (26 June 1958)

Hemingway's enduring commitment to Pound is both touching and bewildering. By the beginning of the 1950s Pound's broadcasts and writings in support of the Axis powers were well-publicised, including his outspoken support for antisemitic laws and policies; simultaneously, the full extent of Nazi mass murder, the Holocaust, was becoming evident to the general public. Hemingway advocated Pound's release on several occasions but beyond the spurious premise of the letter – that writers deserve special treatment by virtue of their uniqueness – he offered nothing that resembled a rational justification of his pleas. Further to this, the unvarying feature of the Hemingway's political affiliations, at least from the mid-1930s, was his contempt for Fascism. The letters from Pound reminded him of the 1920s in Europe, a magical decade in which artists attained an almost superhuman status – at least in their own perception of themselves – exempt from the standard expectations of conscience and principle by virtue of their commitment to the unexplored. Pound in the 1950s became part of Hemingway's exercise in selective time travel. For the sake of a return to the years or their strange fellowship, with Pound allowing him to believe he was his equal among the new elite of the avant-garde, Hemingway was prepared to overlook his friend's subsequent support for Hitler and Mussolini.

The Finca too provided Hemingway with a delusional refuge from of uncertainties of the present day. Cuba was full of American expatriates, sufficient to make it an adjunct to Florida without being accountable to the US or anywhere else. It had become a favourite offshore location for American mobsters, who established hotels, casinos and nightclubs mainly as a means of laundering money. It also reminded him of Spain, the Spain prior to the decisive closing battles of the Civil War when democracy was a fluid, impetuous ideal and Soviet-backed authoritarian communism existed alongside various manifestations of home-grown socialism and anarchy. Optimistic left-leaning pluralism seemed a realistic alternative to a society largely unchanged since the eighteenth century. During the month before Pound's release Hemingway sensed that Castro's

Communist guerrillas and other revolutionary factions were resurrecting the ideals of Spain in the 1930s, making irreversible gains against the Batista government. On the closing day of 1958, Batista – corrupt, dictatorial, but the guarantor of the island's close relationship with the US – fled. On New Year's Day 1959 Cuba had become a revolutionary Communist state barely 70 miles from the American coast.

On 12 April Hemingway wrote to Bronislaw Zielinski: 'This is a very pure and beautiful revolution so far – Naturally I do not know how it will come out. But I hope for the best – So far it is what we hoped for, in intent, when they made the Republic in Spain (and which never arrived). I hope things will go well – the people who are being shot deserve it' (PUL). A few days earlier, in an interview in Havana with Kenneth Tynan, he was a little more reserved: 'This is a good revolution [...] an honest revolution' (Tynan, p. 336). Zielinski, a translator of Hemingway's work, was based in Warsaw and sympathised with the Polish Communist government. His affiliations enabled him to travel: he had visited Hemingway in Havana in 1958 and they had discussed the Communist factions of the anti-Batista uprising. As his letter to Zielinski indicates, Hemingway's support for Castro was excited as much by memories of Spain as by commitment to the future of the island. Shortly before he wrote it he and Mary had made one of their apparently random visits to Ketchum. This time he was not concerned with hunting or fishing. He bought a house, in incautious haste. Hemingway took a particular interest in the architecture and mood of his homes and the fact that this one was exceedingly ugly – it looked as if a prefabricated bungalow had been piled above its equally featureless replica – testified to his sense of desperation. He needed a bolthole if things in Cuba did not 'go well'.

Despite this he never disavowed his belief that Castro could bring equanimity and economic equality to the island that had been his home for almost 20 years. When he left the Finca for Ketchum in July 1960 there was no indication that he would not go back. He took with him only notes that were relevant to his imminent, final, visit to Spain. The Finca was still served by the staff who looked after it during Hemingway's and Mary's absences.

He expected to return because he had begun to treat Castro's state as the fulfilment of, as he put it to Zielinski, 'what we hoped for, in intent, when they made the Republic in Spain (and which never arrived)'. The shift from 'we' to 'they' is revealing: the former recalls his allegiance to a particular faction of the Republican cause, the Communists. Cuba was what he hoped for in Spain, an idealised past that had, against the odds, 'arrived' in the Caribbean and it is for this reason that he revisited Spain, obsessively, in 1959 and 1960. He was resigned to the fact that the dreams of 1936–9 had died, aware that while international opinions on the Franco government varied it was accepted as the immutable status quo. Yet the island once colonised by Spain was becoming a means of exchanging disappointed memory for what might have been.

In an article in *Standpoint* ('Shooting Script', January 2009) James Scott Linville claims to have interviewed a journalist who, with Hemingway, had witnessed one of the mass executions by firing squad of Batista supporters. No specific dates are given but we are treated to a lurid account of how the writer viewed the spectacle from a cane chair while drinking a daiquiri. The story can never be verified, the alleged witness being dead, but it is echoed in Hemingway's private letter to Zielinski where he declared that those 'being shot [...] deserve it'. Note the present tense, and note also that Linville's interviewee stated that these executions were ordered and personally organised by Che Guevara. No one disputes that Guevara played a significant role in such killings but reliable records show that his involvement, specifically during his command of Santa Clara, ceased in mid-January 1959, more than a year before the international press reported the executions. Did Hemingway know of them before the rest of the world? We can never be certain but there are self-evident parallels between what happened in 1959–60 in Cuba and his unapologetic support for the Spanish Communists' policy of causing alleged spies, or even those with suspect political allegiances, to 'disappear'. On several occasions he claimed to have been a member of execution squads, justifying his participation by claiming that those shot were Falangist infiltrators – again those who 'deserve[d] it'.

At the end of April 1959 Hemingway and Mary disembarked from the *Constitution* at Algeciras, Spain, and drove, in a rented open-top Ford, to a gated, luxuriously appointed villa just outside Malaga. This was the home of their hosts, Bill and Annie Davis, who routinely entertained members of the European aristocracy and Hollywood superstars. The source of the Davis's enormous wealth remains unclear as indeed does the reason for the Hemingway's invitation to La Consula as the Davis's permanent guests for more than six months. Bill and Hemingway had met before, but only briefly, and it appears that Davis was obsessed with fame by association. Aside from the fact that he was outstandingly rich he had no claim to significance, and his sycophantic treatment of his guest during 1959 – personally driving him to *corridas*, answering his daily demands for expensive drinks and foodstuffs – caused Hemingway to refer to him as 'my nigger, my slave' (Castillo-Puche, p. 48). The arrangement reminded Hemingway of the 1920s when he, Hadley and Pauline had enjoyed the hospitality of equally generous patrons on the Côte D'Azur.

The ostensible reason for the trip was his contract with *Life* to write a series of articles on the survival of bullfighting in Spain, a revisitation of *Death in the Afternoon*. He was focussing on the rivalry between the most celebrated matadors of the era, Ordonez, whom he regarded as a friend, and Luis Miguel Dominguin. He would represent the latter as a crude, ageing practitioner. In Hemingway's reports, covering fights during the 1959 summer season, Ordonez was the artist, Dominguin the brutal pragmatist, more concerned with getting the job done than respecting the bull's dignity in the duel between man and beast. More impartial observers treated the articles as insulting misrepresentations, and Dominguin later expressed anger at what he saw as a one-sided dramatisation of the differences between the two matadors who, in truth, regarded each other with mutual respect. His distortions and favouritism echoed his obsessive preoccupation with bullfighting as a combination of high art and courage that had first drawn him to Spain in the 1920s. During May and early June he kept Hotchner up to date with the progress of his writing. On 4 May he had produced 92,453 words and three weeks later he had passed 109,000. *Life* wanted three articles, of no more than 8,000–9,000 words each. It appeared that Hemingway had forgotten the specifics of his contract. Instead he was trying to make himself part of the events he was witnessing by refusing to compress them into a conventional piece of journalistic narrative. He recorded what he witnessed, day by day, minute by minute. The words on the page would in some way cement his permanent allegiance to a ritual, a way of life, that seemed to offer some reassurance against fragmentation and uncertainty elsewhere. He was morbidly overweight, his kidneys were in a foul state, as was his liver, and those closest to him were concerned about his mental stability. When the shortened articles appeared, and much later after the full text was published posthumously as *The Dangerous Summer*, commentators and reviewers were drawn to an endemic feature of each: repetition and circularity. An emphatic preoccupation with given words and phrases had manifested itself in his prose since *The Sun Also Rises*, but this was different. The reader is subjected to an unvaried and wearying catalogue of descriptions – from each matador's clothing, mannerisms and technique to an account of the weather, townscape and general mood surrounding one *corrida* after another. There is more than a hint of hopelessness in his dreary listing of everything and his reluctance to inform this with anything remotely acute or perceptive. It was as if he was desperate to preserve something that protected him from thinking about anything else. In the articles and in the book we revisit each fight as an obligation; nothing has altered, nothing will change and the experience will not cease. He is craving stagnation as a way of preserving the past, avoiding the present and postponing the immediate future.

At the end of June, Hemingway agreed to meet Valerie Danby-Smith at a hotel in central Madrid. The background to their encounter remains mysterious. All commentators are satisfied that she represented a Belgian news agency and that Hemingway had agreed to an interview, but no one is able to give the name of her employer. She was Irish, of entrepreneurial working-class stock – her father was a self-employed builder – dark haired, fair skinned, good-looking enough but not distractingly beautiful, and, when she met Hemingway, barely 19 years old. Would an international news agency, albeit unspecified, send a teenaged stranger to conduct an interview with one of the world's most famous writers? There is no record of what happened during their meeting, but within a few days she had a new job, as Hemingway's secretary, on a generous salary of 250 dollars a month. She went immediately to La Consula – apparently without the necessity of moving her possessions from wherever she had lived in Brussels – and what happened thereafter is based on a chronicle of conjecture and lurid, questionable recollections. Castillo-Puche wrote that 'He couldn't keep himself from casting covert glances at the affectionate little Irish girl with the unkempt hair, and touching her [...] She kept stroking herself, and constantly acted more or less like a little bitch in heat. She was a very pretty little creature, who was to lose a great many things at the fiesta.' He then adds that it was 'all [...] rather dull' (Castillo-Puche, pp. 191, 184, 347). Buck Lanham, George Plimpton and Clara Spiegel, a friend of Mary, all thought that they had become lovers or that he had propositioned her, but none had any proof (see Meyers, p. 532), while their host, Bill Davis, was convinced that nothing unseemly had occurred, based on his knowledge of who had been sharing bedrooms in his house.

Valerie, involuntarily, became the focus for suppositions cultivated by those who had known Hemingway for decades and were alert to his addiction to what had gone before – Castillo-Puche's intimations that she was a new version of Adriana are a sordid example of this. Some treated the arrival of Danby-Smith with grim resignation – Lanham suspected that recent history might repeat itself – while others became vultures hoping to prey on evidence of a now inglorious legend.

Hemingway's sixtieth birthday party, arranged by Mary, began at 10.00 am on 21 July in La Consula and soon came to resemble one of Nero's infamous banquets. Forty guests shared 72 bottles of Loire Rosé, 48 bottles of Champagne, plus apparently limitless amounts of whisky, gin and vodka. Cocktails mixed by a team of devoted barmen were constantly available. A van-load of baked hams, seafood casseroles and Chinese sweet-and-sour game dishes were delivered, and in the early hours Hemingway was presented with a candle-laden three-tiered birthday cake, followed by a half-hour display of fireworks. By noon on the following day the majority of the guests were still conscious, though mainly on deckchairs surrounding the Davis's pool. Most would stay until late afternoon, continuing to eat and drink. Hemingway's intimates – including Valerie, Lanham, the Bruces, the Davises, Hotchner, Gianfranco Ivancich and his wife – heroically stayed the course, as did Mary and the Maharajah of Cooch-Behar, the latter not a friend of the Davis's but seemingly invited to add a hint of oriental glamour to the occasion. All who later spoke of the event recalled that Hemingway behaved as though he was reluctant to be there. He was variously abusive and indifferent towards Mary, which was not unusual, but this time it appeared symptomatic of an unfocussed mood of introversion and hopelessness.

The likeliest reason was that the celebrations would have felt bleakly inappropriate, given that they coincided with his demise as a writer. During the previous two months he had been working on the introduction to an anthology of his short stories. Charles Scribner Junior had encouraged him to provide more than a token foreword. It would be his first piece of prose *about* literature, a lengthy reflection on the short story, the genre that many thought he had radicalised. Indeed, Scribner predicted that the volume would become a standard text in colleges and universities, given Hemingway's status within the cultural establishment, and encouraged him to present himself as a sagacious virtuoso addressing eager students. Mary, typing it up, was confounded. When reading his work she had always managed to find room for her reservations as constructive suggestions, but now she had encountered something that, if it went into print, would severely damage his reputation. Boldly, she suggested that he had dealt with Faulkner, as a writer and an individual, with what appeared to be gratuitous spite and that he should do some major revisions (*HIW*, p. 469). Privately, she was aware that the piece was irredeemably disastrous. He had attempted a relaxed colloquial manner, as though addressing the reader directly in a bar, and accordingly the prose shifts from an assembly of short-sentence maxims to an incoherent ramble. Mary bought Hemingway time from Scribner's in the hope that her husband might consider her advice that general revisions would improve his profile as a cultural savant.

Instead he dispatched it to Scribner's unaltered with an accompanying letter demanding it should be promoted as a work that would appeal more to the common reader than the undergraduate, adding that it was for this reason he had adopted such a blunt rough-house manner. Scribner was appalled by what he read, and replied that in his opinion intelligent readers would treat it as a gross act of 'condescension' (Scribner to Hemingway, 24 June 1959, JFK). His first letter of rejection since *The Sun Also Rises* had reached him two days before his birthday party, where he was praised as an artist at the summit of his career. He refused to rewrite the preface and Scribner cancelled the contract for the anthology.

It was eventually published in the *Paris Review* (Issue 17, Spring 1981), unedited and with the ungrammatical passages intact. Few, if any, have commented on it, treating it rather like a photograph of a fatal road crash, the record of a tragedy that speaks for itself. It does, however, deserve more than the attention of the prurient reader. Despite its apparent incoherence it comes closer than any other document to giving us an insight into the real Hemingway. Often he appears to lose track of his subject, but this should not be treated as a symptom of alcoholism or mental instability. It is, rather, a startling example of unrehearsed candour. He is writing about the relationship between his sense of himself and his fiction and frequently, often in a brief paragraph, he is unable or unwilling to differentiate between the real and the invented:

> So I start to invent and I make myself a guy who would do what I invent. I know about the dying part because I had been through all that. Not just once. I got it early, in the middle and later. So I invent how someone I knew who cannot sue me – that is me – would turn out and put it into one story [...] I throw everything I had been saving for into the story and spend it all. I really throw it away, if you see what I mean. I am not gambling with it. Or maybe I am. Who knows? [...] So I make up the man and the woman and put all the true stuff in, and with all the load, the most load any story ever carried, it still takes off and it flies.

Throughout the piece, Hemingway, his fictional alter egos and his reinventions of those he knew coalesce into a unique account of why he became a writer and how he wrote. He was unlike any other novelist, a man who rode the wave between the actual world and the one that spread itself across the page.

On the morning of his birthday he received a letter from his lawyer and accountant Alfred Rice, informing him that due to an error in his 1957 return he was likely to face a demand for at least 29,000 dollars in back taxes. This figure, Rice indicated, could increase, since the Internal Revenue Service (IRS) were alert to further discrepancies and were busily scrutinising his finances since 1957, and before that. Rice later admitted that he was responsible for the miscalculation and volunteered to pay all interest on the amount owed. Nonetheless, the two events – being rejected by his publisher and the sudden threat against his financial stability – made the abundant praise lavished upon him at the party seem like a form of vindictive caricature. Irrespective of what he had already achieved, the present and certainly the future seemed intent on denying him contentment.

His tax problems were not ruinous and Rice should be commended for limiting the damage. At the same time it is evident that the letter marked the onset of Hemingway's conviction that agents of the state, from the IRS to the FBI, were spying on him. What began as a general sense of anxiety evolved during the next two years into paranoia. During the final few months of his life he was certain that men in cars or seated at tables in restaurants were following him, intent on tracking him down and prosecuting him: he felt that his record as a Communist sympathiser, along with his questionable tax returns, would be used against him by a country that had once been his home and was now, he feared, his nemesis. His anxieties would have been infused with memories of the 1940s when he had worked for the OSS and earned enmity from Hoover, the head of the competing agency, the FBI.

Mary left Spain first, flying to New York on 20 September. From Havana she wrote to him on how their friends were dealing with Castro's new regime and included in the same envelope another one marked 'Personal' (JFK archive). It was as though she foresaw a legacy of exchanges that would be pored over by archivists, editors and biographers and was allowing him to separate one narrative from another, perhaps by destroying the intimate letter. It was three and a half pages in length and she presented him with a meticulous, coldly impartial account of how his behaviour over the previous year had been unforgiveable and was now unendurable. Her manner is wearily resigned but she makes it clear that she is planning to rent an apartment of her own in New York. When exactly she rescinded her decision to leave him is unclear, but it is evident that after he returned to America and they met at Ketchum at the end of 1959, pity had replaced her feelings of despair. In 1960 when Mary drove him through Ketchum he seemed unduly preoccupied with lights glowing in the bank. It was night time, the branch had been closed for several hours and after they arrived at the house he announced that 'they' were checking his account. 'Who?' asked Mary. 'The FBI', he replied, 'they want to get something on us'.

In May they travelled to the Finca. It would be his last visit to Cuba and he spent five hours a day on his sequel to *Death in the Afternoon*. By the end of the month the manuscript had gone beyond 110,000 words. He insisted on returning to Spain and flew to Madrid on 4 August to be joined by Valerie on the 20th. Mary was reassured by her note that she was caring for him as her employer, as a writer she greatly respected, and nothing more. Hemingway attended *corridas* obsessively. When he returned to New York on 5 October the book had reached 150,000 words. It is doubtful that Stanley Kubrick was aware of Hemingway's condition when he adapted Stephen King's novel for the film *The Shining*, but the parallels are striking. The novelist, Jack Torrance, played by Jack Nicholson, looks after an isolated hotel to allow him the peace and time to finish his next book. Instead, he becomes deranged, repeating the same passages again and again in a 'novel' that goes nowhere. Unlike Nicholson, Hemingway does not retype the same phrase incessantly but the obsessive returns to the *corrida* in his prose, as if he is unable to release himself from a single recurrent moment, reflects a similar state of mind. Place names and other minor details might vary but it seems as though the bullfight is his last refuge from a world that terrifies him.

Following his return to Ketchum in October 1960, Hemingway was faced with an assembly of phantoms just as unnerving as those that drove Nicholson's figure to his typewriter. He and Mary were met at the railway station by George Saviers, his doctor, and as they left the terminal Hemingway nodded across the road to two men in rain coats who had exited a cafe at the same moment and confided in Saviers that 'they' were 'tailing me out here'. Later, Mary informed the physician that during their stay at her apartment in New York her husband had refused to go outside, convinced that men were awaiting him on the stairwell or in the street, and that he believed the two individuals outside the Ketchum cafe were part of the same surveillance unit and had followed them from the East Coast.

Six weeks later, at the close of November 1960, Hemingway reluctantly followed Saviers' advice and enrolled at the Mayo Clinic in Rochester, Minnesota. His physical condition was scrupulously assessed. His blood pressure and the state of his liver attested to a lifestyle unsympathetic to both but nothing irreversible, let alone fatal, was diagnosed. Psychologists at the clinic were more interested in his apparent symptoms of delusion and paranoia and recommended electro-convulsive therapy. In the 1950s the treatment was seen as exploratory yet largely harmless. It is now regarded as the modern equivalent of trepanning, a crude procedure almost certain to worsen the condition it is supposed to cure. Studies have shown that it has side-effects comparable to rapid and serious bouts of concussion, and since Hemingway had suffered the consequences of regular head injuries since the 1920s these new assaults on his brain were particularly catastrophic.

He had now lost interest in his sprawling sequel to *Death in the Afternoon* and had abandoned the manuscripts of the unfinishable, autobiographical novels. Instead, he bombarded his publisher with letters about what would be his final, completed book, *A Moveable Feast*, which Scribner's were sure would attract global attention and sell in vast numbers. Hemingway wanted Scribner's to cancel or at least postpone publication, anxious, he stated, that those still alive from that period would take civil actions against him.

The book is a piece of fiction, in the sense that he persistently uses real individuals as the models for fabrication, exaggeration and misrepresentation – by parts delusional and vindictive. Yet he presented it as an autobiography. It seemed almost as if, at the end of his career, Hemingway had brought upon himself a bizarre form of natural justice, with the incurable liar turning against the novelist.

On 25 April he returned to the Mayo Clinic for more electro-convulsive therapy. The previous day his hunting companion, Don Anderson, had found him in the living room of the Ketchum house placing two cartridges into his twelve-bore shotgun. He was not grandstanding. He intended to kill himself, but Anderson wrestled the gun away from him. On his way to Rochester, after the plane refuelled, he attempted to walk into its spinning propellers. Further electro-convulsive therapy treatments made him worse, as did his transference to the less brutal Hartford Institute of Living, under Dr Gordon Edren, on 7 June. On 30 June, back in Ketchum, Mary, Hemingway and a few friends were taking dinner in the Christiana Restaurant, and he asked the waitress about two men at the adjoining table. They were, she answered, 'salesmen'. 'They're FBI', Hemingway pronounced to his guests. Three days later, on 2 July, he rose early, went downstairs, loaded both barrels of the same shotgun that Anderson had snatched from him in April and killed himself with it.

All we know of his last hours comes from the fact that next to his body was a file of letters from Agnes von Kurowsky. Mary wrote to Baker (3 June 1962, JFK) that there were 'letters of hers in the stuff I shipped up [to him] from Key West', adding that she had read them. She was perplexed for several reasons. He had never mentioned Agnes to her; Baker had disclosed her existence. But she was less concerned that he had chosen them as his final companion than with their content. She had known for years that he had been something of a fantasist, but the letters showed her that even as a teenager, for his first love, he was an inveterate liar:

> I suspect that Ernest's part in the Monte Grappa offensive was as a spectator, with cane, just as his part in the Fourth Division's offensive in France in the fall of 1944 was unofficial, untrue.

Bibliography

Anderson, Sherwood. *Sherwood Anderson's Memoirs*. New York: Harcourt Brace, 1942.

Baker, Carlos. *Ernest Hemingway: A Life Story*. New York: Scribner's, 1969.

Beach, Sylvia. *Shakespeare and Company*. New York: Harcourt Brace, 1959.

Braden, Spruille. *Diplomats and Demagogues*. New York: Arlington House, 1971.

Brenner, Carlene Fredericka. *Hemingway's Cats*. Sarasota, FL: Pineapple Press, 2011.

Bruccoli, Matthew J. *Scott and Ernest: The Authority of Failure and the Authority of Success*. New York: Random House, 1978.

Buckley, Peter. *Ernie*. New York: Dial, 1978.

Burwell, Rose Marie. *Hemingway: The Postwar Years and the Posthumous Novels*. Cambridge: Cambridge University Press, 1996.

Callaghan, Morely. *That Summer in Paris: Memories of Tangled Friendships with Hemingway, Fitzgerald, and Some Others*. New York: Dell, 1964.

Capa, Robert. *Slightly out of Focus*. London: Random House, 2001.

Carr, Virginia Spencer. *Dos Passos: A Life*. Garden City, NY: Doubleday, 1984.

Castillo-Puche, Jose Luis. *Hemingway in Spain*. Garden City, NY: Doubleday, 1974.

Dearborn, Mary V. *Ernest Hemingway: A Biography*. New York: Knopf, 2017.

De Fazio, Albert J. III, ed. *Dear Papa, Dear Hotch: The Correspondence of Ernest Hemingway and A.E. Hotchner*. Columbia: University of Missouri Press, 2005.

Drew, Fraser. 'April 8, 1955 with Hemingway: Unedited Notes on a Visit to Finca Vigía'. In *Fitzgerald/Hemingway Annual*, edited by Matthew J. Bruccoli and C.E. Frazer Clark, Jr. Washington, DC: Microcard Editions, 1970, pp. 108–16.

Eastman, Max. *Einstein, Trotsky, Hemingway, Freud and Other Great Companions*. 1959; reprinted, New York: Collier, 1962.

Fenton, Charles. *The Apprenticeship of Ernest Hemingway: The Early Years*. 1954; reprinted, New York: Viking, 1965.

Fuentes, Norberto. *Hemingway in Cuba*. Secaucus, NJ: Lyle Stuart, 1984.

Gardner, Martin. 'Ernest Hemingway and Jane'. In *Are Universes Thicker than Black-berries?* New York: W.W. Norton, 2003, pp. 135–43.

Gellhorn, Martha. *Travels with Myself and Another*. New York: Dodd, Mead, 1979.

Griffin, Peter. *Along with Youth: Hemingway, The Early Years*. New York: Oxford University Press, 1985.

———. *Less than a Treason: Hemingway in Paris*. New York: Oxford University Press, 1990.

Hemingway, Ernest. *Death in the Afternoon*. New York: Scribner's, 1932.

———. *To Have and Have Not*. New York: Scribner's, 1937.

———. *Across the River and Into the Trees*. New York: Scribner's, 1950.

———. *A Moveable Feast*. New York: Scribners, 1964.

———. *By Line: Selected Articles and Dispatches of Four Decades*, ed. W. White. New York: Scribner, 1967.

———. *The Dangerous Summer*. New York: Scribner's, 1985.

———. *For Whom the Bell Tolls*. New York: Scribner's, 1995.

———. *The Old Man and the Sea*. New York: Scribner's, 1995.

———. *A Farewell to Arms*. New York: Scribner's, 1997.

———. *True at First Light*. New York: Scribner's, 1999.

———. *The Complete Short Stories*. New York: Scribner's, 2003.

———. *The Garden of Eden*. New York: Scribner's, 2003.

———. *Green Hills of Africa*. New York: Scribner's, 2003.

———. *The Sun Also Rises*. New York: Scribner's, 2003.

———. *Islands in the Stream*. New York: Scribner's, 2004.

Hemingway, Gregory. *Papa: A Personal Memoir*. 1976; reprinted, New York: Paragon House, 1988.

Hemingway, John. *Strange Tribe: A Family Memoir*. Guilford, CT: Lyons Press, 2007.

Hemingway, Leicester. *My Brother, Ernest Hemingway*. New York: World, 1971.

Hemingway, Mary Welsh. *How it Was*. New York: Alfred A. Knopf, 1976.

Hemingway, Valerie. *Running with the Bulls: My Years with the Hemingways*. New York: Ballantine, 2004.

Ivancich, Adriana. *La Torre Bianca*. Milan: A. Mondadori, 1980.

Kert, Bernice. *The Hemingway Women*. New York: W.W. Norton, 1983.

Lewis, Wyndham. 'The Dumb Ox'. *American Review* (June), 1934.

Loeb, Harold. *The Way it Was*. New York: Criterion Books, 1959.

Lynn, Kenneth S. *Hemingway*. New York: Simon & Schuster, 1987.

MacLeish, Archibald. *Riders on the Earth*. New York: Houghton Mifflin, 1978.

Marshall, S.L.A. 'How Papa Liberated Paris'. *American Heritage* 13(3), 1962.

McAlmon, Robert. *Being Geniuses Together, 1920–1930*. New York: Doubleday, 1968.

Mellow, James. *Hemingway: A Life Without Consequences*. Boston: Houghton Mifflin, 1992.

Meyers, Jeffrey. *Hemingway: A Biography*. New York: Harper & Row, 1985.

Moorhead, Caroline. *Martha Gellhorn: A Life*. London: Chatto and Windus, 2003.

Mort, Terry. *The Hemingway Patrols: Ernest Hemingway and His Hunt for U-boats*. New York: Scribner, 2009.

Nagel, James, ed. *Ernest Hemingway: The Oak Park Legacy*. Tuscaloosa: University of Alabama Press, 1996.

Owen, Richard. *Hemingway in Italy*. Chicago: Chicago University Press, 2017.

Parker, Dorothy. 'The Artist's Reward'. *New Yorker*, 30 November 1929, pp. 28–31.

Paul, Bart. *Double-edged Sword: The Many Lives of Hemingway's Friend, the American Matador Sidney Franklin*. Lincoln: University of Nebraska Press, 2009.

Prokosch, Frederic. *Voices: A Memoir*. New York: Ferrer, Strauss and Giroux, 1984.

Reynolds, Michael. *The Young Hemingway*. 1986; reprinted, New York: W.W. Norton, 1988.

———. *Hemingway: The 1930s*. 1997; reprinted, New York: W.W. Norton, 1998.

———. *Hemingway: The Paris Years*. 1989; reprinted, New York: W.W. Norton, 1999.

———. *Hemingway: The Homecoming*. 1992; reprinted, New York: W.W. Norton, 1999.

———. *Hemingway: The Final Years*. New York: W.W. Norton, 1999.

Reynolds, Nicholas. 'Ernest Hemingway, Wartime Spy'. *Studies in Intelligence* 56 (extracts, June 2012).

———. *Writer, Sailor, Soldier, Spy: Ernest Hemingway's Secret Adventures, 1935–1961*. New York: Harper Collins, 2017.

Rollyson, Carl. *Beautiful Exile: The Life of Martha Gellhorn*. London: Aurum Press, 2001.

Ross, Lillian. 'Portrait of Hemingway'. *New Yorker*, 13 May 1950, reprinted, New York: Modern Library, 1999.

Stein, Gertrude. *The Autobiography of Alice B. Toklas*. New York: Harcourt Brace, 1933.

Townsend, Kim. *Sherwood Anderson: A Biography*. Boston: Houghton Mifflin, 1987.

Tynan, Kenneth. *Tynan Right and Left: Plays, Films, People, Places and Events*. London: Longmans, 1967.

Viertel, Peter. *Dangerous Friends: At Large with Hemingway and Huston in the Fifties*. New York: Doubleday, 1992.

Villareal, Rene and Raul Villareal. *Hemingway's Cuban Son: Reflections on the Writer by his Long-term Majordomo*. Kent, OH: Kent State University Press, 2009.

Wilson, Edmund. 'Hemingway: Gauge of Morale'. In *The Portable Edmund Wilson*, edited by Lewis M. Dabney. New York: Penguin, 1983.

———. *The Wound and the Bow*. Cambridge, MA: Houghton Mifflin, 1941; reprinted, New York: Oxford University Press, 1965.

Index

Plate numbers are in *italics*.
Italics are used in headings for names of publications etc.
Hemingway is abbreviated to EH.